THE GREATEST SKI RESORTS IN NORTH AMERICA

Sixth Revised Edition

By Carol Bartholdi

GuideBook Publishing Co.
Vail, Colorado and Reston, Virginia

Cover Photo: The light, airy, deep powder of Snowbird, Utah sprays up and over a joyous skier thrilled by the experience. Photo by Eric Schramm, courtesy of Snowbird Resort.

Library of Congress Cataloging-in-Publication Data

Carol Bartholdi
     The Greatest Ski Resorts in North America

Copyright © 1988, 1989, 1990, 1991 by Robert E. Weber
Copyright 1992,1993 by Carol Bartholdi

ISBN: 0-929498-05-4

First published in 1988 by GuideBook Publishing Co.

GuideBook Publishing Co.
2465 Freetown Drive, Reston, VA   22091

Printed in the United States of America

The paper used in this book complies with the Permanent Paper Standard issued by the National Information Standards Organization (Z39.48-1984).

10 9 8 7 6 5 4 3 2 1

The Lodge at Breckenridge projects from the top of a mountain high above the town and across from the four peaks of the ski resort. The views are spectacular.
Photo by GuideBook Publishing

Trail Maps

Many of these trail maps were updated this year, but some still do not represent the latest 1993-94 trail maps, because they were not available at press time. Please pick up the most recent trail maps when you arrive at these resorts.

Preface

In this sixth edition of **The Greatest Ski Resorts in North America,** *I continue to strive to bring you the most up-to-date information available about the ski resorts included in this review. My aim is to help the skier who is looking for new territory. I hope to help you avoid many of the pitfalls I have experienced when going to a new area. Where are the best runs? How can I avoid crowds, especially at the end of the day? Where can I find child care? What are the names of some good restaurants, both high-priced and some easier on the pocketbook? I want you to know that all of the areas in this book will test your abilities, and will keep you interested, either on the hill or off, for at least one week.*

Most of the prices and many of the trail maps are brand new this year. Despite an effort to get new prices, often during the summer and early fall ski shops and winter businesses have not established their prices, or the people are not available.(Can you imagine that some people take vacations during the summer?!) I hope that even if things are not exact, you will get an idea of what to expect when you get to your destination.

That said, I would like to point out an extraordinary trend among many of the resorts included here.

Like so many large companies, many ski resorts are aiming for **BIGGER!** *Is bigger better? At Aspen this year(see the chapter on Aspen and Snowmass) the purchase of both Aspen Highlands and the Aspen Skiing Company (affectionately known as Skico) could mean big changes at the two areas, and more cooperation. As of this writing, the new owners were planning to consolidate management of mountain operations, while resort development would be set separately. New lifts, new construction of base facilities (especially at Highlands), better transportation between all four mountains, all are hoped for. These changes could lead to a bigger resort with more options for the visitor.*

In Summit County, Colorado the purchase of Breckenridge by Ralston Purina, already the owner of Keystone and Arapahoe Basin, could signal changes there. Already a collective marketing campaign can attract people to the area. Shuttle buses between the areas are going to increase in frequency this winter. They are too far apart to connect physically, but this could mean more development in the valley.

Copper Mountain, the other big resort in Summit County, has applied to make its extreme skiing area a regular part of the mountain, called Copper Bowl. Telluride may extend its bounds in the next few years. Vail Associates has purchased Arrowhead, which could increase Beaver Creek by several hundred acres. Vail also is discussing the opening of two more back bowls. Even Sunshine Village in the Banff area is hoping to install new high speed quads on virgin territory on Goat's Eye Mountain next year.

It remains to be seen whether all of this projected growth can be as exciting as it sounds for all of us who ski, and still not contribute to too much traffic, too much building and too much infringement on the wilderness that makes the quiet turns of skis down a trail as thrilling as it is.

Before going to do more research for next year's book, I must share a discovery my 40-year-old legs discovered during the last ski season.

Last spring I tried "Fat Skis" on a March morning with 21 new inches of powder at Snowmass. I was skeptical. Friends have scornfully spoken about this new "fad" among us skiers. Actually these were Atomic skis which were termed "Diet Fatties" by the ski technician at Gene Taylor's ski shop in the Snowmass Village Mall. All the really fat skis had been rented already at 9 a.m.!

My father, one of the lead researchers for this book, who at somewhat older than 40, and as a Vail resident, has legs to cut through any amount or consistency of the white stuff-- and who still puts my two younger sisters, my brother and myself to shame on the mountain--sliced nicely through the light white feathery snow at the top of Elk Camp, even with his skinny skis. I, fearful with my flatlander legs, despite months of aerobics and walks, pushed forward on the wider slats, wondering if they would help my usual clumsiness in the deep stuff.

They did! I can not say my form was perfect, but those diet fatties floated nicely on the top layers of that gorgeous snow. We both whooped and carved our way down, even when at a slightly lower altitude the snow became thicker and heavier. The solution? We headed up again! And then in need of a change, we headed for the Alpine Springs lift and then over to the Big Burn, and then over to Campground! I highly recommend an experiment with these new sticks if some morning you are faced with beautiful deep powder.

Enjoy!
Carol Bartholdi

The new Ritz Carlton in Aspen is nestled a block from the slopes, and its red brick architecture blends with the nineteenth century western town mood of the town. Photo by GuideBook Publishing

Road and Weather Information

ALBERTA		(800) 661-8888
BRITISH COLUMBIA		(800) 663-6000
CALIFORNIA	Mammoth Area	(619) 934-6166
	Reno Area	(702) 793-1313
COLORADO		
	Eastbound traffic	(303) 639-1111
	Westbound traffic	(303) 639-1234
	Summit County (Keystone, Copper, Breckenridge)	(303) 453-1090
	Pitkin County (Aspen, Snowmass)	(303) 920-5454
	Routt County (Steamboat)	(303) 879-1260
	Gunnison County (Crested Butte)	(303) 641-2896
	Eagle County (Vail)	(303) 328-6345
IDAHO		
	Statewide	(208) 336-6600
	Sun Valley	(208) 886-2266
NEW MEXICO		
	Statewide	(505) 841-9256
	Santa Fe Area	(505) 827-9300
UTAH	Statewide	(801) 964-6000
VERMONT	Statewide	(802) 828-2648
WYOMING		
	Jackson Hole	(307) 733-9966

Contents

The Greatest Ski Resorts in North America

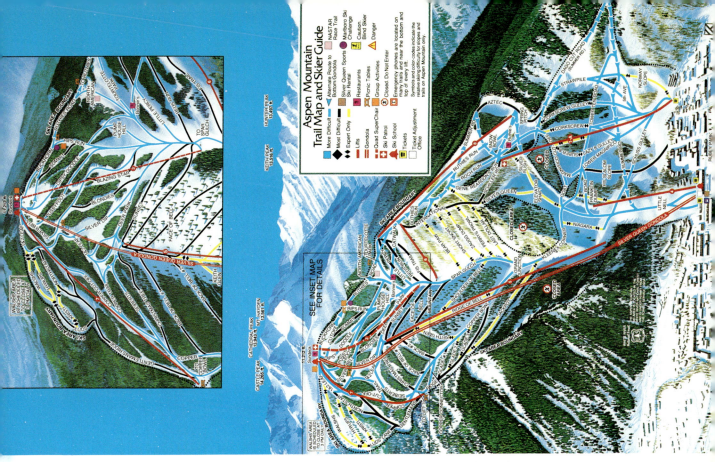

This is not the official 1993-1994 trail for Aspen Mountain. Please pick up an official trail map when you arrive at the area.

This is not the official 1993-1994 trail map for Buttermilk Mountain. Please pick up official trail map when you arrive at the area.

This is not the official 1993-1994 trail map for Snowmass Ski Area. Please pick up an official trail map when you arrive at the area.

Trail map reprinted by permission of Ski Banff/Lake Louise (for Mystic Ridge Norquay)

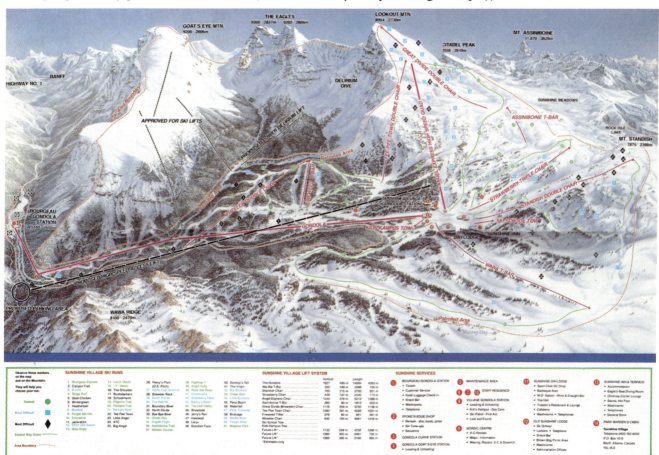

Observe these markers on the map and on the Mountain.
They will help you choose your run.

Easiest ● (green)
More Difficult ■ (blue)
Most Difficult ◆ (black)
Easiest Way Down ------
Area Boundary ·········

SUNSHINE VILLAGE SKI RUNS

1. Bourgeau Express
2. Canyon Trail
3. B-Line
4. Ridge Run
5. Goat Chicken
6. Wintergreen
7. Heatherlael
8. Bluebell
9. Forget-Me-Not
10. Ermaline
11. Jackrabbit
12. Short and Sweet
13. Miss Grass
14. Larch Skate
15. "T" Wenn
16. The Shoulder
17. Bushklazmenn
18. Schoolmarm
19. Pajames Trail
20. Pechans Trail
21. Barriers Bowl
22. Tee Pee Town
23. Little Angel
24. XTC
25. Big Angel
26. Percy's Pitch (D.S. Pitch)
27. World Cup Downhill
28. Brewster Rock
29. South Divide
30. The Fall W
31. Boundary Bowl
32. North Divide
33. Bus Bye Bowl
34. Green Run
35. Angels Flight
36. Assiniboina Trail
37. Melster Course
38. Highway 1
39. Angel Gully
40. Rock iss Road
41. Shoessnaze
42. Strawberry Face
43. Rootry'x Bowl
44. The Dell Valley
45. Showdowl
46. Jerry's Run
47. Hookwall
48. Larya
49. Standish Face
50. Dorsey's Tail
51. The Virgin
52. Big Bunkers
53. Green Run
54. Little Bunkers
55. Pans Basin
56. Waterfall
57. Paris Traverse
58. Bridcage
59. Wahha Bowl
60. Trojan Alley
61. Meadow Park

SUNSHINE VILLAGE LIFT SYSTEM

	Vertical	Rise	Length
The Gondola	1627'	496 m	4393 m
Wa-Wa T-Bar	350'	166 m	2366' — 700 m
Standish Chair	785'	215 m	2793' — 851 m
Strawberry Chair	448'	137 m	2535' — 773 m
Angel Express Chair	1244'	379 m	5212' — 1589 m
Assiniboine T-Bar	295'	90 m	1813' — 553 m
Great Divide (Brewster) Chair	1175'	358 m	3730' — 1138 m
Tee Pee Town Chair	1362'	391 m	4039' — 1231 m
Firewired T-Bar	278'	85 m	921' — 281 m
Wheeler Chair	635'	194 m	3991' — 1218 m
Ski School Tow			
Kids Kampus Tow			
Future Lift*	1732'	528 m	4237' — 1290 m
Future Lift*	1000'	305 m	2461' — 750 m
Future Lift*	1069'	330 m	3158' — 965 m

*Estimates only

SUNSHINE SERVICES

1 BOURGEAU GONDOLA STATION
• Ticketn
• Customer Service
• Hotel Luggage Check-in
• Snack Bar
• Washrooms
• Telephone

2 SPOKEN EDGE SHOP
• Rentals - skis, boots, poles
• Ski Tune-ups
• Souvenirs

3 GONDOLA CURVE STATION

4 GONDOLA GOAT'S EYE STATION
• Loading & Unloading

5 MAINTENANCE AREA

6 **7** **8** STAFF RESIDENCE

9 NORDIC CENTRE
• X-C Rentals
• Main - Information
• Waxing, Repairs, X-C & Downhill

10 SKI SCHOOL

11 SUNSHINE DAYLODGE
• Sport Chek Ski Shop
• Barbeque Area
• W.G. Saloon - Wine & Draught Bar
• The Deli
• Trapper's Restaurant & Lounge
• Cafeteria
• Washrooms • Telephones

12 OLD SUNSHINE LODGE
• Lockers • Telephone
• Snack Bar
• Brown Bag Picnic Area
• Washrooms
• Administration Offices

13 SUNSHINE INN & TERRACE
• Accommodation
• Eagle's Nest Dining Room
• Chimney Corner Lounge
• Sauna, Hot Pool
• Washrooms
• Telephones
• General Store

14 PARK WARDEN'S CABIN

Sunshine Village
Telephone (403) 762-6500
P.O. Box 1510
Banff, Alberta, Canada
T0L 0C0

Trail map courtesy of Sunshine Village

Front Side
South Face

Trail map reprinted by permission of Lake Louise Ski Area

The trail map pictured is not to be used as a guide to the Breckenridge Ski Area. Use the trail maps provided by the resort at the ticket windows.

Trail map reprintd by permission of Keystone

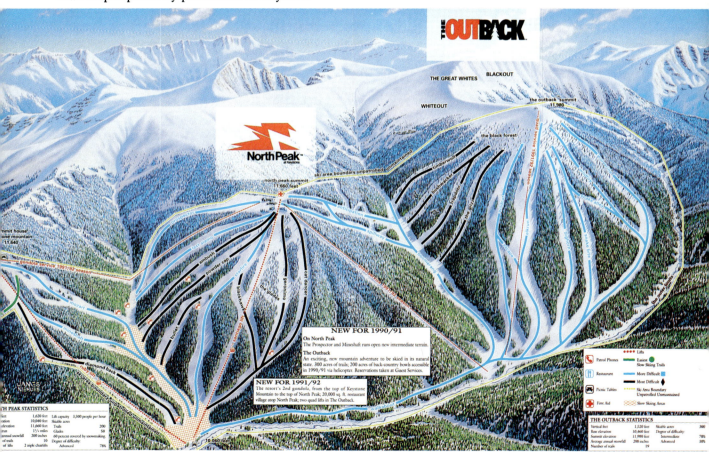

Trail map reprinted by permission of Keystone

Trail map reprinted by permission of Keystone

Trail map reprintd by permission of Copper Mountain Resort

Trail map courtesy of Crested Butte

MAP KEY	TRAIL DIFFICULTY SYMBOLS	TRAIL NAMES	LIFTS	IMPORTANT NOTICE

MAP KEY

Ⓜ MOUNTAIN MAPS

🅟 PATROL PHONE

▲ LIFTS

Ⓡ RESTAURANT

🅦 WARMING HUT (FOOD)

🅢 SKI SCHOOL
MEETING PLACE

✳ SNOWMAKING

〰️ PATROLLED AREA
BOUNDARY—DO NOT CROSS

✖ CLOSED AREAS—SEVERE
AVALANCHE HAZARD AREA

⚠ CAUTION

🔺 YOU ARE HERE

TRAIL DIFFICULTY SYMBOLS

● EASIEST

■ MODERATELY
DIFFICULT

■■ MORE DIFFICULT—
VARIED TERRAIN PLUS
SNOW CONDITIONS
FOR THE BETTER THAN
AVERAGE SKIER

◆ MOST DIFFICULT—
EXPERT

◆◆ MOST DIFFICULT—
EXPERT USE EXTRA
CAUTION

TRAIL NAMES

1. Union Pass Traverse
2. Way Home
3. North Colter Ridge
4. Buffalo Bowl
5. South Colter Ridge
6. Pawnis Bowl
7. Lower Sublette Ridge
8. Rendezvous Trail
9. Bivouac
10. Bird In The Hand
11. Papry Run
12. Alta Chutes
13. Grand
14. South Pass Traverse
15. Dimeoff
16. Lower Tram Line
17. Riverbin Bowl
18. Thunder
19. East Ridge Traverse
20. Expert Chutes
21. Gros Ventre
22. Nez Perce Traverse
23. Amphitheatre Traverse
24. Solitude Traverse
25. Avalanche
26. Downhill
27. Station
28. Sundance! Gully
29. Eagles Rest Cutoff
30. Eagles Rest
31. Posh Bear
32. Antelope Flats
33. Lower Teewinot
34. Lower Teewinot
35. Cross Country Ski Trail
36. Solitude Cutoff
37. Ashley Ridge
38. Beaver Tooth
39. Jackson Face
40. Nez Perce
41. Backtail
42. Surprise
43. Camp Ground
44. Timbered Island
45. Easy Does It
46. Lift Line
47. Sleeping Indian
48. Wide Open
49. Togwotee Pass Traverse
50. Moran
51. Upper Warner
52. Upper Teewinot
53. St. Johns
54. Teewinot Gully
55. Secret Slope
56. North Hobacks
57. South Hobacks
58. Tower Three Chute
59. Paint Brush
60. Lander Bowl
61. Lander Box
62. Hanging Rock
63. U.P. Connection

LIFTS

AERIAL TRAM   2.4 Miles Long
12 Minutes   4,139 Vertical Rise
1. EAGLE'S REST DOUBLE CHAIR   2,260' Long
5 Minutes   330 Vertical Rise
2. TEEWINOT DOUBLE CHAIR   3,060' Long
7 Minutes   425 Vertical Rise
3. APRES VOUS DOUBLE CHAIR   5,000' Long
10 Minutes   1,745 Vertical Rise
4. THUNDER DOUBLE CHAIR   3,770' Long
5 Minutes   1,466 Vertical Rise
5. CASPER BOWL TRIPLE CHAIR   3,490' Long
6 Minutes   1,046 Vertical Rise
6. CRYSTAL SPRINGS DOUBLE CHAIR 4,110' Long
9 Minutes   1,196 Vertical Rise
7. UPPER SUBLETTE RIDGE QUAD CHAIR 4,108' Long
9 Minutes   1,630 Vertical Rise
*8. RENDEZVOUS BOWL SURFACE LIFT 4,108' Long
5 Minutes   824 Vertical Rise
9. UNION PASS SURFACE LIFT   1,360' Long
2 Minutes   150 Vertical Rise

* This lift does not operate during periods of adverse wind, weather or snow conditions.

IMPORTANT NOTICE

FOR SKI PATROL ASSISTANCE,
DIAL 150 ON ANY SKI PATROL TELEPHONE,
OR CONTACT NEAREST LIFT OPERATOR.

This trail map is conceptual in nature and generally represents the location and difficulty of ski trails. The classification of ski runs is based on good weather and snow conditions. During periods of low visibility or other inclement weather and snow conditions, the degree of difficulty of the ski runs may change. For specific trail conditions, ask ski patrol or ski host.

Be aware of changing conditions. Natural and man-made obstacles exist. Grooming activities are routinely in progress on slopes and trails. Use caution, ski in control, and ski only on designated slopes or trails.

Skiing closed areas is a misdemeanor and subject to a fine of up to $100.00.

THE JACKSON HOLE SKI RESORT
IS OPERATED IN COOPERATION
WITH THE BRIDGER-TETON
NATIONAL FOREST.

Trail map reprinted by permission of Jackson Hole

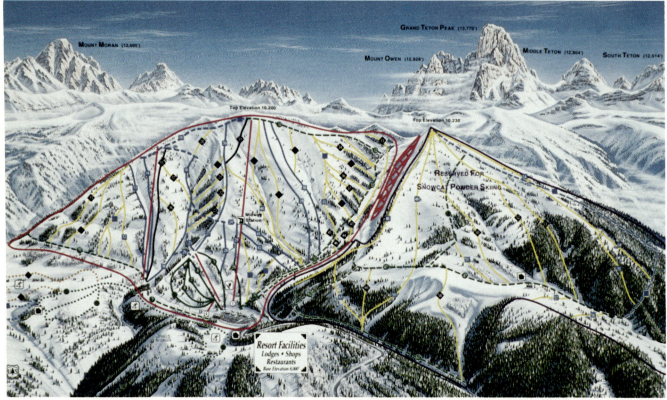

Trail map reprinted by permission of Grand Targhee Ski and Summer Resort

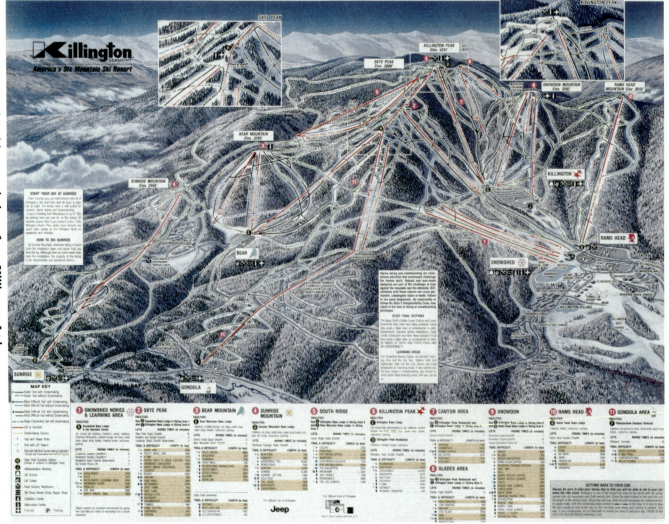

Lift	Length	Verti
Chair 1	3210'	10
Chair 2	3950'	9
Chair 3	2800'	10
Chair 4	4150'	10
Chair 5	4000'	13
Chair 6	1500'	4
Chair 7	2800'	1
Chair 8	3600'	10
Chair 9	6200'	17
Chair 10	4500'	10
Chair 11	2050'	2
Chair 12	3100'	8
Chair 13	2300'	4
Chair 14	5900'	11
Chair 15	5900'	11
Chair 16	6200'	15
Chair 17	3865'	7
Chair 18	5046'	11
Chair 19	2650'	2
Chair 20	2500'	4
Chair 21	2725'	4
Chair 22	3750'	2
Chair 23	2629'	11
Chair 24	5390'	13
Chair 25	4200'	13
Chair 26	2900'	8
Gondola 1	3450'	7
Gondola 2	4450'	14
T-Bar 2	2800'	7
Poma 1	500'	

ABILITY CODE:

🟢 Easier
🟦 More Difficult
◆ Most Difficult
🟨 Slow Skiing Area

Operation Hours

Chairs: 1, 2, 4, 8, 10, 17, T-2 operate 8:30-4
Chairs: 9, 14, 23, Go operate 9:00-3:30
Other Lifts operate 9:00
On weekends & holidays 30 m
Lift operation schedule subject
due to wind, weather & snow co

bin	16 Hully Gully	30 Downhill	44 Drop 18	61 Gravy Chute	77 Critter's	92 Solitude	106 St. Anton	120 The Acts
epy Hollow	17 Cloverleaf	31 Avalanche	45 Stump Alley	62 Silver Tip	78 Secret Spot	93 Face of Five	107 Dave's Run	123 Side Show
dges	18 Round Robin	32 R.C. West	46 St. Moritz	63 Powder Bowl	79 Training Wheels	94 Sanctuary	108 Huevos Grande	124 Festival
iday	19 Spring Canyon	33 Merry-go-round	47 Patrolmen's	64 Fascination 1	80 White Bark Bowl	95 Sliver	109 Climax	125 School Yard
ochet	20 Round About	34 Carousel	48 Over Easy	65 Far West	81 White Bark Ridge	96 Dry Creek	110 Hangman's Hollow	126 Crosswalk
d Hill	21 Hansel	35 Big Bird	49 Phantom's Escape	66 Blue Ox	82 Oops	97 Rooster Tail	111 Cornice Bowl	127 Manzanita
cksilver	22 Gretel	36 Little Bird	51 Mambo	67 Agee's Run	83 Surprise	98 Waterfall	112 Drop Out	128 Juniper
nshine	23 Grizzly	37 Lost in the Woods	52 Forest Trail	68 Terry's Run	84 Hemlock Ridge	99 China Bowl	113 Wipe Out	129 Watertank
ejay	24 Shaft	38 Wall Street	54 Jill's Run	69 Sesame St.	85 Hemlock Bowl	100 Christmas Bowl	114 Scotty's	131 Relief
ckadee	25 Viva	39 Wahzoo	56 Gus' Pasture	70 Sesame St. West	87 Roadrunner	101 East Bowl	115 Paranoid Flat	132 Slot
ll	26 Avalanche Chutes	40 Easy Rider	57 Bowling Alley	73 Bristlecone	88 Arriba	102 Center Bowl	116 Starchute	
itail	27 Dragon's Back	41 Short Cut	58 Thunder Mountain	74 Comin' Thru	89 Santiago	103 West Bowl	117 Repeat 22	
wing	28 Dragon's Tail	42 Coyote	59 Broadway	75 Lodgepole	90 One Chance	104 Saddle Bowl	118 Follow Me	
	29 Rollercoaster	43 Roger's Ridge	60 Wall	76 Ponderosa	91 Spook	105 Gremlin's Gulch	119 Encore	

Trail map reprinted by permission of Mammoth Mountain Ski Area

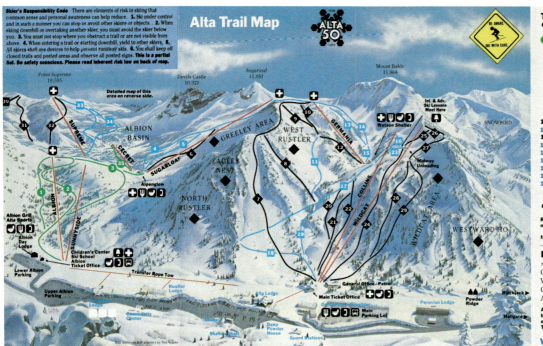

Alta Trail Map

ALTA 50

BE AWARE. SKI WITH CARE

Point Supreme 10,595

Devils Castle 10,920

Sugarloaf 11,051

Mount Baldy 11,068

SNOWBIRD

ALBION BASIN

GREELEY AREA

WEST RUSTLER

GERMANIA

Watson Shelter

Int. & Adv. Ski Lessons Meet Here

EAGLES NEST

Midway Unloading

NORTH RUSTLER

COLLINS

WILDCAT

WILDCAT AREA

WESTWARD HO

Albion Grill Alta Sports

Albion Day Lodge

Children's Center Ski School Albion Ticket Office

Lower Albion Parking

Upper Albion Parking

Transfer Rope Tow

Rustler Lodge

Alta Lodge

Lodge

Community Center

Shallow Shaft

Deep Powder House

Guard Stations

General Office / Patrol

Main Ticket Office

Main Parking Lot

Peruvian Lodge

Powder Ridge

Blackjack ►

Hellgate ►

Map sketches and graphics by Ted Nobels

Trail Names
Only main trails shown

● Easier   ■ More Difficult   ◆ Most Difficult

1. Patsey Marley	19. Corkscrew
2. Crooked Mile	20. Nina Curve
3. Sunnyside	21. Schuss Gully
4. Devil's Elbow	22. Collins Face
5. Roller Coaster	23. Midway
6. Extrovert	24. Bear Paw
7. Alf's High Rustler	25. Warmup
8. Stone Crusher	26. Peruvian Ridge
9. Sun Spot	27. Punch Bowl
10. Race Course	28. Rock Gully
11. Race Course Saddle	29. Wildcat Face
12. Lower Sunspot	30. So Long
13. Mambo	31. Sidewinder
14. Ballroom	32. Supreme Challenge
15. Main Street	33. Big Dipper
16. Aggie's Alley	34. Rock 'n Roll
17. Meadow	35. Sweet 'n Easy
18. Cat Track	

Patrol   Rest Rooms   Food   Ski School Meets Here   Bus   Phones

Run signs are marked to the relative difficulty of the area, and may vary with snow conditions. Hazards may exist at any time. For further information, contact ski patrol, ski school or lift foremen. Do not ski alone off main trails. Please ski safely.

Lifts

Name	Length	Vertical	Name	Length	Vertical
Collins	4,240	1,100	Sugarloaf	5,100	1,300
Wildcat	4,153	1,250	Sunnyside	4,000	730
Germania	3,750	1,125	Cecret	2,610	325
Albion	5,200	850	Supreme	3,850	1,081

Albion, Sunnyside and Cecret Lifts are designed primarily for the beginning and intermediate skier, with the rest of the lifts offering terrain suitable for intermediate to expert advanced. To reach Supreme Lift, you must first take Cecret Lift.

Wasatch National Forest   Revised June 1988

Trail map courtesy of Alta Ski Area

WEST TWIN PEAK

MT. BALDY

HIDDEN PEAK (11,000')

GAD VALLEY

LITTLE CLOUD LIFT

PERUVIAN GULCH

OLLINS GULCH

ALTA SKI AREA

MID GAD RESTAURANT

MID GAD UNLOADING STATION

GAD II LIFT

GAD I LIFT

MID GAD LIFT

PERUVIAN LIFT

AERIAL TRAM

RACE HILL

WILBERE LIFT

CLIFF ACCESS

THE CLIFF

CHICKADEE LIFT

SNOWBIRD CENTER

THE LODGE

THE INN

IRON BLOSAM

(7,900')

Entry

Cottonwood

BROWN

LIFTS:	VERTICAL RISE	TRAVEL TIME	TRAVEL LENGTH	*Skiers per hour
AERIAL TRAMWAY	2,900 ft. 883.9 m.	8 min.	8,395 ft. 2558.8 m.	125 per cab
PERUVIAN	1,000 ft. 304.8 m.	6 min.	2,943 ft. 897.0 m.	1,200
WILBERE RIDGE	668 ft. 207.7 m.	4.5 min.	2,154 ft. 656.5 m.	1,200
GAD I	1,827 ft. 557.0 m.	13 min.	6,704 ft. 2062.8 m.	1,200
GAD II	1,239 ft. 377.6 m.	9 min.	4,397 ft. 1340.2 m.	1,200
MID-GAD	1,315 ft. 401.0 m.	9 min.	4,310 ft. 1314.0 m.	1,100
LITTLE CLOUD	1,304 ft. 398.0 m.	7 min.	3,515 ft. 1072.0 m.	1,200
CHICKADEE	142 ft. 43.3 m.	3 min.	830 ft. 252.9 m.	710

TOTAL LIFT CAPACITY: 8810 skiers per hour

1 Chip's Run •	Black Forest
Primrose Path	Organ Grinder
Silver Fox	Lunch Run
Peruvian Cirque	Big Emma
Dalton's Draw	Bananas
Blackjack	Gadzooks
Chickadee •	Tiger Tail
Little Cloud	Carbonate
Regulator Johnson & Regulator Traverse	Lower Bassackwa
Wilbere Bowl	West Second Sou
Wilbere Chute	Miners Road
Mach Schnell	Bass Highway • (Easiest route to
Rothman Way	Chip's Face
Harper's Ferry East	Great Scott
Harper's Ferry	Upper Cirque
Wilbere Ridge	Cirque Traverse
Wilbere Cutoff •	Gad Chutes
Bassackwards •	Chip's Bypass •
Election •	Mark Malu Fork
S.T.H.	Adager

Snowbird's enthusiastic hosts and hostesses give free ski tours to introduce skiers of all levels to our exciting, varied terrain.

SKI SCHOOL MEETING AREAS
A—Chickadee — All children, adult beginners
B—Big Emma — All adults, above beginner level
C—Children's Center — Level "C", Cliff Lodge
• **DENOTES SLOW SKIING AREAS.** Fast or reckless skiing is not permitted at Snowbird.

ATTENTION SKIERS: ( ) EMERGENCY PHONE
The various difficulty ratings are relative to the Snowbird area. During periods of low visibility or other inclement weather and snow conditions, the degree of difficulty of the ski runs may change. If you are unfamiliar with the area, begin with those runs marked ■ EASIEST and progress to ◆ MORE DIFFICULT or ◆ MOST DIFFICULT as your ability allows. ▲ CAUTION: Check with the Ski Patrol for current conditions.

FOR YOUR SAFETY
Skiing is a mountaineering sport which has inherent risks. While efforts have been made to provide for your skiing safety, there are still hazards which require your alertness and vigilance. Good physical condition, proper clothing, appropriate equipment and a knowledge of the principles of skiing will dramatically reduce your chances of having an accident. Please enjoy skiing Snowbird while exercising common sense and caution. This brochure is not intended for use as a skier's guide.

Trail map reprinted by permission of Snowbird

Trail map reprinted by permission of Alpine Meadows

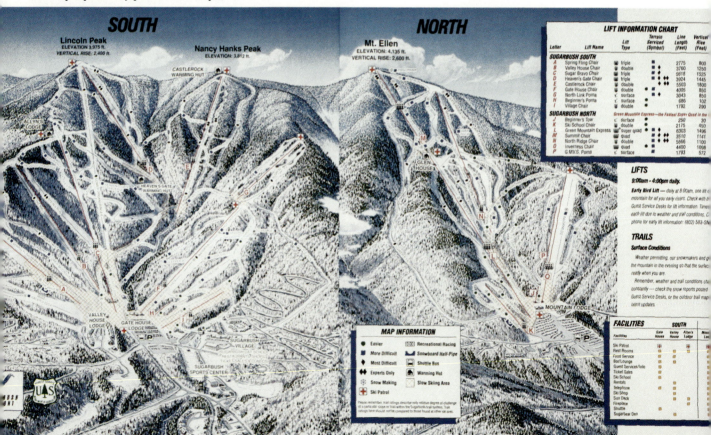

Trail map reprinted by permission of Sugarbush

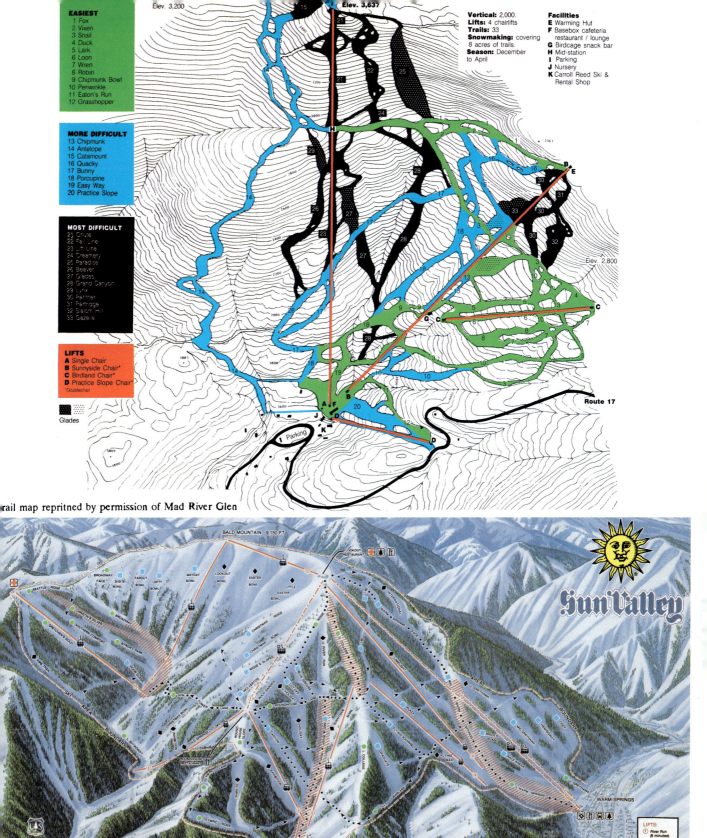

rail map repritned by permission of Mad River Glen

Trail map reprinted by permission of Sun Valley Company

TAOS

Trail map reprinted by permission of Taos Ski Valley

Trail map reprinted by permission of Telluride Ski Resort

Trail map reprinted by permission of Vail Associates, Inc.

Trail map reprinted by permission of Vail Associates, Inc.

Snowmass provides plenty of challenges on its runs in Hanging Valley. The resort hopes to extend its terrain significantly during the next several years.   Photo by Michael Kennedy/Courtesy Aspen Skiing Company

The Silvertree Hotel is conveniently located at the edge of the Snowmass slopes and at the edge of the Village Mall. Above, the morning rush is in full swing. Photo by GuideBook Publishing Co.

ASPEN/Aspen Highlands

P.O. Box 1248
Aspen, CO. 81612

Aspen Reservations and Information (800) 26-ASPEN (303) 925-1221 Snow Report

New For 1993-94

All four Aspen area ski mountains are poised on the edge of big change, but as this book went to print, none of the hoped-for changes were certainties. All of the changes will come about because both the Aspen Skiing Company and the Aspen Highlands ski area this year were purchased by ski-loving developers who want to bring the aging giant up to par with many of their aggressive new competitors, consolidating management and operational activities at all mountains.

While Aspen remains a great ski resort, and a town to dazzle anyone, many of its lifts are old and slow compared to lifts at other resorts which have poured millions of dollars into on-mountain facilities during the past decade.

Since 1985, the Crown family of Chicago has owned a half interest in the Aspen Skiing Company, which operates Aspen Mountain, Tiehack and Snowmass. Last spring they purchased the other 50 percent from the Miller/Davis Companies and announced plans for big improvements at the three mountains. For the 1993-94 ski season, a high-speed quad chair at Tiehack will replace Lift No. 1 from the bottom of the mountain to the top. In addition, the entire base lodge at Tiehack has been rebuilt.

At Snowmass, skiers will be able to reach the top of Sam's Knob and Alpine Springs much more quickly this year thanks to the addition of two new high speed quads.

To aid those families who have children who want to ski at Tiehack, and whose parents want to try some of the Aspen mountains, a new shuttle service will begin during this ski season Dubbed **Max the Moose Express**, this free shuttle will pick up riders at specified stops around town. If you registered for a Tiehack class the night before, you can ride the bus.

This good news has been accompanied by a major change in the offing at the Aspen Skiing Company's sister resort, Aspen Highlands, which is located three miles north of Aspen Mountain between Tiehack and the town of Aspen. Gerald Hines, a Houston-based real estate developer and co-owner of Hines Interests with his son, Jeff, was finalizing the purchase of Aspen Highlands from Harvard University and Whipple Jones. Jones founded the area in 1957, and while it has magnificent skiing, its lifts have not been upgraded in more than 20 years.

The Hines plan for the Highlands will not only transform this versatile skiing mountain from a tough skiing, crude half-sister of Aspen into a modern, inviting resort but also consolidate all 4 areas operations, which can only be good for the visitors' services. During the summer, both new owners announced their plans to share development and operations at Aspen Highlands ski area and base village. The Aspen Skiing Company will use its expertise to manage and improve mountain operations and, as experts in real estate development, the Hines company will organize the changes at the base of the mountain. For more information about future plans, see the Aspen Highland section of this chapter.

How to Get There

While Aspen is a 200-mile drive from Denver, in recent years its accessibility has been immeasurably improved. Not only did the Eisenhower tunnel two decades ago eliminate the old drive over the top of the Continental Divide on Highway 6, but finally in 1992, the 4-lane section of Highway 70 through Glenwood Canyon was complete. For many years that construction, an impressive engineering feat which carved a larger shelf for cars to drive along between Eagle and Glenwood Springs, often caused delays. Now a non-stop, breathtaking drive surrounded by sheer red cliffs, carved sometimes through the mountain and skirting the Colorado River will be a welcome part of the trip. It is especially beautiful at sundown.

Air traffic to the Aspen area continues to increase, making flying to the resort much more convenient. Flights into and out of Aspen's Sardy Field have increased. Sardy is an FAA-controlled airport where instrument landings are possible. Thus, it is necessary to bus passengers from Denver only during the worst storms. The town of Aspen is located only two and a half miles east of Sardy Field and is accessible by taxi (High Mountain), limousine, and courtesy van.

From Denver, Continental and United Express will offer 60 round-trip flights daily between mid December and April. United Express also will offer travelers from Los Angeles and chicago daily non-stop service. Four non-stop flights from Dallas/Fort Worth also will be available.

In addition Eagle County Airport, an 80-minute drive from Aspen, also provides gates to American Airlines for non-stop flights from Chicago, Dallas, Miami and New York. Delta will offer non-stop service from Salt Lake City. America West flies daily from Phoenix and Taesa flies Saturday from Mexico City via Laredo.

At press time, it was not certain whether Denver's new airport would open by December of 1993 or not. At some time during this ski season, however, the changeover will occur. How the transition from Stapleton will be accomplished remains to be seen. If your are driving, remember to allow at least 30 minutes extra for the additional miles to the new airport.

Most major car rental agencies are located at Sardy Field. They provide *skierized* cars equipped with snow tires and ski racks. For a slightly higher price, many rental agencies will provide four-wheel drive vehicles. Travelers are cautioned to reserve these vehicles far in advance of arrival because demand for them is great.

Having a car at Aspen is not necessary and may not even be desirable because the local transportation system is so good. Free shuttle buses run daily between Aspen, Aspen Mountain, Aspen Highlands, Snowmass, and Buttermilk.

Buses that go to Aspen Highlands are not the same buses that shuttle between Aspen Mountain, Buttermilk, and Snowmass. The Highlands has its own shuttle system with buses departing daily from Aspen's Ruby Park every 15 minutes between 8:15 A.M. and 11:00 A.M. These buses stop along Main Street en route. Return rides to Aspen in the evening commence at 3:00 P.M. and continue until 5:15 P.M. Transportation to and from Snowmass is provided every Tuesday and Thursday.

Mountain Information

Aspen Skiing Co. owns three separate mountains, each distinct and unique. Aspen Mountain, known as Ajax to many of the locals, is situated in the center of town and is designated for intermediate and expert skiers only. Tiehack Mountain is located a short distance to the west and offers less challenging terrain, perfect for beginning and intermediate skiers. Snowmass is discussed in a separate section of this book, and is located miles to the north of Aspen.

Aspen Mountain

Aspen Mountain is different from other mountains featured in this guidebook. It is one of only two mountains that does not have beginner slopes (the other is Sun Valley)! It may also be the only mountain where the majority of the trails are short. Ajax appears to have "blown" its top, because much of the skiable terrain is directed from its outer edges into its center crater. Most of the skiing on the upper third of the mountain is intermediate in nature and not particularly exciting.

However, expert skiers will find Aspen Mountain truly exhilarating. The expert runs on Ajax are steep, frequently gladed, covered with enormous bumps, and definitely not for advanced skiers who fancy themselves experts. The main attractions to this mountain are its legendary location in one of the oldest ski resorts in America and its breathtaking view from the top. From the mountain's summit, visitors can view the town of Aspen lying far below and Starwood, a wealthy show-business neighborhood located on the other side of town.

Some of Aspen Mountain's most awesome runs are situated in the middle third of the mountain. As previously mentioned, these short runs terminate on an intermediate run named Spar Gulch. In order to ski the mountain, it is necessary to traverse almost all the way to the bottom of the hill and take the lift up again. This translates to less ski time and more lift time. The runs included in this situation are primarily Bear Paw, Short Snort, Zaugg Dump, Perry's Prowl, Last Dollar, the Face of Bell, and the Shoulder of Bell.

Until the 1981-82 season Aspen Mountain had no artificial snowmaking capabilities. During lean snow years the lower third of the mountain was virtually unskiable. Now, however, snowmaking equipment has been added, and the lack of natural snow should not inhibit anyone from enjoying the lower third.

Located in the White River National Forest, Aspen Mountain consists of 625 skiable acres (253 ha) and has over twenty-three miles (37 km) of trails. Of these trails 35% are rated more difficult, 35% are most difficult, and 30% are expert. "More difficult" relates to the blue square sign used at most resorts to denote "intermediate," while the black diamond denotes "most difficult," which most resorts usually refer to as "expert." Aspen Mountain illustrates its "expert" terrain with two black diamonds.

The base elevation of Aspen is 7,945 feet (2,422 meters) and its summit is 11,212 feet (3,417 meters). This provides the skier with 3,267 vertical feet (996 meters) of skiing.

This terrain is serviced by
1 Gondola (Silver Queen)
1 Quad SuperChair
2 Fixed Grip Quads
4 Double Chairs

Aspen receives an annual snowfall of about 300 inches (762 cm) at its summit and 155 inches (394 cm) at its base. Its average monthly snowfalls are

Nov.	34"	(86 cm)
Dec.	52"	(132 cm)
Jan.	40"	(102 cm)
Feb.	51"	(130 cm)
Mar.	66"	(168 cm)

Ajax has the snowmaking capacity to cover 210 acres (85 ha) which is somewhat limiting, especially during the beginning of ski season. Most of the snowmaking capabilities are located on the lower portion of the mountain near the bottom of the Little Nell lift, where traffic tends to rapidly ski off the base. However, Aspen Mountain's snowmaking equipment assures skiers that there will be enough coverage for them to enjoy the slopes during the entire period of operation.

During the season, weather permitting, it is possible to ski the back bowls of Aspen Mountain. These are powder runs suitable for both intermediate and expert skiers. Reservations are necessary prior to skiing the backside because access to the terrain is via snow-cat. Telephone (303) 925-1227 or (800)525-6200 for reservations.

Tiehack Mountain

Located two miles from Aspen Mountain on Colorado Highway 82, Tiehack/Buttermilk is almost midway between Aspen and Snowmass. For beginning skiers, there is probably not a finer mountain in Colorado on which to learn to ski. Its gentle ski terrain is meticulously maintained throughout the winter season.

Tiehack Mountain, until recently known as Tiehack/Buttermilk, consists of 410 skiable acres (162 ha) and has over 20 miles (32 km) of trails. It is a small mountain by Colorado standards but is completely adequate for beginners and intermediate skiers. This is especially true when one considers the expansive terrain available at Snowmass and Aspen Mountain proper. Of the skiable trails available, 35% are considered easiest, 39% are more difficult, and 26% are most difficult.

The base elevation of Tiehack 7,870 feet (2,399 meters) and its summit is at 9,900 feet (3,018 meters). This provides the skier with 2,030 vertical feet (619 meters) of skiing. This area's longest run is Tom's Thumb to Homestead Road to Spruce. It is 3 miles (4.8 km) long and rated easiest (beginner) its entire length.

Buttermilk receives an annual snowfall of about 200 inches (508 cm) at its summit and 155 inches (394 cm) at its base. Its average monthly snowfalls are

Nov.	33"	(84 cm)
Dec.	43"	(91 cm)
Jan.	38"	(89 cm)
Feb.	47"	(114 cm)
Mar.	59"	(142 cm)

The average monthly temperatures during the season are

Nov.	31°	0° C
Dec.	22°	-5° C
Jan.	20°	-6° C
Feb.	23°	-5° C
Mar.	29°	-2° C

Aspen Highlands

This may be the last year you can ski on some of the old lifts at Aspen Highlands, so if you want to see the old mountain as it has been, you'd better head out there. Plans for the "new" Aspen Highlands are among the most exciting proposed at a ski resort in a long time. Pending a county approval process which usually takes from 12 to 18 months, the changes will return the Aspen area to its glory days as a premier offering to skiers searching for longer, steeper runs, variety and much-needed high speed lifts to whisk them up to its peaks. It also should attract skiers from Aspen Mountain and Snowmass more than it has during the past 10 years or more.

Among capital improvements proposed are first of all the replacement of the aging lodge at Highlands' base with a new pedestrian village including commercial and restaurant space, 105 tourist condominiums, an 82-room hotel and skier support services, such as the ski school and patrol. The company also will also offer single family home sites on either side of the base.   Plans also include affordable housing for local workers.

The first lifts to be changed at the Highlands will be Cloud 9 and Exhibition 2 chairs which are double chairs operating mid-mountain. The 2 high speed quads which eventually are planned for the bottom of the slopes will not be added until plans can be satisfactorily be set for the accommodation of more traffic on the roads leading to the resort.

Other long range plans include the addition of a lift to serve the Aspen Ski Team which will lead from the public schools just down the road, and possibly a lift connecting Tiehack/Buttermilk to Aspen Highlands.

For skiers, planned mountain expansions will make Aspen Highlands tough skiing even more attractive. This year the Hines Interests plan to study the best way to control avalanches in both Highlands and Maroon Bowls, in the hope that they can add lifts and open the terrain to skiers. In addition new lifts and extended runs will increase the skiable acreage in the Steeplechase area from 800 to 2,300 acres!

Aspen Highlands, as it is, is a large mountain nestled between Aspen Mountain to the east and Tiehack to the west. As old as Aspen Highlands is, it has always been overshadowed and outspent by Aspen Skiing Company. Consequently, Aspen Highlands has evolved into a totally different area. There is little of the glitz, glamour, or ambience of Aspen Mountain or Snowmass here. Rather, this area is reminiscent of a past when skiing was a little more primitive and skiers were a little more in touch with nature.

While the physical facilities are somewhat dated, the runs and trails on this mountain have the patina of time etched into them. This is the mountain where the locals ski because it is rarely as crowded as the other three ski areas and the prices are lower. During the 1993-94 season, in fact, the area's management decided again to keep its prices at $30 a day for an adult daily lift ticket. During the past two years the response to this price, lowered from the 1990-91 price of $40 was so great that it made sense to continue the bargain.

Aspen Highlands' mountain is different from other mountains in the area in that its beginner, intermediate, and expert trails run all over the mountain; they are not confined to one or two specific areas. However, the concentration of expert runs is at mountaintop. This is a mountain that one rarely skis all the way down until the end of the day. The center section, primarily beginner and intermediate terrain, is serviced by four chairlifts.

Located in the White River National Forest, Aspen Highlands consists of 550 skiable acres (223 ha) and has over 21 miles (33 km) of skiable terrain. Of these trails, 23% are rated beginner, 48% are rated intermediate, while 29% are rated expert. Of the expert terrain, 14% is double black diamonds. Intermediate terrain is referred to on the trail map as "more difficult" and is identified on the mountain by a blue square. The black diamond shape denotes "expert." In recent years, most resorts have also added the category of double black diamond. This designation identifies runs that are either extremely steep, gladed, moguled, or all of the above. Skiers attempting to ski a double black diamond run should possess enough skill to turn their skis within the length of the skis and to ski in any conditions from deep powder to "crud." Crud is deep snow that has been skied on for several days without grooming and which has melted during the day and refrozen during the evening.

The base elevation of Aspen Highlands is 8,000 feet (2,439 meters) and its summit is at 11,800 feet (3,597 meters). This provides the skier with 3,800 vertical feet (1,158 meters) of skiing. Aspen Highlands offers the most vertical feet of skiing in Colorado.

Aspen Highlands is served by

9 Double Chairlifts
2 Poma Lifts

Snowmaking capabilities at Aspen Highlands have grown to cover 110 acres. Snowmaking throughout the Aspen area is limited due to restrictions on the use of water. Fortunately, the area is blessed with abundant natural snowfall, and the only time man-made snow is needed is early in the season.

The longest beginner run at the Highlands is Nugget to Park Avenue. It is approximately two miles (3.2 km). Most of this run is a catwalk, and it is the most popular way down the mountain in the evening. The longest intermediate run is Golden Horn to Thunderbowl, approximately two miles (3.2 km). Golden Horn and Thunderbowl are terrific cruising runs. Always groomed and wide open, they rival the Big Burn at Snowmass. These are the runs one takes to work on technique or just to get the feeling back into his legs after a summer's layoff from skiing.

The longest expert run is Moment of Truth. It is nearly one mile (1.6 km) long and is a double black diamond.

The natural terrain of the mountain lends itself to many double and triple fall lines. Very few of the trails go straight down the face of the mountain but tend instead to be alongside the mountain's ridge, particularly near the top. The expert skiing terrain at Highlands is among the best in the country. The newly opened Steeplechase on the east upper part of the mountain is steep and gladed. Try this area after a big snowfall and learn why everyone raves about tree skiing. On the other side of Aspen Highlands' mountain is Olympic Bowl—not so much a bowl as a series of open, steep runs. Some of the runs in "Oly" bowl are gladed, but not enough to intimidate competent skiers. In fact, many of the runs in Oly are intermediate and among the best on the mountain. These include Olympic Glades, Pyramid Park, and Grand Prix. For intermediates who love to ski bumps, there is Scarlett's Run. Formally known as Flora Dora, this run is short and adds new meaning to the term, "ski the bumps." This is the site of the annual bump ski contest which is a real challenge. Beginning skiers will feel at home on Apple Strudel and Red Onion. More advanced skiers should avoid these runs because they frequently are crowded with classes.

Skiers who have a fear of heights are advised to avoid taking the Loges Peak lift. Just before skiers exit this chairlift, it passes over a ravine that is 800 feet (244 meters) deep! Naturally, it's not as frightening on a snowy day as it is on a bright, sunlit one.

Expert skiers who are unsure of their ability to ski double black diamonds should consider skiing The Wall. This is a short, steep run and somewhat typical of most double black diamonds. If skiers can negotiate The Wall without trouble and enjoy the experience, they will no doubt enjoy the other double blacks here and at other resorts, as well. It is always a wise idea to try the run when there is good snow because one rarely is injured by falling into soft, deep snow.

Aspen Lift Ticket Prices (1993-94)

Aspen Skiing Company offers many different lift ticket rates for individuals, as well as for groups, persons over 65, the physically challenged, and combination lift ticket/ski lesson packages. Lift tickets are discounted 10% during value season. If you know you will be skiing at any of the four Aspen area mountains for several days, you can say a fair amount of money by purchasing tickets at least 14 days before your arrival. Call 1-800-525-6200, ext. 3594 to charge tickets in advance, and save more than $12 per day!

The full day lift ticket prices had not been announced at press time, but during the 1992-93 season, they were $43.

14 Day Advance Purchase Adult 3 Mountain Rate (1993-94):

Value Season (Nov. 25-Dec. 17, 1993)	**Regular Season**
March 26 - Apr. 10, 1994	**Dec. 18, 1993 - Mar. 25, 1994**
$180 6 of 7 days	$234
$150 5 of 6 Days	$200
$124 4 of 5 Days	$164
$ 93 3 of 4 Days	$126

14 Day Advance Purchase Rates for Children aged 7 to 12 and seniors, 65 to 69, 70 and over ski free. Children 6 and under ski free.

$144 6 of 7 Days
$125 5 of 6 Days
$104 4 of 5 Days
$ 78 3 of 4 Days

Aspen Highlands Lift Ticket Prices (1993-94)

$ 22 Adults Half-Day (A.M. or P.M.)
$ 30 All-Day
$ 58 2 of 7 Consecutive Days
$ 78 3 of 7 Consecutive Days
$115 5 of 7 Consecutive Days
$ 22 Daily Student Rate (Proper ID Required)

Lift ticket prices for children over twelve

$ 15 All-Day
$ 28 2 of 7 Consecutive Days
$ 39 3 of 7 Consecutive Days
$ 60 5 of 7 Consecutive Days
$ 15 60 years and older

In addition to offering its own lift ticket prices, Aspen Highlands cooperates with Aspen Skiing Company and is included in the four-mountain coupon book program. Under this plan there are two seasons: Value and Regular. Four-mountain coupon book prices during the 1993-94 season are priced as follows:

$240 6 of 7 Day Regular Season
$164 4 of 5 Day Regular Season

Hours of Operation

9:00 A.M. to 3:30 P.M., Aspen Mountain
9:00 A.M. to 3:30 P.M., Buttermilk Mountain
9:00 A.M. to 4:00 P.M., Aspen Highlands

Lift Ticket Purchase Locations

Lift tickets are sold at the bases of the Silver Queen Gondola, the Little Nell Quad Chairlift, and the 1-A Chairlift at Aspen Mountain. Tiehack Mountain lift tickets may be purchased at the base of the Main Buttermilk Lift, located just behind the Inn at Aspen. Lift tickets may also be purchased at the base of Lift # 3 at West Buttermilk and at the edge of the Tiehack parking lot by the Race and Events Center.

Regardless of where tickets are purchased, they will be honored at Aspen Mountain, Tiehack and Snowmass. The special four-mountain rate also includes Aspen Highlands.

How to Avoid Crowds on Aspen Mountain

In 1987 Aspen Skiing Company spent millions of dollars improving Aspen Mountain. The addition of the Silver Queen Gondola and the Quad SuperChair™ significantly changed the demographics of the mountain. Although the additions were designed to improve the mountain's uphill services, they had the unplanned effect of increasing the number of persons who ski Ajax. Formerly many people skied Snowmass in order to avoid the crowds on Aspen Mountain. However, with the improved lifts, many skiers apparently decided to return to Aspen Mountain. The result is that the mountain is now as crowded as it ever has been.

One of the ways skiers have discovered to avoid crowded lift lines is to hire an instructor for the day. By doing this, they can break into lift lines, a viable alternative to waiting in line if one is not opposed to spending $250 per day for an instructor. Most people who choose this option also treat the instructor to lunch. Those without a large wallet should try avoiding the gondola and lift number three.

The most common way down Ajax mountain at the end of the day is via Spar Gulch to Little Nell. This is a narrow ravine which becomes very crowded with skiers of all ability levels. In the evening particularly, use caution and ski slowly when returning to the base. One of the reasons that now snowboarding is allowed on Aspen Mountain is because of the natural "half pipe" shape of Spar Gulch. Mountain managers feel that if snowboarders were added to the natural funneling of the crowds at the end of the day it would be dangerous.

As an alternative to negotiating traffic on Spar Gulch, take Ruthie's Run to Dago Cut Road or to Magnifico. By doing so, you will exit the mountain a little further north of Little Nell, but you will avoid the congestion. If this is not acceptable, exit onto Tower Ten Road. This catwalk, located very near the bottom and bisecting Franklin Dump, will return the skier to Little Nell.

How to Avoid Crowds at Aspen Highlands

During busy days most crowds seem to congregate at the Cloud 9 and the Exhibition II lifts. To avoid lift lines and still enjoy the same runs, try the Grand Prix poma lift. It runs parallel to the Exhibition lift. The Loges Peak lift is not usually as crowded as some of the other lifts, and it is convenient to ski the intermediate and expert runs near the top of the mountain from here. The Thunderbowl lift also frequently is not crowded, and skiing is great in this area. However, it is low on the mountain so snow conditions usually are not as good as they are farther uphill.

In the late afternoon the most crowded runs are Park Avenue and Golden Barrel. Avoid these high traffic areas by returning to the base via Golden Horn, Thunderbowl, or Upper Jerome Bowl. If snow conditions are good, the expert skier should return by skiing Lowerstein—it's a great way to finish!

Aspen Ski School

Aspen Skiing Company employs over four hundred certified ski instructors. However, most of these instructors teach at Buttermilk and Snowmass. Because there are no beginner runs nor easy intermediate runs on Aspen Mountain, ski classes are limited to advanced intermediates and experts. The 1993-94 rates may be found in the section of this book dealing with Snowmass.

Aspen Highlands Ski School

Aspen Highlands Ski School employs sixty full-time instructors and another fifteen during peak periods. It teaches a modified American Teaching System (ATS), formerly known as the American Teaching Method (ATM). Instructors also teach Graduated Length Method (GLM). The GLM system has fallen into disrepute of late and is no longer offered at most resorts. However, the instructors at Highlands believe there is a place for it in their teaching programs, so they employ GLM for a brief time with rank beginners.

Ski classes meet daily at the base facility, close to the bell. Classes run from 10:15 A.M. through 3:30 P.M. daily. However, classes of fewer than four students end at 1:00 P.M.
Prices this year probably will be similar to those offered by the other Aspen mountains.
Aspen Highlands also conducts special classes designed for skiers who want to learn a particular skill such as telemark, snowboard, and mono-ski. Additionally, it organizes clinics for racing, for powder hounds, and a special clinic just for ladies which includes a picnic lunch and video critique.

Equipment Rental

There are more than twenty ski-rental locations in Aspen. As at all ski resorts, the prices for rental equipment are similar. Rates for skis only are usually between $15 and $20 per day. If boots and poles are required, the rate will usually vary from $17 to $22 per day. An up-charge of 10 to 20% for performance skis is typical, and most (if not all) shops offer performance packages. Aspen ski-rental shops will usually discount their rates for equipment if it is to be rented for three or more days. A cash or credit card deposit must be posted at the time the rental agreement is made.

Ski Tuning And Repair

Aspen offers an excellent selection of stores and companies in various locations for ski tuning and repair. Most rental establishments repair skis; in addition, there are companies that only sell new skis and companies that only repair older ones. Almost without exception, the shops do a competent job of repairing or waxing skis. However, a few stores have state-of-the-art ski-tuning equipment. All things being equal, skiers should consider having their skis and bindings tuned or repaired where this up-to-date machinery is utilized. See the Snowmass chapter for an idea of prices this year for tuning and repair.

Aspen Mountain Dining

Four mountain restaurants are found on Aspen Mountain. All are cafeterias except Darcy's. **Darcy's** is located in **Ruthie's Restaurant** at the top of the 1-A Lift. Although originally built as a lunch and dinner restaurant, the town of Aspen never granted the restaurant a permit to operate at night. It remains, however, the only restaurant with table service on Ajax. This restaurant is named after Darcy Brown, an original member of Aspen Skiing Company's Board of Directors. He was responsible for running the company from 1957 through 1979. He was also the husband of Ruthie, for whom the cafeteria part of the restaurant is named. (When Darcy and his crew were cutting runs on Ajax, Ruthie complained that Roch Run and Silver Queen were too difficult and offered to invest $5 thousand in the company if an easier way down the mountain could be cut. And that is how Ruthie's Run came into existence). Darcy's was formerly the Coyote Grill, and those who are familiar with it will welcome the changes in management and menu. Service is prompt and courteous and the food is excellent. Whether enjoying a simple cup of black bean soup or mesquite-grilled salmon, guests will be pleased. There is a long list of appetizers, soups, sandwiches, and specialties, as well as a very extensive wine list available to make lunch on the mountain memorable. Few mountain restaurants afford visitors as spectacular a view as does Darcy's—with the town of Aspen spread directly below.

Bonnie's Restaurant, located at Tourelotte Park high on the mountain, is convenient to the Quad SuperChair™. The views from its sizable deck are of Snow Bowl. Bonnie's serves cafeteria-style food which is typically nondescript. The ambience, however, is unique. The restaurant has a pseudo-beach decor with thatched, umbrella-topped tables outside, and a similar thatch-topped bar which is open when weather permits. It is a popular place to stop at the end of the day before embarking down the mountain.

At the top of the Silver Queen Gondola another cafeteria, **The Sundeck**, serves fare similar to that found in other restaurants on the mountain. From its outside deck in clear weather, skiers can enjoy spectacular views of the Maroon Bells.

Tiehack/Buttermilk Mountain has four mountain restaurants. **The Cliffhouse**, a cafeteria-style restaurant located at the top of the #2 Lift, serves Swiss specialties as well as traditional fare.

Another cafeteria, **Cafe Suzanne's**, is located at the base of West Buttermilk. Suzanne's is smaller and more intimate than most mountain restaurants. Try the excellent crepes.

Anneliese's, located at the base of Eagle Hill on Tiehack, is open for public dining and is frequently used by clubs and groups. This restaurant offers table service as well as cafeteria service.

The Main Buttermilk Restaurant (still another cafeteria) is located at the base of the Main Buttermilk chairlift. On warm, bright days its deck is a favorite place to relax and watch skiers negotiate their way down Government or Spruce Face.

Aspen Highlands Mountain Dining

Two mountain restaurants and a restaurant at the base comprise the Highlands' food service. The largest mountain restaurant is the **Merry-Go-Round**, situated at the top of the Exhibition II lift and at the base of the Cloud 9 lift. This restaurant serves typical cafeteria-style food. On Fridays, resting skiers can enjoy the Friday Freestyle contest held in front of this restaurant at noon. The **Cloud 9 Restaurant**, located at the top of the Cloud 9 lift, is smaller but the food is similar to the Merry-Go-Round's. However, this restaurant has something no other mountain restaurant has: ski patrol members jump over its outdoor deck several times a week at noon, weather and workload permitting. Thrill to the patrolmen's antics as they soar over the restaurant's
65-foot long deck! For a bird's-eye view, try to catch a ride up the Olympic lift while they are performing; they will appear to almost land in your lap!

Child Care

Because Aspen is one of the country's oldest established ski resorts, many services have simply evolved rather than having been planned. Child day care is an example of a service that was needed but not planned. The result is that it is inconvenient for skiers to place their children in day care. There are three services, all of which are located out-of-town. In order for skiers to place their children in such facilities, they must either drive to the centers or take the shuttle to and from the service.

Aspen Sprouts is located in the Airport Business Center midway between Aspen and Snowmass, near Buttermilk Mountain. Care for children between the ages of one and five is available Monday through Saturday. Reservations may be booked by telephoning (303) 920-1055.

Little Feet, also located in the Airport Business Center, will accept some walk-in visitors. However, it is primarily a service for working parents in Aspen. Little Feet will accept children aged six weeks through eighteen months. The 1990-91 rate was $45 per day or $30 per half-day. Three meals a day were provided. As with all day-care centers, diapers and formula should be provided by the parents. Operating hours are from 7:30 A.M.to 5:30 P.M. Telephone for advance reservations: 303/920-1548. Skiers should be sure to confirm child-care arrangements when they book accommodations.

Much more convenient facilities are available for children old enough to be enrolled in either ski school or in **The Powder Pandas** at Tiehack Mountain, which operates from 8:30 A.M. through 4:00 P.M. and accepts children aged three to five. Lunch and specialized ski instruction are provided for all ability levels.

Aspen Highlands' **Snowpuppies Ski School** accepts students aged three through six. Classes begin at 9:30 A.M. and continue until 3:30 P.M. each day.

Recognizing that existing day-care facilities are limited, Aspen Skiing Company has established a day-care center in the newly remodeled Timbermill Restaurant, located slopeside at the west end of the Village Mall in Snowmass. This facility accommodates children eighteen months through six years. Children aged eighteen months through three and a half may be enrolled in **The Snow Cubs**. Children three years through six may be enrolled in the **Big Burn Bears**. For more information, telephone (303) 925-4444.

Baby sitters are available in Aspen by telephoning the Aspen Resort Association at (303) 925-1940 or the Snowmass Resort Association at (303) 923-2000.

Medical Facilities

Injuries which occur on the slopes are treated on an emergency basis by the ski patrol. Broken bones are immobilized and trauma is contained. Once emergency treatment has been rendered and the patient has been stabilized, he is transported to Aspen Valley Hospital for specialized care as needed.

Aspen Valley Hospital is a full-service hospital with all the equipment and expertise one expects of a large city hospital. The hospital staff's credentials are impressive. Many staff members received their training at some of the most prestigious institutions in America such as Johns Hopkins, Columbia, Yale, UCLA, Cornell, NYU, and Harvard.

Cross-Country Skiing

Track skiing is available through the Ute Nordic Center on the Aspen Championship Golf Course, located on Highway 82 near Sardy Field. Lessons and tours are offered. A retail shop on the premises has complete lines of clothing and cross-country ski equipment. Rental equipment is also available for the three-pin skier.

The largest cross-country ski company is **Ashcroft Ski Touring**, located twelve miles west of town along Castle Creek. Ashcroft has thirty kilometers of groomed double tracks offering spectacular views of the Maroon Bells and the White River National Forest. Huts, stocked with firewood and hot drinks, are placed along the trails for skiers' convenience. Ashcroft offers all levels of instruction and provides guides for longer tours which can last up to several days.

Each evening at 6:00, groups head for dinner and night skiing at the **Pine Creek Cook House**. At the trailhead in Ashcroft's parking lot, participants are provided with miners' headlamps to light the way—usually unnecessary if a full moon is out. Non-skiers can visit the Cook House by sleigh. Telephone (303) 925-1971 for additional information or to make reservations for specific trips.

Back-country skiing has received a great deal of bad press in recent years due to deaths caused by avalanches. The early 1987-88 season saw a great deal of avalanche activity. The back-country skier should be aware of potential dangers **before** embarking on such a journey, **always** wear a beeper and know how to use it, **never** travel alone, and use a competent guide familiar with the area to be traversed.

There are few feelings as exhilarating as being in the wild, away from everybody for several days. Many people recognize the joys of this activity and reserve such trips several months ahead. Advance reservations to use the hut system are essential in order for skiers to avoid being stranded on the mountain at night without shelter. However, once a reservation is made, it cannot be readily rescheduled. Many skiers, therefore, find themselves in the unenviable position of forfeiting their deposits and their cross-country experience if avalanche danger prevents them from leaving at their reserved time. Unfortunately, people have been known to put pressure on guides to go out during marginal conditions, and as a result, deaths due to avalanches have occurred. Please use good judgment and if the conditions are not right, reschedule at the earliest possible date, even if it is not until the following year. Information and reservations may be made by telephoning the Tenth Mountain Trail Association at (303) 925-5775.

Special Events

The single biggest event each year at Aspen/Snowmass is the Wintersköl celebration, or Festival of Snow. Each January for five days, events such as canine fashion shows, beauty pageants, pancake breakfasts, ice sculpting, free-style contests, recreational ski races, bartenders' drink contest, avalanche awareness presentations, live concerts, ice hockey, hot air balloon races, telemark bump contests, sky-diving demonstrations are scheduled all day and late into the evenings. There is even a chili shootout on the Snowmass Mall and a terrific fireworks display accompanied by music on a local radio station. As if this were not enough, additional events during the year generally include one or more races on the Pro Ski Tour, USSA races, Coca-Cola Challenge, NASTAR finals, and Golf on Skis Weathermen's Cup.

Accommodations

Aspen has a greater variety of accommodations to fit visitors' tastes and pocketbooks than perhaps any other ski resort in the country. The Aspen experience offers visitors two completely different choices in local ambience—Aspen's upbeat, small-town chic or Snowmass's ski in/ski out convenience.

Hotels

The Little Nell hotel has proven to be among the most popular hotels in Aspen. Offering guests only 92 rooms, of which 13 are actually suites, The Little Nell is located on Durant St. less than one hundred steps from the Aspen Mountain Gondola. This is a warm hotel decorated in soft colors complementing the native stones, woods, and flowers found throughout the establishment. This is the only hotel in a U.S. ski resort which AAA awarded its prestigious Five Diamond Award, signifying an exceptional level of service, striking, luxurious facilities and many extra amenities. Another indication of the quality of this hotel is the fact that it was accepted as a member of the prestigious Relais & Chateaux, an international association of small luxurious inns.

The ground floor, while naturally containing the check-in, concierge, and central lobby, is festooned with some of Aspen's toniest shops including Oilily (children's clothes), Oxbow Outfitting Co. (everything one could possibly need for an outdoor Aspen adventure), Ute Alpinist (clothes for the more athletic, such as mountain climbing gear and paraphernalia, Sport Stalker (fashionable ski and resort wear).

Separating the Aspen Mountain Gondola from the hotel's central lobby is a beautiful outdoor heated swimming pool and hot tub. The pool deck is constructed from concrete dyed to match the mountain's red color. The pool itself is slate gray gunnite with a descending waterfall which creates its own small maelstrom. During good weather, the deck is open for lunch dining and après-ski. What a great way to wind down after a challenging day on Bell Mountain!

For those who have exerted themselves too much or who are partial to activities other than skiing, there is a well-outfitted spa just one flight down from the main lobby. The spa sports two Stairmaster 4000 PT's as well as free weights, Lifecycles, Cybex UBE, and Nautilus equipment. The locker rooms, though small, are beautifully appointed with deep-pile Berber carpeting, dark oak paneling, and Charlie Brown granite counter tops. Massage rooms and a steam shower complete this special facility dedicated to pampering.

Each of the hotel's rooms and suites is different. The difference may be only in the use of color or it may be more substantial due to the unusual nature of the hotel's building site. Regardless, all rooms are finely appointed with all the amenities one could wish for away from home. Management has taken into account the special needs of skiers and planned accordingly. Therefore, the rooms are oversized compared to most hotels—providing room to move about in ski boots and bulky ski suits. Complimentary bathrobes are provided as are conditioners, shampoo, lip balm, bath oils, etc. Fully stocked mini-bars, TV's, VCR's, as well as two telephone lines are found in all rooms. Fax rentals and The latest movies on VCR can be provided by the conscientious concierge. In the suites, the mini-bars are replaced with full wet-bars; some also have full-size dining tables. Suites' baths have theatrical lighting, Jacuzzi tubs, and steam showers. There are two televisions, full stereo systems, and lots and lots of live, luscious plants.

The Little Nell is one of Aspen's most expensive (and most exclusive) hotel with rates comparable to those found in only the world's best hotels. Room prices vary according to the time of year. The least expensive rates (April 5 through June 5) begin at $170 for a standard room and will increase to $350 a night during the Christmas and New Year's period. The most expensive suites during the same times begin at $1,000 per night and will increase to $2,200, respectively.

Although it is always difficult to pick the best of anything, the **Hotel Lenado** and its companion, **Sardy House** must rank as two of the finest hotels not only in Aspen, but at any ski resort. Both hotels were renovated by well-known Aspen architect Harry Teague during the past decade.

Located at 200 S. Aspen Street, the Lenado is convenient to Aspen Mountain and the free shuttle bus which transports guests to Tiehack, Aspen Highlands, and Snowmass.

The Lenado's architecture makes it unique. In fact, the hotel received the prestigious American Institute of Architects Award in 1984.

In the multi-story lobby large windows overlooking Aspen Mountain are framed by angled staircases on either side. The 28-foot rough concrete and red sandstone fireplace dominates the Lenado's living room and its two vertical pine columns accentuate its height. The masculine ambience is softened by the liberal use of fine, soft woods and overstuffed red and green plaid sofas. The rustic, luxurious feel of these rooms is accented by the custom-designed, black, flowered carpets. One does not notice that there is not a picture to be found anywhere in the hotel. The hotel and the scenes outside its windows are the artwork; nothing else is needed to decorate it.

The reading room off the lobby is amply stocked with newspapers, magazines, and books. In another corner is the lounge, finished in soft woods. Markham's is an adult bar—quiet, elegant, and comfortable. The breakfast room across from the lobby is sunny and bright and affords visitors a view of Shadow Mountain, the sunset or Aspen's streets. In total, the atmosphere is comforting, enabling guests to prepare mentally for tackling the slopes of Ajax.

The same care and attention given the lobby and other public rooms is evident in the guest rooms. Windows are fitted with naturally finished shutters; the beds are constructed locally from willow and native applewood. Headboards and footboards are made from thin apple limbs twisted into an architectural form. Each unique bed is covered with a beautiful feather comforter. Wood-burning fireplaces are perfect for casting a warm glow in the room, and built-in Jacuzzi tubs provide a "finishing touch" to guests' relaxing evenings.

Another unique feature which separates The Hotel Lenado from run-of-the-mill hotels is the placement of boot and glove warmers in the lobby. Imagine getting into warm boots and gloves first thing each morning!

During the 1993-94 ski season, rates begin at $119 per night for a twin bedded room, $199 per night for a deluxe king or queen bedded room, and peak at $279 and $369 per night, respectively, during the holiday season.

Sardy House, a gracious turn-of-the-century, 2 1/2-story red brick Victorian retains the traditional atmosphere of one of the finest older Aspen homes, and offers modern travelers all of the privacy and comforts they are accustomed to. A carriage house addition to the original structure expanded its size, but the hotel has only 14 rooms and 6 suites. All of the bathrooms have whirlpool baths and heated towel racks. The Fireplace Suite is only a few steps from the heated outdoor pool and contains a huge feather bed, complete stereo, color TV with HBO, a VCR, Jacuzzi, and heated towel racks.

Upon entering Sardy House, guests might feel as if they were entering someone's living room were it not for the registration table opposite the front door. **The Sardy House** restaurant, renowned in Aspen, is small; therefore, dinner reservations are necessary. **Jack's Bar**, an intimate space next to the dining room, will remind you of an old English pub. Seating is also limited here, but Aspen visitors should certainly make a point of visiting the **Sardy Bar**. Only the conversation affirms that guests are in a ski resort.

During the 1993-94 regular season, rates vary from a low of $135 for Room Five in the Main House, which contains a queen bed and an antique bath, to $350 for the O.J. Wheeler Suite which contains two bedrooms, a whirlpool bath, steam shower, stereo, VCR, and bar.

Those who have visited Aspen in the past are certainly aware of the **Hotel Jerome**, established in 1889. Renovations made during 1985 restored the Belle of the Roaring Fork Valley to her former self, no doubt with many improvements original designers never even considered.

With $22 million having been spent on its public areas, ballroom, and 93 guest rooms, a Victorian "gem" has emerged with a mixture of old and new skillfully woven together. The outdoor heated swimming pool and spa continually plume steam into the cold Aspen night air while guests and visitors mingle in the spacious public areas. **The Century Room** dining room, elegant and comfortable, provides a welcome respite from the day's activities. A private dining room can be reserved for larger parties.

Jacob's Corner, a tastefully furnished and comfortable restaurant located off the pool promenade, is open for breakfast and lunch. The Jerome's **Antler Bar** is available for special functions.

Hotel Jerome remains one of the "in" places for après-ski and before-dinner cocktails. Rooms at the Hotel Jerome during the 1993-94 season start at $229 per night and peak at $1,500 for the Grand Parlor Suite.

Last year's opening of the **Aspen Ritz-Carlton** has been a welcome addition to the grande dame of American ski resorts. The immense red brick facade of this 257-room hotel reflects the Victorian mining heyday style of this town. Many of its rooms and the first floor lounge face an inner court containing a pool and fountain and also look up the mountain to the slopes of Aspen Mountain which many of its visitors can contemplate and try first hand every morning. The hotel lobby is a short, two-block walk from the Silver Queen Gondola and Lift 1A, or the hotel provides a free shuttle to any of Aspen's four mountains. A free ski equipment storage service is provided in the Aspen Sports shop directly across from the hotel lobby, where rentals, lessons, lift ticket sales and planning for other sports also are available. A complete fitness center with exercise and weight room, steam, sauna, massage and lockers is available to guests. The hotel offers 18,000 square feet of meeting space and a team to help plan and coordinate special events.

The solid, large feeling of this hotel and its employes' attention to personal service and details compliment the name of the Ritz. After a visit to this wonderful hotel, one can understand why the hotel chain itself won the coveted Malcolm Baldridge award for quality of service a year ago. All of its employees go out of their way to make guests feel welcome and to help them in any way they can.

During the 1993-94 low ski season, minimum prices for a room at the Ritz-Carlton begin at $145 per night and top at $1,000 per night for The Ritz-Carlton Suite. During the Christmas season, the same rooms will cost $330 and $2,700, respectively.

Those who want to spend a little less for lodging should try the recently restored **Independence Square Hotel**. Situated on Aspen Mall at 404 South Galena Street, the Independence offers a convenient location with modern, tastefully decorated rooms.

Comprising only twenty-eight rooms, the hotel is a renovation incorporating the most often requested amenities including cable TV, wet bar/refrigerator, queen-size beds, and individual ski lockers. Nightly turndown service is available by requesting it from the concierge. Although the rooms are small, available space has been put to good use. For example, the queen-size beds, modern versions of the old Murphy bed, fold into the wall during the day. Even most of the cabinetwork, such as dressers, is built-in to conserve space. A Jacuzzi on the hotel's roof affords bathers spectacular views of Aspen Mountain and the town of Aspen.

The Independence Square Hotel during the 1993-94 season advertises rates ranging from $79 per night for a room with no view during the off season to $210 per night for the same room during the Christmas holidays. A large room with a mountain view will start at $210 and peak at $300 per night.

For skiers whose fancy runs to more traditional lodging facilities, there are numerous hotels in town that are small, family-owned facilities, such as the **Innsbruck Inn** located at 233 W. Main Street. Convenient to a shuttle bus stop, it is owned and operated by Karen and Heinz Coordes. The rooms are imaginatively decorated and convenient to everything Aspen has to offer. The room rate at the Innsbruck includes Continental breakfast served in the upstairs lounge. Furnished in a Swiss/Austrian style complete with Bauernsthle seating and potted geraniums, the lounge is typical of Europe's famous bed and breakfast establishments. The Innsbruck also features a small outdoor heated pool and whirlpool. A sauna is located in the basement.

Rates at the Innsbruck begin at $623 and peak at $875 per week (double occupancy) during the 1993-94 ski season.

Another great value in lodging is found at the downtown **Limelight Lodge**. Clean, large rooms with queen-size beds and down comforters are the norm. The hotel offers a year-round heated pool, cable TV, sauna, whirlpool, coin laundry, and some in-room refrigerators. The base price during the beginning of April and pre-Christmas ski seasons is $58 per night, peaking at $148 during the holidays. For a larger room rates for the same period would be $98 and $188, respectively. With its proximity to Aspen's ski lifts, the Limelite is a good value.

Condominiums

One of the most distinctive rental properties in Aspen has to be the **Brand Building**. Situated in mid-town at Galena and Hopkins where "the action" is, the Brand Building is an extensive renovation of a turn-of-the-century building. It is divided into six one and two-bedroom apartments, each unique unto itself.

The largest apartment, the Silver Queen, consists of 2,000 square feet of living space. It is very contemporary in design and is furnished with large, colorful abstract paintings and white pickled woodwork. The upstairs bedroom features a gas fireplace and marble bath complete with a French shower! Although the kitchen is small, it is adequate and includes all the GE appliances one could desire. Should arriving guests have any special bedding requirements such as the size of the beds, on-site management will be pleased to accommodate the visitor's needs. During the 1991-92 ski season this apartment rents from a low of $865 per night to a high during the Christmas holidays of $2,300 per night.

The Durant is a very contemporary and masculine apartment. Furnished in stark white, the bedroom is cantilevered over the entry and is accessible by a spiral staircase. An electrically controlled canopy opens to the roof, affording guests a 360° view of Aspen Mountain and Red Mountain. A gas grill is on the roof. The Durant rents for between $345 and $750 per night during the 1991-92 ski season.

The Cascade apartment is as feminine in motif as the Durant is masculine. Furnished in a traditional style bordering on Victorian, the Cascade is all ruffles and flowers. During 1991-92 it rents for between $375 and $775 per night.

Three apartments at the Brand Building feature their own private gas grills on the roof. They also come complete with 36 channels of cable TV, two-line telephones, VCR's, and complete stereo systems. Each apartment is complemented with objets d'art particularly suited to it.

The Brand's basement, completely outfitted as a luxury spa, offers free weights, Universal Gym, steam showers, a shallow therapy pool and is enhanced by a motor-driven roof canopy. On the way to the spa, the guest is immediately intrigued by the artwork on the wall. At first it is difficult to identify the subject. However, upon closer examination, one discerns that the artist was inspired by the existing art of New Mexico's Indians. Starting with an old wall, he composed a massive painting to decorate it. However, he only painted portions of the scene, thus creating an image that is a faithful representation of ancient Indian paintings which have partially deteriorated due to age and weather. The artistry offers an excellent commentary on the old 1890 Brand Building.

Located just south of town are the **Aspen Club Condominiums**. Constructed primarily of gray barnboard, they resemble button mushrooms. Highlighted with native stone, they blend in well with the ubiquitous aspen and birch trees.

Available in two, three, and four-bedroom configurations, these family units carpeted in dark green wool and trimmed in mahogany offer spectacular accommodations. A moss-rock fireplace in the living room adds cordiality to the room, and a second fireplace graces the master bath. Comfortable seating for eight surrounds a glass dining room table and the small, adjacent bar is convenient for serving cocktails.

In the master bedroom walk-in closets, an intercom, and a king-size bed with its handmade patchwork quilt assure guests that every comfort and amenity has been provided.

The kitchen offers guests the finest appliances including a Jenn-Air range, convection and radiant double oven, as well as matching washers and dryers.

The Aspen Club, located on the same grounds as the Aspen Club Condominiums, is a 60 thousand square foot, three-level private club. The Club features a small restaurant which serves nutritious health food for diet-conscious guests, a Nautilus room, a free weights room, a room for aerobic exercise equipment, and a full-size gym for volleyball, basketball, and aerobic dancing. There are also six racquetball courts, three indoor and seven outdoor tennis courts, three squash courts, and an indoor lap pool. Dr. Julie Anthony, a founder of the Aspen Club and former sports psychologist to the Philadelphia Flyers, and other well-known fitness experts are often on hand to give seminars on health, fitness, and stress management to sports enthusiasts.

Visitors should not confuse the Aspen Club Condominiums with the Aspen Club Lodge. The Lodge is directly to the left of Aspen Mountain's base facility. The renovation which took place in 1985 has placed the Aspen Club Lodge on the list of nice, convenient lodges with reasonable nightly rates. An improved dining and bar area is very accessible to guests. Lodge guests are offered full access to the Aspen Club and are provided free shuttle service between the two facilities.

Many other lodging accommodations are available in Aspen. To receive a complete price list, write to the Aspen Resort Association, 303 East Main Street, Aspen, Colorado 81611, or telephone (303) 925-1940 and ask for "Aspen Resort Association Rates and Accommodations."

Restaurants

It is fair to say that Aspen's restaurants are as diverse as its lodging. There is truly something for everyone.

A superb Southwestern style restaurant located at 105 S. Mill is **Pinons**. This is a very upscale Aspen restaurant, with upscale prices to match, but the food is very fine, the wine list excellent, and the food preparation creative and delicious. Try the elk tournedos sauteed with ginger and pink peppercorn sauce. The meat is thick and very tender, and cooked with a nice amount of spice-tasty but not overwhelming. The blackened pork tenderloin with madeira and apple onion compote is tangy and satisfying. And to complement it all, the vegetables are crisply cooked to perfection. Call (303)920-2021 for reservations.

Another creative and delicious restaurant in Aspen is **Syzygy**. A dramatic second-floor restaurant bathed in pastels upstairs at 520 E. Hyman, its two eating areas are separated by a wall of water which flows down a glass partition and offers a soothing atmosphere to its patrons. Chef Alexander Kim's edible works of art please the eye as well as the palate. But, please don't hesitate too long to eat Mr. Kim's food: the vegetables are crisp and hot, cooked to perfection, and the sauces are delightful.

One of the most unique eateries anywhere has to be **Boogie's**. Located in downtown Aspen at 534 E. Cooper, Boogie's is a two-storied structure, the first floor being a chic and trendy retail clothing shop similar to an Esprit Warehouse. Elvis Presley's red Corvette dominates the decor of this floor. The upstairs restaurant is modeled after a 1950's diner and serves short-order food that is very good. Even if one does not eat here, Boogie's exciting and enjoyable atmosphere provides an environment that both teen-agers and their parents find appealing. Waitresses dressed in period costumes of very short skirts, tri-cornered aprons, and caps add drama to the setting.

One of Aspen's most elegant dining rooms, the **Century Room**, is located in the Hotel Jerome on East Main Street. Soft piano music, a romantic fireplace, and superb wine selections are certain to help guests unwind. Featuring nouvelle cuisine with traditional service, the Silver Queen is designed with the diner's comfort in mind. Expensively embroidered banquettes and a large floral arrangement which dominates the dining room attest to the extent the owners have gone to create an ambience complementary to excellent dining.

The menu features a wide selection of appetizers including Sevruga caviar. The house spinach salad with raspberry vinaigrette and duck breast is highly recommended. All entrées are cooked to order, using only the best and freshest ingredients. The Dover sole, always a difficult dish to prepare, is truly wonderful. Although expensive, the Silver Queen's meals are worth the expense, thanks to an excellent chef. (303)925-1220

Many people would agree that the best Oriental restaurant in Aspen is **Asia**, located on Main street. The only truly oriental aspects of its ambience are its waiters, waitresses, and red walls. Otherwise, it is a typical Aspen establishment created by joining two houses together. The restaurant features an extremely long l00-year-old bar which was originally located in Liverpool and brought to Aspen especially for Asia. The extensive bill of fare rivals that of any Chinese restaurant found anywhere, and the prices are most reasonable.

Poppies Bistro Cafe, beautifully set in a century-old residence at the corner of Park Ave. and Cooper Ave. (Hwy. 82), is a highly regarded Continental restaurant. The former home is divided into several rooms for general dining or large seatings. The bar and its adjacent dining area are particularly comfortable and remind one of an old English gentlemen's club. The kelly green tartan colors and patterns are enhanced by the warmth of the bar's Honduran mahogany. Tiffany period lamps cast a glow on the tables, and their diffused light illuminates the snow-covered lawn just outside the windows. An impressive wine cellar assures that all meals can be accompanied with the proper varietal.

Poppies' menu reads as elegantly as any Mayfair restaurant's. For appetizers there are fresh potato pancakes, smoked duck & goat cheese belleno, steak tartare, or wild mushroom salad. The most requested entrée is probably the steak au poivre prepared with cognac and heavy cream. Other entrées include a vegetarian dinner, consisting of carrot and leak in filo, steamed broccoli, dauphinoise potatoes, fritters, and a daily fresh vegetable; hunter's loaf, from buffalo venison saddle and lamb rack, served with wild mushrooms, California cabernet sauvignon grape and apple-onion confit. Chef Alan Mello will also prepare for his guests medallions of Scottish red deer resplendent with fresh berries and cranberry-jalapeño jelly. For reservations telephone (303) 925-2333.

Other good restaurants include:

Ute City Banque, 501 E. Hyman Ave., formerly a real bank. The vault is open for inspection. Featuring an eclectic menu, the Ute City Banque typically serves dishes such as Mayan swordfish, fettucini with grilled duck, rack of lamb, and veal Val D'Ostana. (303)925-4373

The Cantina, 411 E. Main, decorated in bright Mexican colors, is a great après-ski gathering location. Only the exceptionally brave should try the 27 oz. Margarita served in a glass as large as a fish bowl.(303)925-3663

The Mother Lode, 314 E. Hyman, an Italian restaurant and an Aspen landmark, is moderately priced and offers a superb menu selection of really good Italian cuisine.(303)925-7700

The Golden Horn, 320 S. Mill, is known for its veal. Although a bit expensive, this Swiss/Austrian style restaurant is a must for Aspen visitors. (303)925-3373

The Aspen Mine Co.,428 E. Hyman, is a great place to take the children. Diners get the real feeling of being in a mine at the turn of the century. Try the ribs in this moderately- priced eatery. (303)925-7766

The Crystal Palace, 300 E. Hyman, a dinner theater, has long been a favorite of Aspenites. Waiters and waitresses serve guests and then provide musical entertainment after dinner. Only one seating is available at 8:00 P.M. each evening. Reservations are required. (303)925-1455

Activities

Although Aspen's reputation as one of America's great ski areas is well deserved, it is also one of the greatest all-around winter resorts where numerous non-skiing activities can be enjoyed.

The T-Lazy-7 Ranch has hundreds of snowmobiles available at reasonable rental rates. Located on Maroon Creek Road just past Aspen Highlands Ski Resort, the T-Lazy-7 is convenient to all accommodations, and its access road is always clear. Rent a snowmobile and take the one and a half-hour tour to the Maroon Bells and around Maroon Lake. If snowmobiling is a new experience, the T-Lazy-7 staff will be happy to provide instruction. If one can drive a lawn mower, one can easily maneuver a snowmobile.

Take a sleigh ride through Aspen or the surrounding countryside. Hansom cabs await customers at the Hyman Avenue Mall.

Tailwinds Aviation offers Aspen visitors scenic flights lasting just under one hour. The management will even organize special flights for photographers.

For a more leisurely look at the mountains, try Unicorn Balloon Company. The hot-air balloons depart daily, weather permitting, from Snowmass and from an area near Aspen. The gondola accommodates up to eight persons, and each flier receives a certificate, a cloisonné pin, and a flight log. Trip durations will vary, as will destinations. Plan on three hours to complete each balloon ride. Reservations can be made by telephoning (303) 925-5752.

Aspen offers more than thirty art galleries. The Aspen Fine Art Dealers' Association publishes a brochure and map showing each member's location. These brochures are available in most hotel lobbies or from the Aspen Resort Association.

Indoor ice skating is available at the Aspen Ice Garden located at Hyman and Second Street.

Services

Sporting goods stores, apparel stores, pharmacies, grocery stores, liquor stores, furniture, bath shops, and specialty stores are all within Aspen proper. In addition, there are antique shops, massage services, bakeries, hair salons, bookstores, florists, an historical society, movies, the Aspen Little Theater, banks, churches, dry cleaners, optical services, and baby-sitting.

The Big Burn on Snowmass goes on and on, offering intermediate and expert runs, wide open spaces and glade skiing. Photo by GuideBook Publishing Co.

SNOWMASS

P.O. Box 1248
Aspen, CO. 81612

Snowmass Reservations and Information (800) 598-2004 (303) 925-1221 Snow Report

New For 1993-94

Although a protest by an environmental group halted construction on new lifts at Snowmass late last summer, skiers will be glad to know that two new high-speed quads have been put in place at Snowmass. Both the Alpine Springs and Sam's Knob lifts will now whisk skiers to their summits at a quicker pace.

An Aspen Skiing Company proposal for a major expansion at Snowmass presently is pending before the United States Forest Service. If approved, a 3-phase expansion and improvement plan for the mountain would begin in 1993 with a base to summit two-stage gondola, 5 high speed chairs, 450 new acres of intermediate and expert terrain, a new mountain restaurant and environmental center and 360 acres of snowmaking coverage.

The new trails would be added to the upper Burnt Mountain area of Snowmass. The slopes will resemble those advanced intermediate runs on the Big Burn. One lift will serve this new area, and a new lower lift will provide a new access point to Snowmass from a new 400 car parking lot.

How to Get There

Snowmass is a 195-mile drive from Denver, 6 miles from Aspen's Sardy Field and 12 miles from the town of Aspen. Like its business partners, Tiehack and Aspen Mountain(Both are owned and operated by the Aspen Skiing Corporation) in recent years its accessibility has been improved. The recent completion of the 4-lane section of Highway 7 through Glenwood Canyon should eliminate long delays drivers suffered through during the past several years. And the drive through the canyon is breathtaking.

Driving to Snowmass from the east or west is as simple as hopping onto I-70 and turning south on Colorado Highway 82. The only major delay you might face is bad weather.

Skiers from the North and from the South can easily drive to Snowmass by taking I-25 to Denver and getting onto I-70. Visitors from the West can pick up I-70 in Utah.

During the 1993-94 ski season, air traffic to the Aspen area continues to increase, making flying to the resort much more convenient. During the past couple of years flights into and out of Aspen's Sardy Field have increased. Sardy is an FAA-controlled airport where instrument landings are possible. Thus, it is necessary to bus passengers from Denver only during the worst storms.

From Denver, Continental and United Express will offer 60 round-trip flights daily between mid-December and April. United Express also will offer travelers from Los Angeles and Chicago daily non-stop service. Four non-stop flights from Dallas/Fort Worth also will be available.

In addition, Eagle County Airport, an hour's drive from Snowmass, also provides gates to American Airlines for non-stop flights from Chicago, Dallas, Miami and New York. Delta will offer non-stop service from Salt Lake City. Call your travel agent or call Aspen to confirm flight schedules for subsequent seasons.

Once the skier reaches Aspen Airport, Snowmass is only 12 miles west and accessible in numerous ways, including taxi (High Mountain), limousine, courtesy van, and rental car.

Most major car rental agencies are located at Sardy Field, and they provide *skierized* vehicles equipped with snow tires and ski racks. Many rental agencies can provide four-wheel drive vehicles. The traveler is cautioned to reserve these vehicles far in advance because the demand for them is great.

One of the nicest things about Snowmass, however, is that once you get there, you really don't need a car. Shuttle buses run constantly among the resorts of Aspen Mountain, Aspen Highlands, Tiehack and Snowmass. Much of the lodging is close enough to the mountain to walk, or right on the mountain, enabling you to ski to and from the slopes.

Mountain Information

The single feature that sets Snowmass apart from most other resorts is its mountain. Snowmass is a family mountain. It contains ample, varied terrain from beginner to advanced expert and has an abundance of intermediate runs.

The Village of Snowmass is arranged roughly parallel to Fanny Hill and Assay Hill, both of which are beginner runs. It is extremely convenient for guests to leave their accommodations in the morning, drop the kids at ski school, and catch a ride up one of the longer lifts which serves the rest of the mountain. In the evening it is equally easy to ski down to the ski school, pick up the kids, walk around the village, and then return to your lodging.

Snowmass is located in White River National Forest and contains five principal areas: Sam's Knob, The Big Burn, High Alpine, Campground, and Elk Camp. Snowmass consists of 2,500 (849 ha) skiable acres and has over 55 miles (88 km) of trails. Of these trails, 10% are considered easiest, 51% are more difficult, 18% are most difficult, and 21% expert.

The base elevation of Snowmass is 8,223 feet, and its summit is at 12,310 feet. This provides the skier with 4,087 vertical feet of skiing.

This abundant terrain is serviced by the following lift equipment:

3 Quad SuperChairs™
9 Double Chairlifts
2 Triple Chairlifts
2 Platter Pulls

Snowmass is most famous for its Big Burn area. Legend has it that the Ute Indians, revolting against the white man's mining activities and establishment of towns in the vicinity, forced the white settlers to flee. In the process the Utes set fire to the mountain and, to this day, the region has not been reforested to any appreciable degree. This has created a huge snowfield which is mostly intermediate terrain. The Burn is almost a mile wide and a mile and a half long and thus truly a cruiser's paradise. Occasionally it is possible to ski the Burn while the rest of the resort is snowed-in. It is an amazing feeling to be skiing above the clouds in bright sunshine and then to disappear into a storm, only to ride the lift out of it again and again.

Most beginner runs at Snowmass are located near the bottom of the mountain, while most of the intermediate trails are in the center. The expert terrain is at the top. Notable exceptions to this rule of thumb are the Big Burn and the runs served by the Campground Lift.

At the top of Sam's Knob is a restaurant; trails located behind it and down to the skier's left are expert. Not, "I know I will die before I get down" expert runs, but difficult enough to let skiers know they have to work to ski them well. Those skiers who are just in their prime (twenty to sixty years old) will be particularly interested in skiing Lower Powderhorn, Campground, Bear Claw, Wildcat, The Slot, and Zugspitze. Some poling may be required to return to the lift station from Wildcat, The Slot, and Zugspitze. To minimize this, it is advantageous to take a left turn onto the service road near the bottom and follow it to Campground's base which, through a short series of washboard, deposits you at the Campground Lift. Make certain to time late afternoon runs so as not to become stranded because the lift closes at 3 P.M. It would be an almost impossible walk back to the village at night wearing ski boots.

The truly expert skier or the crazed teen-ager should find Hanging Valley Glades and the Hanging Valley Wall a memorable experience! Slightly less difficult, but interesting to say the least, are KT Gully and Rock Island. These two trails will remind well-traveled skiers of Tourist Trap at Vail, before Vail Associates decided to widen it. They are also similar to Pallavicini at Arapahoe Basin.

During days when the weather is less than cooperative, the intermediate skier will want to forego the Burn because it is too windy, cold, snowy, or all of the above. This is the best time to ski the Elk Camp area or the High Alpine area. Elk Camp has been carved out of the forest, and the trees shield skiers from the wind and provide contrast in flat light. The mid-portion of High Alpine is a great refuge; runs such as Naked Lady, Lodgepole, and Bottoms Up can be very satisfying.

Snowmass receives an annual snowfall of approximately 300 inches (762 cm) at its summit and 155 inches (394 cm) at its base. Its average monthly snowfalls are

Nov.	12.6"	(25 cm)
Dec.	45"	(132 cm)
Jan.	40"	(104 cm)
Feb.	50"	(104 cm)
Mar.	66"	(173 cm)
Apr.	17"	(43 cm)

Snowmass has portable snowmaking equipment which it moves around as needed.

The average daily temperatures in Snowmass during the season are

Nov.	31°	0 C
Dec.	22°	-5° C
Jan.	20°	-6° C
Feb.	23°	-5° C
Mar.	29°	-2° C
Apr.	39°	4° C

No discussion of Snowmass would be complete without mentioning that Aspen Mountain, Aspen Highlands, and Tiehack Mountain are within 12 miles of the resort. These are very large mountains in their own right, and guests at Snowmass are encouraged to ski at least one other mountain during their visit. If one considers these other mountains, the skiable terrain is more than doubled.

Lift Ticket Prices (1993-94)

Snowmass has many different prices for lift tickets. Space does not permit the inclusion of all of them, other than to mention that special rates are available for groups, individuals over 65, handicapped persons, and combination lift ticket/ski lesson packages. See the Aspen section of this book for details on prices.

If you know you will be going to the Aspen area, and you know you will not be skiing anywhere else during the time, you can save a lot of money by purchasing your tickets in advance. Last year the daily price of a lift ticket was $43, and it certainly will not go down. By buying ahead of time you can decrease the price of skiing to between $30 and $32 per day. To buy in advance, call 1-800-525-6200 and ask for ext. 3594 if you will be staying in Aspen, and ext. 4554 if you are staying in Snowmass. Tickets may be picked up when you arrive either at any of the will call desks at Aspen Mountain, Snowmass or Tiehack.

Hours of Operation

8:30 A.M. to 3:30 P.M.
Campground lift 9:00 A.M. to 3:00 P.M.
Fanny Hill and Assay Hill close at 4:00 P.M.

Lift Ticket Purchase Locations

Visitors find it is easy to ski from their lodging to any of the lift ticket windows. Lift tickets are sold in the Village Mall which is easily identified by its unique clock tower, in the "A" parking lot, at the base of the Assay Hill lift, the base of the Fanny Hill lift, the base of the Wood Run lift, and at the base of the Campground lift. (This latter location is only approachable by automobile before the lifts open). All major credit cards are accepted.

How to Avoid Crowds

Because the ratio of skiable acres to uphill lift capacity is so favorable, crowd control is minimal. There really are not a lot of crowds at Snowmass. However, as with all resorts, some areas do become congested. In the early morning and after lunch, congestion occurs at the top of Sam's Knob as skiers line up to ski Max Park. Max Park is the major avenue to Big Burn, so many skiers traverse it on their way to the Big Burn and Sheer Bliss lifts. Traffic can be avoided by taking the Sunnyside or Pipeline trails. These are moderately difficult to easy runs, depending on conditions.

The only other potential area of congestion, and it is slight, may be found where Dawdler and the terrain off the face of Sam's Knob converge. Around 3:00 P.M. to 4:00 P.M. many skiers of differing abilities begin making their way down to lodging, bars, or the village shops. Traversing this short distance will not be a problem if care is taken.

Ski School

Snowmass employs 300 instructors trained to teach adults, children, and the physically challenged. Traditional group and private lessons are available daily. In addition, Snowmass Ski School offers some unique programs. Its Mountain Masters program is for skiers who are good enough to get down almost any slope but who cannot always do it with the ease and style they would like. This approach requires four days, and the instructors utilize video, races, and other techniques to sharpen the advanced skiers' ability.

Snowmass has an attractive approach for teaching teen-agers and younger children first grade and older. Lessons are divided into groups according to age and experience. Instructors aim to make the classes more fun by planning on-mountain picnics and fun races and visiting other mountains. For no additional cost, the ski school arranges some ice skating and pizza parties during the evening. Meeting place for the morning lessons is directly across Fanny Hill from the Snowmass Mall. Most teen-agers who have been skiing for a while do not have trouble negotiating the slopes, but they do have trouble being entertained during the evenings. This program helps to fill this need.

Children 18 months to 3 years can be enrolled in the Snowcubs program at Snowmass for $40 for a half day, $62 per day, $310 for 5 days. This is a licensed day care center located downstairs in the

Timbermill Building at the ski slope end of the Snowmass Village Mall. It is open from 8:30 a.m. to 3:30 p.m. Children younger than 3 will not ski, but, weather permitting, will play outside for part of the day. Skiing instruction begins for 3-year-olds who will enjoy playing and trying their luck on the boards in an enclosed "contoured ski area."

Older children aged four through kindergarten may be enrolled in a child-oriented ski instruction program called **Big Burn Bears**. Small groups of supervised children receive hot lunches, snacks, and a lift ticket. They also meet downstairs in the Timbermill Building.In this program, children will work with same instructor each day all week. 1993-94 rates are $62 for a whole day, $40 for a half day. Hours are from 8:30 A.M. through 3:30 P.M. daily. Evening child care is available at $5 per hour from 5:30 P.M. through 11:00 P.M. Telephone (800) 525-6200 for information and reservations.

There is an active ski program available to blind skiers and handicapped individuals. Snowmass's BOLD (Blind Outdoor Leisure Development) has been training skiers since the program's inception. For information, handicapped skiers should telephone Peter Maines at (303) 925-2086. Handicapped skiers may be eligible for complimentary lift tickets, lessons, and rental equipment. However, it is imperative that handicapped skiers first contact the Snowmass Ski School and arrange an appointment. Telephone (303) 923-4873.

The 1993-94 ski season prices for adult lessons are

Group Classes
$ 48   All Day, 1 Day(10:30 - 3:30)
$126   All Day, 3 Days
$275   (plus lift ticket Mountain Masters (4 days)
$ 99   Learn to ski package, 3 days

Children\Teens Classes
$50   All day
$42   Half day-beginners

Equipment Rental

Among the ski rental companies located in Snowmass are **Aspen Sports** in the Snowmass Center, **Gene Taylor's Sports**, **Christy's**, and **Stein Eriksen's**, all on the mall.

In 1993-94 Gene Taylor's will offer a Basic rental package consisting of Rossignol and K2 skis, Salomon boots, poles and bindings for $14 per day. A DeLuxe package consisting of Rossignol skis, and Salomon boots, poles, and bindings was $18 per day. A High Performance package will cost $22, and Demos will go for $25. All children's skis are brand new Blizzard skis and will be priced at $7. Snowboards and boots will cost $22 per day. Discounts of 10 percent will be given for rentals of 3 to 5 days, and 20 percent for 6 days or more.

At Aspen Sports, which has shops on the Village Mall, in the Silvertree Hotel and at the Snowmass Center, prices are different. A basic package of K2 or Rossignol skis, Salomon boots and poles will cost $15.50. The sport package of Rossignol, Elan or K2 skis will cost $21.50, and the performance package will cost $27.00 with almost any of the skis they sell, and a variety of boots. A children's package will cost $12.50, with a 50 % reduction in the price with the 5-day rental of an adult package.

There are also many shops in the town of Aspen. For information, see the section of this book entitled *Aspen.*

Ski Tuning and Repair

All the Snowmass rental stores will tune and repair skis. **Sunset Ski Repair**, located on the mall near the Popcorn Wagon, will also tune or repair skis.

The 1993-94 prices for tuning at the Gene Taylor's on Snowmass Village Mall are listed here. Prices elsewhere will probably be within a few dollars of these.

$ 5   Hot Wax
$18   Sharpening and Wax
$25   Complete Tune-Up(This is a base price. If the job gets very involved, it may cost more!k)
$20+   P-tex

Mountain Dining

Snowmass has some truly nice and unique mountain restaurants. The quality of food is better than that found either on Aspen Mountain (with the exception of **Darcey's**) or Aspen Highlands.

Cafeteria service is available at **Sam's Knob**, **High Alpine**, **Elk Camp**, and **Ullrhof**. Table service is available at **Gwyn's** at High Alpine, **Dudley's** at Sam's Knob, and at **Krabloonik** near the base of the Campground lift. A full breakfast is available at all mountain cafeterias.

An absolute must for skiers who crave an unusual dining experience while demanding quality food and service is **Krabloonik**, located near the Campground base.[1] The name Krabloonik is Eskimo for "big eyebrows," the Eskimos' name for white men. Krabloonik is also the name of the restaurant owner's first sled dog.

This restaurant is truly unusual. The only heat emanates from a wood-burning stove located in the middle of the restaurant seating area and light is provided by individual gas lanterns hanging from ceiling rafters. In the evening the glow of the gas lights and the warmth of the fire create a cozy, intimate atmosphere not easily duplicated.

The menu, complemented by an extensive wine list, includes such delicacies as smoked trout, wild game tartare, baked brie with pears and lingonberries, and, sometimes,smoked buffalo tongue. Typical entrées include salmon, monkfish velouté, Muscovy duck breast with red currant cassis, pheasant breast Veronica, noisettes of caribou sauce poivrade, elk loin with sage sauce, wild boar schnitzel, and for the less adventurous, tenderloin of beef with sauce Diane.

Krabloonik is more than a restaurant; it is also a sled dog kennel. There are 220 dogs on the premises, and the cacophony is deafening during feeding time, usually between 4:00 P.M. and 4:30 P.M. Even when skiing the Campground lift, you frequently can hear the Malamute, Eskimo, and Siberian huskies barking. Krabloonik employees manufacture dog sleds on location from ash and hickory wood. Some of these dogs and sleds find their way to the annual Iditarod race in Alaska. During the past year, a Krabloonik team placed 21st out of the more than 70 teams entered.

It is possible to go for a sled ride before or after lunch. The countryside around Krabloonik is beautiful, and being a part of a twelve to fifteen-dog team racing through the aspen groves on a cold, clear day is quite an experience. The 2-hour ride costs $175 for each adult, and $110 for a child.

---

[1] Krabloonik is not on the Snowmass property but is within walking distance of the Campground Lift. Reservations are imperative because the restaurant is frequently fully booked for lunch. Telephone (303) 923-3953.

Reservations for dog-sled rides are booked far in advance; therefore, be sure to make ride reservations at the time lodging is booked. Telephone (303) 923-3953.

On the other side of the mountain at High Alpine, **Gwyn's** offers more traditional fare. The restaurant's Austrian/Swiss decor, complete with chintz curtains on windows overlooking the slopes, is charming. Gwyn's tends to become crowded during the high season; therefore, it is advisable to make reservations. Telephone (303) 923-5188.

Dudley's at Sam's Knob is in a lovely setting overlooking Lower Powderhorn and Garret Peak. Diners can enjoy service at linen-covered tables. As with Gwyn's, this restaurant can become crowded, so reservations are advisable. Telephone (303) 923-3516.

Child Care

During the 1988-89 ski season Aspen Skiing Company opened its own 8 thousand square foot child-care center in the lower level of the Timbermill Restaurant on Snowmass Mall. Infants eighteen months through three years of age may be enrolled in the **Snow Cubs** program, a snow play program combining indoor programs with outdoor activities. The facility is filled with attractions for young children, such as a life-size teepee, a covered wagon to play in and an indoor sandbox. Groups are kept small and children receive abundant attention. There is a separate nap room; hot lunches are served daily. Reservations are requested. and if you can not bring your child, a 24-hour cancellation is asked for. Price is $62 per day during 1993-94 for the first five days, dropping to $60 for additional days. Telephone (800) 525-6200 for information and reservations.

This facility also offers Night Hawks at Snowmass, evening child care. A child must be three years or older to participate. For one child the cost is $7 per hour, for 2, $10 per hour and for 3, $15 per hour. For information call 1-800-525-6200, or 303-923-1220.

Medical Facilities

Injuries which occur on the slopes are treated on an emergency basis by the ski patrol. Broken bones are immobilized and trauma is contained. Once emergency treatment has been rendered and the patient has been stabilized, the injured skier is transported to the Aspen Valley Hospital for specialized care as needed.

The Aspen Valley Hospital is a full-service hospital with all the equipment and expertise one expects of a large city hospital.

Cross-Country Skiing

Three pinners will love the trails at Aspen and Snowmass. They are probably the most extensive in America, comprising nearly eighty kilometers of groomed tracks. No wonder locals refer to the cross-country terrain as "Aspen's fifth mountain!"

Easy to moderate trails are located east of Aspen at the site of the Aspen Club. Meandering from open meadows through aspen groves, these trails are perfect for an afternoon's adventure.

On the other side of the valley is the Rio Grande Trail whose trail head is on the bus route, near the post office. This trail follows the old railroad right of way, and during good weather it is groomed all the way to Woody Creek.

Tracks on the Aspen Golf Course are available for the beginner or those who want to take it easy before tackling more difficult slopes. As one would expect, this is primarily flat terrain. There are also special skating lanes for those who want to perfect the latest craze in racing technique. A bridge across Maroon Creek enables the adventuresome to travel all the way to Snowmass utilizing Owl Creek Trail.

Owl Creek Trail is considered by many as being among the most beautiful trails in the Rocky Mountains. This track ties in directly with the trail network at Snowmass. Its trails are the most demanding of the free system.

The Snowmass Club trails encompass every conceivable type of terrain, from golf course flat to steep terrain located above Owl Creek Road. Check in at the Snowmass Club Touring Center and arrange for a catered lunch to be served at Tepee's Cabin, located in an open meadow on one of the trails.

Twelve miles up Castle Creek is the Ashcroft Ski Touring Center. It features thirty kilometers of groomed and set tracks, available for a nominal fee.

Special Events

Each year in mid-January Aspen and Snowmass celebrate Wintersköl with parades, torchlight processions down the mountains, and fireworks. Winterskol 1994 takes place Jan. 12 through 16. Mardi Gras in February is also celebrated with many skiers dressing in costume. Celebrations culminate at that evening's Mardi Gras ball.

There are also innumerable special events that change yearly but which normally include professional ski races, USSA races, and World Cup.

Accommodations

There is no shortage of accommodations of every description and price in Snowmass. Generally, however, the older properties are arranged along Brush Creek Road which runs roughly parallel to the slopes. All of these facilities are close enough to the runs to be described as ski-in/ski-out. Newer units being built along Woodrun are also ski-in/ski-out.

A security gate is located at the entrance to the resort—approximately one and one-half mile from the runs and accommodations. The guard at the desk has a list of all guests' names and will give directions to lodging facilities. Parking at Snowmass is restricted, and only guests with parking permits affixed to their cars are allowed to park close to their accommodations and to the slopes. Day skiers from Aspen may park free further downhill near the guard's gate in the rodeo lot and take a free shuttle up to the lifts and ticket offices. This is a great convenience for Snowmass guests. Guest cars without a parking permit may be towed or at least fined. The fine is substantial.

Hotels

One of the premier hotels at Snowmass is **The Snowmass Lodge and Club**. A AAA 4-diamond rated facility, the club is situated at the Touring Center and offers rentals, lessons and tours. The club is away from the hustle and bustle of the mall and includes two tennis courts protected from the weather by a huge plastic bubble. Other features are two racquetball courts, two squash courts, an outdoor heated olympic-size swimming pool, a Jacuzzi, Nautilus, free weights, and a cardiovascular room including Airdyne and Life Cycle stationary bikes. Guests also can enjoy the sauna, steam room, pro shop, and exceptionally well-appointed locker rooms. Personal trainers, massages and regular aerobics classes are also a part of this facility's services. There is even a private nursery for guests' children. Aerobics classes are offered on a regular basis and are taught on a wood, air cushion floor.

Rooms at the Snowmass Lodge and Club are decorated in country French style and all have private balconies. Each room contains a small refrigerator, coffeemaker, cable TV, and bathrobes.

The lobby of the lodge is finished in fine wood, and its furniture is upholstered in rich wool fabrics. Its restaurant, **The Four Corners**, serves breakfast, lunch and dinner. Entertainment is available in the adjacent bar with complimentary hors d'oeuvres from 4 to 7 P.M. daily. Transportation to the ski area and concierge service is provided gratis by the Club. Complimentary ski equipment storage can be found at the Timbermill Building on the Snowmass Village mall. Skis will be tuned upon request.

Country Club Villas are located adjacent to the Snowmass Club, and their guests enjoy member privileges at the Club. The Villas are one, two, and three-bedroom condominiums. Prices for 1993-94 at these condominiums range from $175 to $490 per night for a one bedroom; $265 to $585 for a two bedroom; and $350 to $695 for a 3 bedroom. Prices vary according to the time of the ski season.

Prices for Snowmass Lodge rooms for the 1993-94 season start at $125 per room to $200, and peak at $300 and $375, respectively for the same rooms. Use of the tennis courts requires an additional fee. For information call (800)525-6200 or (303)923-5600 for information. Ask about ski package rates, which save you money on skiing tickets.

The only ski-in, ski-out full service hotel in Snowmass is the **Silvertree Hotel** located at the slopeside edge of the Village Mall. The large hotel offers nicely furnished rooms, many with beautiful views, a ski concierge, massage, a small health club, heated pools and whirlpools, on-site full service ski shop and storage, room service and a lounge and two restaurant. During the past summer, all bedspreads were replaced and coffee pots updated in each room.

The hotel has three restaurants: **The Conservatory**, with a lounge near the main lobby of the hotel; **Brothers Grill**, which serves moderately priced American fare for breakfast lunch and dinner; and **Cowboys**, a gourmet restaurant with a Southwest flare located next to the hotel. Conference facilities also are available. Prices vary according to the time of year and type of room. For 1993-94 regular season, from Feb. 12 to Mar. 25, a standard room rents for $205, and a slope view room for $325. The slope view price includes a breakfast in the Conservatory Restaurant. During the Christmas holidays, the same rooms will cost $250 and $390, respectively.

Hotel Wildwood is located adjacent to the slopes, on the Snowmass Village Mall. All DeLuxe rooms and suites at the Wildwood have a private balcony or patio with a view of the slopes. All rooms feature two queen- or king-size beds, a refrigerator, coffeemaker, and TV with remote control. All rooms have been newly-decorated.

Wildwood's amenities include a heated outdoor pool, Jacuzzi, and a men's and a women's sauna. A Continental breakfast is complimentary during the ski season and free transportation to and from Aspen Airport is available.

The hotel has an après-ski bar, and **Pippin's** restaurant specializes in classic American dishes such as prime rib, New York strip steak, rack of lamb, baked chicken breast, fresh salmon and live Maine lobster. Lodging prices during the 1993-94 season are quoted from a low of $108 per night to a high of $245 for a hotel room. For a suite, prices range from $193 to $615 per night.

The Stonebridge Inn is located just a short walk from the Snowmass ski slope. Another full-service hotel, guests are provided with free transportation to and from Sardy Field, 24-hour front desk and switchboard, daily maid and bell service. Each room has a coffee maker, small refrigerator and cable television. On the grounds are a heated swimming pool, jacuzzi and bathhouse with sauna and changing rooms. Prices vary according to season, but during the value season(Jan. 2 to Feb. 12) a standard room will cost $128, and during New Year's week it will cost $ 187. During the same periods, a suite will cost $158, and $217, respectively.

Condominiums

There are so many condominiums in Snowmass, it would be difficult to list them all. Here are a few:

Among the newer condominium offerings at Snowmass is the twenty-nine unit **Chamonix** located along the Woodrun Chairlift. These two and three-bedroom condos are run like a quality hotel, with a central lobby and concierge services. Upon guests' arrival, management provides a complimentary ski wax or arranges rental skis for them.

Rooms at Chamonix are nicely appointed with traditional furnishings. All have balconies and sun rooms furnished with rattan furniture. Kitchens are completely supplied with all the utensils one could possibly need. The ranges are Jenn-Air, and both microwave and regular thermal ovens are available. Washers and dryers are provided in every condominium, as are ironing boards and humidifiers.

The master baths are well appointed with steam showers or Jacuzzi tubs and double sinks.

From its underground parking to its heated outdoor pool and its soaring ceilings, the Chamonix is a great retreat—a wonderful place in which to celebrate a week or two in ski country.

During the 1993-94 season the Chamonix rent for between $249 to $700 for a 2 bedroom, and $334 to $890 for a 3 bedroom.

Woodrun Place, another condominium complex, is located diagonally across the street from the Chamonix, and is a very comfortable lodge. Woodrun is managed by Snowmass Lodging Company; their staff will bend over backwards to help guests feel comfortable. Staff members will grocery shop for skiers, chauffeur them, or arrange for breakfast, lunch, or dinner to be prepared and served in their condo.

All Woodrun Place condominiums feature contemporary furnishings from quality manufacturers. The color and fabric selections are warm. Kitchens are completely equipped and contain laundry facilities as well. Fireplaces and whirlpool baths are standard features.

This fifty-five unit complex has a beautiful outdoor pool and therapy pool, as well as a ski locker room. Exercise facilities are located on the premises. The only drawback to Woodrun may be for the guest who books a single condominium and finds that all the other units are occupied by members of a conference. Woodrun is a conference center which attempts to book groups.

Rates for condominiums during the 1993-94 regular season are between $196 and $482 per night for a 1 bedroom; $249 to $647 for a two bedroom; and $334 to $853 for a 3 bedroom.

The **Woodrun V** condominiums are reached by first crossing a small bridge which may not be evident after heavy snowfalls. Entry is through a small foyer, and the living/dining, kitchen, and master bedroom are upstairs. All other accommodations are located down from the foyer on the first floor.

The interiors are constructed from brick and redwood and the decorations are traditional. Handmade Mexican tiles provide a distinctive touch to each kitchen. The fully equipped kitchens feature Kitchenaide appliances and Jenn-Air grills. There are even trash compactors. Separate formal dining rooms and step-down living rooms add dimension to these unique condos. Off the living rooms are nicely appointed sitting rooms. The many large windows provide a panoramic view of Snowmass Resort. Guests will also find stereos, VCR's, remote-controlled cable TV's, copperclad fireplaces, and a heated outdoor swimming pool. Rates during the 1993-94 ski season are from $329 to $726 per night for a two bedroom; and $408 to $1,049 for a three bedroom.

Restaurants

A relatively recent restaurant addition to the Snowmass scene is **Cowboys**, associated with and next door to the Silvertree Hotel. Busy and friendly, the food is good, not too expensive and a great western band plays nightly. Attractive western artwork by Linda Loeschen hangs on the walls and is available for purchase. It is also a pleasant place to come for a drink. Try the vegetable strudel with fresh seasonal vegetables and cheeses, wrapped in paper bread and baked. It is delicious! So are the oven roasted Colorado lamb loin marinated in achiote and the onion crusted salmon with roast corn and asiago cheese. Every night Chef Kendzior offers a wild game selection. A children's menu is offered.

Among Snowmass' offerings is singer John Denver's **Tower Restaurant**. The restaurant is in a landmark building on the Mall and thus is visible from most places in the resort. The Tower features traditional steak dinners, pasta dishes, poultry such as Hawaiian chicken, and several fresh fish selections.

Also on the mall is **Hite's**. Entrées are similar to those of the Tower, although the menu selections are greater and more varied. Other restaurants are found in some of the hotels such as the Silvertree; several short-order food establishments are also conveniently located in the Village.

Chez Grandmère is the finest Continental restaurant in Snowmass. Located at 15 Kearns Road in Snowmass Village, it features a fixed price menu at $30 per person which includes an aperitif, hors d'oeuvres, salade maison, freshly baked french bread, choice of entrée, three vegetables, dessert, coffee or tea. Although the menu changes daily, typical entrée choices may include swordfish, breast of pheasant, veal steak, or similar dishes. Hors d'oeuvres typically include carrots in fresh ginger and sea scallops. Chez Grandmère is a 1989 recipient of the coveted *Wine Spectator* award for excellence in wine lists. For reservations, telephone 303/923-2570.

Situated in a snug corner of Snowmass Mall, **La Bohème** is a clean-cut version of Chez Grandmère. Its ambiance is more functional than elegant; its service is more utilitarian than gracious. Guests enter the restaurant through a bar, as if the restaurant itself were being punished for its lack of elegance. This is not a noisy restaurant, a welcome atmosphere, different from the noisy glitter of nearby Aspen. La Bohème's menu is extensive, featuring such diverse items as striped bass in parcheuiu paper with tomato, wild mushrooms, and lemon basil; hot smoked Norwegian salmon with sorrel beurre blanc and caviar; grilled scallop of veal with spinach and artichokes, candied peal onion in lemon veal juice; and roasted herb-marinated farm chicken with potato mushroom pancakes. For reservations, telephone 303/923-6804.

Activities

Because Snowmass and Aspen Mountain are so close together and the uphill lift companies are the same, it is reasonable to expect activities to be shared by the two resorts. Therefore, to learn about the activities of the area, consult the section of this book that deals with Aspen.

Services

Snowmass is a complete village where sporting goods stores, apparel stores, pharmacies, grocery stores, liquor stores, and specialty stores can be found. Other services are located in Aspen.

Village Map

Krabloonik
Kennels & Restaurant

Corey
Glade
Lift

to Campground
Lift

Conference
Center

Silvertree
Plaza

Shuttle
Transportation
Center

Village Mall

Bus
Station

Burlingame
Lift

Fanny Hill
Lift

Wood Run
Lift

Snowmass
Center

Funnel
Lift

Assay Hill
Lift

Anderson
Ranch
Arts Center

Melton
Ranch

The
Snowmass
Club Touring
Center

The
Snowmass
Club

The
Snowmass Club
Cross-Country
Trails

Rodeo Grounds
Parking and Shuttle Bus

to Highway 82

Snowmass
Stables

BANFF/LAKE LOUISE

Ski Banff/Lake Louise
Box 1085
Banff, Alberta, Canada T0L 0C0

(800) 661-1676 Reservations
(403) 762-4561 Information
(403) 277-7669 Snow Report

New for 1993-94

No new trails or lifts have been added to any of the three ski areas in the Banff/Lake Louise region during the past year, but a new, large luxury hotel has joined the other large resorts. Rimrock Resort Hotel, owned by the Sumitomo Trust of Japan, opened its doors to 345 rooms in August of 1993. Located on Sulphur Mountain, about a 10-minute drive from downtown Banff, many of its rooms offer gorgeous mountain views. Athletic facilities include an indoor swimming pool, whirlpool, sauna, steam room, weight room, squash court and games room. The lobby houses a lounge, and an entertainment lounge also is available in the hotel. Heated underground parking is available and welcome on winter nights.

The hotel provides a free shuttle to Banff at a quarter after and a quarter to the hour, and a return shuttle can be taken from town one the half hour and hour.

Rooms are priced by view, with the least expensive having a view obstructed by trees or buildings. During the low season these rooms start at $125 per night and peak during the Christmas season at $175. The most expensive rooms, with view of the Bow or Spray Valleys, start at $155 per night and peak at $205. Summer rates will be higher. Call (800)661-1587 from Canada and USA, and (800)372-9270 from Alberta, for information and reservations.

Introduction

Skiing in the Banff/Lake Louise area is a different experience from skiing at any other resort featured in this book because Banff consists of three mountains, without any substantial lodging at the resort proper. These three separate ski mountains (Sunshine Village, Mystic Ridge\Mt. Norquay, and Lake Louise Ski Area) comprise a destination resort where guests will enjoy both spectacular mountain vistas and friendly Albertan hospitality.

The town of Banff itself is located away from the slopes—5 miles (8 km) east of Sunshine Village ski area, and 35 miles (58 km) southeast of Lake Louise Ski Area and 4 miles southwest of Mystic Ridge/Mt. Norquay.

All the true destination resorts featured in this book have a village or facilities at their bases to afford both skiers and non-skiers adequate activity for six days and seven nights, and Banff/Lake Louise considered together easily meets this activity criterion. However, the base accommodations' requirement is another story. While there is a small village located 2 miles west of Lake Louise Ski Area and also a small hotel located at the base of Sunshine Village's ski lifts, neither resort can claim a traditional base area. In fact, the hotel at Sunshine Village is only accessible by riding the gondola that runs from the parking lot to the base ski area. Thus, guests staying at Sunshine Inn are usually limited to coming and going only during the gondola's operating hours. The reason that Banff/Lake Louise cannot meet the base facilities' requirement as defined in this book is due to the fact that the Canadian Parks Service controls every aspect of the resorts' operations. The park service has been fundamentally opposed to expanding on-hill development. They do, however, after painstakingly careful review allow improvements to existing facilities. Under this premise the Canadian Park Service allowed Lake Louise to install two high-speed quad chairlifts during the summer of 1989. They also allowed Mystic Ridge\Norquay to double its skiable terrain for the 1989-90 season.

In spite of these problems of accessible base facilities and adequate accommodations, the area taken together is indeed worthy of inclusion as one of the continent's greatest ski areas. American skiers cannot fail to be impressed with Albertans' friendly concern that they enjoy their vacation and Canadian ski experience.

How To Get There

Vacationers flying to Banff/Lake Louise land at Calgary International Airport, served by Wardair, Air Canada, Canadian, American West, Continental, Delta, United, and several European carriers. Once skiers arrive at the airport, several transportation options are available to them. Regularly scheduled bus service between the airport and Banff/Lake Louise is available from Greyhound, Brewster, and Pacific Western Transportation. Adult fares, subject to possible change, are expected to be $26 from Calgary to Banff, and $32 to Lake Louise, during this ski season. Telephone Brewster at (403) 762-6767. Pacific Western also offers bus service to Lake Louise and Banff for $28 and $30, respectively. Reservations are recommended. Call 1-800-661-1668 or (403) 762-4558 for current schedules and prices at Pacific Western.

Although having a car is not necessary to ski the entire area, it is recommended for the flexibility it provides. Access to a car will greatly enhance one's ability to visit all the attractions the area has to offer. Rental cars are available from all major U.S. rental companies as well as Tilden (a Canadian car rental agency).

Avis	(403)762-3222
Budget	(403)762-4565
Hertz	(403)762-2027, Banff Springs Hotel
	(403)522-3969, at Chateau Lake Louise
Tilden	(403)762-2688

Avis, Hertz, Budget, and Tilden are also available in Banff proper. Driving time to Banff from Calgary International Airport is, of course, determined by weather, but on a clear day with dry highways the 85 miles (135 km) can be driven in an hour and twenty minutes. Lake Louise is another half-hour's drive.

Bus transportation between the town of Banff, Sunshine Village, Mt. Norquay, and Lake Louise Ski Area is offered four times per day by Pacific Western. During the 1990-91 season the round-trip fee between Banff and Sunshine was $10, Banff/Norquay was $8, and Banff/Lake Louise was $12[1]. The buses stop at most major Banff hotels as well as the bus depot. For information or current departure and arrival times, telephone (403) 762-4558 or (403) 762-2241.

Mountain Information

The town of Banff is closest to Mt. Norquay and Sunshine Village. Lake Louise is generally considered a little out of the immediate Banff vicinity. However, since Lake Louise offers the most ski terrain of the three mountains, it is dealt with first.

Lake Louise

Of the three ski areas that comprise Banff/Lake Louise, Lake Louise Ski Area is the largest, consisting of 4,000 skiable acres (1,619 ha) and 3,250 feet (1,000 meters) of vertical. Two high-speed quad chairs, Friendly Giant Express and Top of the World Express have been added to the front of the Lake Louise mountain and increased the speed and capacity for carrying skiers up. In addition the Ptarmigan double chair which rises up the back of the mountain has been replaced with a fixed grip quad.

As noted earlier, skiers who have only skied in the United States will be disappointed in its meager base facilities. Although they are the most extensive of the three mountains, they would only qualify as a day-skier facility in the United States. Even by British Columbia standards, the facilities in Banff/Lake Louise area are primitive. The Canadian Parks Service wardens continually monitor all the slopes of the three resorts. Management has its hands tied when it comes to making decisions or changes on the mountain. Park wardens tell the ski patrol which runs they can open and when. The wardens, not the ski patrol, are responsible for all avalanche work and determining when there is a threat or when a threat has been removed. They even tell the mountain management which runs are to be groomed and when! As long as this restrictive situation is allowed to exist, the area will remain an anachronism in world skiing.

In spite of these problems, Lake Louise is a great mountain and should be on every skier's agenda to ski sometime. From its base elevation of 5,400 feet (1,645 meters) to its peak of 8,650 feet (2,637 meters) it offers skiers of every ability level fantastic conditions and spectacular views not duplicated anywhere else on the continent. Lake Louise is really two mountains with four faces. The front face is gladed for two-thirds of its length, while the upper third offers bowls or open snowfields. A comfortable mix of all ability levels exists on this face almost from top to bottom. Beginning skiers will particularly like Wiwaxy because it is long and scenic. In inclement weather it is protected, and the natural snow conditions on it are usually excellent. Ride Olympic Chair to reach the top of Wiwaxy and follow signs down to the base. Intermediate skiers will want to freshen their skills on Meadowlark and then try some of the runs higher on the mountain like Skyline or Upshoot Trail. Experts will want the thrill of skiing the Canadian men's and ladies' downhill courses. Both start at the top of Glacier Chair and run non-stop to the base area. These runs are frequently well moguled for recreational skiing, unlike their condition during actual racing events. Although cold and windy conditions may be experienced by skiers riding the Summit Platter above the tree line, it remains the most popular lift for the mountain's "regulars." It is the highest conveyance on the mountain and services intermediate and advanced terrain but most importantly, it often has large pockets of untracked snow—perfect for powder enthusiasts.

Lake Louise's second mountain, Larch, is its most sheltered mountain. This is where most skiers go when the weather closes in. To reach it, ride any of the chairs from the base to their terminus

---

[1] All dollar amounts in the Banff/Lake Louise chapter are quoted in Canadian dollars. At the time of this writing, the U.S. dollar was approximately equal to $1.15 Canadian.

and follow the signs to Eagle Chair, or take the new high-speed quad to the saddle at the top of the mountain. If Eagle Chair is selected, ride it to the top of the south face and drop off down the north or east faces to the base of Larch Chair. All runs down this face are expert except Pika, which is clearly marked and easy to locate. From the top of the new Top of the World quad follow the green "balls" down the north face. This is the only marked trail from this chair to the backside. Novices should follow these markers around the bowl. Advanced skiers will, no doubt, choose to follow one of the more direct fall lines to the bottom. Either way, all trails lead to Pika and Larch Chairlift.

Larch is best described as an intermediate mountain. There is only one expert run shown on the trail map; all others are either intermediate or beginner. However, there is a gladed area of larch trees two-thirds of the way up Larch Chair. Riders of this lift will find many skiers working their way down these interesting glades. Many hours of enjoyment can be derived from skiing this area, but caution should used until you are familiar with it. From the top of the lift there is a run called The Ski Out. It is an intermediate run until the base of Larch is reached. However, if one skies this run past the intersection of Look-Out near the base of Larch Chairlift, he is committed to skiing all the way back to the base lodge.

The north and east faces of Lake Louise offer expert skiers some of the most interesting skiing in the area. The runs served by the Ptarmigan 2 Chair are trails cut among the abundant trees. These are the best mogul runs on the mountain. Open bowl skiing can be reached by skiing Paradise Chair or by skiing over the top from Summit Platter, where some really excellent ridge runs such as Whitehorn One or broad, snowfield skiing on Shoulder Roll are accessible. However, skiing these runs requires a long run-out to get to the lift for additional runs. It is similar in length to the run-out from Mongolia Bowl at Vail.

The longest runs at Lake Louise are Wiwaxi for beginners at 3 miles (4.8 km), Boomerang for intermediates, also at 3 miles (4.8 km), and for experts Outer Limits to Men's Downhill at 5 miles (3.2 km).

The average monthly temperatures at Lake Louise are

Dec.	24°	-5°C
Jan.	21°	-7°C
Feb.	31°	-1°C
Mar.	37°	3°C

Lake Louise's annual snowfall is between 350 and 400 inches annually. The monthly snowfall is

Nov.	58"	(147 cm)
Dec.	73"	(185 cm)
Jan.	67"	(170 cm)
Feb	47"	(119 cm)
Mar.	56"	(142 cm)
Apr.	45"	(114 cm)

Sunshine Village

In order to get from the parking lot of Sunshine Village to the base of the mountain, it is necessary to ride the 7,621 ft. (2,323 meters) gondola to Canada's highest elevated resort at 7,082 feet (2,160 meters). The ride takes twenty minutes. Sunshine is a gem: located high among Canada's tallest and most picturesque peaks, it is only developed to a fraction of its potential. It is the only Banff/Lake Louise ski area which offers any on-mountain accommodations(see lodging information later in this chapter). For the skier, it is an area consisting of long, open runs, hidden trails among tall pines, and sunlit meadows. Sunshine boasted the only high-speed quad chairlift, The Angel Express, in the

Banff/Lake Louise area until Lake Louise Ski Area installed its two quads in the summer of 1989. From its terminus, intermediate skiers can enjoy large open-field skiing similar to that found on Snowmass's Big Burn. However, skiers should remember that skiing at this high altitude of 8,954 feet (2,730 meters), so far north, on an unprotected slope can spell trouble if the weather turns bad. In fact, Sunshine practices snow-farming. That is, they use extensive snow fences and snowcats to harvest the snow and prevent it from blowing away during the high winds that usually accompany storms in this part of the world.

Other than Angel Express, most of Sunshine's lifts are old and functionally obsolete. Small double chairlifts and T-bars are the rule in this part of the Canadian Rockies. It is interesting, however, to note that Sunshine is the oldest and highest ski area in the Rockies and the only one on the North American Continent that crosses the Continental Divide. It also crosses the provincial boundary between Alberta and British Columbia. All the lifts are relatively short, as are the runs. One should not come here expecting to find long runs such as are available at Whistler or Blackcomb. No doubt if they are ever allowed to re-lift the mountain, management will increase the length of the runs presently available. The Canadian Park Service has approved a plan to add three lifts, possibly high-speed quads up the face of Goat's Eye Mountain, which will add some spectacular open fields of snow and steep treed areas to this area's terrain. Currently this mountain is not lift serviced. Its addition to the area would be welcomed by all Sunshine skiers. Construction is projected to begin during the summer of 1994.

The best expert runs at Sunshine are found off Tee Pee Town Double Chair where steep bump runs are usually available. This is also the site of the best tree skiing. Tree skiing, though excellent, is somewhat limited as the majority of the resort is above the timber line. The best intermediate skiing is located under Angel Express and Great Divide Double Chair. These are among the longest runs at Sunshine as well. They are all above the timber line and always immaculately groomed. Beginners will love all the terrain available just for them. Whether skiing Green Run from the top of Angel Express or Meadow Park as it meanders around Wawa, beginners are unhindered by more aggressive skiers constantly crossing their tracks or scaring them by skiing too fast and too close.

Sunshine Village consists of 20% beginner slopes, 60% intermediate, and 20% advanced.

Sunshine's annual snowfall is 374" (949 cm). The monthly snowfalls are

Nov.	35"	(89 cm)
Dec.	45"	(114 cm)
Jan.	69"	(175 cm)
Feb.	69"	(175 cm)
Mar.	76"	(193 cm)
Apr.	45"	(114 cm)
May.	35"	(89 cm)

The average monthly temperatures are

Dec.	24°	-5° C
Jan.	21°	-7° C
Feb.	31°	-1° C
Mar.	37°	3° C

Sunshine's longest beginner run is Bourgeau Express at 3.6 miles (5,787 m); its longest intermediate is Ladies Downhill to Whiteway at 1.6 miles (2,587 m), and its longest expert run is North Divide to Tee Pee Town at one mile (1,690 m).

Mystic Ridge\Norquay

Mystic Ridge\Norquay still is the smallest of the three mountains in the Banff area, but it recently added 70 new acres of terrain with the development of Mystic Ridge. The ownership of the resort petitioned the National Parks Service for a major expansion in 1988. This area opened the first Canadian chairlift in 1948. Now two new high speed quad chairlifts, the Mystic Express and the Spirit Quad Chair whisk skiers to previously undeveloped intermediate trails, which make up 45 percent of the area. Previously this area was known mainly for beginners and experts, with little in between. The rest of the terrain is divided between 16 percent expert trails, 28 percent advanced, and 11 percent beginner. One hundred percent of the area is served by snowmaking equipment. Now the area has five lifts, with a base elevation of 5,350 feet(1,636 meters) and a summit elevation of 7,000 feet(2,133 meters). Norquay is the only local area open for skiing at night, once a week on Wednesdays. For information, call(403)762-4421, or the 24-hour Snowphone at (403)221-8259.

Lift Ticket Prices (1993-94)

Lake Louise

$ 39.50 Adult, All-Day
$ 34.   Adult, Half-Day
$ 35   Youth, 13-17, Student with photo ID, 17-25, and Senior 65+)
$ 10   Child, (6 through 12)
$180   Adult, 5 out of 7 days
$146   Youth, Student and Senior, 5 out of 7 days
$204   Adult, 6 out of 7 days

Sunshine Village

$ 37   Adult, All-Day
$ 32   Adult, Half-Day
$ 32   Student, All-Day (13 - 25 with school photo ID) (Senior, Older Than 65)
$ 28   Student, Half-Day
$ 13   Child, (6 through 12)
$ 63   Adult, 2-Day
$ 87   Adult, 3-Day
$112   Adult, 4-Day
$140   Adult, 5-Day

Mystic Ridge\Norquay

$29.90   Adult, All-Day
$25.   Adult, Half-Day
$15.   Night Ski, Wednesdays only
$25.   Youth, Student, and Senior(55+), All-Day
$13   Junior (6 to 12 years)

Hours of Operation

Lake Louise

8:30 A.M. through 4:00 P.M. (May be open longer during Spring)
8:30 A.M. through 3:45 P.M. Ptarmigan Chair

8:30 A.M. through 3:30 P.M. Larch Area

Sunshine Village

Sunshine Village gondola opens daily at 7:30 A.M. and closes at 5:30 P.M. Saturday it closes at 7:00 P.M., and on Fridays and Sundays it closes at 10:30 P.M. All other lifts operate from 8:30 A.M. through 4:00 P.M. Angel Express High-Speed Quad may be open until 6:00 P.M. Fridays and Saturdays during the spring.

Mystic Ridge\Norquay

9 A.M. through 5 P.M. daily
Night skiing begins Dec. 15 on Wednesday only until 9 P.M.

Lift Ticket Purchase Locations

Lake Louise lift tickets are sold at the Whiskeyjack Base Area. Sunshine Village sells its lift tickets at the base of the gondola. Mystic Village/Mt. Norquay tickets can be purchased at the customer service center at the base of the mountain.

How To Avoid Crowds

Lake Louise is similar in size to Vail, although its lift system is nowhere as extensive. Even on the sunniest days the runs are never crowded, but some lifts do experience long lines. Thanks to the new quad chairlifts, lift lines on the south face are not as much of a problem on weekends and holidays as they once were. The crowded lift will be Larch and Ptarmigan, but if this area is skied in the morning or during the traditional lunch period, the afternoon rush can be avoided. Even some of this problem has been alleviated by replacement of the Ptarmigan double chair with a quad. Ski the south face in the afternoon. Avoid eating at Temple Lodge during crowded weekends and holidays. The service will be faster at Whiskeyjack and Whitehorn Lodges.

The Larch area is the best area to ski during periods of flat light when its trees will provide contrast. The top of Lake Louise's mountain is barren, and during windy weather it can become bitterly cold. Snow must be farmed and conserved as the wind will otherwise blow it all away. Snowmaking has been added to the top of the Top of the World Express near the Temple Lodge to help improve this problem. This man-made base tends to get skied-off, and when this happens, the runs are icy with conditions similar to those that frequently plague Keystone.

Because there is only one way up to the ski area at Sunshine Village, its gondola can become crowded on weekends and holidays. The best way to avoid delays is to arrive early and get on the hill before most of the skiers arrive from Calgary. Once in the ski area, the least crowded runs appear to be the ones off Wheeler Double Chair, Firewheel T-Bar, and Wawa T-Bar. During periods of heavy snow and cold, blowing winds, the sheltering trees of Wheeler Double Chair are especially appreciated.

Ski School

Canadian ski schools teach a different skiing method than their United States' counterparts. In Canada the standard teaching method is the International Skiing Standard established by the International Ski Instructors Association and administered by the Canadian Ski Instructors Alliance (CSIA). Instructors at both Lake Louise and Sunshine are certified by CSIA. Rather than beginner, intermediate, and expert levels of proficiency, the CSIA defines its students as exhibiting "bronze", "silver", or "gold" abilities. Bronze students can make controlled wedge turns; silver level students can make controlled basic parallel turns and a controlled skate stop, while gold students are proficient at making controlled dynamic parallel turns and short radius turns in the bumps.

Lake Louise (1993-94)

$22   Adult, Group Lesson, 1 3/4 hours
$50   Private, 1-2 persons, One Hour ($32 if started before 9 A.M. or after 3 P.M.), $16 for each additional person
$31   GM Kinder Ski: Ages 3 - 6, supervised day care and 2-hour lesson
$33   GM Kids Ski: Ages 7 - 12, Full Day instruction , lunch and lift

All A.M. group lessons at Lake Louise last for one hour, forty-five minutes, and classes meet at 10:15. All P.M. classes are for two hours and meet at 1 P.M. The reason for the extra fifteen minutes in the afternoon is that afternoon classes are not usually as crowded as morning classes and management wants to encourage more skiers to take afternoon lessons.

Sunshine Village (1992-93)

Never-ever-before skiers can enroll in Sunshine's Never-Ever Pack sponsored by Labatt's "Skiing is Believing." This package includes rental equipment, lift tickets and a two and one-half hour lesson for the price of a lift ticket alone! Other ski lessons are priced as follows:

$ 15   Adult
$ 20   Short Turn Clinic
$ 48   Adult, Private Lesson
$160   Adult, All-Day
$ 10   Wee Angels (3 - 5, 1:30 to 2:30 P.M., includes equipment, lesson)
$ 35   Young Devils (6 - 12, includes equipment,lunch and lesson, 11 A.M. to 3 P.M.)

All lessons are for one and one-half hours and quoted rates do not include equipment or lift tickets unless noted otherwise. Private lessons meet on the hour 9:00 A.M. through 4:00 P.M. Never-Ever Pack classes meet at 10:00 A.M. for registration at the Bourgeau customer service area at the base of the gondola. Their lessons begin at 10:30 A.M. Regular group lessons meet at 10:50 A.M. and 12:50 P.M. All classes meet in front of Sunshine Village Hotel at the top of the gondola station.For advance reservations, call (403)762-6560.

Mystic Ridge/Mt.Norquay(1993-94)

$30   Adult learn-to-ski package, lift, lesson, rental and 1/2 price lesson coupon
$25   Child learn-to-ski package
$20   Adult group lesson, 1 hour for 2 people or less, 2 hours for 3 people or more
$15   Child, 6 to 12 years, group lesson, 2 hours
$25   Child Full-Day lesson, lunch not included, 10:30 - 12:30 and 1:30 - 3:30
$35   Private lesson, one hour

Equipment Rental (1993-94)

Lake Louise Ski Rental, located across from Whiskeyjack Lodge at the base of Lake Louise, rents adult alpine, Nordic, or snowboard equipment for $18 per day with a twenty percent discount if it is rented for three or more days. High-performance packages are available featuring K2 5500, Head CRSL, Dynastar GS, Atomic ARC, Fischer RC4 RS, Kastle RX12, and Kastle National Team GSM skis, Salomon SX 81 boots or Nordica 555 boots, and Salomon 957 or 747 bindings. High-performance packages start at $40 per day with a twenty percent discount on three or more days rental. Children's ski packages start at $12 per day and are likewise discounted. Cross-country ski equipment is available for $12 and telemark at $23. Snowboards are $31 for a full day. Boots for use with snowboards are also available, although price was unknown at press time.

Numerous rental shops are found in and around Banff and Lake Louise. If skiers plan to rent equipment during peak seasons, it is advisable to reserve skis in advance as the shops rent out their skis quickly during Christmas and Easter.

In Banff Springs Hotel, **The Ski Stop** carries a complete line of all types of recreational and high-performance rentals. During the 1992-93 season the standard package rented for $17 per day with discounts applicable with three or more days rental. Equipment consists of Rossignol Edge skis, Salomon 447 and 357 bindings, Salomon SX 31, 41, 60 or 70 boots, and Kerma poles. The high-performance package will consist of Rossignol DV series skis, Salomon 457 or 357 bindings, Salomon SX 52, 61, 71, 72, or 82 boots, and Kerma poles. High-performance packages start at $28 per day and were discounted for three or more days. For reservations or additional information, telephone (403) 762-5333, ext. 6515. The Ski Stop also rents a full line of ski apparel by the day or week.

Sports Rent at 208 Bear St. in Banff also rented recreational through high-performance skis. New rates were unavailable at press time. For reservations or information, telephone (403) 762-8222.

At Mystic Ridge/Norquay equipment can be rented for $15 for an adult set of skis, boots and poles; for children the same can be found for $10. High performance sets cost $25. Snowboard and boots will cost $23.

Ski Tuning and Repair

At press time, rates were not available, but call any of the rental shops mentioned here and they will give you the latest.

Mountain Dining

Lake Louise

All three on-mountain restaurants at Lake Louise are cafeterias, and food is marginal compared to that served at other resorts featured in this book. At **Whiskeyjack Lodge** located at the base area, a small buffet is served daily, but its offerings are limited and its food quality is less than discriminating diners would expect.

Temple Lodge, located at the base of Larch Chair, is the most popular dining spot on the mountain. This is the newest facility at Lake Louise and its rough-sawn cedar interior no doubt contributes to its popularity. On the second floor, **Sawyer's Nook** offers soups, sandwiches, and daily specials served as a small buffet. Diners can carry their selections to tables decorated with red and white checkerboard vinyl tablecloths. Many knowledgeable locals order their hamburgers and fries in the downstairs cafeteria and carry them upstairs to eat in Sawyer's Nook. This is a good idea if one cannot afford the time go into town and dine at the Post Hotel for lunch!

Sunshine Village

The best on-mountain food is found at **The Chimney Corner Lounge** located in Sunshine Village Inn. Bathed in the natural sunlight which streams through its glass-enclosed east wall and ceiling, The Chimney Lounge features mountain nachos (a reference to the quantity, no doubt), chicken fingers, steak sandwich, veggie dip, and its locally famous Sunshine burger. An abundance of natural light and an oak interior finish provide the ideal environment for hanging baskets of vines and flowers. At the far end of the bar, there are two dos-à-dos fireplaces constructed out of Banff-quarried granite with mounts of bison and antelope. Since this is not only a great mountain restaurant but also a lively après-ski bar, it is not unusual to find any number of people climbing up the chimneys. Close examination will reveal numerous signatures and graffiti on the ceiling where it abuts the fireplace.

Other mountain dining at Sunshine centers around the gondola station, either in the **Old Sunshine Lodge** or in the **Daylodge**. Burgers and salads and other simple fare may be found on the third level of the Daylodge in **Trapper Bill's Lounge**. On the second level of the same building is found the cafeteria with the usual day-ski-area food and beverages. On the main floor of the Daylodge is the **Sunshine Deli** where hungry skiers can create their own sandwiches while enjoying their favorite beer or wine.

Just slightly uphill from the Daylodge is the **Snack Shack** which occupies the main floor of the original Sunshine Village daylodge. Short-order items are the specialty here. It is also the only area where skiers can eat their "brown bag" lunches.

Child Care

Sunshine Village **Kids Kampus Daycare Centre** is located adjacent to Sunshine Inn at the top of Bourgeau Gondola. Kids Kampus is a government-approved facility utilizing indoor and outdoor activities. Care is for children from nineteen months through six years of age. Reservations in the Kids Kampus is recommended. Telephone (403) 762-6560. Sunshine also has its Wee Angels program for children aged three through five. At $10 per hour students receive one and one-half hours of ski lessons daily and three hours of day care. Six through nine-year-olds should enroll in the Ski Angels. The Ski Angels is an all-day program including lunch and instruction. A similar program called Big Angels is available for children ten through twelve years of age.

At the Lake Louise base area, a nursery and child-care center accommodates children from eighteen days through twelve years of age. Reservations are only required for infants. The nursery accepts children up to twenty-three months. The 1993-94 cost for this service is a modest $21 per day or $4 per hour for infants. Older children aged two through six have their own play area, and their indoor and outdoor activities are closely supervised by an attentive staff. The fee for this service was $3.75 per hour.

Children three to seven may participate in a combination program that features two one-hour ski lessons with indoor play. This program is called **Kinder-Ski**. Seven through twelve-year-olds can enroll in the **Kids-Ski** program. This program encourages children to learn the mountain by skiing with an instructor all day. There are some indoor or outdoor activities at the beginning and end of each ski day, too.

Medical Facilities

The ski patrols at both Lake Louise and Sunshine Village render emergency service to injured skiers. They will administer trauma treatment, stabilize broken bones, and transport injured skiers downhill by sled to First Aid Stations, located at the base of the Olympic Chair at Lake Louise and at the gondola station in Sunshine Village.

From either resort, seriously injured skiers will be taken by ambulance to the Banff hospital at the corner of Wolf and Lynx streets.

Cross-Country Skiing

Cross-country skiing at Banff/Lake Louise is wonderful. Whether on the tracks at Sunshine or on any of the numerous trails maintained by Parks Canada throughout the region, one will be overwhelmed by beautiful scenery. The rugged majesty of the mountains within Banff Park is not found anywhere else on the continent. The beauty of skiing across Lake Louise on an ice surface the color of Caribbean waters is not duplicated elsewhere in the Americas. This unusual coloring apparently is the result of minerals being introduced into the water from the continual movement of the Victoria Glacier just above the lake. In fact, several frozen, emerald green waterfalls drain into the lake and provide climbing opportunities for the adventuresome.

At Sunshine, too, the sheer awesomeness of the mountain peaks surrounding the groomed 12.5 k track is without parallel.

For more information and free trail maps of the entire area, telephone (403) 762-4506 and ask for *Nordic Trails in Banff National Park,* or stop by the Banff Information Centre at 224 Banff Ave in Lake Louise. Local area maps are also available from the Emerald Lake Lodge Nordic Centre at (403) 343-6321 or from Castle Mountain Village at (403) 762-3868.

Accommodations

Banff

Perhaps the most famous hotel in Canada—certainly in the Canadian Rockies—is the Canadian Pacific's **Banff Springs Hotel**. Featured on television shows, brochures, postcards, and in the movies, the Banff Springs Hotel is unique. With its Elizabethan-style turrets, copper gables, and wind-snapping flags, this hotel is an institution. Constructed during Canada's western expansion by Canadian Pacific Railroad, it was originally intended to draw tourists from the eastern provinces to view the beauty of western lands and to encourage people to inhabit the area. This is a large hotel with 841 rooms, an indoor swimming pool, game arcade, shopping arcade, numerous restaurants, lounges, steam and sauna rooms, ballrooms, and every amenity imaginable. The rooms tend to be on the small side and are generally in need of remodeling. High ceilings, furniture 20 to 30 years old, and vintage carpet are the norm. The motif of the hotel is Elizabethan with soaring arches, embroidered fabrics, and dark wood finishes. There are, however, several rooms that are truly exceptional and would be worthy of four stars in anyone's guide. Request room 916 or 917, for example, and enjoy living in a garret high above the forest with views of Mt. Rundle, the golf course, lakes and streams frequented in the early dawn or late dusk by foraging herds of mountain goat, elk, deer, or big horn sheep. Beautiful marble baths and wonderfully appointed suites provide a surrounding anyone would be pleased to occupy for a romantic ski week.

Forty percent of Banff's visitors hail from Japan, so it is not surprising to learn there are numerous Japanese restaurants in the area. One of the better ones is located on the lower level of the Banff Springs Hotel and is called **Samurai**. This restaurant features typical Japanese decor and dishes such as shabu-shabu and sukiyaki cooked at your table or at the counter, should you choose to eat at the bar.

The Banff Park Lodge is a 210-room hotel located at 222 Lynx in the center of downtown Banff. This AAA 4-diamond award-winning hotel's rooms feature free cable TV, balconies, twin queen-size beds, and a few contain extra sinks. All rooms have views of Mt. Cascade, which is definitely one of the better views in North America. Upgraded rooms feature steam baths, king-size beds, and a Jacuzzi tub right in the room! All rooms are soundproofed for pleasant sleeping regardless of the partying group down the hall.

Banff Park Lodge's features include a magnificent cathedral ceiling in the main reception area and adjoining Glacier Lounge. Suspended from this ceiling is an old chairlift from days long gone by. This is a warm and inviting area in which to partake of après-ski. The welcoming rock fireplace is built from slate and granite mined on Mt. Rundle, known as Rundle rock. On the lower level of the hotel, there is a hot tub and unique indoor swimming pool where the odor of chlorine is totally absent. The ventilation system around which this pool has been built is as exceptional as the attention to detail in its finishing. Dark redwood-paneled walls and comfortable iron furniture encourage conversation among fellow bathers. Changing rooms, as well as steam and sauna rooms, are adjacent to the pool.

A 130-seat family-style restaurant called **Chinook** is located on the mezzanine. The restaurant is justifiably proud of having its own pastry chef. There is also a smaller, more intimate restaurant called **Terrace**. Its partial glass ceiling affords views of the evening snowfall and bright stars.

All major credit cards (except Master Card) are accepted. The new rates were not available at press time, but during the 1992-93 ski season regular rooms rented from a high of $175 per night based on double occupancy to a low of $95 per night. The hotel's most expensive rooms during high season went for as high as $260 per night, based on double occupancy.

The **Douglas Fir Resort & Chalets** are located minutes from downtown Banff on Tunnel Mountain Road. The complex of 133 condominiums offers studio units to two bedroom units and 2- or 3-bedroom A-Frame chalets with very reasonable prices. All units have cable tv, full kitchens and wood burning fireplaces. The complex includes an indoor pool, children's pool and two huge indoor waterslides, which spiral 220-feet and 190-feet around and above the pool. Also included are a steam room, sauna, children's pool, fitness room with universal, cycling and rowing machines, and a games room, and tennis court, racquetball and squash courts. On site is located a grocery store and a coin laundry. Rates start at $92 for studios and $132 for 2 bedroom units and chalets, and peak at $144 and $184 per unit respectively, during the Christmas holidays. Summer rates will be higher. Call (800)661-9267 for information and reservations. Free indoor parking is available.

Sunshine Village

The only accommodations at Sunshine Village are those of **Sunshine Inn**, located at the top of the gondola. These are also the only accommodations available in Banff/Lake Louise that are directly adjacent to ski slopes! This is a small hotel with only 84 rooms, vaguely reminiscent of the small hotels found at Taos Ski Valley, but with a slightly foreign flair for Americans. In addition to regular hotel rooms that are, more or less, the same all over the world, they have what they refer to as *terrace rooms*. Terrace rooms are detached from the main hotel complex, and each two-room configuration shares a common bath and toilet area. Because of the hotel's location, access is limited to the hours of the gondola's operation. Once skiers are at the hotel in the evening, there is no opportunity to go to Banff or Lake Louise for dinner or entertainment. For this reason, the hotel seems to cater to families more than ski clubs or young college students. Standard rooms do not have any TV's, but a "family room" located on the hotel's "B" level contains a large screen TV, as well as a well-stocked library. It is a comfortable room with tables, chairs, sofas, a fireplace, and flagstone floor. Most guests utilize the room as a "sort of baby sitter" while they become acquainted with other guests. The hotel boasts an outdoor heated swimming pool with adjacent changing rooms and a co-ed sauna.

Typical guest rooms are plain but clean. They contain one queen-size bed and one single bed. Recently redecorated in mauves and grays, the rooms are furnished with a chest of drawers, telephone table, and two side chairs. There are no closets, but a clothing bar is provided. The bathrooms are small and contain a combination tub and shower.

Because of the evening isolation of the hotel, entertainment is provided in the adjacent **Eagle's**

Nest restaurant and Chimney Corner Lounge. The dining room comfortably seats 105 persons in its rustic setting of terra-cotta tile floors, beige and green table linens, and beech ladder-back chairs. The dining room overlooks the illuminated Standish and Strawberry chairs. During the 1993-94 low season, the rate for a regular room ranges from $75 per person, based on double occupancy to a high of $135 per night. A lift ticket included. During the high season just after Christmas, prices range from $100 per person to $299 per person/ Other options are available such as American plan and weekend-only rates. Since 1934 the Sunshine Inn has hosted six and seven-night "Ski Weeks." Similar to the ski weeks offered at Taos, Sunshine ski weeks include room, board, lessons, nightly entertainment, day care, and other entertainment. When booking reservations check current offerings.

Lake Louise

Chateau Lake Louise is beautifully positioned on the shore of Lake Louise. Guests should request rooms that face the lake and Victoria Glacier, a massive ice sculpture suspended high above the lake. This is a beautiful setting: a pristine natural forest, craggy mountain peaks, emerald waters, and fluffy, white, powder snow. Poised on the shore, the hotel resembles a modern-day castle with its angular shape and peaked blue towers. Owned and operated by Canadian Pacific Hotels (the same as the Banff Springs Hotel), it is currently undergoing renovations. The older, unrenovated rooms are small, and their furnishings dated. The newly renovated rooms are charmingly decorated in a Swiss-mountain motif. However, they are small and little or nothing has been done to improve the acoustics. These rooms are noisy!

The hotel has a very large central lobby with two-story glazed doors opening onto the lake. The lake is kept clear of snow for skaters' pleasure. The lobby has comfortable seating and desks are available for guests to write letters and postcards. As a full-service hotel, numerous retail shops, gift stores, and amenities are offered. In the lobby there is **The Lobby Bar**, cozy with plush seating and views of Victoria Glacier and skaters on Lake Louise. The Lobby Bar features full lunch service every day except Sunday, and après-ski favorites include chicken fingers, french fries, as well as several mulled wines.

Located 6 km from the Lake Louise ski area, the Chateau offers shuttle service for a reasonable fee.

The finest hotel in either Lake Louise or Banff is the **Post Hotel Lake Louise**. A member of the prestigious Relais & Chateaux group of inns, it was constructed mostly with hand tools in the summer of 1942. The hotel has continually undergone change and improvement. Originally named Lake Louise Ski Lodge, it changed its name to Post in 1978 because of the confusion between its name and that of Chateau Lake Louise and because there was a small post office on the adjacent property. The hotel was sold in 1978 to Barb and George Schwarz who have operated it ever since. In 1986 the Lake Louise area was considered ripe for tourist development by many at a time when Husky Oil Co. was looking for an investment in the tourist industry. They purchased a share of the Post Hotel, and today Husky and the Schwarz family own and operate it.

Upon entering the hotel through its grand lobby furnished in waxed, natural pine and decorated in mauve and sea foam, one is immediately aware of the quality of his surroundings. Just off the lobby is nestled the small, inviting **Norman Lounge** with its granite fireplace and mounted moosehead. This room is sensual and intimate like the lounge at Sardy House in Aspen. Further down the corridor from the lounge is an award-winning dining room, discussed at length in the section of this chapter entitled *Restaurants*.

Unlike many hotels that make guests feel crunched or squeezed, Post Hotel has wide corridors which make it easy for guests to pass and for bellmen to move luggage from the reception area to individual rooms. Rooms are comfortably large and decorated in the same fashion as the lobby with mauves and sea foam being the dominate colors. Furnishings have been custom built from native pine and contribute to the hotel's atmosphere of a small Swiss inn. Satellite TV, a small desk, Jacuzzi tubs, and ample closets promise the guest a comfortable stay here at Post Hotel in Canada's winter paradise. Hotel amenities include a unique hypo-cell indoor salt pool. This swimming pool does not utilize chlorine for purifying the water; rather, the water is purified through osmosis and a hypo-cell. Guests will also enjoy a hot tub and steam room.

The hotel's 83 rooms are arranged in 13 different configurations. The simplest configuration is type A with two double beds; it is also the most plentiful. Type B rooms contain a king-size bed, whirlpool tub, and a fireplace. Type A & B rooms represent more than fifty percent of the available rooms. Teype A rooms contain two double beds. Type B have a king sized bed, whirpool tub and fireplace. The others are highly specialized and contain numerous amenities such as kitchens and additional sleeping accommodations. At press time, the 1993-94 rates were not available, but for the 1992-93 ski season, Type A and Type B rooms rented from a low of $100 per night to a high of $215 per night. Other specialty rooms ran as high as $250 per night. For specific definitions of these unique rooms, telephone the hotel directly at (403) 522-3989 or in the U.S.A. (800) 661-1586.

Restaurants

Banff

The Yard restaurant located at 206 Wolf Street offers some unusual fare, such as Tex-Mex, B.B.Q., and blackened dishes. A simple decor of blue, exposed girders, ivy-filled hanging planters, oak tables, and captain chairs make this restaurant a perfect choice for families. The buffalo wing appetizers are served as either mild, hot, or suicide! Serving sizes are abundant. The tostados are crisp and the salsa hot with a hint of garlic. This would be a favorite restaurant for everybody except Texans who might find the fare a little too mild. Telephone (403) 762-3848 for reservations.

A favorite of the locals is **The Rose and Crown Pub** on Main Street. Located upstairs, it is a dark, typical British pub. Pints and half-pints are served in traditional English glasses, and three dart boards receive constant attention. A fireplace warms the room and a wide-screen TV featuring Warren Miller-style films provides entertainment, if just watching the clientele is insufficient. Between 7:00 P.M. and 9:00 P.M. every Thursday the bartenders serve "pub grub". These are very plentiful servings of daily specials. Typically items such as three huge beef ribs served on top of rice pilaf and a BIG fresh salad would be featured. A second non-beef offering is always available, too. The 1990 price for this extravagant meal was only $3.95. Of course, the management hopes its clients will make up the cost of the meal in liquor purchases. No reservations accepted.

Italian food lovers should try **Giorgio's La Casa** at 219 Banff Avenue. There is an upstairs and a downstairs Giorgio's. The upstairs restaurant is the formal dining room and is referred to as La Casa. The downstairs is less formal and referred to as **La Pasta**. The better value is found in the downstairs La Pasta location. La Casa is intimate with Italian love songs quietly playing in the background, candle light, sparkling crystal, white table linens, and a respectable wine list offering French, American, or Italian wines. The minestrone alla paesana is excellent, full of quartered ripe tomatoes and other fresh vegetables. Entrées are served hot and presented colorfully. Saltimbocca alla romana and tortellini alla panna are recommended dishes. Menus are the same upstairs or downstairs; only the prices are different. For reservations, telephone (403) 762-5116.

Some of the best meals in Banff/Lake Louise will be found in the dining room of the **Post Hotel** in Lake Louise. Fantastic dishes prepared by Chef Kenneth Pitcomb are served in the original building of the Post Hotel. A feeling of Provence is imparted to the scene with the use of hand-hewn wooden beams to support the stucco ceiling and the log walls; the room is further enhanced by a quaint stone fireplace where a welcoming fire dances. Relax and enjoy a house pinot noir while watching one of the trans-Canada scenic trains whistle by.

A sample of the Post's menu includes terrine or pâté du jour, slices of air-dried beef, smoked bacon and cured ham, sautéed shrimps with a touch of calvados, and steamed apple for appetizers. The Belgian endive in mustard dressing is an excellent salad. Fresh fish may include trout filets with herbs and cream sauce or Caribbean jumbo shrimps "provençale". Meats may include chicken breast in red wine sauce, boneless rack of lamb provençale, strips of beef tenderloin "stroganoff", or filet of beef with green peppercorns in cream sauce. As one might expect, dining at the Post Hotel is not an inexpensive event, but it is not overpriced and the food is a fair value. For reservations, telephone (403) 522-3989.

The Edelweiss dining room at The Chateau Lake Louise is reminiscent of seventeenth century English manor homes with their soaring ceilings, Gothic arches, and heavily embroidered fabrics. Table settings are impressive and the service is attentive. The menu seems a bit unusual, featuring such items as sausages Albertville, pasta of the day, and the "full-meal" burger at relatively high prices. For reservations, telephone (403) 522-3511.

The Walliser Stube located on the arcade in The Chateau Lake Louise is very comfortable and serves a limited but interesting menu. Newly renovated in dark mahogany woods and bright brass fittings, the Walliser Stube is squeezed in on two floors. An unusual dumbwaiter is used to speed food to both levels. Prices are moderate.

Other places to try in the Banff area include a variety of choices at the Banff Springs Hotel. Stop by for a drink at **Grapes**, a wine bar.

The Balkan, upstairs at 120 Banff Ave., is a popular restaurant which features Greek food, steaks, seafood, pasta and vegetarian dishes. Favorite entrees include the Greek combo of spanakopita and tyropita for $13.95, and also the moussakka, $12.95. All entrees include a Greek salad, and potato or rice.

Le Beaujolais, 212 Buffalo St., (403)762-2712, a French restaurant with an excellent menu awarded four diamonds by AAA. Reservations advised.

Boccalino Grotto, corner of 8 Avenue and 10 Street in Canmore, (403)678-6424, has great pasta and fondue in new elegant surroundings.

Buffalo Mountain Lodge, on Tunnel Mountain Road in Banff, (403)762-2400, a beautiful dining room decorated with natural wood offering an array of gourmet choices.

Earls, at the corner of Banff and Wolfe St., (403)762-4414, is a popular spot for meat burgers and veggie burgers, as well as salads, chicken, steaks, and stir fried dishes. Try the Hunan Kung Pow or the Garden Burger or Caesar Salad. A full bar is available, and Earls offers only 5 white and 5 red wines. This place is casual, plays good rock and roll, and charges moderate prices, with entrees ranging from $7.95 to $15.95.

Grizzly House, 207 Banff Ave., (403)762-4055, specializes in fondues, raclette and exotic meats such as buffalo, venison, rabbit, alligator, rattle snake, kangaroo, shark, swordfish and frogs legs. The most popular complete dinners, ranging in price from $26.95 to $29.95 include a salad, a cheese or vegetable fondue as an appetizer, an entree of meet or fish and a chocolate fondue as dessert.

Joshua's, 204 Caribou St. in Banff, (403)762-2400, a local favorite, with good service and a delightful menu, including lamb carpaccio, wild mushroom ravioli, and duck breast and poached pears.

La Fontaine, 124 Banff Ave., (403)762-3311, AAA awards this restaurant 4 diamonds, and calls the dining room intimate and semicasual with luxurious oak furnishings. Reservations are recommended.

Santa Lucia, 710C Eighth St. in Canmore,(403)678-3414, a very good and moderately priced Italian restaurant, specializes in authentic Italian pizza, pasta, veal, chicken and fish. The average pasta dish is priced at approximately $7.50 and meat dishes cost around $11-$12.

Activities

Helicopter skiing is a great pastime in the Canadian Rockies because much of this vast area is inaccessible by any other means. Several helicopter ski companies work out of the Banff/Lake Louise area. Among them are **Selkirk Tangiers Helicopter Skiing Ltd.**, (403)762-3889; **Purcell Helicopter Skiing**, (604) 344-5410; **Heli-Ski Panorama**, (604) 342-3889.

Dog-led tours of scenic trails near the Banff Springs Hotel and on Spray Lakes near Canmore are offered by **Mountain Mushers Dog Sled Co.**,(403) 678-5742. At Chateau Lake Louise, call 522-3511 and at the Emerald Lake Lodge, call (604)343-6321. The 6-foot sleds carry two adults and a driver and are pulled by 7 to 9 Siberian huskies.

Bus tours of the Banff/Lake Louise area are available. These five-hour motor coach tours visit the lovely Bow Falls, the Hoodoos, Tunnel Mountain Drive, Sulphur Mountain Gondola, Vermilion Lakes, and Castle Mountain. For information and reservations, telephone (800) 661-1152.

Visitors may use the fitness facilities at **Sally Borden Building**, at the Banff Centre, which has a 25 m. pool, gym, squash, racquetball courts, weight room, jacuzzi, and sauna. (403)762-6450.
See the accommodations above for a description of facilities at the **Douglas Fir Resort**.
The **Banff Rocky Mountain Resort**, at Tunnel Mountain Road and Banff Ave., charges $5 a day for use of its squash courts, exercise facilities, pool, whirlpool, sauna and steam room. (403)762-5531.
Banff Community Fitness Centre, 335 Beaver Street, has free weights and fitness machines for public use. Drop-in aerobics classes are held at Banff High School, Beaver and Wolf Streets, for $3.50. Call for times. (403)762-1229.

Cross-country skiers may be interested in a late-afternoon departure to the legendary **Skoki Lodge** located deep in the woods of Banff National Park. Built in 1930 this lodge and its adjoining cabins provide comfortable accommodations with a rustic ambience. Facilities include a lodge and 3 surrounding cabins with enough room for 22 guests. Cabins are heated by wood stoves, and lighted by kerosene lanterns. Outhouses are the only toilet facilities. This offers wonderful access to cross country skiing. For information or reservations, telephone (403) 522-3555.

Services

A full complement of sporting goods stores, apparel shops, pharmacies, grocery stores, liquor stores, furniture, bath, and specialty shops is within the immediate town of Banff. In addition there are antique shops, art galleries, bakeries, beauty salons, book stores, florists, massage and tanning studios.

BRECKENRIDGE SKI RESORT

Breckenridge Ski Area
Box 1058
Breckenridge, CO. 80424

(800) 800-2732 Reservations
(303) 453-5000 Information
(303) 453-6118 Snow Report

New For 1993-94

An exciting addition at Breckenridge this year will be its expansion to include 315 new acres for skiing at Peak 7. Adding to the area's expanse of bowl skiing, the adventurous can now try 210 new acres of open bowls in the area, as well as 15 acres added to the top of Imperial Bowl at Peak 8. Breckenridge now boasts 785 acres of bowl skiing between these two mountains. In addition, the area includes 90 acres of glades before leading skiers back to Peak 8 runs. Skiers will reach Peak 7 via Peak 8's T-Bar.

During the past year the Ralston Purina Company of St. Louis, owner of Keystone and Arapaho Basin Ski Areas, has purchased the Breckenridge Ski Resort. Between the two resorts, over 2.4 million skier days were recorded last season, making it the most popular of ski complexes in the U.S. The resorts are 17 miles apart, but this year "Breck-stone" management promises more frequent free buses between all of its ski slopes.

How to Get There

Breckenridge is served by all major airlines through Denver's Stapleton International Airport. All major car rental agencies are represented at Stapleton. At the airport proper visitors will find

Avis	(800)221-1212
Budget	(800)527-0700
Dollar	(800)421-6868
Hertz	(800)654-3131
National	(800)328-4567

Other car rental agencies are located outside airport property and offer free airport pickup and drop-off; among them are

Alamo	(800)327-9633
Enterprise	(800)325-8007
Thrifty	(800)367-2277

Breckenridge is 85 miles from Stapleton, 98 miles from the new airport. It is around a 2-hour drive in clear weather on dry roads. From Denver take I-70 west to the Frisco exit at Highway 9. Follow Highway 9 until it becomes Main St. in Breckenridge.

All rental agencies provide their clients with free maps. Due to possible road restrictions, travelers to Breckenridge are advised to always rent cars that are *skierized*, i.e. equipped with snow tires and ski racks. For a slightly higher price, many rental agencies can provide four-wheel drive vehicles. The traveler is cautioned to reserve these vehicles far in advance because the demand for them is great.

Several companies offer shuttle service to Breckenridge from either the new airport or Denver's Stapleton Airport. **Resort Express** provides door-to-door transportation to Summit County during the 1993-94 season for $38 each way, $74 round trip on Saturdays, and $69 other days. Reservations are required. Call (800)334-7433. All major credit cards are accepted.

Vans to Breckenridge provides a similar service daily from the airports for varying rates, depending on the season. Regular fares will be $35 one way, $62 round trip, with fares rising to $38 and $74 respectively for Saturdays and holidays. Call (800)222-2112 for reservations and information.

Once skiers reach Breckenridge, the mountain and most accommodations are within walking distance. Additionally, free shuttle transportation to the mountain's two base areas is offered. Transportation is either by the Breckenridge Free Shuttle, owned and operated by Breckenridge Ski Area, or the Free Town Trolley, which is owned and operated by the town of Breckenridge. The Free Shuttle operates from 8:00 A.M. to 5:30 P.M., and the Free Trolley operates from 10:00 A.M. to 11:00 P.M. Free schedules are available at all lodging accommodations and from the Chamber of Commerce. For more information, telephone (303) 453-2368, Ext. 272.

The Summit Stage also operates a free shuttle service throughout Summit County which encompasses Breckenridge, Copper Mountain, Keystone ski areas and the towns of Breckenridge, Dillon, Frisco, and Silverthorne. This year some routes have been extended and the express routes have been quickened. For more information on the Summit Stage, phone (303)453-1241.

Mountain Information

Breckenridge is a large resort; there are more than 1,915 skiable acres consisting of 126 trails. Sixteen percent of the trails are classified as "easiest" (beginner), 27% as "more difficult" (intermediate), and 57% as "most difficult" (expert). It is easy to understand how skiers of all ability levels can enjoy Breckenridge for more than a week.

The longest run is from the top of Peak 8 to the village at the base of the mountain. It is a beginner run named Four O'Clock and is 3.5 miles long. Centennial and Crystal are the longest intermediate runs, each at 1.3 miles (2 km). The longest expert run is Cimarron at two-thirds of a mile (894 meters).

Four mountains comprise Breckenridge Ski Area: Peak 7, Peak 8, Peak 9, and Peak 10. These bland names were adopted by the U.S. Forest Service for designating the ten peaks which begin in Frisco and are in a line going south just to the west of Lake Dillon. From a base of 9,600 feet (2,926 meters) to a summit of 12,998 feet (3,723 meters), there are 3,398 vertical feet (796 meters) of wonderful skiing. All the mountains are interconnected by 16 lifts which include four Quads, 1 Triple Chairlift, 8 Double Chairlifts, and 3 Surface Lifts and give the resort an uphill lift capacity of 24,430 skiers per hour.

One of the joys of Breckenridge is the ability one has to move around the three mountains. This mobility assures intermediate and expert skiers uncrowded slopes and fresh snow. However, it takes some time to learn how to use the lift system to best advantage. The ideal place to begin the day is at Peak 8. This base area is less congested than Peak 9, and it provides the most diverse runs of all three peaks.

Breckenridge presents the skier with a myriad of options on its four mountain peaks: traditional carved trails; above tree line and bowl experiences. Photo by GuideBook Publishing Co.

If you would like to try all four of Breckenridge's mountains in one day, start at the Colorado SuperChair at the bottom of Peak 8 first thing in the morning and then ski to the T-Bar. From its summit, you may traverse north in to the Peak 7 bowls. Be forewarned the new bowls contain some of the steepest pitches anywhere at Breckenridge, sometimes approaching 36 degrees.

For a real physical challenge, skiers can hike from the top of the T-Bar to the top of Peak 8 - - 12,998 feet above sea level! From there you will be able to ski across the ridge between Peaks 8 and 7, and choose your own spot from which to descend into the bowls. The glades at the bottom of Peak 7 dump you back on the runs like Claim jumper on the far side of Peak 8.

Rest your legs during the return trip up the SuperChair before skiing to the #6 Lift. From the top of this lift, numerous choices for skiing are offered. Experts will want to test Contest and Horseshoe Bowls; intermediates will enjoy taking Four O'Clock to Columbine. Next, skiers should test themselves by skiing the runs paralleling Horseshoe Bowl's T-bar: Pika, Ptarmigan, White Crown, or Forget-Me-Not. All are short and can be skied in just an hour or two. After skiing these runs, the morning can be finished off by skiing to the bottom of Colorado lift via either Duke's Run, Northstar, High Anxiety, Boreas, or Little Johnny.

After skiing the top of Peak 8, it will be time to journey to Peak 9. From the top of The Colorado SuperChair, experts will relish any of the double black diamond runs which lead to the C-Lift. Runs with names like Mach 1, Goodbye Girl, Tiger, and Southern Cross offer challenging terrain. Intermediates will enjoy Frosty's. From the C-Lift's terminus, acres and acres of intermediate terrain are accessible. Super runs such as Upper Lehman, Cashier, Bonanza, and Peerless are long, wide, and groomed nightly. Experts will enjoy the North Face of Peak 9 where all the runs are double black diamonds. Similar to the back bowls along the #6-Lift, these are gladed runs whose northern exposure insures the snow will always be good. These glades are especially nice on spring afternoons when conditions on less-sheltered runs begin to deteriorate.

After spending some time on Peak 9, move to Peak 10. Centennial is Summit County's equivalent of the Big Burn at Snowmass — a wide, groomed, cruising run. Test your stamina by trying to ski top to bottom without stopping. Experts should concentrate on The Burn. Steep, moguled, and gladed, the Burn is only open late in the ski season when the snows have accumulated enough to cover fallen trees that litter the area. If there is not enough snow, ski Cimarron, Mustang, Spitfire, or Corsair.

With the exception of the double black diamond areas, the single black diamond runs are generally not beyond the ability of moderately strong intermediates. Of course, conditions do change a trail's particular characteristics and this should be taken into account before attempting a new run for the first time.

Individuals skiing for the first few times will find a great many beginner trails on the face of Peak 9. Long runs on which to practice skills learned in lessons include C Transfer, Red Rover, and Lehman.

Breckenridge's abundant snowfall totals over 320" (813 cm) annually. Monthly totals over the last several years have averaged

Nov.	36"	(91 cm)
Dec.	31"	(79 cm)
Jan.	32"	(81 cm)
Feb.	45"	(114 cm)
Mar.	58"	(147 cm)
Apr.	54"	(137 cm)

Average mid-mountain high temperatures are

Nov.	26°	-3° C
Dec.	21°	-6° C
Jan.	21°	-6° C
Feb.	23°	-5° C
Mar.	29°	-2° C
Apr.	34°	1° C

Lift Ticket Prices (1993-94)

$ 39	Adult, All-Day, for Breckenridge, Keystone and Arapaho Basin.
$ 74	Adult, 2 of 3 Days
$108	Adult, 3 of 4 Days
$136	Adult, 4 of 5 Days
$160	Adult, 5 of 6 Days
$180	Adult, 6 of 7 Days
$ 28	Adult, Half-Day P.M. Only
Free	Adult, 70+
$ 17	Child (6-12) or Senior (60-69 years), All Day
$ 30	Child, 2 of 3 Days
$ 45	Child, 3 of 4 Days
$ 60	Child, 4 of 5 Days
$ 75	Child, 5 of 6 Days
$ 90	Child, 6 of 7 Days
$ 15	Child, Half-Day P.M. Only
Free	Child, 5 and Under, Seniors, 70 and over.

Discounting of lift tickets for the entire Summit area is rampant. Each resort has made its own arrangements with retailers in the county and along the front range. These tickets are sold at a discount to the merchants who will resell them. Prices for discounted tickets will vary from one location to another, and it is possible to shop around for the best rate.

Ski the Summit

"Ski the Summit" passes may be purchased at any Breckenridge ski ticket location. Summit passes are good at Keystone, Copper, Arapahoe Basin, and Breckenridge. Prices for these passes during 1993-94 are

$148	Adult, 4-Day
$222	Adult, 6-Day
$ 68	Child, 4-Day
$108	Child, 6-Day

Hours of Operation

9:00 A.M. to 3:45 P.M. daily. High-speed Super Quads open at 8:30 A.M. After March 1, lifts remain open until 4:00 P.M.

Lift Ticket Purchase Locations

Lift tickets may be purchased at the base of Peaks 8 and 9 or at the base of the Mercury Quad at Beaver Run Resort.

How to Avoid Crowds

Because Breckenridge welcomes so many guests each year, crowd control is a real concern. Peak 9 is the most crowded of all the mountains. No doubt this is because it has the most beginner and intermediate runs of the three mountains and also because it is the mountain that exits directly into the town of Breckenridge. The best way to avoid crowds is to ski Peaks 8 and 10. Avoid the SuperChairs because they will be more crowded than the conventional two and three-place chairs. If one has the ability to ski expert runs, use the #6 and #4 lifts, the T-Bar, and the E-Lift as there is seldom any waiting at these areas.

In the evening it is important to remember to return to the correct base area. It is frustrating to have to wait to catch a shuttle from Peak 9 if your car is in the lot at Peak 8. Plan ahead and pay attention to the signage. The mountains are very well marked. All signs are color coded to identify the mountain one is skiing and to give the direction of other mountains. For example, all the trail signs on Peak 8 are blue, on Peak 9 orange, and on Peak 10 yellow. One must be high enough on the mountain at 3:00 P.M. to find trails leading to other mountains, if the ultimate destination is other than the mountain being skied at the time.

Be particularly careful in the late afternoon when skiing Sawmill, Sundown, and Silverthorn. These are the main exit points used by more than 50% of the skiers, many of whom will be flying down the hill. Most injuries today are not broken legs but are more serious in nature and frequently are caused by out-of-control skiers who collide with others. Be alert and pay attention to other skiers.

Ski School

Breckenridge Ski School's 330 instructors teach the ATS (American Teaching System) method of skiing. This is a universal system of skiing that is taught at most major ski resorts in the United States. It is possible, therefore, for students to take lessons at more than one resort without having to learn a new system at each location.

Never-ever and beginning skiers meet at the Quicksilver SuperChair at the base of Peak 9 or just to the left of the Colorado SuperChair on Peak 8. Classes commence at 10:15 A.M. and 1:45 P.M. daily.

Intermediate and expert skiers meet for their lessons either at Peak 9 Restaurant or at Vistahaus Restaurant at the top of Peak 8.

Lessons may be arranged at any of the ski school offices, located at the base of the Quicksilver SuperChair, Mercury SuperChair, or The Colorado SuperChair adjacent to the lift ticket windows. During the 1993-94 season, lesson prices are

$ 48......All-Day, with beginner terrain lift ticket
$ 38......Half-Day, with beginner terrain lift ticket
$ 72......All mountain lift ticket and all day lesson
$ 70......1 Hour, Private

For children an all day lesson with all-terrain lift ticket and lunch will cost $53. A half-day children's lesson with no lunch or lift ticket will cost $35.
In addition, special lessons are offered from time to time, depending upon conditions and demand. For example, during heavy snowfall periods, lessons in powder are offered. If enough skiers want to learn how to improve their ability on the moguls, classes are arranged to fill this need.

Special instruction is also available for handicapped skiers. Breckenridge has done a commendable job of working with handicapped persons.   Call the Breckenridge Outdoor Education Center (B.O.E.C.) at (303)453-6422 for information or write them at Box 697, Breckenridge, CO 80424.

Equipment Rental

Numerous rental shops are found in and around Breckenridge. If skiers plan to ski during the peak season, it is advisable to reserve skis in advance as the shops rent out their supply of skis quickly during Christmas and Easter.

The **Mountain Haus**, located in Centennial Square at the corner of Main and Jefferson and offers three rental packages. The basic package designed for never-ever and beginning skiers is the called the Standard. During the 1993-94 season, it consists of Rossignol Edge skis, Salomon boots and bindings and poles, for $15 per day, $10 per day for a rental of 5 days or more. If you reserve your equipment ahead of time, and pay ahead of times, or if you use a ski discount card, you stand to save a significant amount of money.

The Performance package consists of various models of K2, Rossignol or Volkl skis, Salomon or Nordica boots, Salomon bindings, and poles for $20 per cay. Demos are available for $30 per day, with up to 3 days being refundable upon purchase. Equipment reservations are available by telephoning Mountain Haus at (800) 843-6864.

Blue River Sports, in the Der Steiermark Building, across the street from the Peak 9 base area, at 600 S. Park Avenue, offers a basic package of K-2 skis, and Salomon boots and bindings for $12 a day, $8 for juniors(weighing 90 lb. or less shoe size 6 or less). Deluxe equipment includes K-2 skis, Salomon boots and bindings for $3 more. Performance equipment, designed for the intermediate to advanced skier, includes K-2 TR Comp skis, Salomon 777 and Quadrax 7 bindings and Salomon 83 EXP boots. Competition equipment, for advanced skiers, include Dynastar, K-2, Salomon, or Fischer skis, Salomon boots and bindings for $23 per day. Snowboards go for $19 per day. Discounts are available for multi-day rentals.

Ski Tuning and Repair

Tuning and repair services are available at all ski-rental shops and sporting goods stores. Skis should be warm before waxing. Therefore it is a good idea to drop the skis off at the end of the day and pick them up the next morning.

Rates for tuning will be within a dollar or two in price from shop to shop. At press time, many area shops had not set this year's prices, but they will be around what Blue River Sportsand Mountain Haus will be asking:

Blue River:	Mountain Haus:
$ 3 Hot Wax	$ 8
$35 Full Tune Up	$ 35
$15 Bindings Adjusted	$ 12
$15 Sharpen and Wax	$ 25, basic tune, repair and P-Tex

Mountain Dining

Two mountaintop restaurants are available at Breckenridge. Both are cafeterias where table service is not offered.

The **Vista House** at the top of the Colorado SuperChair is marginally better than the **Peak 9 Restaurant** located at the top of the C-Lift and the Mercury Super Chair. The usual hot and cold sandwiches are available, as well as pizza, french fries, stews, and so forth. Bar service consists of beers, wines, and spirits. Other cafeterias are located at the Bergenhof(Peak 8 base), The Copper Top (at

Beaver Run) and The Maggie (at the Village).

Considering the trend among resorts to offer table service and gourmet meals at noon, Breckenridge is lacking. Hopefully, the resort will see fit to remedy this situation in the near future. Meanwhile, if a quality luncheon is desired, the skier will have to try one of the 12 restaurants located within walking distance of the base of Peak 9 or in the town of Breckenridge.

Child Care

The Breckenridge Resort offers two child care centers and ski schools for young children, based at Peaks 8 and 9. Infants 2 months to 2-years-old can only be cared for at Peak 8. The all day program in 1993-94 will cost $45, from 8:30 a.m. to 4:30 p.m. Half-days in the mornings or the afternoons will cost $35. Parents must bring proof of immunization at registration, and also provide diapers, wipes, formula, bottles, food and a change of clothes.For the over 1-year-old, please bring the same equipment. Lunch and two snacks will be provided.

At the Peaks 8 and 9 **Children's Centers** children from 3 to 5 years can participate in snow play with no skiing for $45 for an all day program, $35 for a half day. For the same price an introductory ski school lesson is offered at both areas. The Peak 8 facility is in the base lodge, not in the Kids' Castle. 303-453-1643, ext 7227. At Peak 9 the Children's Center is in the Village Resort. 303-453-1643, ext. 7327.

The **Kinderhut Children's Center** is located at the Mercury SuperChair near the Beaver Run Resort. This is a fine, clean facility that accepts children one to three years in the day-care program and children three to six in the children's ski school.

Children enrolled in the day-care program are treated to indoor and outdoor activities. Snow play and sledding are the main outdoor attractions; while indoors, the children participate in creative painting, crafts, listening to stories and music. A quiet time, lunch, and snacks are included. At press time the new rates were not available, but in 1992-93 the base price of $49 per day. Children may be left for half-days for $39. Rentals are included.

The Kinderhut opens at 8:30 A.M., and parents are expected to pick up their children between 3:30 P.M. and 4:00 P.M.

Those children enrolled in the ski program may arrange for rental equipment through any of the town's rental establishments or directly from the ski school. Actual ski instruction is two hours each morning and two hours each afternoon. Lunch features children's favorite foods such as spaghetti, hot dogs, grilled cheese sandwiches, as well as the old reliable peanut butter and jelly sandwiches. The daily rate for children enrolled in the ski program is the same as for those enrolled in day care.

Reservations for the Kinderhut should be made by telephoning (303) 453-0379.

Medical Facilities

The Breckenridge Ski Patrol will only render emergency aid for skier injuries. The patrol will administer trauma treatment, stabilize broken bones, and transport the injured skier downhill by sled to one of two clinics, located at the base of Peak 8 or Peak 9. The clinic located at the base of Peak 9 is well equipped to treat ski emergencies. Should an injury or illness be more serious than the clinic can handle, arrangements will be made for ambulance transportation to Summit County Medical Center in Frisco where the patient will be stabilized and then flown via helicopter to one of Denver's major hospitals.

For medical emergencies not related to skiing, dial 911 on the telephone for assistance. Two additional medical emergency centers in Breckenridge are Breckenridge Medical Center at 410 French

St., telephone (303) 453-6934 and Parkway Medical Clinic at the Parkway Center, telephone (303) 453-4336.

For eye injuries telephone (303) 453-4300. There are two dentists in town: Dr. Edgar Downs at (303) 453-4244 and Dr. John Warner at (303) 453-9615.

Cross-Country Skiing

Cross-country skiing is very popular in Breckenridge. In fact, the town may even be considered a mecca for Nordic skiing.

The Breckenridge Nordic Ski Center is located midway up Ski Hill Road, the main road to the Peak 8 parking lot. Owned and operated by Gene and Therese Dayton, the Center boasts 24 km of groomed tracks meandering through open meadows and dense woods. There are three loops: an easier loop, a more difficult loop, and a most difficult loop. From these loops, the skier experiences numerous beautiful views of the town below and the alpine ski runs above.

The lodge where the Nordic ski school is located, as well as the trail head, was formerly the base area at Peak 8. It is quaint and contains a retail store, rental shop, as well as basic food and beverage service. The lodge is very picturesquely nestled among tall pines away from the hustle and bustle of Breckenridge's crowded streets and alpine slopes.

Special Events

Breckenridge's calendar is always full of special events. The largest and most popular event is the Ullr Fest, honoring the Norwegian god of winter. Staged in mid-January, Ullr Fest features ice sculptures, parades, fireworks, and a torchlight parade down the mountain.

Other special events include Women's Ski Seminars, held four times each year for one-week periods. These programs are for women, by women and attempt to bond the ski experience with the emotional needs of the participants. The Swatch Freestyle World Cup may become an annual function. This snowboard event is new to skiing, and Breckenridge is on the forefront of its promotion.

In the spring, the annual Telemark Returns are staged. This is a 10-km race benefiting the Breckenridge Outdoor Education Center. Classic telemark turn competition and dual slalom telemark racing are featured, along with an 1880's costume contest.

In addition to the above events, there are Pro Mogul Tour contests, a Snow Beach Party, Figure 8 Contest, and the Breckenridge Bump Buffet.

Accommodations

Hotels

Three of the better accommodations at Breckenridge are to be found right at the bottom of the lifts at Peak 9.

The **Beaver Run Resort,** located only fifty feet from the Mercury SuperChair on Peak 9, enjoys a perfect location. This is a large complex resembling a college campus more than a hotel. Accommodations run the gamut from simple hotel rooms to large suites. Some rooms even boast their own spas, while others have fireplaces, kitchens, and balconies with views of the town or of the slopes. Constructed of concrete and pine, the facility epitomizes the power of the surrounding mountains in much the same way as The Cliff Lodge at Snowbird defines its terrain. During the season, a hotel room rents for between $105 and $205 per night, while a three-bedroom suite, capable of sleeping up to eight persons, rents for between $340 and $655 per night depending upon the season. Tastefully appointed and well maintained, the Beaver Run Resort is a village unto itself. It is entirely self-contained with shops, restaurants, a swimming pool, disco, miniature golf, and hot tubs.

Across the street from Beaver Run is the **Breckenridge Hilton**, another deluxe hotel with 208-rooms and all the services and facilities one expects from a large hotel. The entire hotel underwent renovation during the past summer and is decorated in beautiful Southwestern style. Nearly all of the rooms have beautiful views of the mountains and many have private balconies. All have wet bars, refrigerators, color TV's, stereos, and in-room movies. Guest facilities include a formal dining room and a lounge. During the 1993-94 season rooms containing either a king-size or a queen-size bed rent from a low of $115 per night to a high of $225 per night, depending upon the season. This year, for the sixth time in 7 years, the Breckenridge Hilton has won first prize in the "Taste of Breckenridge" competition.

The Village at Breckenridge is located with ski in-ski out convenience to the Quicksilver Super-Quad chairlift and is a 455-room hotel which includes studio to 3-bedroom condominiums. The facility houses a full health club, 2 heated pools and 12 hot tubs. Call (800) 800-7829 for information and rates.

If you have a car and do not mind driving just a few miles to the slopes, **The Lodge at Breckenridge**, also known as **The Breckenridge Spa Resort**, 112, Edwards Drive, is a beautiful place to stay. This wooden lodge building is located on 32 acres, perched on top of a mountain across the valley from the Breckenridge Ski Resort. Rooms are spartanly furnished with beautiful wood, but are equipped with televisions, telephones, and balconies with breathtaking views in every direction. The hotel offers a complete health club, with a weight room, aerobics classes, personal trainers, indoor swimming pool, and saunas and jacuzzis. Local shuttle and concierge services are available. Call (303)453-9300 or (800)736-1607.

A lovely, new bed and breakfast opened its doors in Breckenridge last year. The **Allaire Timbers Inn** is a huge log home with 8 tastefully decorated large rooms, including 2 suites with private baths and decks. All guests have access to the outside hot tub, a reading loft, and a beautiful common area with cathedral ceiling and stone fireplace which invites guests to relax and warm themselves after skiing. A hearty breakfast is included. This place would be a cozy retreat for getting away from it all. Prices range from $120 to $210 per night based on double occupancy. (303)453-7530.

Condominiums

Finding a place to stay in Breckenridge became easier last year with the implementation of a new central reservations system, reached by calling (800)800-BREC (2732). The system represents 95 percent of the available short-term lodging in the Breckenridge. There are no truly great condos here such as are found in Aspen, Vail, Telluride, Sun Valley, or Keystone. There are, however, a great number of average units suitable for most visitors' needs. Be aware that many of the properties for rent are different from one another, even if located within the same complex. Generally, most properties are over five years old; many are substantially older. The majority of individual property owners have not made a conscientious effort to remodel and upgrade the units. Most of the units need updating and their furnishings have become shopworn.

One of the better condominium complexes is a ski-in/ski-out development situated just above the base area of Peak 8. The **Skiwatch** condos offer covered parking and hotel-type furnishings. The living areas are small but comfortable and feature wood-burning fireplaces. Although there is no dining area, a large service counter separates the kitchen from the living area. The kitchens contain Jenn-Air ranges, disposals, microwaves, and adequate utensils for preparing meals.

Located at the corner of Ski Hill Road and Park St., **Ski Hill Condominiums** offer covered parking and elevator service to the units. Many of these condos have bright kitchens and earth-tone decors. Fireplaces with glass doors radiate heat during cold, snowy evenings. Spiral staircases lead to upstairs sleeping lofts with spacious sleeping accommodations, full baths, and small balconies. Adjacent to the dining areas are the master bedrooms, complete with private baths.

Cedars Condominiums, located across the street from the Hilton, appropriately derive their name from their cedar exterior. All units include private garages with electronic garage door openers. The first floor of the two-floor layout contains a living area, kitchen, and bath. The living area offers a fireplace, stereo, and cable TV. Some of the interior walls are cedar sided. The kitchen contains most necessary amenities such as an ice maker, disposal, microwave, and dishwasher. A washer/dryer is also included. These are ski-in/ski-out units located just below the D-Lift and just above the Quicksilver SuperChair. Some units seemed to have trouble with melting snow, and the balconies off some of the bedrooms are not usable because plastic sheets had been draped over the sliding glass doors.

Restaurants

Hearthstone Restaurant like many in Breckenridge is situated in an old Victorian house at 130 S. Ridge St. Its food is so delicious and casual atmosphere so inviting that it is often visited by skiers more than once during their usual week's tour of this town. The restaurant does not open its doors until 6 p.m., but the upstairs bar is often crowded with apres-skiers who enjoy not only the drinks but a fabulous view of the ski mountain from its large front windows. For dinner try the baked brie or spinach stuffed mushrooms. The lamb and the steaks are succulent and spiced nicely and the pasta dishes are also very good. Reservations are recommended, call (303)453-1148.

Cafe Alpine also is a casual and inviting restaurant nestled in a Victorian home and open for breakfast, lunch and dinner. A 1993 winner of the "Taste of Breckenridge" the Cafe Alpine is known for its apres-ski "tapas," a variety of small snacks accompanied by a fine selection of wines by the glass. Examples of the tapas are hummus, vegetable pate, chicken empanadas, stuffed grapes with mussels and rice, and stuffed artichokes. Each dish costs less than $3.50. Dinner entrees include fresh pasta of the day, vietnamese stir fry and bohemian chicken curry as well as New York strip steaks. Call(303)453-8218 for information.

The Breckenridge Hilton Resort is home to **Swan's Restaurant** won first prize in the "Taste of Breckenridge" competition in 1993 for the sixth time in seven years. The restaurant is open for breakfast, lunch and dinner but it is known for its wild game cuisine. Elk, buffalo, antelope, trout and pheasant are among its selections. A new chef will add some New Orleans influence to the Colorado cuisine, and a new sous-chef from the popular Keystone Ranch will add his own flare. For more information or reservations call (303)453-4500.

Spencer's at Beaver Run features American cuisine. Located on the mezzanine level of the hotel, its lackluster ambience belies the creativity of its chef and variety of his offerings. Typical appetizers may include tortellini pesto, escargot Milan, or oysters Rockefeller. Entrées feature roast prime rib of beef, filet mignon béarnaise, tournedos Chesapeake, roast honey lemon duck, seafood pasta, vegetarian delight, fresh Pacific salmon, fresh Rocky Mountain rainbow trout, and shrimp scampi. Prices are moderate. Credit cards are accepted and a children's menu is available. (303)453-6000.

Difficult to find but definitely worth the search, **Pierre's** must be considered one of the best restaurants in Breckenridge. Look for its Main Street entrance, climb (or take the elevator) up three stories, cross a terrace, and you find yourself in a quaint, cozy dining room. Pierre Luc not only supervises his staff, but also prides himself on being actively involved in all food preparation.

Menus vary from summer to winter and each day creative specials are offered. Typical entrées include seafood choices like filet of trout (sauteed with diced tomatoes, shrimp, and basil), poached salmon (with onion, tomato, green olives, capers, olive oil, sherry vinegar, and fresh oregano), or grilled sea scallops served on black pasta with a curry sauce. Selections like grilled chicken with pineapple-tomatillo salsa , veal loin and cumin-flavored lentils, medaillons of lamb, and steak (try the New York steak with bordelaise sauce and mini cheese ravioli!) round out the menu. Save room for the daily variety of fresh desserts - impressive! Pierre's is open for lunch and dinner Tuesday through Sunday. Call (303)453-0989 to make reservations.

The **Blue Moose**, at 540 S. Main, (303)453-4859 is a fun restaurant with an eclectic menu. One can order standard fare such as steaks, Caesar Salads and burgers, but the restaurant also serves fresh pastas with a variety of sauces; "Yakisoba:" fresh vegetables and soba noodles with Indonesian peanut sauce or spicy ginger-soy sauce with tofu, chicken or beef or shrimp; or fresh fish or Mexican flavored treats such as "Moose Mess"or "Veggie Burrito."

Weber's, located in a renovated Victorian house on Main Street, serves American and German dishes. All entrées are accompanied with rolls, homemade soup, tossed green salad with poppy seed dressing or marinated herring in sour cream, red cabbage or sauerkraut, spaetzles or baked potatoes, dessert and coffee.

The German specialties of the house include sauerbraten, wienerschnitzel, kassler rippchen, and bratwurst. American dishes include calves liver, pork chops, filet of sole, as well as a variety of steaks. Telephone (303) 453-9464 for reservations.

Poirrier's Cajun Cafe, located in the middle of Main Street at 224 S. Main at Adams, specializes in Cajun-creole cuisine. Furnished in what may best be described as Louisiana deli-style, the Cajun Café is a comfortable retreat for those persons who want an out-of-the-ordinary meal that will warm them on even the coldest days. Reservations are not required but may be made by telephoning (303) 453-1877.

Above Main Street on Ridge Street is **Fatty's**. This is a ramshackle pizzeria loaded with ambience, and it features excellent pizza and sandwiches. Fatty's is an institution in Breckenridge, and no visit would be complete without dining there at least one evening. Reasonably priced, it is a great place to take the family.

Other fine restaurants in Breckenridge include **Mi Casa, Breckenridge Cattle Company, St. Bernard**, and the **Whale's Tail**.

Activities

Reportedly, more than 50% of Breckenridge's visitors during the ski season do not ski. In response to their needs, numerous non-skiing activities are available, including

Ice-Skating on Maggie Pond
Ballooning
Snowmobiling at Tiger Run
Dinner Sleigh Rides
Movies at the Village Cinema
Shopping
Live Theater
Walking Tours of the Historical District

Several health clubs are also available in Breckenridge including the Breckenridge Athletic Club located on French St. This full-service club offers daily aerobics classes, racquetball, Nautilus, Olympic free weight training, hot tub, steam room, tanning, massage, and men's and women's locker rooms. Monthly and annual memberships are available.

The $ 6.5 million Breckenridge Recreation Center, located just past the City Market Complex, opened its doors in 1992. Local residents and visitors can use the new complex for a daily fee ..... The facilities include an indoor pool, hot tubs, racquetball, tennis, weight rooms and aerobics classes.

Services

Sporting goods stores, apparel shops, pharmacies, grocery stores, liquor stores, furniture, bath, and specialty shops are within the immediate Breckenridge area. In addition, there are antique stores, massage services, art galleries, bakeries, beauty shops, bookstores, florists, movies, live theatre, banks, churches, alterations, dry cleaning, optical repair shops, and baby-sitting services.

Skiers take a breather on a run called Mozart leading them toward the Outback area at Keystone.
Photo by GuideBook Publishing Co.

KEYSTONE RESORT

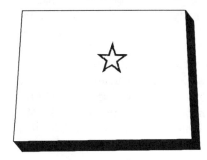

Box 38
Keystone, Colorado 80435

(800) 222-0188
Reservations and Information
(303) 468-4111 Snow Report

New For 1993-94

The news at Keystone this year is that its owner, Ralston Purina, purchased the Breckenridge Ski Resort Breckenridge last spring. The resulting combination dubbed "Breckstone" by some, will be a formidable marketing package. Last year one quarter of all the people who skied in Colorado skied at a resort owned by the pet food company: Keystone, Breckenridge and Arapahoe Basin.

We mentioned this last year, so it is not brand new, but the changes made at Keystone during the past few years have upgraded this area to entice skiers to try all of the new variations in its terrain. Keystone spent $32 million two years ago on expansion and opened its fourth mountain, **The Outback.** Comprised of 889 acres of advanced intermediate and expert terrain, this mountain is primarily gladed skiing, narrow chutes, and ungroomed cruising runs—17 trails and 2 bowls. A 6-person gondola was added to improve the lift capacity of North Peak, and The Outpost, a 26,000 square foot restaurant was built. Two new high speed quads were added, as well as more snow-making equipment.

The investment paid off with a record increase in skiers visiting Keystone for two years in a row.

How To Get There

Keystone is served by all major airlines through Denver's International Airport.

Please refer to the Breckenridge Ski Area section of this book for information about renting cars in Denver.

Keystone is 90 miles from Denver International Airport via I-70. Exit in Dillon to U.S. 6 and travel 6 miles east to the resort. The trip from the airport takes 1-3/4 hours to drive in clear weather on dry roads.

All rental agencies provide their clients with free maps. Due to possible road restrictions, the traveler to Keystone is advised always to rent a car that is *skierized*, i.e. equipped with snow tires and ski racks. For a slightly higher fee, many rental agencies can provide four-wheel drive vehicles. The traveler is advised to reserve these vehicles far in advance because demand for them is great.

Skiers interested in traveling throughout Summit County to ski and to dine should seriously consider renting a car for flexibility. However, it is not necessary if one is willing to put up with some inconvenience, because both Keystone and Summit Stage provide bus service on a scheduled basis.

Transportation from Denver International or Stapleton airport to Keystone is provided by Resort Express. Resort Express provides door-to-door transportation to Summit County during the

1993-94 season for $38 each way, $74 round trip on Saturdays, and $69 other days. To book reservations on Resort Express, telephone (800) 334-7433 or (303) 468-7600. All major credit cards are accepted.

Vans to Breckenridge also will provide door-to-door service daily from the airport for varying rates depending on the season. Regular fares will be $35 one way, $62 round trip, with fares rising to $38 and $74 respectively for Saturdays and holidays. Call (800)222-2112.

Once at Keystone the **Summit Stage** operates a free shuttle service throughout Summit Country, including the other nearby ski areas, Arapaho Basin, Breckenridge, and Copper Mountain, and the town of Breckenridge, Dillon, Frisco, and Silverthorne. This year some routes have been extended and the express routes have been quickened. For more information on the Summit Stage, phone (303) 453-1241.

The bus is convenient, but depending on it may be a little limiting if you want to visit other areas or go out to dinner, or even to the discount stores in Silverthorne.

Mountain Information

Keystone has four distinct mountains, the main one being Keystone with a vertical drop of 2,340 feet (713 meters). Its base is located at 9,300 feet (2,835 meters) and its summit is at 11,640 feet (3,548 meters). The skiable terrain comprises 599 acres and is serviced by

1 Gondola
2 High-Speed Quads
2 Triple Chairlift
6 Double Chairlifts
4 Surface Lifts

The longest beginner run is Schoolmarm which runs for three miles (4.8 km) from Keystone's summit to the base of the mountain.

The longest intermediate run is Spring Dipper which begins at the summit. It is 1.5 miles (2.4 km) in length.

The longest expert run is Go Devil, which is slightly shorter than either Schoolmarm or Spring Dipper.

Keystone's second mountain, North Peak, is located directly south of Keystone Mountain. Access to North Peak is from the summit of Keystone Mountain via Mozart, considered an intermediate run, or via Diamond Back, an expert run.

The base of North Peak is located at 10,040 feet (3,060 meters) and it has a summit of 11,660 feet (3,554 meters). Its vertical drop is 1,620 feet (494 meters), and the mountain is served by one triple chairlift, 1 quad chairlift and 1 gondola.

North Peak's longest intermediate run is Mozart which is two miles (3 km) long. Geronimo is its longest expert run at one and a half miles (2.4 km).

North Peak has 249 skiable acres.

The Outback is Keystone's third mountain, and its newest. Its high-speed quad brings skiers to 17 "ballroom" trails and perfect glades. From its 10,460 foot (3,138 meters) base to its 12,200 foot (3,660 meters) summit, The Outback represents 1,740 vertical feet (522 meters) of steep chutes or wide intermediate trails. Its longest run is 2.5 miles (4km). One high-speed quad chairlift serves the area.

Keystone's fourth mountain is Arapahoe Basin. This mountain is located on the Continental Divide, approximately five miles (8 km) east of the main mountain and resort accommodations. Free shuttle service is available every ten minutes between the various mountains and Keystone Lodge.

Arapahoe Basin's base is at 10,800 feet (3,240 meters) with its summit at 13,050 feet (3,915 meters). The vertical drop at A-Basin is 2,250 feet (675 meters). Access to the runs is via

    1 Triple Chairlift
    4 Double Chairlifts
Keystone mountain consists of thirty-nine trails of which Keystone considers

    13% Advanced
    55% Intermediate
    32% Beginner

North Peak's terrain consists of

    53% Advanced
    37% Intermediate
    10% Beginner
The Outback's trails are rated as
    81% Advanced
    19% Intermediate
    0% Beginner

Arapahoe Basin's trails consists of

    40% Advanced
    50% Intermediate
    10% Beginner

Keystone's annual snowfall is 230 inches (508 cm). Its average monthly snowfalls are

Oct.	9"	(23 cm)
Nov.	25"	(63 cm)
Dec.	27"	(69 cm)
Jan.	40"	(102 cm)
Feb.	17"	(42 cm)
Mar.	44"	(112 cm)

All trails' actual degrees of difficulty are subject to change depending on snow conditions. As a general guide, the descriptions are accurate. It should be pointed out, however, that the expert and advanced trails at Keystone Mountain are not nearly as difficult as the expert and advanced slopes at Arapahoe Basin. In fact, many of the runs at Arapahoe Basin are so difficult they are identified with a double black diamond. With the exception of the lower portion of Go-Devil and Last Hoot, advanced intermediate skiers should have no difficulty handling any of Keystone's terrain. The problem with the lower portions of Go-Devil and Last Hoot is that they tend to be skied off, thus exposing base conditions which can be equated with the term "ice," though not in the same sense as experienced skiers will find on the slopes of the eastern United States.

North Peak's intermediate runs tend to become skied off and icy. The expert runs on North Peak are usually heavily moguled and may also be icy. The moguls found on Keystone and North Peak are typically made by skiers using shorter skis. As a result, they tend to become flat on the top, and the valleys are closely arranged making it difficult for skiers with longer skis to establish a path through them. Unlike the expert runs on Keystone Mountain, the expert runs on North Peak are best left to expert skiers only.

In contrast to this, moguls at Arapahoe Basin are usually made by longer skis, and their tops are more rounded than those at Keystone. The valleys are longer making it easier for skiers to pick a path through the bumps. The expert trails at Arapahoe Basin are truly "expert," and skiers who do not have a great deal of experience should not attempt them. Most of the runs at A-Basin are either gladed (meaning among trees) or steep with triple fall lines. The intermediate runs are located mainly at the top of the mountain. There are virtually no trees on the top of A-Basin. During snowstorms or periods of flat light, it is extremely difficult to "feel" which way is down. As a result, vertigo is a common complaint. It is suggested that beginner and intermediate skiers only go to Arapahoe Basin on clear, sunny days. Expert skiers will love the place under all conditions.

Although the trails at Arapahoe are narrow, steep, and gladed, the opposite is true at Keystone Mountain and North Peak. Here the runs are wide, meticulously maintained ego boosters!

Keystone has installed extensive artificial snowmaking capabilities which afford it the distinction of being the first ski resort to open each year. Keystone can now make snow on 849 acres (340 ha). On Keystone Mountain, fully 599 acres, 100 percent, have snowmaking equipment. At North Peak, 150 acres are covered and at the Outback, another 100 acres have snowmaking coverage. There are no snowmaking capabilities at Arapahoe Basin. Due to A-Basin's high altitude, snowmaking is not necessary because the area catches snow early in the season and it stays late into the spring. Frequently Arapahoe Basin is the last mountain in Colorado to close. When it does close it is usually not due to a lack of snow, but rather due to a lack of motivated skiers.

Keystone continually grooms its beginner and intermediate slopes. Grooming of expert or advanced trails is limited and usually does not consist of more than chopping down moguls that have grown too formidable. Each day the mountain's management meets and decides which trails will be groomed, and this information is posted conveniently at the base of each lift. Such attention to grooming assures beginner and intermediate skiers of a consistent soft pack for skiing. At Keystone there is usually little hard pack and rarely any ice. There also is almost never any powder of consequence. If weather conditions bless the slopes with abundant powder, Keystone skiers should seek out the advanced and expert runs at North Peak and Arapahoe Basin and the Outback. The powder in the Colorado Rockies is generally very light and relatively easy to ski if one understands the necessary technique.

Average daily temperatures during the season taken at the top of Keystone Mountain:

Oct.	43°	(6°C)
Nov.	31°	(0°C)
Dec.	30°	(-1°C)
Jan.	29°	(-2°C)
Feb.	28°	(-2°C)
Mar.	34°	(1°C)
Apr.	44°	(6°C)

Night Skiing

Beginning and intermediate skiers have 2,340 vertical feet available from dark until 9:00 P.M. each evening for night skiing. Twilight tickets (2 P.M.——10 P.M.) are available at $27 for an adult; children's lift tickets are $16. Night Tickets (4 P.M.——10 P.M.) are $22 for adults and $16 for children. Late night tickets (7 P.M.——10 P.M.) are $15 for adults and $15 for children. Uphill transport is via the Skyway Gondola.

Lift Ticket Prices (1993-94)

$39	Adult, Full Day
$108	Adult, 3 out of 4 days
$136	Adult, 4 out of 5 day
$160	Adult, 5 out of 6 days
$17	Child Under 13, Full Day
$45	Child, 3 out of 4 days
$60	Child, 4 out of 5 days
$75	Child, 5 out of 6 days
Free	Children 5 and under

All major credit cards accepted.

Special "Ski the Summit" lift tickets that are exchangeable for lift tickets at Copper Mountain and Breckenridge, both located within thirty minutes' drive from Keystone, are available. Free shuttle bus service is offered.

Hours of Operation

8:30 A.M. to 4:00 P.M.
Upper Lifts Close at 3:30 P.M.
The Skyway Gondola and several chairlifts at Keystone Mountain are open for night skiing until 9:00 P.M.

Lift Ticket Purchase Locations

Lift ticket purchase sites are conveniently located at the base of Keystone Mountain and at Arapahoe Basin. Tickets may also be purchased at Keystone Lodge, the Activity Desk, the Ski School, and at designated locations throughout metro Denver.

If lift tickets are purchased at the base of the mountains, waiting in line usually is no longer than five minutes except during Christmas, New Year's, and Easter weeks. During these times the wait can be as long as twenty minutes.

How To Avoid Crowds

As would be expected, the longest lift lines occur at the base of Skyway Gondola. Other lines form at the base of Argentine Lift, Peru Lift, Saints John Lift and Exhibition Triple Lift at Arapahoe Basin. Lines at these lifts from 9:00 A.M. until 10:30 A.M. can exceed fifteen minutes. Similar delays should be expected from 1:00 P.M. through 2:00 P.M. daily.

Crowd avoidance can be achieved during peak periods by skiing at Arapahoe Basin or North Peak rather than Keystone Mountain. At Keystone Mountain proper, plan to ski trails served by the Erickson, Montezuma, and Ida Belle lifts. The Summit House restaurant area (including the area where the gondola terminates and Mozart begins) is frequently congested and regularly exhibits very hard-packed to icy conditions.

Ski School

Keystone's Ski School's two locations are at the base of the gondola in River Run Plaza and at Keystone Mountain Plaza base area.

These locations are convenient to the slopes, mountain restaurants, ski rental and repair shops, apparel shops, transportation, and day-care facilities.

The ski school's staff consists of 150 instructors trained in the American Teaching System (ATS) of skiing. Classes consist of no more than eight students of similar ability levels. Group lessons are from 10:00 A.M. to 12:00 P.M. and from 1:00 P.M. to 3:00 P.M. daily.

Private lessons by the hour or day can be arranged at any of the ski desks.

Group lesson rates are $30 per two and one-half hour segments, with class size limited to 8. Private lessons are $70 per hour.

Beginning skiers can take advantage of beginner packages which include lift tickets good on Tip Top, Checkerboard, and Molly Hogan lifts as well as skis, boots, and poles at a rate of $50 per day.

Special lessons are available from time to time depending on weather conditions and sufficient skier demand. These lessons include

Handicapped
Racing Clinics
Powder

Equipment Rental

Keystone's own equipment rental shops are located in both the River Run Plaza and the Keystone Mountain Plaza, as well as at the base of Arapahoe Basin. These locations are convenient to the slopes, mountain restaurants, ski schools, transportation, and day-care facilities.

Equipment Rental Rates, 1993-94

$17 Recreation Package consisting of skis, boots, bindings and poles
$23 Sport Package consisting of skis, boots, bindings and poles
$29 Premium Package consisting of skis, boots, bindings, and poles

Reduced rental rates are available for multi-day, half day, and night use. Keystone's rental equipment is excellent. Each year new equipment is purchased. Thus, equipment renters are assured of superior rental equipment that is fitted by factory-trained technicians.

A rental deposit of $100 is required for theft and breakage protection. Upon return of the equipment, the deposit is returned. Cash or credit cards are accepted.   Prior to renting equipment, skiers are required to sign a "hold harmless" form relieving Keystone of liability should renters be injured while using the equipment.

High-performance skis may be *demoed* (rented) from sporting goods stores located at Keystone for a day or a week unless snow cover is inadequate.

Ski Tuning and Repair

Tuning and repair services are available at all ski rental shops and sporting goods stores. Skis must be warm before waxing. Therefore, it is a good idea to drop the skis off at the end of the day and pick them up next morning.

Rates for Tuning (estimated 1993-94)

$ 6	Hot Wax
$12	(Pair) Edges Sharpened
$35	Complete Tune-up
$15	Bindings Adjusted
$ 7+	P-tex (minimum with tune-up)

Mountain Dining

The Alpenglow Stube is one of the best on mountain gourmet restaurants at any resort. Even non-skiers can enjoy getting to this restaurant: ride the Skyway Gondola from the base of Keystone Mountain and transfer to the Outpost Gondola to the Summit of North Peak. The views are breathtaking and the ride smooth and protected from the elements bringing you to a culinary adventure known for its locally influenced fare with a hint of Germany. Of course the chef changes the menu every year, but some favorite dishes have been the carpaccio of venison, rack of wild boar and breast of pheasant. The salads are beautifully prepared and the desserts are very tempting: sacher torte, apple flan and gratin "Stube." This restaurant is open evenings also.

The other side of the Outpost restaurant at the Outback serves good cafeteria food.

The Summit House located at the summit of Keystone Mountain has cafeteria-style service on all three levels. In addition to the usual assortment of hot and cold food, special items such as pizza, barbecue, and fresh pastries are available. The Summit House is open from 8:30 A.M. through 4:00 P.M. Breakfast is not served here. Wine and beer service is restricted after 2:00 P.M.

At the base of Keystone Mountain similar services are available at **River Run Plaza** and **Keystone Mountain Plaza**. These locations do serve complete hot and cold breakfasts. Food and beverage service is also available at **Keyster's Cafe and Bar** in River Run Plaza. **Gassy's**, located in Keystone Mountain Plaza offers complete sit-down meals at reasonable prices. Also at Keystone Mountain Plaza is a colorful outdoor wagon where delightful hot crepes and soft drinks are sold. Spirits are available from **Last Lift Bar**, located on the second floor of the Mountain Plaza building. A gourmet cookie stand is available for a quick bit, as well as the Mountain House cafeteria and Ernie's Pizzeria.

On warm, clear days the staff at Keystone will generally set up a grill at the base of Santiago Lift at North Peak. This is a comfortable setting where skiers can bask in the sun and enjoy a quick hamburger or hot dog.

Food and beverage service at Arapahoe Basin, though quite adequate, is not of the same caliber as at Keystone Mountain.

Child Care

Keystone's **Children's Center** is located only one hundred feet west of the Mountain Plaza building near the base of the Argentine and Peru lifts; at Arapahoe Basin the Children's Center is located under the restaurant at the base of the mountain. Both locations are staffed with individuals trained and licensed by the state of Colorado. Typical attendant/child ratios vary between 1:3 for infants and 1:6 for toddlers. Programs are available for children to take ski instruction or to participate in play groups. Programs are available for half-day or full-day care. Full-day care includes a nourishing meal. Ages accepted: two months through eight years. Reservations should be made at the time accommodations are booked. The center will provide a beeper to wear while they ski, so they can be contacted if they are needed. Telephone (800) 255-3715 or (303)468-4182.

During night skiing, the center stays open and will provide evening babysitting until 9 p.m. for guests at Keystone accommodations.

1993-94 child care rates are $45 per full day for children aged two months through eight years and $35 for half-day. Baby-sitting services in the Lodge or in the condominiums are priced at $8 per hour. Keystone sponsors movie nights for children in the lodge each evening to accommodate parents who would like to go out for dinner. For teenagers Keystone features evening activities once a week.

Children aged three through twelve may be enrolled in **Children Only** ski instruction programs. The classes begin at 8:30 A.M. and end at 4:30 P.M. These programs provide supervised play, ski lessons, and lunch. Equipment rentals can be included in this program. Only eight children are allowed in any one class, and they have their own section of mountain to ski that is "off limits" to adults.

Medical Facilities

Keystone's medical facility is located in the Snake River Health Services building at the base of Keystone Mountain Plaza just below the Argentine Lift. This modern clinic is staffed from 8:00 A.M. through 6:00 P.M. with local doctors on call 24 hours per day. At least one doctor is an orthopedic specialist. Day surgery is available and minor or emergency surgery is possible. For serious illness or injuries that cannot be handled by the clinic, there is a helicopter pad directly adjacent to the health facility with air ambulance service to any of Denver's hospitals. Ground transportation via commercial ambulance is also available. Prescription drugs on a limited basis are dispensed by the clinic when prescribed by one of the staff physicians. Other prescription needs can be filled by the pharmacies located in the towns of Dillon or Silverthorne, six miles west of the resort.

Cross-Country Skiing

The cross-country skiing point of embarkation is located at the colorful Ski Tip Lodge deep in the heart of Arapaho National Forest. A total of 46 kilometers of trails, twenty-seven of which are groomed, make up the majority of the cross-country terrain. Equipment rentals and instruction are available from mid-November through early April.

Special Events

NASTAR races are held daily in Keystone Mountain's Packsaddle bowl. Registration can be completed at any of the ski school locations. The fee is $6 for two runs; additional runs may be purchased for $1 each.

Marlboro coin-operated, self-serve slalom racing is also available in Packsaddle Bowl for $ .50 per run.

From November through June, Phil and Steve Mahre offer specialized training to skiers of all abilities. This training course consists of five-day and 3-day sessions.

Special events vary from day to day and month to month at Keystone. However, they will typically include functions such as sleigh rides, moonlit cross country ski tours, snowmobiling through the beautiful Arapaho National Forest, and special interest seminars. Movies are shown nightly in Keystone Lodge and in nearby Dillon.

Accommodations

Hotel

The only hotel at Keystone is **The Lodge**, located approximately a half mile from Keystone Mountain Plaza. Rooms are tastefully decorated with a superior quality furniture, unusual at most ski resorts. The Lodge has been the annual recipient of the prestigious American Automobile Association's Four Diamond Award and the Mobil Travel Guide's 4-Star rating. Most rooms in the Lodge have private balconies from which spectacular views of either Keystone Mountain or adjacent peaks can be seen. Some rooms have separate sitting rooms and loft bedrooms. All Lodge guests have access to the heated swimming pool, therapy pool, and sauna. The Lodge is a full-service hotel with valet, room service, daily housekeeping, travel agency, and nightly bed turn-down. All rooms have color television, free HBO cable service, and a Servibar. Loft rooms without balconies are approximately ten percent larger than loft rooms with balconies. Each year Keystone refurbishes about fifty to sixty rooms so guests are always assured of well-decorated accommodations. Accommodations in The Lodge run from a low season rate of $190 to a Christmas holiday rate of $205 based on double occupancy.

Within the Lodge are two cocktail lounges and three restaurants offering a variety of service and menus.

Condominiums

All services available to guests of the Lodge are also available to guests of Keystone's condominiums. Amenities include a central switchboard, 24-hour check-in service, and room service. All guests are given their own Keystone credits card which can be used at any of the resort's shops.

Four grades of condominiums are available: Resort I, Resort II, Village, and Mountain Premium.

Resort I: Key Condo, Wild Irishman, Flying Dutchman, and **Keystone Gulch** townhouses. Resort II includes those at the **Pines, Soda Spring, Soda Spring II, Homestead/Lodgepole, Quicksilver, Saints John**, and **Tennis Townhouses**. All are located in varying directions about one mile from the slopes. Keystone's private coach service makes daily ten-minute runs between all the condos and the Lodge, shops, and mountain bases. All accommodations are clean and modern with fully equipped kitchens including garbage disposals and dishwashers. All units have fireplaces and are stocked with firewood; daily maid service is provided. Resort I townhomes are older than the Resort II and so are priced slightly lower. Condominium rates during the 1993-94 ski season for Resort I townhomes vary from a low season $130 per night for studio accommodations to a holiday season rate of approximately $730 per night for a four-bedroom unit. For resort II accommodations, rates begin at $140 per night for a studio during the low season to a high season rate of $225 per night for the same room. No 4-bedroom units were available at press time, but last year's rates started at $380 during the low season.

Village: Argentine, Plaza, Mall, Edgewater, Lakeside, Willows, Montezuma, Lenawee, and **Decatur**. These condos are situated around Lake Keystone but are convenient to The Lodge and most of Keystone's shops. Several restaurants are also located within easy walking distance. During much of the winter, a beautifully lighted Christmas tree decorates the center of the lake. Spending an evening by the fire, overlooking the skaters on the lake is a moment in time to cherish. Village condos rent during the 1993-94 ski season from a low of $160 per night for studio accommodations to a high of approximately $890 per night for a four-bedroom unit during the holiday season.

Mountain Premium: Chateaux d'Mont, Slopeside Inn, River Bank. The Chateaux is Keystone's most expensive lodging. Each Chateaux unit contains its own private hot therapy pool, Jenn-Air range, Whirlpool ice maker, individual room thermostats, humidity control, clothes washer and dryer, private balcony, private ski locker, and Sub-Zero refrigerator. The interiors of several units were professionally designed and furnished by world famous Ginsler & Associates. All the amenities afforded guests at the Chateaux are also provided to guests at the Keystone Mountain Inn and River Bank including use of the swimming pool, central switchboard, message center, and wake-up calls. Daily maid service is provided. The 1993-94 rate for Mountain Premium during low season is $240 for the one-bedroom unit, per night; it reaches a high of $1,000 per night during the holidays for the three-bedroom condo.

Slopeside Mountain Inn consists primarily of efficiency units complete with one queen bed with an additional murphy bed, so the capacity is for four persons. Space is limited here, but the amenities provide a comfortable setting in which to relax after a day on the slopes. Studio units at Keystone Mountain Inn during the 1993-94 low season rent for $185 per night, while one-bedroom units rent for a holiday season high of $240 per night.

Ski Tip Lodge

Located east of River Run Plaza, the **Ski Tip Lodge** is a twentieth-century anachronism. A restored 1860 stagecoach stop, the Ski Tip is steeped in mountain tradition and lore. Guests are treated to rooms without telephones or television. Meals are no longer served family-style in the dining room, but the food is still excellent and there is a different menu each evening. Nestled among lodgepole pines, Ski Tip Lodge is the center for cross-country and telemark skiing. Visitors are guaranteed that their stay at "The Tip" will be a memorable vacation. Space is limited so interested individuals or groups are urged to make reservations early. Keystone has a separate reservation number for the Ski Tip: (303) 468-4202.

Restaurants

Among the major restaurants located within Keystone Resort, several are owned and operated by the resort itself. Perhaps the finest restaurant in the entire county is the **Keystone Ranch**, located on Keystone's Robert Trent Jones-designed golf course. Winner of the Four-Diamond AAA award, the restaurant itself is in an exquisite log building that was originally home to a local ranching family. The decor and ambience of the dining room are reminiscent of the ranching and mining enterprises that originally occupied area residents. Each day a prix fixe menu consisting of seven courses is offered. The food's preparation and its presentation are peerless. The Ranch is truly a world-class restaurant. Its wine cellar is stocked with the finest vintages of rare wine, as well as a complete offering of medium-priced varietals. The building, the view of the snowcapped peaks, the food, and the service definitely make the Ranch a treat for hungry skiers interested in a formal dining experience.

Located in the Lodge at Keystone is another equally enjoyable restaurant, the **Garden Room**. This restaurant offers fare similar to that of the Ranch, but on a menu basis. The view from its floor-to-ceiling windows is of the ice skating rink, brilliantly decorated with twinkling lights, and of Keystone Mountain's brightly illuminated ski trails. The service and ambience of the Garden Room are faultless.

Adjacent to the skating rink is **The Commodore**, a fine seafood restaurant. Also owned by Keystone, the Commodore flies fresh fish in daily. Its atmosphere is less formal than that at either the Ranch or the Garden Room.

Nestled away underneath The Commodore restaurant is **Montezuma's Rock and Roll Saloon,** one of Keystone's night entertainment offerings. Drinks, pizza and appetizers are available and during the ski season live music has this place jumping. Pool tables and video games also are available for entertainment. Telephone 468-4021.

If you don't feel like cooking or going out, call Pizza on the Plaza for a delivery: 468-9501.

In nearby Silverthorne the **Old Dillon Inn** (ODI) is a landmark. Originally built in 1869 as a stage coach stop, it has been relocated three times before finally coming to rest in its current location. The ODI is a typical old West bar and is similar to The Red Onion in Aspen; in fact, it is under the same ownership. Separated from the raucous bar is a Mexican dining room. The restaurant shares the same eclectic features of the bar itself. A relaxing ambience has been created with the use of dimly lit faux-Tiffany ceiling lamps, checkered table cloths, and a low ceiling. The food served at the Old Dillon Inn is excellent. Reservations are not accepted, and diners should be prepared to wait up to one hour for seating during peak holiday periods. Prices are reasonable.

Other fine restaurants abound within the resort and without, as well. Because Keystone is located in Summit County, Colorado, all the fine dining establishments located at Copper Mountain, Breckenridge, Frisco, and Dillon are convenient. Among those to be visited are **The Snake River Saloon** (seafood and Italian), **Weber's** (German), **The Blue Spruce** (American), **Farley's** (American), **Charity's** (American), **The Plaza** (Continental), **Barkley's** (Mexican and prime rib).

There is also a full complement of McDonald's, Wendy's, Pizza Hut, Arby's and similar fast food restaurants to keep the youngsters happy.

Activities

Keystone's winter activities include swimming in the Lodge's heated indoor/outdoor swimming pool, tennis in its indoor facility, aerobics classes, free weights, a Marcy Apex machine in the health facility, racquetball, ice skating, snowmobiling, dog sled rides, sleigh rides, and tours of the mountains in snow cats. Nightly movies in the Lodge are offered for a nominal fee.

Services

A complete range of sporting goods stores, apparel shops, pharmacies, grocery stores, liquor stores, furniture, bath, and specialty shops is within the immediate Keystone area.

On their way to the Outback at Keystone, a boy and his father stop to admire the beautiful view. Photo by GuideBook Publishing Co.

COPPER MOUNTAIN RESORT

P.O. Box 3001
Copper Mountain, Colorado 80443

(800) 458-8386 Reservations
(303) 968-2882 Information
(303) 968-2100 Snow Report

New For 1993-94

No new snowmaking, lifts or trails have been added at Copper this year, but the resort has applied to make its presently "extreme" skiing area a permanent part of the resort. The areas which are "hors le piste"(outside the trails) comprise around 300 acres, so an extra 200 are included in the proposed annex. To be known as Copper Bowl, the new area would be an attractive addition for intermediate and advanced skiers, and would include three lifts and 500 acres on the back side of Union Peak and the north face of Tucker Mountain. The vertical drop will be at least 1,215 feet. It is hoped that the new construction could begin during the summer of 1994.

For the eighth year in a row, Copper Mountain Resort earned a Four Diamond Award from the American Automobile Association.

How To Get There

Copper Mountain is served by all major airlines through Denver's Stapleton International Airport or its new airport.

Please refer to the Breckenridge Ski Area section of this book for information about renting cars in Denver.

Copper Mountain is seventy-five miles from Denver on I-70, a one and a half-hour drive in clear weather on dry roads.

All rental agencies provide free maps to their clients. Due to possible road restrictions, travelers to Copper Mountain are advised to always select a car that is *skierized*, i.e. equipped with snow tires and ski racks. For a slightly higher price, many rental agencies can provide four-wheel drive vehicles. The traveler is cautioned to reserve these vehicles far in advance because they are very popular.

Skiers traveling to Copper Mountain should seriously consider renting a car. Although Summit Stage provides reliable bus service between Copper, Breckenridge, and Keystone, its schedule is fixed. Remaining solely at Copper Mountain for a week may be too confining for many persons. However, Vail, Breckenridge, and Keystone are only about twenty-minute drives from Copper.

For those skiers who do not want to be bothered with automobile rentals, **Resort Express** and **Vans to Breckenridge** both provide door-to-door transportation to Copper Mountain. The prices will be $38 each way , $74 round trip on Saturdays, and $69 others on Resort Express. Call (800)334-7433 or (303)468-7600 for reservations and information.

Vans to Breckenridge will provide service to Copper for $35 each way, $62 round trip, with fares rising to $38 and $74 respectively for Saturdays and holidays. Call (800)222-2112 or (303)668-5466.

Mountain Information

Copper Mountain comes about as close as any mountain to being described as "perfect." In terms of topography it faces north, and its skiable terrain progresses from expert on the east to beginner on the west. This mountain is just naturally divided into three segments of expert, intermediate, and beginner topography.

Copper Mountain has 2,760 vertical feet (841 meters). Its base is located at 9,600 feet (2,926 meters) and its summit is at 12,360 feet (3,768 meters). The skiable terrain consists of 1,360 acres and is serviced by

2 High-Speed Quad Lifts
6 Triple Chairlifts
8 Double Chairlifts
4 Drag Lines, i.e. Poma

The longest beginner run at Copper is actually composed of two runs, Soliloquy and Roundabout, whose total length is more than two miles.

The longest intermediate run is Andy's Encore, a great cruising run. It goes for 1.6 miles (4.1 km) which begins at the top of the B-1 lift and descends to the base of the F-lift.

There is no single longest expert run at Copper Mountain, although several trails parallel one another in length on the mountain's A-lift side. Far East, Too Much, and Triple Treat all afford expert skiers lots of excitement.

Of the 1,330 acres comprising Copper, 22% of the trails are for beginning skiers and 27% are for intermediate skiers. A full 51% of the skiable acreage is dedicated to experts' use.

The definitions of beginner, intermediate, and expert are closely adhered to by Copper. Guests should not have any difficulty skiing any of the slopes by relying on Copper's trail markings. The only area where skiers can get into trouble is below the American Flyer lift, which tends to ice-up due to the heavy skiing received daily. The American Flyer lift, located at The Center of the resort, usually receives more than its share of the action. Skiers who look for soft, packed powder, intermediate runs should seriously consider spending the majority of their slope time skiing the runs off the I and J lifts. These are long, well-maintained runs that challenge intermediate skiers without intimidating them. The expert skier who does not have much powder experience should try to ski these runs early in the morning following a "big dump." This is an exceptional area in which to learn powder skiing because it is just steep enough to propel the skier downhill without creating uncontrollable fear.

The beginning skier at Copper Mountain is treated to one of the most expansive beginner areas in the country. In order to avoid crowds, the beginner should make a beeline to the Union Creek base facility. This is the terminus for the H and K lift systems that provide access to acres and acres of barely tracked, broad runs as gentle as the backside of a baby and as long as two miles.

For the expert, Copper offers several areas of unique skiing. One such area, Union Bowl, is similar in terrain to that found in the finest California resorts centered around Lake Tahoe. By taking the S-lift to the top of Union Bowl, one skis along a ridge and finding a suitable place, drops off the cornice into broad fields of snow and bumps. The areas serviced by the S lift are also lightly gladed, which some experts might prefer. All the runs have triple fall lines, of course, due to being situated in a bowl.

From the top of the B-1 lift, it is a short distance to the Storm King drag line which takes expert skiers to the top of Copper Mountain, and from there down into Spaulding Bowl, and thence into some of the greatest gladed, expert skiing anywhere. Runs such as Widowmaker, Highline, Cabin Chute, and Sawtooth emanate from this bowl.

Copper will continue to offer skiing "hors le piste," that is out of bounds, to the more expert and adventurous skiers. These Extreme Experience guided adventure tours make available an additional 35 acres of expert terrain on the south side of Copper Peak. Ask at the ticket window or ski school to find out more about this adventure. A bus will bring you back to the base of Copper Mountain Resort after you finish your run.

Copper Mountain receives an annual snowfall of about 255 inches (648 cm). Its average monthly snowfalls are

Nov.	34"	(86 cm)
Dec.	51"	(130 cm)
Jan.	38"	(97 cm)
Feb.	38"	(97 cm)
Mar.	51"	(130 cm)
Apr.	37"	(94 cm)

Copper Mountain's snowmaking capabilities are substantial. As many as 270 acres (109 ha) can be covered with artificial snow. Most of this snowmaking equipment is situated along the beginner and intermediate areas.

Average daily temperatures during the season are

Nov.	26°	(-4° C)
Dec.	19°	(-7° C)
Jan.	16°	(-9° C)
Feb.	18°	(-8° C)
Mar.	23°	(-5° C)
Apr.	33°	(0° C)

Lift Ticket Prices (1993-94)

$ 38	Adult Daily
$ 72	2-Day out of 3
$105	3-Day out of 4
$136	4-Day out of 5
$165	5-Day out of 6
$186	6-Day out of 7
$ 24	Ages 60-69
$ 17	Beginner, and Child, 12 and under
Free	70+ and child 3 and under

Ski The Summit pass

$148	4-Day
$222	6-Day

$ 68   Child 4-Day
$108   Child 6-Day

Copper Mountain represents one-third of the available skiing in Summit County, Colorado. The other Summit resorts are Keystone, Arapahoe Basin and Breckenridge. All these resorts honor "Ski the Summit" passes issued at one another's resort. Caution, however, is advised because only "Ski the Summit" passes are interchangeable. Do not purchase a lift ticket for Copper Mountain if it is anticipated that skiing at the other resorts is a likelihood. Purchase a "Ski the Summit" pass in this situation!

Hours of Operation

8:30 A.M. to 4:00 P.M. weekends
9:00 A.M. to 4:00 P.M. weekdays
Upper lifts close at 3:30 P.M.

Lift Ticket Purchase Locations

Lift ticket sales are conveniently located at the Clubhouse situated at the base of the B-lift, at The Center near the base of the American Flyer lift, and at Union Creek near the base of the H-lift. During peak periods such as Christmas through New Year's and Easter, additional ticketing locations are opened at the base and in Copper's Transportation Center.

The most congested area in which to purchase lift tickets is The Center. During peak periods, generally from 9:00 A.M. to 10:30 A.M., the wait can be as long as a half-hour. Waiting can be avoided altogether if tickets are prepurchased after 3:00 P.M. the previous day or at any of the other-mentioned ticket locations.

How to Avoid Crowds

Crowds at Copper should be a concern to skiers because of the mountain's proximity to Denver and two other major ski resorts. However, crowds can be avoided if skiers use some judgment about where they ski. The worst crowding always occurs around 10:00 A.M. and between 1:00 P.M. and 2:00 P.M. During these times or during major holidays, avoid skiing runs serviced by the following lifts: American Flyer, G, I, J, B. Abundant skiing is available for skiers of all abilities without utilizing these lifts.

It should also be noted that in order to avoid a long walk in skis, do not ski Treble Cliff to its end. Just before the end of this run there is a large depression; stop here and observe a track to the left through the trees. This path is created each year and makes it easy to cut through the trees and exit onto the lower portion of Rosi's Run, thus avoiding the long hike back to B-lift. By all means do ski Treble Cliff, especially during or just after a large snowfall as it is an excellent powder run for the expert.

Ski School

Copper's Ski School meets in three locations daily: The Center, Union Creek, and Solitude Station. Solitude Station is the mid-mountain restaurant located at the top of the American Eagle lift and at the base of the E-lift.

These locations are convenient to the slopes, mountain restaurants, ski-rental shops, ski repair shops, apparel shops, transportation, and day-care facilities.

Adult classes are scheduled to begin promptly at 9:30 A.M. (lasting until 12:00 P.M.) or at 12:30 P.M. (lasting until 3:00 P.M.). They are designated for persons twelve years and older. The rate for group lessons during the 1993-94 season is $37. Private lessons are available at 8:30 A.M. and 2:30 P.M. Classes are for one and a half hours or a half-day. A full-day private lesson is also available in 1993-94 at $225. Private lessons for up to four persons are available for $295 per day. This class option is an excellent way for a family to learn the mountain and to get tips on their skills at the same time.

Copper offers various lesson plans which include lessons, equipment, and lift tickets. There are also special classes available for advanced and expert skiers.

Copper Mountain's ski school guarantees its students complete satisfaction with their lessons, or it will do whatever is necessary to achieve their satisfaction.

Newcomer and advanced snowboarding lessons are available in two and one half hour classes at 10:00 A.M. and 12:30 P.M. 1993-94 snowboard lessons are $37.

For children, classes are divided by age and ability. All day classes begin at 10 a.m., include lunch, and end at 3:15 p.m. The cost is $45, and with a lift ticket, $50. A kids value package is available which includes lesson, rental, lift and lunch for $54. Registration is from 8:30 to 9:45.

Equipment Rental

Copper provides rental equipment at the Skier Services Center and at Union Creek. Its basic equipment is found in the Novice Package. This package rents during the 1993-94 season for $17 per day and consists of Rossignol Edge skis, Rossignol boots, Salomon bindings, and poles. Children's rates are $14 per day. Top-of-the-line rental equipment consists of a full line of demo skis, Tecnica, Rossignol or Dachstein boots, Salomon bindings, and poles. This High Performance package rents for $28 per day.

Several private sporting goods stores are situated conveniently at The Center, the B-lift base, and at Union Creek. **Christy Sports**, located at The Center, has a particularly large inventory of high-performance skis and abundant ski apparel to meet various price points.

Ski Tuning and Repair

Tuning and repair services are available at **Breeze**, located at the base of the B-lift, or at **Christy Sports** in The Center. In addition all ski-rental and sporting goods stores in the nearby towns of Frisco, Breckenridge, Silverthorne, and Dillon offer ski tuning and repair.

Mountain Dining

Unlike many major ski resorts, Copper Mountain has the majority of its long ski runs situated along its lower lifts. Because of this unusual arrangement, most of the restaurants are found at the various base points. There is one true mountain restaurant situated at the top of the American Eagle lift called **Solitude Station**. Its food service is typical ski resort fare. Food service is cafeteria style, served hot and fresh. Anything from fresh, homemade pizza to hot dogs, hamburgers, and wine and beer is available. Breakfast is served at all base restaurants. On warm, clear days the staff at Solitude will set up an outdoor barbecue and grill hamburgers and bratwurst.

Numerous excellent restaurants are situated throughout the Copper complex; these are discussed in the section entitled *Restaurants*.

Child Care

Copper's day care and particularly its children's ski program have received national recognition by *Ski* magazine as being among the best day-care programs in the country.

For children aged two months to two years, there is the Belly Button Babies program. Copper provides special care and low supervisor ratios to assure parents that their children will receive adequate and caring attention. Persons planning to enroll their children in this program should be prepared to provide their own formula, diapers, and wipes as well as an extra set of clothes, a favorite toy or blanket and warm outdoor clothes and sunglasses or goggles. It is also important that reservations be made early. It is best to make day-care reservations at the same time accommodations are being booked.

The full-day rate during the 1993-94 ski season for children enrolled in the Belly Button Bakery\ Babies is $45 and includes lunch. Additional days are discounted to $39 each; the half-day rate is $35. Reservations are required. Call (800)458-8386, ext.5 or (303)968-2318, ext. 6345.

Children two years and over can be enrolled in the Belly Button Bakery. This innovative program incorporates snow play and skiing (for children over three years). Lunch is included and snacks are provided in the afternoon. With careful supervision, the children help to bake cookies. This class meets daily at 8:30 A.M. and children must be picked up by 5:00 P.M. It is always a good idea to provide the children with an extra change of clothing.

Fees for children enrolled in the Belly Button Bakery are identical for children enrolled in the Belly Button Babies program.

All day-care facilities are located in the lower level of the Mountain Plaza building. The Mountain Plaza building is the large, red-roofed, multi-story building in The Center of the resort complex. It is easily identifiable and convenient to all adult ski class meeting places, shops, restaurants, and rest rooms.

Baby-sitting in the evenings is available by making early reservations at the Belly Button Bakery. The rate for this service during the 1993-94 season is $6 per hour plus $1 per additional child.

Medical Facilities

Copper Mountain maintains a complete medical facility in order to handle emergencies or family medicine. Located in the Bridge End Complex close to The Center, it is open daily during the season.

For serious illness or injuries that cannot be handled by the staff, a helicopter pad adjacent to the clinic facilitates air ambulance service to any of the Denver hospitals. Ground transportation via commercial ambulance can also be arranged if needed. Prescription drugs on a limited basis are available from the clinic if prescribed by one of the staff physicians. Other prescription needs can be filled by the pharmacies located in the towns of Frisco, Silverthorne, Breckenridge, or Dillon.

Cross-Country Skiing

Nordic enthusiasts will have to go a long way to find a better place to ski than Copper Mountain. Copper maintains 25 kilometers of trails, commencing at the Union Creek Base and meandering up and through the Arapaho National Forest. All of the cross-country tracks work their way up Vail Pass through beautiful glades and past roaring streams. For the beginner, there are one and a half hour lessons available for $32 including the fee for using the track and rentals. Telemark lessons are also available for $44. All lesson fees include lift tickets. Rental equipment is available at the Union Creek base.

During the 1993-94 season, track passes which include one ride on the K-Lift are $8 per adult without a Nordic lift ticket and $14 with a lift ticket. Children and seniors are $6.

Special Events

Each year Copper Mountain hosts a long list of featured events. A staple among its events, however, has always been the NASTAR racing program. Located at the top of the G chairlift and running parallel to Loverly, the NASTAR course is open from early December between 1:00 P.M. and 4:00 P.M. daily. NASTAR costs $6 for two runs with additional runs priced at $1 each. Parallel to the NASTAR course is a self-timer. The fee for using the self-timer is $1 per run.

Other events include ice skating, sleigh rides, moonlit cross-country tours, snowmobiling, and movies. For information or reservations, telephone (800) 458-8386, ext. 5.

Accommodations

All of Copper Mountain Resorts accommodations are rated 4 diamonds by AAA, the highest rating they give.

Copper's largest hotel is the **Mountain Plaza Hotel**. Located in The Center, the Plaza is convenient to the slopes, shops, and restaurants. Typical of many of Copper's older properties, the Plaza is beginning to show its age. These are good, standard facilities not unlike accommodations found in countless hotels throughout the United States. The rooms are arranged in modules of three, i.e. two standard hotel rooms with a studio between them. This affords management the option of renting a single room or a two-bedroom unit from the same module.

Similar accommodations may be found at the **Copper Mountain Inn** and at the **Spruce Lodges**. 1993-94 rates for a standard hotel room at Copper Mountain vary from a low of $110 to a high of $225. Of course, all rates are higher during holiday seasons such as Christmas. A one-bedroom hotel room or condo will run between $135 and $280 per night.

Condominiums

Recently Copper Mountain has begun a condominium expansion program near the base of the B lift and the golf course. Unlike the initial condos, these are being built and managed by Copper Mountain. Copper's management believes it is imperative to provide a consistent, high-quality housing environment. In response to this perceived need, it has constructed two new projects: **The Woods and Legends of Copper Creek** and **The Greens at Copper Creek**.

Of the two developments, The Woods is the premier property. Each unit shares no more than two common walls with other units. These are essentially stand-alone two or three-bedroom units tastefully furnished and equipped with all the amenities one would expect from a property of this type. The views from this project's windows are of the spectacular Ten-Mile range and the A and B lift-serviced runs, a vista without parallel. These accommodations include cathedral ceilings, parquet entries, fireplaces, master bath suites, and garage parking. Kitchen appliances include ice makers, self-cleaning ovens, dishwashers, and garbage disposals. Many units also have washer/dryers,whirlpool tubs, and microwave ovens.

The Greens are designed for sale as interval ownership property. However, until all the units are sold, they are available for rent. Tastefully decorated, these efficiency units offer the same views as the Woods. Enclosed parking is also available, and the kitchens are completely appointed with appliances and cooking utensils. Two bedroom, one bedroom, and studio units are available. In the two-bedroom units, one of the bedrooms may be converted into a sitting room. Fireplaces are constructed of stucco in the style of the Southwest. Southwest colors are represented with the use of warm greens, teals, peach, and similar colors. Neither of these projects offers swimming pools nor hot tubs because management believes that the need for such amenities is filled by the Copper Mountain Racquet and Athletic club.

1993-94 ski season rates for condominiums at the Woods and the Greens are identical. The Depending on the time of year, rates for a two-bedroom unit vary between $215 and $385 per night. Three-bedroom units rent for between $275 and $480 per night.

Restaurants

There are enough restaurants in the Copper Mountain complex to satisfy all but the most discriminating gourmets. The best restaurant is **Pesca Fresco** located across from the lift ticket kiosk at The Center. Its luncheon and dinner menus offer wide varieties, and the daily fish and pasta specials are worth considering. The Plaza's modern decor of warm woods and kelly green ultra-suede wall treatments is enhanced by many indoor plants. Service is attentive and prices are moderate. Pesco Fresco is open for breakfast and a jazz piano bar is open during après ski and evening.

At the base of B-lift is **Farley's Tavern and Restaurant**, named after the owner's dog. Farley's is only open for dinner. From time to time it will open for lunch, but one should not count on it because the schedule is erratic. Farley's is a cozy, informal restaurant featuring American cuisine. There is a similar restaurant just down the street in Frisco called **Barkley's Bar and Restaurant** which is also under the same management. It is unclear if the owners once had a dog named "Barkley." Both restaurants feature unique fare and provide excellent value for the discerning client.

Another fine restaurant, located in Copper Mountain's Racquet and Athletic Club, is appropriately named **"Rackets."** Situated at the top of an impressive staircase, the restaurant offers a civilized respite from the rigors of alpine skiing and other athletic activities. Rackets is decorated in what is best described as "mountain traditional." Blue and white table linens are complemented by the lovely silver service and classical le Corbusier seating. A large fireplace and oak bar complete the ambience. Because the restaurant is not located conveniently to the slopes, it is not open for lunch. It is open, however, for dinner every evening. Entrées include broiled salmon, Bar-B-Que scallop kabob, skewered lamb medallions, and roast prime rib au jus.

Numerous other restaurants scattered around Copper feature regional dishes such as Mexican and home-style cuisine. A current listing of all restaurants will be available upon checking into accommodations.

It must be noted, however, that there are additional excellent restaurants in the nearby towns of Breckenridge, Keystone, Silverthorne, and Dillon. One of the best restaurants in the entire area is probably **The Ranch at Keystone**. Also the Breckenridge Hilton houses a wonderful restaurant called **Swan's**. The best steak is found at **The Blue Spruce** in Frisco. The best German food is at **Weber's** in Breckenridge. The best Italian food is found at **Risterante Al Lago** located in Dillon; the best seafood is at **The Commodore** at Keystone.

In nearby Frisco and Silverthorne there is a full selection of fast-food establishments such as Arby's, McDonalds, Wendy's, Pizza Hut, Kentucky Fried Chicken, and Dairy Queen.

Activities

In addition to the 35 shops and restaurants found at Copper Mountain, there is a $3 million athletic club with racquetball courts and two indoor tennis courts, a twenty-five yard, four-lane lap pool, complete Nautilus, free weights, aerobics and exercise classes, tanning salon, hot tubs, saunas, steam rooms, a massage therapist, nursery, and restaurant. All guests of Copper Mountain may use the facilities free of charge. The club is open from 6:00 A.M. to 10:00 P.M. weekdays and from 8:00 A.M. to 10:00 P.M. weekends.

Services

A full complement of sporting goods stores, apparel shops, pharmacies, grocery stores, liquor stores, furniture, bath, florist, ice cream, and other specialty shops is located in The Center area. The Center is, as one might expect, at the hub of the resort complex adjacent to the Mountain Plaza hotel and the Plaza restaurant.

Village Map

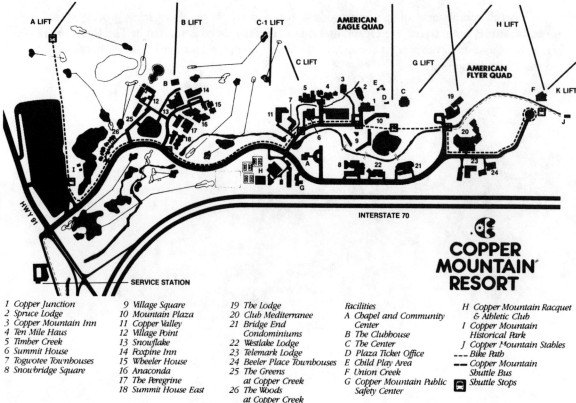

SERVICE STATION

INTERSTATE 70

COPPER MOUNTAIN RESORT

1 Copper Junction
2 Spruce Lodge
3 Copper Mountain Inn
4 Ten Mile Haus
5 Timber Creek
6 Summit House
7 Togwotee Townhouses
8 Snowbridge Square

9 Village Square
10 Mountain Plaza
11 Copper Valley
12 Village Point
13 Snowflake
14 Foxpine Inn
15 Wheeler House
16 Anaconda
17 The Peregrine
18 Summit House East

19 The Lodge
20 Club Mediterranee
21 Bridge End
   Condominiums
22 Westlake Lodge
23 Telemark Lodge
24 Beeler Place Townhouses
25 The Greens
   at Copper Creek
26 The Woods
   at Copper Creek

Facilities
A Chapel and Community
   Center
B The Clubhouse
C The Center
D Plaza Ticket Office
E Child Play Area
F Union Creek
G Copper Mountain Public
   Safety Center

H Copper Mountain Racquet
   & Athletic Club
I Copper Mountain
   Historical Park
J Copper Mountain Stables
--- Bike Path
━━ Copper Mountain
   Shuttle Bus
🚌 Shuttle Stops

CRESTED BUTTE

Crested Butte Mountain Resort
P.O. Box A
Mt. Crested Butte, CO. 81225

(800) 544-8448 Reservations
(303) 349-2211 Information
(303) 349-2323 Snow Report

New For 1993-94

In order to provide some more moderately-priced lodging close to the bottom of its lifts, this year the Crested Butte Mountain Resort will open the doors of a new hotel, the Mountain Lair. Owned by the resort itself, the new hotel's doors are only 200 yards from the Silver Queen quad chair. Visitors also will have but a 30-second walk to the town center where free shuttle are available to the town of Crested Butte. Each room at the new hotel is similar: 405 quare feet, two king-size beds, color television, telephones. The hotel's amenities will include a 2 outdoor hot tubs, laundry facilities, vending machines, and gift shop. Depending on the time of year, rooms will rent for between $80 and $170 per night. Half of the Mountain Lair's 126 rooms will open by the first day of Free Ski Lift Period, Nov. 19, with the rest being open before the summer season.

Again this year Crested Butte will offer free lift tickets from Nov. 19 to Dec. 18. There are no strings attached to this offer: no lodging requirement nor special package to buy, no asterisks, and no fine print! Free skiing will be available to everyone regardless of age, whether they are guests or locals. In addition, free lessons will be provided for never-ever skiers who are over 7-years-old! This offer was made at the beginning of the last two ski seasons and was such a success in drawing new skiers to the area that they've decided to do it again.

For those who can't be there during the Free Lift Ticket period, keep in mind that this resort also offers a **QuickStart** special rate for first-time skiers. The ski school will provide 1-1/2 days of ski lessons, and two days of lift ticket for only $79. At the end the two days, the resorts guarantees that a new skier will be able to ski down from the top of the Keystone lift using wedge turns. If the individual can not do that, he can get his money back or keep returning until he gets it right! If you know someone who wants to learn how to ski, this sounds like an attractive deal.

How To Get There

Crested Butte is located 230 miles from Denver, 196 miles from Colorado Springs, and 160 miles from Grand Junction. The drive to Crested Butte from any direction is one of the most beautiful in Colorado. From Denver take Colorado Highway 285 south to Highway 50 in Salida; follow this until it intersects Highway 135 in Gunnison; turn north and follow the road to Crested Butte. Once in Crested Butte, be sure to note that the town is not the same as Mt. Crested Butte. Mt. Crested Butte is the ski resort where most of the accommodations are located and is only about three miles from the town of Crested Butte. The directional signage is very good.

From the West take Interstate Highway 70 to Grand Junction; turn south on Highway 50 to Gunnison. Be careful to notice that Highway 50 makes a ninety-degree turn east in the town of Montrose. Once in Gunnison, take Highway 135 north to Crested Butte. If the weather is suspect, stop in Montrose and check on the road conditions to Gunnison. During storms Highway 50 will frequently be closed around the Blue Mesa Reservoir, and there are no accommodations between Montrose and Gunnison.

Flying into Crested Butte is easy. During the 1993-94 ski season, American Airlines will offer daily direct service to Gunnison from Dallas/Fort Worth.

Delta's service from Atlanta to Gunnison will be expanding this year. For most of the ski season Delta Airlines will run a daily flight, and then for about one third of the season, a Delta flight will fly to Gunnison on Wednesday, Saturday and Sunday. Continental offers Saturday service from Houston's Intercontinental Airport. Continental Express provides 5 daily connections through Denver's airport in Denver. Finally, Mesa Airlines will fly from Denver 4 times per day.

Crested Butte is a scant twenty-eight miles from Gunnison, and the road (Highway 135) is good. At the time accommodations are booked, guests should also request ground transportation and indicate to the reservationist their flight number and time of arrival. Transfers via Alpine Express during the 1993-94 season are $32 round trip. For children 12 and under, the fare is $22. This company operates a fleet of 32 vehicles. Telephone (800) 822-4844 to book reservations on Alpine Express.

Major car rental agencies are represented at the Gunnison Airport. Full-size cars, vans, and four-wheel drive vehicles are available. To reserve a car, telephone Budget at (303) 641-4040, Hertz at (800) 654-3131, or National at (800) CAR-RENT.

A car, though a convenience, is not necessary because Crested Butte is the only ski resort in the area, and all activities center around it or the town of Crested Butte. A free daily shuttle runs every thirty minutes from 7:15 A.M. until midnight during the ski season.

Mountain Information

Mt. Crested Butte is an extremely versatile mountain with 1,160 acres of skiable terrain. Of that area, 145 acres are classified for beginners, 349 acres for intermediates and 118 acres for the advanced skiers. In addition, 550 acres are designed as the "Extreme Limits," for experts only, 100 percent double-black diamond, ungroomed terrain. The intermediate and beginner terrain is intermingled nicely, and the runs are long. Most beginners who are not in classes usually gravitate to the Keystone Lift. The long, gentle runs in this area provide just enough downhill slope to keep moving without worrying about falling hard.

The intermediate skier will love the long, wide runs off the Paradise and Teocalli lifts. Trees which line the sides of all the trails provide good visual contrast even in poor light. All beginner runs and most of the intermediate runs are groomed regularly. Take a run down Treasury. This intermediate trail is the longest in the resort and has enough challenging terrain to test one's skills on moguls, soft pack, and steep slopes.

One of the most unique features of this mountain, however, is its notoriously underrated expert terrain. The North Face of the Extreme Limits provides some of the best skiing found at any resort!

The Extreme Limits is unique because it receives no attention from the resort's mountain maintenance people. The patrol limits its involvement there to avalanche control, emergency rescue, and a nightly sweep. Otherwise, the area is skied as nature created it. Although there is lift service to the general area, many of the specific runs can only be reached by climbing.

Under no circumstances should skiers attempt to ski the Extreme Limits the first few times without a guide. It is possible to make a wrong turn which could put the skier at extraordinary risk. The North Face is best described as a series of small bowls arranged contiguous to one another. Of these runs, the easiest is probably found in The Glades. The Glades is moderately moguled at the top. Bumps have been formed by good skiers with long skis, and the troughs associated with skiers traversing are nowhere in evidence. The most difficult runs are Phoenix Bowl, Staircase, Slot, and Cesspool. The primary reason a guide is necessary is so skiers can learn the way out of the bowls without having to exit through one of these extremely tight, steep, rocky chutes.

In order to reach Spellbound Bowl's summit, it is necessary to climb from the top of the North Face Lift for about one-half hour. It is worth the effort, however, since you can usually find powder somewhere on it. From this bowl, you can ski into Phoenix Bowl. From there, more walking is required before finally exiting onto Black Eagle. If the skier is not inclined to walk to the top of Spellbound Bowl, it is possible to enter just below the summit via Million Dollar Highway. This is a cut between the rocks which separate Hard Slab from High Life. The map identifies this cut as Phoenix Entrance, and it usually is too rocky to be used without damaging your skis.

On the Front Face is a run called Horseshoe Springs identified on the map by a single black diamond. No indication of its short length is given. Horseshoe Springs is also extremely steep! Those who have enjoyed the exhilaration of The Wall at Aspen Highlands or Mach One at Breckenridge will love Horseshoe Springs.

For those skiers who do not shy away from hiking, runs such as Peel and Upper Peel to the right of the Silver Queen Lift are very steep and challenging. A word of caution, however; this area does not hold snow very well and tends to become skied off quickly. Try Upper Peel and Peel if they are open, though—Wow!

Many skiers at Crested Butte begin their morning by taking the East River Lift. This lift is the first to enjoy the morning sun, and as the day progresses, most skiers follow the sun around the mountain and finish the day skiing the Silver Queen Lift.

Mt. Crested Butte's base is located at 9,375 and its summit is at 12,162 feet. The vertical drop is 3,062 feet. The longest beginner run is Houston at 1.8 miles (2.9 km). The longest intermediate run is Treasury at 1.9 miles (3 km), and the longest expert run is International at 1.4 miles (2.2 km).

Although located only thirty-one miles from Gunnison which is noted for its very cold weather, Mt. Crested Butte has relatively moderate temperatures. Its average in-town temperatures during the season are

	High		Low	
Nov.	36°	2° C	12°	-11° C
Dec.	28°	-2° C	-8°	-22° C
Jan.	28°	-2° C	-10°	-23° C
Feb.	32°	0° C	-3°	-19° C
Mar.	39°	4° C	5°	-15° C

Receiving over 300 inches (762 cm) of snow annually, Crested Butte normally does not have to rely on its extensive snowmaking capabilities. Snow is generally made only during the early days of the season, principally to guarantee good coverage during Thanksgiving and occasionally during Christmas.

The average monthly snowfalls are

Nov.   38"   (96 cm)
Dec.   58"   (147 cm)
Jan.   64"   (162 cm)
Feb.   48"   (121 cm)
Mar.   50"   (127 cm)
Apr.   25"   (64 cm)

Lift Ticket Prices (1993-94)

$ 41......Adult, All-Day	Child, Under 13........$25
$ 29......Adult, Half-Day, P.M. only	Child..................$19
$ 82......Adult, 2-Day	Child, 2-Day...........$50
$123......Adult, 3-Day	Child, 3-Day...........$75
$148......Adult, 4-Day out of 5	Child, 4-Day...........$96
$185......Adult, 5-Day out of 6	Child, 5-Day...........$110
$216......Adult, 6-Day out of 7	Child, 6-Day...........$114

Children 12 and under still ski free with a paying adult all year long except between December 26 and January 2 and March 12 and 26.

Multi-day tickets purchased prior to December 26 or March 14 that carry over into the exception periods are honored if the bulk of the stay falls in the non-exception period. Lift tickets purchased during the exempt period which carry over beyond it are charged on a pro rata basis. Proof of age is requested at the discretion of the ticket seller. Only birth certificates and passports are considered acceptable proof!

Crested Butte became a trend setter during the 1989-90 ski season with the introduction of their innovative **Learn To Ski Free** program. For the 1993-94 season "never-ever skiers" will receive free lessons and free lift tickets for however long it takes them to learn to ski during the free lift tickets period, Nov. 19 to Dec. 18. Crested Butte is to be commended for recognizing that skiing has not been producing enough new, young skiers.

Hours of Operation

9:00 A.M. to 4:00 P.M.

Lift Ticket Purchase Locations

Lift tickets may be purchased at the Gothic Building Lift Ticket Office which is located at the foot of the Keystone Lift, convenient to all lodging and to Gothic Cafeteria. Ticket wickets open at 8:00 A.M. and close at 4:00 P.M. During busy seasons it is a good idea to prepurchase the next day's lift ticket after 3:00 P.M.

How To Avoid Crowds

Even though crowds generally are not a concern at Crested Butte, they will occur at certain lifts during some periods and at the base area in the late afternoon. During the Free Lift Ticket season, the area will become a little crowded especially on weekends. But, so far even crowds during that period have not been a terrible problem.

Paradise Lift is one of the lifts that seems to develop crowds more readily than others. The best way to avoid these lines when they occur is to ski the area around the Teocalli Lift where crowding is rarely experienced. Even though the runs off the Teocalli Lift are beginner and intermediate, they are very good and should be skied in any event. After 3:00 P.M. when most skiers are making their way down the mountain, crowding occurs on the trails leading to the base of the Keystone and Silver Queen lifts. Since this is the only way down in the evening, crowds are impossible to avoid. Caution should be exercised, and fast skiers should slow down. The ski patrol is usually positioned on the slopes, urging returning skiers to slow their speed and to ski defensively.

Ski School

Crested Butte Ski School is under the direction of Jean Pavillard. In addition to group and private lessons, the ski school offers lessons and services for handicapped skiers. Consistent with other major resorts, the Crested Butte Ski School teaches the ATS (American Teaching System). For information or to register for ski school programs, call 1-800-544-8448, ext. 2251. If you are in town, call (303) 349-2252.

Group lessons meet at 10:15 A.M. and 1:15 P.M. daily and begin 15 minutes later. Private lessons meet at 9:00 A.M. and 3:00 P.M. All lesson participants meet in the blue fenced area in front of the Gothic building.

For those persons who have never skied before, the ski school offers **QuickStart**, a first-time skier group lessons. *See the first page of the Crested Butte chapter for a description of this program, under* **New for 1993-94.** *Or try a never-ever full day ski lesson, with rentals for $46, $34 for a half day. These prices include lift tickets.*

Group lessons are taught in two-hour segments.

$28	1 Half-Day
$50	2 Half-Days
$60	1 Full-Day
$72	3 Half-Days
$116	5 Half-Days

Private lessons - Reservations are required:

$ 72	1.5 hours, plus $20 for each additional person
$ 92	2 Hours
$135	3 Hours
$245	6 Hours

Special programs:

$40	Bump and Powder, or parallel workshops
$28	Snowboard

Crested Butte offers its Butte Busters program for children aged seven through twelve. A full day of lessons, including lunch will cost $42. Children in the Butte Busters program must register prior to 9:30 A.M. and have their own ski equipment. Sunscreen and eye protection (either goggles or sun glasses) are requested. Operating hours are from 8:30 A.M. to 3:30 P.M.

Equipment Rental

Rental equipment is available from any number of shops at Mt. Crested Butte or in town. Rates for equipment are comparable. Shops typically offer three types of equipment packages: Recreational, Sport, and High Performance.

The Recreational package is the most basic and is intended for novice or beginning skiers. Usually the rental equipment offered is manufactured especially for this use.

Most intermediates who want to rent equipment will select from the slightly higher priced Sport ski package. The skis offered under this designation are almost always production skis often referred to as "recreational" skis. Do not confuse the designation "recreational ski" with the package designated "Recreational ski package."

For skiers who want a high-performance ski or who want to demo a ski prior to a possible purchase, the High Performance package makes the most sense.

The largest rental shop in Mt. Crested Butte is **Crested Butte Ski Rental** located in The Gothic Building(the same building as the ski school and ticket office) and the Grande Butte Hotel. Crested Butte Ski Rental offers recreational packages from $12 for the 1993-4 season. This rate is discounted if four or more days' rental is contracted. Children's rates for one day are $8 and are discounted the same as adults' for extended periods. To qualify for the children's prices, a skier must be 10-years-old or less, and must wear a size 4 boot or smaller.

Crested Butte Ski Rental's Sport Package consists of rear-entry Salomon boots, step-in bindings, skis, and poles. During the 1993-94 season, single day rental is $15.

Crested Butte Ski Rental's High Performance Package consists of top-of-the-line skis from K2, Rossignol, or Dynastar, Salomon SX-91 boots, and Marker bindings. This package is priced from $21 per day during the 1993-94 season.

One of Colorado's largest ski rental companies, **Christy Sports**, has a convenient location in the Treasury Center, near the base area lifts and ski school. Christy's features "Regular", "Sport", "Premium", and "Junior" rental packages. During the 1992-93 season the "Regular" package rents for $12 per day, the "Sport" package for $16 per day, the "Premium" package $23 per day, and the "Junior" package for $8 per day. After two consecutive rental days the rates are discounted. Demo skis are available at $30 per day with no discount for consecutive days. Boots, poles, or skis may be rented separately at a reduced rate, as well. To reserve skis telephone (303) 349-6601.

Gene Taylor's, located on Emmons Loop close to the bus stop and lifts, is one of Crested Butte's oldest and most respected ski rental shops. Taylor's recreation package consists of K2 4500 skis, Salomon SX 51 boots, Salomon 747 or 337 bindings and rents for $8 per day. A multiple day rate of $7.20 is suggested if skis are to be rented for more than one or two days.

The sport package at Gene Taylor's consists of Rossignol 275 or Quantum skis. Rent the Quantum if the snow conditions are powdery and the 275's if hard pack conditions exist. With this package the same Salomon bindings and boots are provided. The daily rate for the sport package is $11 per day and the multiple day rate is $9.90 for four or more days.

Taylor's top rental package, the High Performance package, offers the serious skier the choice of either Rossignol 4S, Strato skis or Atomic Arc HVRC skis. Utilizing the same Salomon SX 51 boots and 747 bindings, this package rents for $14 per day or $12.60 for four or more consecutive days.

For the new breed of shredders that seems to be increasingly on the scene, snowboards are available. To reserve any skis or other equipment call Gene Taylor Sports at (303) 349-5386.

It appears that Treasury Center has become the center of attention for visiting skiers. It is an enclosed mall which protects guests from harsh elements while providing a focal point for the resort. Among the many shops and restaurants located here is **Flat Iron Sports**. Flat Iron's recreation package is called the "Sport" package and consists of K2 EET 21, K2 4500, or Olin 700 skis, a choice of either Koflach, Raichle, or Salomon boots, Salomon 447, Tyrolia 02 special rental bindings. The rental rate for the sport package is $11 per day or $10 if rented for four or more days.

Flat Iron's sport package is referred to as their "Select" package. It typically consists of either various Blizzard or Atomic models of skis. Head Radial or K2 TRC skis are available as well. Salomon SX 61 or 81 boots may be rented or Koflach rear entry boots may be substituted. Salomon 457 or 957 Equipe bindings are standard. This package rents for $18 per day or $16 per day if rented for multiple days.

The High Performance package is called the "Pro" package at the Flat Iron. A wide range of premium skis is available including Atomic 735 GS, 733 SL, Blizzard V20SL or V20RS Thermo. Virtually any boot requested can be provided as can most bindings, though the Marker Titanium and the Salomon 957 Equipe are the most requested. The daily rate for the "Pro" package is $22 or $20 if rented for multiple days. To reserve skis, telephone (303) 749-6656.

Ski Tuning and Repair

Tuning and repair services are available at any of the fine ski shops at Crested Butte. Among the most popular shops are those offering either stone grinding or hand tuning. These shops include, but are not limited to, Gene Taylor's, Flat Iron, Christy Sports, and Mt. Crested Butte Ski Rentals. Hot wax applications vary from $4 to $5; flat filing and waxing can run as high as $28 at Flat Iron or as low as $10 at Christy Sports. Full tunes can be as low as $20 at Gene Taylor's or as high as $30 at Christy Sports. It pays to shop around for the best rate for the amount and quality of tune needed.

Tune-up shops throughout the United States are typically very flexible in their pricing. If someone has a lower rate, they will usually meet it or they will change their rates throughout the season depending on competition.

Rates for these services were not available at the time of this writing. However, rates certainly are comparable with those being charged at other Colorado ski resorts featured in this book.

Mountain Dining

There are two mountain restaurants at Crested Butte. **Twister Warming House** located at the base of the Twister Lift may be reached via any of the runs serviced by Twister Lift. Beginners and intermediates may reach it by skiing Peanut. Nestled among the tall pines, this is a short-order restaurant with a large sun deck.

The larger and principal mountain restaurant is located at the base of the Paradise Lift and is named, appropriately enough, the **Paradise Warming House**. The Paradise features a large, common dining room with cafeteria service. This restaurant is scrupulously clean, and its furniture and fixtures are well maintained. The food offerings are creative and very good. The menu features assorted grilled dishes, deli foods, wine, beer, soft drinks, and fresh salads made daily. The staff also serves lasagna, chili, beef stew, egg rolls, prime rib, and homemade pies. The prices are very reasonable and the ambience is cordial.

Bubba's located within the Paradise is a full-service restaurant featuring table service and an extensive menu. This excellent restaurant is equal to Darcy's on Aspen Mountain or Gwynn's at Snowmass.

Child Care

Day care is available at the Buttetopia Nursery and Day Care. Situated on the ground floor of the Whetstone Building and located only a few steps west of the Grande Butte Hotel, the Buttetopia accepts infants from six months through six years. The facility is divided into two separate areas, one for infants six months through six years and one for children seven years through 12 years.

Care is available by the half-day or full-day. Full-day care includes lunch unless the child is still on formula, which the parents must provide. Diapers for non-toilet-trained children should also be provided. Snacks such as animal crackers are provided by the staff.

Updated rates were not available at press time, but nursery rates during the 1992-93 season were $38 for a full-day and $28 for a half-day. Day-care rates are $35 for a full day and $25 for a half-day.

A variation of the day-care program is also offered at the Buttetopia. This is a program where children aged two to seven can learn to ski. The younger group, ages 2 to 3, join a class called the mites, and enjoy indoor and outdoor play, and some limited ski playing. The Miners, ages 4 to 7, participate in a group less. Offered as half-day or full-day programs, the 1993-94 fee is $39 per half-day and $49 for a full day. Lunch and supervised activities are included in the program, as well as ski instruction.

Medical Facilities

The ski patrol will only render emergency service to injured skiers. The patrol will administer trauma treatment, stabilize broken bones, and transport the injured skier downhill by sled to a clinic located in the Axtel Building at the base of the mountain. This is directly across from the Silver Queen Lift. Should additional medical treatment be necessary, patients are transported to a hospital in Gunnison.

Cross-Country Skiing

For the 1993-94 season the **Crested Butte Nordic Center** is building a new warming shelter and rental shop in Big Mine Park in downtown Crested Butte at the corner of Whiterock and Second Street, just one short block from the Mountain Express bus stop. Operating from 9:00 A.M. to 4:00 P.M. daily, the Nordic Center offers 25 km. of groomed tracks on scenic rolling terrain with enough variation that beginners as well as experts will find something they like.

Along with a new building(the facility used to be housed in the nearby Crested Butte Athletic Club), the center has a new director, former NCAA competitor and U.S. ski team member Mike Bush. Bush and his fellow cross country instructors will offer beginner nordic ski lessons from 10 a.m. to 11:30 a.m. for $20 everyday. Advanced techniques such as track ski racing, back-country mountaineering, Nordic Telemark, and turns (stem christies, stem, parallel, and telemark) are also taught.

Track fees during the 1993-94 season are $6. For senior citizens and children under 15, the price is $3. Private lessons for 90 minutes can be arranged by appointment for $35. Full day back country tours are $30.

Complete rental equipment is available at the Center, and the 1993-94 rate is $12 for a basic cross country package. For additional information, telephone (303) 349-6201.

Nordic skiing is also available at the Irwin Lodge. Be sure to review the section entitled *Activities* for more information on this unique approach to cross-country skiing.

Accommodations

Information about almost all of the accommodation listed here may be had by calling the Crested Butte Vacations reservation line -- 1-800-544-8448.

The Grand Butte Hotel at Mt. Crested Butte has to rank as one of the finest mountain resort hotels in the country. It dominates the foreground of the landscape and is positioned against a spectacular mountain backdrop.

The 262-room structure seems to overawe the winding entrance road which leads to a cavernous underground garage and valet parking. The reception area is on the second floor and is serviced by two elevators from the parking garage. The capacious reception area and lobby has a large moss-rock fireplace which provides a central feature to the room. The plaid seating and tooled leather cocktail tables add just a hint of formality to an otherwise casual decor. The cedar siding used throughout the hotel perfumes the air with a whisper of its scent. This is an active room with people milling around the piano bar or discussing the evening's plans with the hotel's concierge. Across the lobby Christy Sports is usually busy as skis are rented or tee shirts are purchased for friends and relatives.

Another somewhat quieter lounge area is located on the floor immediately below the reception area and lobby. Group meeting rooms are located on this floor as well as a swimming pool, sauna, steam room, and exercise room. As on the main floor, the central lounge area is dominated by a large, native stone fireplace.

The tastefully decorated hotel rooms offered by the Grande Butte are superior to accommodations at most other resort hotels. The two queen-size beds are comfortable, and the dressers provide enough space to store sweaters, ski pants, and so forth for a full week. A small writing table, remote-control color TV, upholstered reading chairs, and footstools contribute to guests' comfort. For guests who wish to cook, a mini-kitchen is disguised as a country French armoire. This mini-kitchen while functional is purely basic, and you should not expect to prepare large meals with its humble features.

Standard rooms at the Grand Butte Hotel during the regular 1993-94 ski season rent from a low of $110 per night to a high of $180 per night.

The Grande Butte Hotel has two fine restaurants: **The Roaring Elk and Giovanni's Grand Cafe**. The Roaring Elk Saloon features nightly entertainment and dancing. Separated from the main lobby by etched glass windows of "roaring" elks, it is an après-ski gathering place. The decor features a beech and brass bar, cedar ceiling, plush leather seating, and plantation shutters.

From the Grande Butte's lobby guests will find that it is fewer than 100 steps to the mountain's lift system. In addition, many other shops, restaurants, and services are located conveniently around the hotel. The hotel is indeed the center of this resort's activity.

The Crested Butte Lodge, part of Crested Mountain Village, located near the center of the resort's activities, is only steps away from the lifts. It boasts an indoor swimming pool found next to **Wong's Chinese Restaurant** on the main floor. As with most mountain properties, geraniums and ferns line every available inch of window space around the pool.

Both penthouse suites and condo units are available at Crested Mountain Village. Although each unit is furnished differently, a common theme is repeated throughout. All units have brick fireplaces, natural oak furniture in a country French style, and a fully equipped kitchen. The bedrooms have queen-size beds
with Laura Ashley print comforters. A Jacuzzi bathtub and double sinks complete the accommodations. Penthouses at the Lodge are available as one bedroom/one bath; two bedroom/two bath; three

bedroom/three bath units. During the 1993-94 ski season, accommodations range from a low of $53 per night and peak at $221 per night.

Only slightly removed from the Mt. Crested Butte hub, but still only 80 yards from the lift, is the **Plaza**, with a large number of condominium units. The central lobby of the Plaza is three stories high and lighted with industrial-style mercury vapor lights. Its ceiling consists of painted ductwork and steel roof tresses. An enclosed hot tub and vending machines are found on the lower floor of the lobby.

Each condominium is well equipped. The kitchens have most of the appliances one could ever use including a refrigerators with ice makers, microwave ovens, convection ovens, dishwashers, disposals, toasters, and coffee makers. Dining areas comfortably seat six. All units have fireplaces and cable TVs with HBO.

Bedrooms at the Plaza tend to be spartan and appointed with functional, natural finish furniture. Master bedroom contain queen-size beds, and the second bedrooms have twin beds. All condominiums contain central humidifying systems, very welcome in the dry mountain climate.

During the 1993-94 ski season, condos at the Plaza rent from a low of $122 per night to a high of $525 per night during Christmas holiday.

The Crested Butte Club is a Victorian hotel and spa located across the street from The Slogar Restaurant in downtown Crested Butte. Newly renovated and very quaint, it offers only seven suites furnished in period pieces, but furnishes all the modern conveniences travelers have grown accustomed to such as CATV, room service, wet bar, and amenities packages. Each room features a uniquely beautiful copper and brass bathtub different from other Victorian tubs. They must be seen to be appreciated. In addition to great rooms and service, the Club has restored the original structure's bar, built by the valley's Croatian coal miners. The original Croatian Hall is on the Register of Historic Landmarks. A large screen TV and piano player promise great après ski in **The Club Pub**. The back bar is the oldest in Gunnison County.

For non-residents, the Club is convenient to the free shuttle bus stop. Weekly, monthly, and annual memberships are available. The Club offers an indoor swimming pool, Jacuzzi, free weights, Universal Gym, Life Cycles, a full range of weight machines, sauna and steam rooms. A special floor for aerobics classes has been installed, and high and low impact aerobics classes are offered: one class at 8 a.m. and one at 5:30. One word of caution for smokers: the entire club is non-smoking. Smokers should not attempt to book rooms unless they are prepared to not smoke in the rooms. Violators of this policy will be billed for the cleaning and redecorating costs necessitated by their habit. Prices during the regular 1993-1994 ski season will range from $125 to $165 per night. For additional information telephone (303) 349-6655.

Restaurants

As at most Colorado resorts, the food quality and service presentation at Crested Butte is excellent. One unique restaurant located in the town of Crested Butte is **The Slogar**. The Slogar is situated in an historic building and decorated in Victorian style. The menu is served family-style and there are only two choices of entrées: skillet-fried chicken or steak. Entrées are complemented with a sweet and sour coleslaw taken from a Pennsylvania Dutch recipe. Mashed potatoes, gravy, and fresh baking powder biscuits with honey butter and strawberry preserves make dining at The Slogar a memorable event. Children's portions are available, as is full bar service. Reservations are recommended. Open 5:00 P.M. to 9:00 P.M. only. (303)349-5765.

The Artichoke at Mt. Crested Butte is a typical fern bar à la California. Just off the slopes in the Treasury Center, next to the Grand Butte Hotel, it is a natural luncheon spot for hungry skiers. The lunch menu at the Artichoke is extensive but leans toward burgers, sandwiches, salads, and soups. Typical selections include "Godfather," "Good Ol'Boy," "Guac," and "ABC" burgers. The staff also prepares chicken chimichangas, artichoke quiche, steamed artichoke, Dagwood sandwiches, bratwurst, taco salads, and many other items. With its moderately priced lunches, the Artichoke is an inexpensive place in which to celebrate great snow, a terrific run, or the fantastic sunshine. In the evenings the

Artichoke modifies its menu to more traditional fare including prime rib, teriyaki, steaks, seafood such as lobster and shrimp. Dinner prices are moderate, generally in the area of $12 to $20 per entrée.

On the more elegant side, try **Giovanni's** located on the lower level of the Grande Butte Hotel. The interior is slick, modern, and crisp. The grey wool carpeting, terra cotta, and brown marble details are accented by black lacquer seating and alabaster walls.

The Grand Cafe specializes in Continental dishes such as shrimp sauté basil, veal citron, breast of chicken en croute and numerous other excellent dishes. Items are moderately priced; reservations are suggested, telephone (303)349-7561.

At the end of Elk Avenue, **Timberline Restaurant** is located inside a 100+ year-old building. Its ancient steam-covered windows glisten. Inside, bare-bulb light fixtures cast interesting shadows on the old clapboard interior. Elegant table settings of mauve tablecloths, bright, delicate floral arrangements, and sparkling silverware provide a gracious counterpoint to the rustic walls.

Timberline's menu is as eclectic as its architecture and interior design. Several vastly different selections are listed on the daily menu. Appetizers may include roasted garlic crepes (spinach, mushrooms, walnuts, and feta cheese served with a lemon caper sauce), roast duck on angel hair pasta (shallots, tomatoes, and roast duckling in a rich brown sauce), or goat cheese Napoleon (layers of eggplant, sun-dried tomatoes, goat cheese and puff pastry).

Entrées are typically served with "harvest" selections like zucchini, butternut, and other squashes. Daily specials are augmented with hearty, tasty staples such as galantine of turkey with cracked pepper and fresh thyme or roast pork loin with rosemary and honey. The seafood cassoulet with saffron and orange is memorable, as is the blackened mahi-mahi served on cucumber noodles.

Prices are moderate and reservations are suggested. There are two seatings per night, one at 6:30 P.M. and another at 8:30 P.M. On Saturdays and Sundays, brunch is served from 8:00 A.M. to 1:00 P.M. For reservations telephone (303)349-9831.

Many other fine restaurants and bars are found in the historical district of Crested Butte. Whether you dine at the **Wooden Nickel** (a local hangout), **Soupcon**, **Le Bosquet**, or **The Bakery Cafe**, your meal will be well prepared and your service attentive. You will want to return to Crested Butte time and time again.

Activities

Activities at Crested Butte are extensive. There are National Standard Races (NASTAR) off the T-Bar and a Marlboro course with a coin-operated self-timer. Sleighride dinners, ice fishing, live theater, movies, snowmobiling, indoor tennis, balloon rides, nightclubs, and dancing are all available to visitors.

One of the finest activities available anywhere is **Irwin Lodge's** snowcat skiing. The Lodge is situated among tall pines high in Gunnison National Forest. Starting from its 12,500 ft. (3,811 meters) ridges, alpine and Nordic skiers of all ability levels can learn to master the abundant powder that falls on this 2,400-acre paradise. Runs from the ridges are typically two miles (3.2 km) in length and 2,000 vertical feet (500+ meters).

The lodge, decorated in the style of the roaring 1890s, contains 25 upstairs guest rooms. Resembling a South Pacific long house, it is 60 feet X 160 feet. The main floor has a common dining and lounge area. All electricity at the Lodge is created by generator. Television programs are provided by video tapes run on a VCR. At 12:00 midnight, it's lights-out; if it is necessary to get out of bed or to read, it must be done with a flashlight!

Irwin Lodge's room rates during the 1993-94 ski season are between $230 and $280 per day, per person, including all meals and activities.

Since 1988-89, activities offered at the Lodge have increased. Formerly only guided snowcat skiing was available. Now, however, guests have a choice of many activities including snowmobiling, cross-country skiing, telemark skiing, alpine skiing, snow shoeing, and ice fishing.

This year, Irwin Lodge will not be participating in the Free Lift Ticket period by providing a shuttle into town every day. They will only be open to snowmobile tours until Dec. 19, when, they hope, there will be plenty of snow for snowcat tours and skiing.

Irwin Lodge has matured from its humble beginnings into a rather incredible resort. Today the Lodge can access over 2,400 acres with six snowcats carrying from 9 to 20 passengers each, qualifying it as the largest snowcat operation in North America (possibly the world). For those persons who would like to try snowcat skiing but hesitate because they worry that they or their spouse might not be able to ski deep powder, Irwin Lodge maintains a limited area of groomed intermediate and beginner trails All things considered, Irwin Lodge offers an unusual ski experience for those bold enough to stray from the more rigid confines of a contemporary (if exceptional) ski resort.

Just getting to Irwin Lodge can be exciting. Transportation from the trail head to the lodge is via snowmobile or snowcat; the trip takes 35 minutes to 1.5 hours depending on the mode of transportation. The scenery is breathtaking. The pristine beauty of the Rocky Mountains and its forests and frozen streams provides a memory not easily forgotten. One word of caution: If snow conditions are poor, be forewarned that you will have a very quiet few days at Irwin Lodge. Other activities include, 2 8-foot hot tubs, large screen TV/movies, pool table, darts, library and a huge fireplace for quiet contemplation. This truly is getting away from it all. The lodge provides buffet breakfast and lunch and an eclectic candlelight evening meal. A full service bar is on the premises. There is nothing to occupy the time if one cannot ski. For additional information, telephone (303) 349-5308 or 1(800)2-IRWIN-2.

Services

A full complement of sporting goods stores, apparel stores, pharmacies, grocery stores, liquor stores, furniture stores, bath stores, and specialty stores is within the immediate town of Crested Butte. In addition, there are antique stores, massage services, art galleries, bakeries, beauty shops, bookstores, florists, movies, a theater, banks, churches, alterations, dry cleaning, optical shops, and baby-sitting services.

Village Map

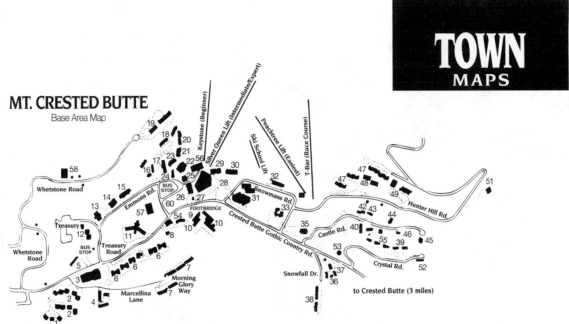

MT. CRESTED BUTTE
Base Area Map

TOWN MAPS

Keystone (Beginner)
Silver Queen Lift (Intermediate/Expert)
Ski School Lift
Peachtree Lift (Easiest)
T-Bar (Race Course)
Whetstone Road
Emmons Rd.
BUS STOP
FOOTBRIDGE
Treasury
Treasury Road
BUS STOP
Whetstone Road
Marcellina Lane
Morning Glory Way
Snowmass Rd.
Crested Butte Gothic Country Rd
Castle Rd.
Hunter Hill Rd.
Crystal Rd.
Snowfall Dr.
to Crested Butte (3 miles)

1 - Ski Jump Condominiums
2 - Outrun Condominiums
3 - Three Seasons Condominiums
4 - Mountain Sunrise Condominiums
5 - Elk Ridge III Condominiums
6 - Chateaux Condominiums
7 - Eagle's Nest Condominiums
9 - Alpine Condominiums
10 - Snowcrest Condominiums
11 - Manor Lodge, Casey's Restaurant
12 - Ponderosa Condominiums
13 - Nordic Inn
14 - Evergreen Condominiums
    Crested Butte Sports
15 - Redstone Condominiums
16 - Crested Mtn. North Condominiums
17 - Crested Butte Lodge
    Wong's Chinese Restaurant
18 - The Buttes Condominiums

19 - Columbine Condominiums
20 - Crested Mtn. Condominiums
21 - The Mall at Crested Mountain
    Tin Cup Restaurant
22 - **SKI AREA CENTRAL**
    Guest Services, Gothic Cafeteria,
    Rafters, Info Desk, Ski School, Rental,
    Lift Tickets
23 - Crested Mtn. Village Conference Center
    Penthouse Condominiums, The Saloon
24 - Gene Taylor's Sporting Goods
25 - The Avalanche Restaurant,
    Butte and Company Ski and Dry Goods
26 - Emmons Building, Village Center Rentals
27 - Bakery at Mt. Crested Butte
28 - Grande Butte Hotel - Roaring Elk Rest-
    aurant, The Dugout Sports Bar & Grill,
    Giovanni's Grande Cafe, CBMR Ski
    Rental

29 - Axtel Building
30 - Whetstone Building, Buttetopia
31 - The Plaza,
    Rocky Mountain Steaks Restaurant
32 - Gateway Condominiums
33 - Woodcreek Condominiums
35 - Mountain Edge Condominiums
36 - Elk Ridge II Condominiums
37 - Crest House Condominiums
38 - Snowfall Point Condominiums
39 - Chadlington House
40 - West Elk Townhouses
42 - Crystal View Condominiums
43 - Elk Ridge I Condominiums
44 - Solar Sixplex
45 - Snow Castle Condominiums
46 - Edelweiss Condominiums
47 - San Moritz Condominiums
48 - Paradise Condominiums

49 - Timberline Condominiums
51 - Overlook Condominiums
52 - Hunter Hill Townhouses
53 - Shibumi Village
54 - The Gardens
    C.B. Medical Clinic
55 - Castle Ridge Condominiums
56 - **TREASURY CENTER**
    Artichoke Restaurant & Bar, Atrium
    Cafe, Eflin Sports, Flatiron Sports,
    Christy Sports, Retail Shops
57 - ***NEW IN 1993** - The Mountainlair Hotel
58 - Shenandoah Buttes

HISTORIC CRESTED BUTTE
Town Map

to Mt.Crested Butte
(3 miles)
GOTHIC (To Mt. Crested Butte)
GOTHIC
MAROON
ELK AVE.
SOPRIS
WHITEROCK
BELLEVIEW
FIRST ST.
SECOND ST.
THIRD ST.
FOURTH ST.
FIFTH ST.
HIGHWAY 135
TOTEM POLE PARK
Bus Stop
Bus Stop
Parking
Parking
TOWN PARK
To Kebler Pass
to Gunnison

1 - Elk Mountain Lodge
2 - Soupçon
3 - Kochevar's Bar, Karolina's Kitchen
4 - Forest Queen Hotel & Restaurant
5 - Penelope's Restaurant
6 - Slogar Restaurant & Bar
7 - Le Bosquet Restaurant
9 - Post Office
10 - Oscar's Bar & Cafe
11 - Bacchanale Restaurant
12 - Wooden Nickel Bar & Restaurant
13 - Talk of the Town
14 - Gourmet Noodle Restaurant
15 - Town Hall
16 - Paradise Cafe
17 - The Bakery Cafe
18 - Donita's Cantina
19 - Angello's Pizza & Deli
20 - Whiterock Lodge,
    Copper Mine Restaurant
21 - C. B. State Bank
22 - True Value
    Crested Butte Drug Store
23 - McDell's Market
24 - Old Town Inn

25 - C.B. Marketplace
26 - Christina Guesthaus
27 - Purple Mountain Lodge
29 - Claim Jumper Lodge
30 - Tudor Rose
31 - Crested Butte Club
    Crested Butte Nordic Center
32 - Rocky Mountain Rentals
33 - Powerhouse Bar Y Grill
36 - Timberline Restaurant
38 - The Alpineer
39 - Cook Works
40 - Shopping Mall
41 - Idle Spur
42 - Shopping Mall
43 - Gothic Inn
44 - Jimmy's Fish & Grill
45 - Crystal Inn
46 - Crested Beauty
47 - Alpine Lace Bed & Breakfast
48 - Elizabeth Anne
49 - Butte Bagels Feed Shack
50 - Rocky Mountain Chocolate
    Factory

FOR RESERVATIONS & INFORMATION CALL:
CRESTED BUTTE VACATIONS 1·800·544·8448

Grand Targhee powder is a must-see it to believe it experience; close to 500 inches of light powder fall on its mountain every year. Photo provided by Grand Targhee resort.

JACKSON HOLE/GRAND TARGHEE

Post Office Box 290
Teton Village, WY. 83025

(800) 443-6931 Reservations
(307) 733-2292 Information
(307) 733-2291 Snow Report

New For 1993-94

No major changes will take place on the mountain at Jackson Hole this year, but big changes could be in the offing. Last year the area was purchased by two long-time Wyoming residents, John L. Kemmerer III and John Resor. The new owners say they have spent the year initiating master plans for the mountain and the base areas. They have a new slogan for advertising -- "Dedicated to Preserving the Old West" and we all look forward to seeing whether this company can maintain the "wild" in Jackson Hole and enhance quality of service and facilities on the mountain without hurting that. Good luck!

Readers of **SKI** magazine this year said Grand Targhee's grooming is tied for first place with Alta, Utah. It also rated number 5 in the top 10 ski areas for value: where you get the most for your money. With an average of 500 inches of wonderful powder per year, and lift tickets of $29 per day, and half-day lessons for children for $14, this area tucked away in the Grand Tetons is a great deal! The small base area also won a design award from Snow Country in 1991. If you visit Jackson Hole, Grand Targhee beckons.

How To Get There

It once was difficult to reach Jackson Hole, but not anymore! Thirteen flights land daily at Jackson Hole Airport, including a direct flight during the winter from Chicago on American Airlines. American also flies daily year-round from Salt Lake City. Delta Airlines and SkyWest offer daily non-stop service Salt Lake City, and Continental Express flies daily into Jackson from Denver. United Express provides daily commuter service through Denver.

The Jackson Airport is located 22 miles from Teton Village, which is at the base of the Jackson Hole Ski Area. Flying into Jackson can be one of the most beautiful, scenic flights available anywhere in the world. The airport is situated in a long north-south valley at the foot of the Tetons and is slightly south of Yellowstone National Park. On a clear day it is easy to see Yellowstone, the Tetons, Jackson Hole, and the town of Jackson from the landing or departing aircraft. Because the airport is located in a very long and broad valley, it is not a difficult airport in which to land even during snowstorms. The reliability of the air service is quite good.

Transportation either to Jackson Hole at Teton Village, to accommodations in town, or to the Jackson Hole Racquet Club is convenient via shuttle bus service. Shuttles meet every inbound and outbound flight. Taxi service and limousine charters are also available at the airport.

Although a car is not a necessity, it is a convenience at Jackson Hole. START Bus (Southern Teton Area Rapid Transit) provides shuttle service between Teton Village and Jackson ten to fifteen times each day between the hours of 7:00 A.M. and 12:00 A.M. National chains and local car rental agencies are located at the airport. It is also possible to rent cars from Budget or Nez Perce, both located in Teton Village. Budget also has an office in Jackson, as do Rent-A-Wreck and Teton Motors.

Traveling by car to Jackson is easy. Take I-80 to the Rock Springs interchange at Highway 191; turn north until Jackson. Once in town, it is only twelve miles to Teton Village on Highway 390. Approaching Jackson from the West on I-80, take the first exit after Evanston, Wyoming, onto Highway 189 and follow it until it becomes Highway 191 and thence into Jackson. There are no major mountain passes to climb, so weather is rarely a factor.

Grand Targhee is located 42 road miles west of Teton Village and is reached via Teton Pass. This is a short 45-minute to one hour drive in clear weather. However, Teton Pass can be treacherous during snow storms. Grand Targhee Resort runs bus service between Targhee, Jackson, and Teton Village. The 1993-94 charge for the combined bus service and lift ticket is $39. Tickets may be purchased at any shuttle stop the evening before departure. If Targhee skiers want to experience remarkable powder skiing, they should reserve space on the snowcat by telephoning (800) 443-8146 in advance. Snowcats transport only 10 persons each day, so reservations are important!

Mountain Information

Jackson Hole is located in Bridger-Teton National Forest, one of the most rugged and striking ranges in America. The ski area is among the largest in North America, encompassing over 2,500 acres of skiable terrain. During its last survey, Snow Country magazine reports that its readers rated Jackson Hole first in the Northern Rockies for its fantastic skiing terrain, and second in views.

Jackson Hole has had a reputation among avid skiers as a difficult mountain with some of the best and most challenging expert runs in the world. This reputation is justified. But, on the other hand, it also has some of the best intermediate and beginner runs available anywhere. Over the years the management of Jackson Hole recognized the need to provide substantial intermediate and beginner runs in order to compete with other American resorts. To this end, they have spent countless millions on development of the resort's skiable terrain. The first problem management had to overcome was the simple fact that over 90 inches (229 cm) of snow were required before intermediate slopes could be groomed. Management attacked this problem from two directions: first, it began a program of dynamiting the large rocks which obstructed the runs and were responsible for the high quantity of snow needed. Second, it installed snowmaking equipment. These improvements have now made it possible to groom the intermediate trails with only 60 inches (152 cm) of snow accumulation.

Two mountains comprise Jackson Hole at Teton Village. The lower mountain where all the beginner and a majority of the intermediate runs are located is called Après Vous. Adjacent to Après Vous is Rendezvous Mountain. Rendezvous is the mountain responsible for Jackson Hole's reputation of being difficult.

This is a big mountain. The base elevation is 6,311 feet (1,924 meters) and the elevation at the summit of Rendezvous is 10,450 feet (3,185 meters). A vertical drop of 4,139 feet (1,262 meters) offers skiers the most vertical feet of skiing of any major United States ski resort.

The mountains consist of 10 percent Beginner trails, 40 percent Intermediate trails, and 25 percent Expert trails. All the area within the boundaries of the resort is considered open for recreational skiing. A look at the trail map shows lines which indicate runs, but in fact the runs are mostly open areas with numerous ways down. For example, trails numbered 3 through 7 are referred to as the "Hobacks," and it would appear there were only five ways down. In fact, there are as many ways down as there are skiers. A person could spend several days just skiing these runs and not ski down the same way twice.

It is imperative that one pay attention to the signs when skiing at Jackson Hole. This mountain is so big it is easy not only to become lost, but also to find oneself in an area that could be dangerous. Always pay attention to signs that alert you to cliffs. These signs are not exaggerating; the cliffs are real and are **not** skiable! There are many trails identified with signs that are not on the trail map. Do not ski any of these runs unless in the company of a guide or unless you are a very accomplished skier. If the skier wants to get an idea of the kind of runs not shown on the trail map without actually skiing one of them, he should ride the Upper Sublette Ridge Quad Chairlift. On the left just before the chair arrives at the bull wheel, the skier can see Corbet's Couloir and the Alta Chutes. These are avalanche chutes that go straight down and are only about 400 cm wide. In other words, they are about twice as wide as most skis are long. Persons skiing these short runs usually build up a speed close to 60 miles per hour. The Couloir used to contain a large rock just at the chute's exit. Fortunately it was removed a few years ago because its position was considered extremely dangerous.

The mountain is so vast that on flat light days it is possible to experience vertigo even on the catwalks. There is so much vertical that several weather systems frequently coexist. It is not unusual for the temperature on Rendezvous to be 10° or even 20° warmer than temperatures in the valley. Jackson frequently undergoes weather inversions, and temperature differential is a rather common phenomeon.

Both mountains are serviced by a modern lift system that includes

1 Aerial Tram
1 Quad Chairlift
1 Triple Chairlift
5 Double Chairlifts
1 High-Speed Poma Lift

Although every type of imaginable ski terrain is available, Jackson Hole is most noted for its large bowls. There are many of them, and all offer exceptional skiing. Beginning at the top of Rendezvous Peak where the 63-passenger aerial tram stops is Rendezvous Bowl, a broad, wide open, steep bowl. Down the center of this bowl are black sticks with large black circles mounted on top. These are placed to aid skiers who might otherwise have difficulty skiing down during flat light or during snowstorms. Looking downhill from the top, a few gladed runs are visible to the left. These are the only areas of Rendezvous Bowl that develop moguls. Although the bowl is never groomed, bumps do not become very large because of the abundant snowfall.

After skiing Rendezvous Bowl, a skier can elect to continue down via Cheyenne Bowl or Larami Bowl; both are steep and exciting to ski. From the bottom of either of these bowls, one can continue to ski the upper mountain or return to the base via any of the Hobacks. The only problem with taking the Hobacks down is that this route requires another ride up the aerial tram to the top.

During the summer of 1989, Jackson Hole replaced its aging gondola cars with new ones. These new cars still hold the same number of skiers, but have been enlarged by twenty square feet.

The longest beginner run is Eagle's Rest at 2,300 feet, with only a 300 foot vertical drop. The longest intermediate run is Gros Ventre. It is 4 miles long. The longest expert run is Rendezvous Bowl at a length of 4,000 feet with a 1,630 foot rise.

Jackson Hole's annual snowfall is 384 inches.

Dec.   65 "
Jan.   67 "
Feb.   62 "
Mar.   55 "
Apr.   13 "

The average monthly temperatures at mid-mountain are

	Low		High	
Dec.	3°	-16° C	17°	-8° C
Jan.	7°	-14° C	25°	-4° C
Feb.	19°	- 7° C	31°	0° C
Mar.	20°	- 6° C	37°	3° C

The sheer magnitude of the mountain is emphasized by the "Go for the Gold" program instituted by Jackson Hole in 1978. Visitors are encouraged to keep track of the quantity of vertical feet skied each day. In fact, they are given a scorecard. After each run or at the end of the day, skiers enter the names of the runs skied and total the vertical feet. Upon achieving 300 thousand vertical feet, they are awarded a bronze Jackson Hole belt buckle. After reaching 500 thousand, they are given a silver buckle, and after reaching the ultimate one million vertical feet, they are awarded a 14 kt. gold buckle.

Since 1978, the resort has awarded in excess of 1,191 bronze, 627 silver, and 236 gold belt buckles. Most skiers will require up to ten years of skiing to achieve the vaulted status of a gold buckle, but there are exceptions. One eighty-two-year-old skier did it in two years, and an eight-year-old girl totaled 790 thousand vertical feet in only two years. Approximately 30,000 skiers have participated in the program.

The "Go for the Gold" program is an honorary system, but individual achievements must be validated by Jackson Hole's Public Relations Department. Skiers who attain goals of 100 thousand and 150 thousand feet in one week will be awarded achievement medals. A goal of 100 thousand vertical feet in a one-week period is not out of reach for most people when one considers that the mountain is nearly five thousand feet in length. Twenty runs spanning the length of the mountain or forty runs for just half its length will enable the skier to qualify for an achievement medal.

Grand Targhee Mountain Information
1-800-443-8146

Grand Targhee is located on the western side of the Grand Tetons. In summer a trail connects Jackson Hole with Targhee, but in the winter it becomes impassable so skiers must commute between the two areas via Teton Pass.

Vistas from the top of Grand Targhee are truly spectacular. The massive Tetons are so close they overpower mere mortals. One imagines oneself skiing in the French Alps or the rugged Canadian Rockies. In fact, skiing conditions at Grand Targhee are probably the best in the world due to Targhee's consistent weather. The resort annually receives over 500 inches (1,250 cm) of light, fluffy powder, 100 inches (250 cm) more than does Jackson Hole. The reason for this abundant snow is that winter storms first drop the majority of their snow on the western slopes, leaving Jackson with whatever is left in the storm. This is very similar to Park City's situation vis à vis Snowbird.

Grand Targhee consists of 3000 acres (1,200 ha), approximately half of which are served by four lifts and half by snowcat only. Needless to say, snowcat skiing is incomparable because there are never more than 20 persons skiing each day and snowfalls are almost a daily occurrence. There is simply never a shortage of fresh powder. The lift-serviced area is the best place in North America to learn to powder ski. The runs are long (over 2,200 vertical feet) and varying in difficulty. A perusal of the trail map indicates numerous expert runs (black diamonds). In reality, however, these do not require the same degree of skiing ability similarly designated runs at Jackson Hole require. These black diamonds are more similar to those found at Vail or Snowmass. Targhee offers such a nice transition between intermediate and expert terrain that skiers can naturally, and usually without much difficulty, learn to ski deep, almost bottomless powder in only a few days. The instructors at Targhee are well versed in teaching packed-powder and hard-pack proficient skiers the finesse they need to master powder.

On those rare days when the sun is brightly shining and the powder is getting a little shredded, adventuresome skiers can always find fresh, untracked powder on North Boundary. Most skiers who think they are at the northern most extreme of Targhee are actually only at Lost Squaw. To find North Boundary, follow the ropes separating the resort from the out-of-bounds. When the rope ends and the only way is down, you are at North Boundary. The run is lightly gladed its entire length. This is typical of all the runs at Targhee, since most are wide, open meadows on top which gradually descend into sparsely treed runs. This is perfect for the weather conditions Targhee often experiences because skiers are thus not subjected to bad light conditions without any contrast. In fact, when the light is bad at Jackson Hole, it may be a perfect day to visit Targhee.

All the intermediate-designated runs at Targhee are groomed every evening. If one is hesitant about skiing powder, there is always a groomed run only a few yards away on which to regain confidence. The steepest runs at Targhee are found just off of Sitting Bull and are named Good Medicine, the Ugly, and Bad Medicine. Bad Medicine is the steepest; with its deep powder, it skis more like an intermediate run. These runs can only truly be considered "expert" after a one or two-day snow drought when they are "bumped out."

Peaked Mountain, the Grand Targhee area served by snowcat is very unusual in that its terrain is the most perfectly suited for this type of skiing found anywhere. There are numerous open glades dotted with small stands of pine, a perfect setting for learning how to ski powder without the added psychological impediment of worrying about dodging trees. Entire 2,800 vertical foot runs can be made one after the other, up to 10 or 12 times daily. For those experienced deep-powder skiers seeking a little more thrill, tight tree skiing is available. It is advisable, however, to form a group of like-minded skiers since the guides will defer to the less skilled and insist on open glade skiing if a wide diversity of skiing ability exists. For a half-day snowcat powder lesson for intermediates, the price is $105and includes a snack. For Grand Targhee lodging guests, a full day of snowcat skiing with hearty lunch, snacks and beverages will cost $135. For those not staying at the resort the cost is $155. As their flyer for Peaked Peak warns, "Bring your snorkel!"

Jackson Hole Lift Ticket Prices (1993-94)

Because the mountain is so rugged, it requires more snow than many resorts in order to be skiable. Therefore, Jackson Hole usually does not open until early December. There is not a "high" or a "low" or a "value" season here. There is only "ski season!" While in the past, Jackson Hole only sold single ride tickets for its tram, this year the resort is offering skiers the option of purchasing single rides for $2 with a chairlift ticket, or limitless tram rides for an additional $4 charge for your lift ticket. The ski area management believes that by charging an additional fee for the tram, it has successfully reduced waiting time for tram rides. There are enough other lifts at Jackson Hole so that it is not necessary for one to ride the tram more than once or twice daily. Also, because all runs served by the tram are expert, the additional charge may discourage some intermediate skiers from skiing above their ability level.

$ 39	Daily Adult	$ 43	all lifts, including tram
$ 30	Afternoon Adult	$ 33	all lifts, including tram
$152	Adult, 4-Day	$168	all lifts, including tram
$185	Adult, 5-Day	$205	all lifts, including tram

14 Years & Under/65 Years and Over:

$19	1-Day	$ 22	all lifts, including tram
$15	Afternoon	$ 17	all lifts, including tram
$74	4-Day	$ 86	all lifts, including tram
$90	5-Day	$105	all lifts, including tram

Grand Targhee Lift Ticket Prices (1993-94)

$29	Adult Full-Day
$19	Adult Half-Day
$15	Child, 6 to 12 years
$15	Senior Citizen, Over 65
Free	Senior citizen, over 70
Free	Children 5 and under

Jackson Hole Hours of Operation

All lifts open at 9:00 A.M. The aerial tram's last departure is at 3:20 P.M. The Rendezvous Poma closes at 3:30 P.M. The Crystal Springs, Thunder, and Upper Sublette Ridge chairlifts' last departures are at 3:40 P.M., while the Casper chairlift's is at 3:50 P.M. All remaining chairlifts close at 4:00 P.M. These different closing times are necessary in order for the ski patrol to "sweep" the mountain. Closing times basically follow the sweep.

Grand Targhee Hours of Operation

9:30 A.M.— 4:00 P.M.

Lift Ticket Purchase Locations

Lift tickets may be purchased at the base of the aerial tram station in the center of Teton Village.

Tickets for Snow King Ski Resort in the town of Jackson are also available at the tram station.

How to Avoid Crowds

With one of the lowest ratio of skiers to available terrain found at any U.S. resort, crowds rarely exist. Even during the Christmas holidays when there is not an extra room to be had, there are few crowds. If crowding does exist, it is only at the aerial tram station. However, even here the wait usually never exceeds one tram departure (approximately 20 minutes).

Ski School

The Jackson Hole Ski School offers numerous programs. A popular choice is the three half-day package. The skier receives a lesson each morning with the same instructor and then is able to practice the newly-acquired skills in the afternoon while becoming familiar with the mountain. These classes are available Monday through Wednesday, or Wednesday through Friday at 9:45 A.M for $75. Lesson and rental packages will cost $111.

Students who want a more comprehensive program can elect to go into the full five-day package program or can upgrade at any time from the half-day to the full-day program. The full-day is from 9:30 to 3 and costs $45. A lesson and rental package will cost $57. However, in order to upgrade, six or more students of the same class must upgrade as well.

For those skiers who do not need lessons, Jackson Hole offers its Mountain Experience at 8:20 A.M. for $65. These classes emphasize skiing powder, skiing steep terrain, and skiing runs not indicated on the trail map. This is a great way for skiers to learn their way around the mountain without the expense of a private instructor.

The highest level of skier education is available at Jackson Hole. The Ski Meisters program is a 4-day, 3-hour per day package including intensive mogul, powder, and racing techniques. A video evaluation is provided. Class size is limited to 2 to 6 students, all of whom must pass a qualifying ski-off to enter the class. Meet at 8:30 a.m. in front of the Ski School Chalet.

Private lessons are also available, including skiing with Jackson's ski school director, Pepi Stiegler. In addition, racing clinics and guided Alpine ski trips are offered. 1991-92 rates are

$ 75	Adult, 3 Half-Day (2 hours per morning)
$150	Ski Meisters
$ 65	Mountain Experience
$ 35	Half-day group lesson
$ 45	Full-Day group lesson
$ 55	Private 1 hour, (1 Student)
$250	Private All-Day, (1 Student)
$310	Private All-Day, (2-3 Students)

SKIWEE CHILDREN (6-13)

$ 90	3 Full-Day
$138	3 Full Days With Lunch
$ 35	1 Full-Day
$120	1 Half-Day, Private Lesson

Lunch and child care will cost and additional $14.

Rough Riders group lessons are available for children ages 3 to 5. Private lessons are $35 per hour. A full day of lessons with child care from 8 a.m. to 5 p.m. with 2-hour lessons at 9:45 a.m. and 1:45 p.m. is $58. Just the lessons will cost $35. Lunch can be added for $14.

Grand Targhee Ski School

$6	Snowplay group lesson, 4 years and younger

$14   Powder Busters, 5-7 years, half day
$16   Targhee Tigers, 8-12 years
$18   Adult group lesson
$42   One-hour private lesson, $15 each additional person
$175   All-Day private lesson
$30   One-hour child's private lesson

Equipment Rental

There are three rental and repair shops in Teton Village. Additional shops are available in the town of Jackson at slightly lower rates, no doubt. Some 1993-94 prices were not available at press time.

Jackson Hole Ski Corporation owns and operates the **Jackson Hole Ski Shop** which only rents Kastle skis. During the 1993-94 season the shop offers three types of rental packages. The first, called the Recreational Package includes skis, boots and poles for $14 a day for 3 days, $13 for 4 to 7 days, and $12 for more than 7 days. Store also offers a High Performance Package for $19 a day for the first 3 days, $16 a day for 3 to 7 days, and $15 days for more than 7 days. The Demo package will cost $29 per day, $24 for more than 4 days, and $24 for more than 7 days.

Snowboards can be rented with boots for $22 a day, $16 for the half-day. With lessons, a snowboard will cost $45. The board alone costs $14.

Located on the lower level of the **Crystal Springs Inn** in the heart of the Teton Village, **Teton Village Sports** offers recreational skis during the 1993-94 ski season for $13 per day, performance packages at $18.50 per day, demo skis for $22 for Rossignol, K2 or Salomon, and $25 for Volkl. A snowboard can be rented for $23. A discount is available for rentals exceeding four or more days. To reserve skis in advance, telephone (307) 733-2181.

Ski Tuning and Repair

Tuning and repair services are available at all ski rental shops and sporting goods stores.

Skis must be warm before waxing. It is a good idea to drop your skis off at the end of the day and pick them up the next morning. The following prices will be charged at Teton Village Sports in 1993-1994:

$ 4   Hot Wax
$25   Minor Tune-up
$30   Major Tune-up
$20   Bindings Mount with Torque Test

On-Mountain Dining

A mountain restaurant is located in Casper Bowl at the top of the Crystal Springs double chairlift and at the bottom of the Casper Bowl triple chairlift. This two-story nine thousand square foot facility is nicely furnished with wooden tables and chairs. Food is served cafeteria-style, and the menu includes hamburgers, hot dogs, soups, french fries, and the like. Beer and wine is available at a separate service window around the corner from the food service.

A small snack bar is located inside the warming hut located at the top of Rendezvous Peak.

At Grand Targhee, as mentioned at the beginning of this chapter, the on-mountain dining earned rave reviews from visitors last year. Skadi's, a restaurant in the base complex, now not only provides gourmet lunches for snowcat skiers, but will sell picnic lunches also.

Child Care

Child care is provided by the Jackson Hole **Cowboy Kids Ranch**. Infant care for ages two months through 18 months is available on an hourly or weekly basis. To make reservations for children, telephone (307) 739-2691 and ask for the nursery. Parents are expected to provide diapers and formula for their children. The 1993-94 rates are $35 per half day and $50 per day.

Child care without skiing for children one and a half through 5 years of age is available during 1993-94 at the same rate as infant care.   Child care for this group includes lunch and snacks.

Child care at the base of Grand Targhee takes place at the **Kids' Club**. Director Melissa Dicken says that the club is physically separated into two area: one for the 2 month-olds to 3-year-olds, and one for the 3- to 9-year-olds. For infants, the center has a 1:3 ration for babies to caretakers. Children three-years-old and up can take half-day lessons with a group; 2-year-olds may take private lessons.

As at other resorts, another option is for snow play, if your children do not want to ski. They can try out little toy skis which hook on street boots, and enjoy the outdoors with several supervised activities, including painting the snow with colored water. Inside, the 2- to- 9-year-olds are offered a variety of arts and crafts. Call 1-800-443-8146 to make reservations, or call Ms. Dicken, who is very willing to describe her program to you.

Medical Facilities

For ski injuries, the ski patrol will render only emergency service. The patrol will administer trauma treatment, stabilize broken bones, and transport injured skiers downhill.

Jackson Hole at Teton Village has a very complete clinic. Located adjacent to the main parking lot and next to the Mangy Moose Saloon, the clinic treats most ski-related injuries. If an emergency or illness exceeds the clinic's capabilities, patients will be transferred to St. John Hospital in the town of Jackson, only twelve miles away.

Cross-Country Skiing

Cross-country skiing at Jackson Hole is nothing short of spectacular. Miles of double-tracked trails lead off in two directions from the trail head in Teton Village. The **Jackson Hole Nordic Center** in Teton Village is the hub of cross-country activity. From this convenient starting point,you can enter 22 groomed trails.

Trail passes for all day in 1993-94 are $7 for adults and $3.50 for children aged 6 through 14. Children under 6 ski for free. Half-day lessons during the 1993-94 season are $32 for adults and $16 for children and seniors. Private lessons are $50 per hour.

The staff at the Center offers telemark clinics, cross-country track clinics, alpine touring, and a terrific tour of Grand Teton National Park and Teton Pass. The center also has an excellent selection of rental equipment.

At **Grand Targhee** 10 km. of groomed track are available, as well as guided tours of the backcountry. Lesson rates are $18 for a group which meets at 10:30; and $40 per hour for a private lesson at your convenience. Trail pass rates are $6/day for adults, and $3/day for seniors or children. Call Targhee Nordic at 1-800-443-8146, ext. 1352 for information.

Accommodations

Lodging is located either in Teton Village, Jackson Hole Racquet Club Resort, or in the town of Jackson. Hotels in town are twelve miles from the resort. There is daily shuttle service to and from Teton Village. The Racquet Club is approximately two miles from Teton Village, and it is also on the shuttle's route.

Hotels

The Best Western Inn at Jackson Hole is located on the slopes of Teton Village. All rooms recently were renovated. Ski lockers are located by the pool or on the main floor. The Inn has a small, heated swimming pool, 3 jacuzzis and a sauna. Bar service is available in the pool area. Cable TV is available in every room. The ice machine is located in its own room outside on the main floor. Double occupancy for a room with two double beds for 7 nights with 5 days of lift tickets for each person during the 1993-94 ski season ranges between $363 to $1,065 per person.

The Alpenhof, also in Teton Village, is one of the better hotels. Its rooms are clean and sound-proof. Most of the rooms have balconies and king-size beds. There is a heated outdoor swimming pool, spa, sauna, game room, and laundry room. Cable TV is standard in every room. Double occupancy rooms in the Alpenhof during the regular 1993-94 season are priced between $499 and $1,553 for 7-day packages with lift tickets.

The Alpenhof's dining room is featured in the restaurant section.

Directly next door and north of the Alpenhof is the **Sojouner Inn**. This hotel has large, comfortable rooms with adequate storage for all the sweaters, shirts, and slacks skiers seem to travel with. Separate ski lockers for guests are available next to the heated outdoor swimming pool and adjacent to the jacuzzi and sauna. **The Stockman** bar is a lively spot for après-ski with free snacks from 4-6 P.M. and continuous showings of Warren Miller ski films. The Sojourner's lobby is comfortably furnished with plush seating and warming fireplaces—a handy place to stretch out before dinner or to enjoy a free cup of coffee in the morning. Regrettably, the Stockman's restaurant should be avoided at all cost. With so many good restaurants available in Teton Village and the town of Jackson there is no reason to put up with the poor food and service this restaurant offers. Double occupancy rooms in the Sojouner Inn during the 1993-94 season or 7-day ski packages are priced between $485 and $1,0985 including lift tickets.

Other hotels in Teton Village and the town of Jackson include **Crystal Springs Inn, Hostel, Village Center, Antler Motel, Parkway, Rawhide, 6-K Motel, Western Motel, Wort Hotel.**

Grand Targhee is not only a day skier area, but it also functions as a destination resort, which now can accommodate close to 400 guests. **Teewinot Lodge, Targhee Lodge** and the Teewinot Navajo are the only hotels in the area. Prices range from $80 per night for 2 queen beds without phone or television to $129 per night with phone, bath and television at the Teewinot Navajo.

Condominiums

Located a scant half-mile from the aerial tram, the **Wind River Condominiums** are situated in a meadow and have a wonderful view of Rendezvous Mountain. These condos offer free shuttle service every twelve to fifteen minutes to the tram station. In the evenings this service provides hourly pickup and return from restaurants in the village.

The Wind River Condominiums are three stories high and feature impressive living areas which occupy two floors. The large fireplaces are made of native stone and the L-shaped seating is comfortable. Cable TV and stereos provide entertainment for stay-at-home guests. All condos are equipped with humidistats. Increasing humidity provides great relief from the dryness always present in the mountains. A separate formal dining room can comfortably seat eight.

The kitchen is small but everything is very convenient. General Electric appliances include an ice maker, dishwasher, disposal, convection oven, microwave oven, and blender.

The lower floor consists of two bedrooms and two baths as well as a laundry room with washer and dryer. One of the baths is a two-person Jacuzzi.

Two other bedrooms including the master bedroom are located on the third floor. Based on eight-person occupancy, Wind River Condominiums with 4 bedrooms rent for $1,427 and $4,521 per person for 7 nights, and 5 days of lift tickets per person. However, Wind River as well as all other condominiums listed for Jackson Hole are managed by more than one property management company, and the rates for the exact same units will vary. Two bedroom packages will cost $688 to $2,060 for the same package.

The **Teewinot Condominiums** are named in the same French terminology as the Grand Tetons, a Teewinot meaning "many pinnacles." Teewinot condos are available as two or three-bedroom units. The rooms are smaller than those of the Wind River, and these living areas do not include a formal dining area. Each living room has a wet bar, fireplace, and TV. All appliances are GE and identical to those found in Wind River Condos.

Among the least expensive condominiums located in Teton Village are the **Rendezvous**, next door to Teewinot and Wind River. The Rendezvous, however, may offer the best value since their furnishings are not very different from those found in the more expensive units. Amenities include stone fireplaces and dining rooms that comfortably seat eight. Rendezvous units are available as either two or three-bedroom condos. Prices are similar to those listed above.

Other condominiums in Teton Village include **Tensleep/Gros Ventre**, **Timber Ridge**, **Nez Perce**, and **Sleeping Indian**.

Grand Targhee's **Sioux Lodge** offers overnight guests condominium accommodations configured as studios, lofts, or 2-bedroom units. All units have been freshly renovated and offer all the conveniences typically associated with major destination resorts: wood-burning fireplaces, complete cooking utensils, dining areas, and complimentary amenities package. The 1992-93 per person rate for studio units varies from a low season rate of $145 to a high season rate of $189. Loft units rent for a low season rate of $179 to a high season rate of $225. Two-bedroom rates are $225 during low season and $285 during high season. Rates vary depending upon the number of occupants and number of days stayed. For reservations telephone (800) 443-8146.

Restaurants

Teton Village's best restaurant is the **Alpenhof Dining Room**, a AAA 4-diamond winner. Dining at the Alpenhof is truly a culinary treat. Furnished in a Swiss/Austrian-style motif, the restaurant is dominated by natural stone walls, and its exterior windows overlook tall conifers. The soft, yellow light from its windows casts warm shadows on skiers returning for the evening, while the aerial tram station's Italian lights twinkle in the freshly fallen snow.

The Alpenhof's waiters are friendly, courteous, and very knowledgeable about the extensive menu and abundant wine selection. Try the potato soup with dill for starters, if it is available, but soup choices change daily. The chicken picatta is recommended for a delicious entrée. It is served smothered in garlic, anchovies, and a rich tomato sauce. This is a Mobil 4-star restaurant, and the award is justly deserved. Reservations are recommended.

The same management that owns the Alpenhof owns the adjoining **Dietrich's Bar & Bistro**. This is the best place for après-ski. From its warm, wood interior to its numerous baskets of hanging blooms and ivy, Dietrich's is comfortable. The central feature of the room is a carved glass windowpane on which is etched the figure of a mountain climber ascending a majestic peak.

Among the beverage offerings are typical ski resort drinks such as Union Jack, Tennessee Mud, and Snow Blind! Dietrick's offers one of the better tables of complimentary hors d'oeuvres. It includes spicy buffalo wings, Mexican pizza, nachos, potato skins, and tostados served with spicy or sweet salsa.

A hardy lunch featuring items such as bratwurst, tortellini primavera, and gourmet pizza is also served.

The **Mangy Moose** is a Teton Village institution, and the largest volume restaurant in Wyoming, Montana and Idaho. The Moose is many things: a restaurant, a bar, a pizza parlor, gift shop, liquor store, and the only place in the Village that features live entertainment, often nationally renowned acts. Most of the time there is a cover charge for the entertainment. The dining room is dominated by a large stone fireplace with a "mangy" moose mounted above its mantle. Antique barber chairs are available for those who need to sit while waiting for a table. Ceiling fans, pseudo-Tiffany lamps, and mirrors complete the Western motif. This is a family restaurant with large tables that encourage people to mix and meet one another. Children's menus are available. The menu includes steaks, Mexican and oriental dishes, and seafood.(307)733-4913

Cafe Christine, located only five miles south of Teton Village on Highway 390 is a comfortable and intimate dining spot. Formerly a private home, it seats only 26 persons, making reservations imperative. The dinner menu changes weekly, but a sample of entrées may include such delectable items as lamb chops roasted with dried apricots, whole shallots, finished with lamb demi-glacé, and served with spaetzle; filet of salmon in a light marsala beurre blanc, garnished with fresh orange segments; or boneless chicken breast sautéed with roasted garlic, topped with julienne of green pepper and sun-dried tomato, finished with a slice of melting brie.

Cafe Christine has a credible wine list featuring numerous varietals as well as a complete card of spirits and beers. Smoking is not permitted in the dining room due to its small, intimate size and proximity to the open kitchen. Visa and Mastercard are accepted, but American Express is not. For reservations telephone (307) 733-1199.

On the square in downtown Jackson Hole, right next to the famous **Million Dollar Cowboy Saloon**, is situated a throwback to Hollywood during its 1940's heyday. **The Cadillac Grille** is decorated in the same Empire style popularized during the reign of such movie greats as Katherine Hepburn, Spencer Tracy, James Cagney, Jimmy Stewart, and Jane Russell. The mood of the decor is so authentic one would not be surprised to see Clark Gable saunter in and say, "Frankly, my dear, I don't give a damn!"

An upscale version of Boogie's in Aspen, The Cadillac Grille features fresh seafood, flown in every other day. Service is courteous and prompt. Fish specials change daily. Typical menu items may include fresh Chilean swordfish grilled and served with hazelnut sauce, fresh mahi mahi in oriental mint marinade, grilled and served with a fresh pineapple salsa. The menu also contains a section entitled "Game du Jour" which obviously is a daily listing of available game dishes. Medallions of elk sautéed and served with lingonberry butter sauce is a local favorite. Of course a full offering of poultry, beef, lamb, and fresh pasta is also prepared daily. All major credit cards are accepted; for reservations telephone (307)733-3279.

In the front of the Cadillac Grille is located a 50s-style diner which has been voted the best burger in town. **Billy's Giant Hamburger** is an extension of the Cadillac's bar and serves freshly ground, half-pound burgers.

The Inn at Jackson Hole houses three restaurants. Jenny Lee's is a moderately priced eatery for breakfast and lunch. **Beaver Dick's,** a restaurant and lounge, caters to the apres-ski crowd and serves sandwiches and drinks. **The Range,** a more elegant choice, serves gourmet, wild game dishes and is open only for dinner. Reservations are recommended.

Activities

One of the more exciting activities available in Jackson Hole is High Mountain Helicopter Skiing. Back-country skiing in the Snake River Range and Palisade Mountains just southwest of Teton Village can be arranged for $400 (1992-93 rates). Typically, this will encompass six runs of 12,000. One-run Nordic trips are available at $150. Telephone (307) 733-3274 for information and reservations.

National Standard Races (NASTAR) are held every Tuesday and Thursday at 1:00 P.M. Participants should sign up at the Ski Chalet between 8:30 A.M. and 11:30 A.M. the day of the race. The Ski Chalet is located just behind the tram station. Cost to run NASTAR is $4 for adults and $3 for children.

Coin-operated self-timed racing is also available, located on Lower Amphitheatre at $ .50 per run.

The Aspens Athletic Club is approximately one mile from Teton Village and offers daily, weekly, seasonal, or annual membership rates. Its facilities are clean and properly maintained. Offerings include indoor/outdoor tennis courts, Nautilus, free weights, basketball, volleyball, aerobics,(including low-impact), jacuzzi/sauna/steam, ice skating, outdoor swimming pool and much more. Phone 733-7004 for more information. A week's membership will cost $45 a week for the ski season. Open Monday through Friday 10:00 A.M. to 4:00 P.M.

Ride a horse-drawn sleigh to visit the National Elk Refuge. It is the largest elk refuge in the United States. Sleigh rides are continual from 10:00 A.M. to 4:00 P.M. through the end of March.

Take a snowmobile tour of Yellowstone or Granite Hot Springs. Dress warmly but take a swimming suit and enjoy the hot, thermal waters. Telephone (307) 733-6850 for reservations.

Shop in unique downtown Jackson. There are over thirty art galleries and fine stores, including Benetton and Ralph Lauren. Visit the Million Dollar Cowboy Saloon or the arched antler entrance at each corner of the central business district's park.

Services

A full complement of churches, sporting good stores, apparel shops, pharmacies, grocery stores, liquor stores, furniture, bath, and specialty shops is located in Jackson.

Beginning at 9 A.M. every day and continuing on the hour, ski hosts and hostesses position themselves at the top of the tram next to the large trail map. These guides are knowledgeable about Jackson Hole and can answer most visitors' questions.

Teton Village map

1 VALLEY STATION TRAM BUILDING
Cafeteria   Public Rest Rooms
Ticket Office   Sheriff's Office
Public Relations

2 CUSTOMER SERVICE CENTER
Central Reservations/Village Travel
Jackson Hole Realty Property Mgmt.
Bus Stop

**3 VILLAGE CENTER/
MOUNTAINSIDE MALL**
Lee's Tees   Raindance Traders
Wildernest Sports   Shades Cafe
Bear Claw Cafe   Powder Shots Photo
The Ski Locker   Village Store

4 CRYSTAL SPRINGS INN
Teton Village Sports
High Mountains Helicopter Skiing
Real Estate of Jackson Hole
Teton Village Property Management

5 MANGY MOOSE
Mangy Moose Restaurant & Saloon
Mangy Moose Liquor/Moose Gifts
Rocky Mountain Oyster Restaurant
Sirk Shirts
Snake River Trading Co.
Rocky Mountain Chocolate Factory
Game Room

6 THE HOSTEL
Teton Video
Pooh Corner

7 THE INN AT JACKSON HOLE
Beaver Dick's Saloon
Jenny Liegh's Restaurant
The Range Restaurant

8 TETON VILLAGE CLINIC
9 TETON VILLAGE MARKET
10 U.S. POST OFFICE
11 SOJOURNER INN
Restaurant/Lounge/Fondue
Game Room

12 ALPENHOF LODGE
Alpenhof Dining Room
Dietrich's Bar & Bistro
Jack Tennis Sports

13 MULTI-PURPOSE CENTER
Kinderschule
Ski Rental Shop

14 JACKSON HOLE SKI SCHOOL
15 GRAND TETON MUSIC FESTIVAL
**16 ROSSIGNOL CROSS-COUNTRY
SKI CENTER**

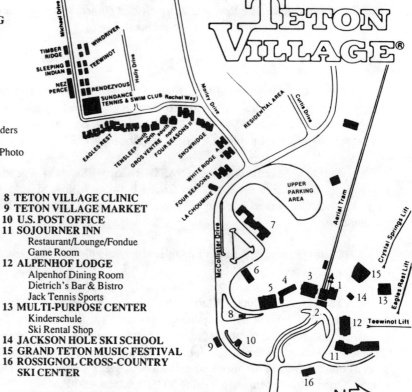

KILLINGTON, LTD.

Killington, Vermont 05751

(800) 621-MTNS Reservations
(802) 422-3333 Information
(802) 422-3261 Snow Report

New For 1993-94

While last year the East's largest ski resort concentrated its efforts on mountain expansion, this year the emphasis and most of $5 million are being poured into mountain base facilities. At the Snowshed base lodge, a 3-story, 10,000 square foot addition has been built to house a new Introduction to Skiing Center. Killington has taught more new skiers than any resort in the country --more than 20,000 last year alone -- and they aim to make it less complicated, less expensive and more comfortable for people with this center. On the second floor visitors will find 400 new seats in its dining area and a new food court.   Also, this year Killington will open its first shop specifically for snowboarders at the Killington base lodge.

A new 3,000 square foot deck has been added to the outside of the Killington base lodge, affording tired skiers a place to rest in the sun and get a beautiful view of the Canyon Quad area and the new snowboarding half pipe added to the SuperStar run on Killington Peak.

Killington was voted by Snow Country readers as having the best Apres-Ski at the bottom of the mountain and best night life around the resort.

How To Get There

Killington can be reached conveniently from Vermont's Rutland Airport. This is a small airport located only eighteen miles from the mountain. Direct flights from Boston's Logan Field and New Jersey\ New York's Newark Airport are via Eastern Express. These flights typically utilize commuter aircraft and can seat approximately forty persons.

Car rental agencies at the Rutland Airport include Hertz and Avis. Because the quantity of automobiles is limited, it is wise to have a reservation. Be sure to request a car with snow tires and ski racks. The ski racks provided are of a highly portable nature. They do not have a rigid construction, and it is entirely likely that upon the traveler's arrival at the car rental counter, the ski racks will be handed to him in a plastic bag. It will be up to the renter to attach the rack to the car. These racks will accommodate only four pairs of skis.

Killington is located at the junction of U.S. Highway 4 and Vermont Highway 100 in Sherburne. Both of these are good, hard-surfaced roads, and they are kept scrupulously clean by the Highway Department.

Mountain Information

Killington is the largest ski resort in the eastern United States. It consists of six peaks which are referred to as separate mountains: Sunrise Mountain, Bear Mountain, Skye Peak, Killington Peak, Snowdon Mountain, and Rams Head Mountain. All these peaks can be skied by skiers of every ability level, and it is easy for all skiers to move from one mountain to another.

Killington has an awesome lift capacity considering the number of acres served. In all, there are eighteen lifts consisting of

  5 Double Chairlifts
  4 Triple Chairlifts
  7 Quad Chairlifts (2 detachable)
  2 Surface Lifts
  1 Gondola

Interestingly, the three and one-half mile gondola is the longest lift in North America. Killington's total skiable area is 721 acres (288 ha) with a vertical drop of 3,175 feet (968 meters). There are five bases or entry points to the mountain, with the lowest elevation at the gondola at 1,160 feet (353 meters). The highest point is Killington Peak at 4,220 feet.

Killington maintains 107 trails or open slopes. Its 6 mountains area interconnected by 77 miles of trails Of these, 44% are rated as beginner, 20% as intermediate, and 36% as expert. Expressed in actual numbers the total skiable trails are as follows:

  48 Beginner
  21 Intermediate
  38 Expert

The longest beginner run is Juggernaut which spirals from the top of Killington Peak to its base at Northeast Passage. It is 10 miles (16 km) long and winds through some of Vermont's prettiest countryside. The longest continuous intermediate run is Timberline, though Chute is almost the same length. The longest expert run is Cascade.

The maximum number of skiers transported per hour on Killington's mountains is 35,427. Clearly, Killington can be crowded. Management also has a policy of selling lift tickets as long as there are people willing to purchase them. Therefore, the potential for crowding at all of the base facilities is even greater than on the mountain itself. The person who is considering a Vermont ski vacation should consider the potential crowding that occurs during the peak periods of Christmas and Easter. Because Killington is close to the East's major population centers, its resultant crowding may be reason enough for skiers to consider one of the many Rocky Mountain resorts.

There are ways, however, to minimize the inconvenience of Killington's crowds. The most crowded base areas are Snowshed and Killington. Crowds are much lighter at Sunrise Mountain base and the Gondola base. Likewise, Sunrise and Bear Mountains do not have as many skiers as the other peaks. Both of these areas offer skiing for all levels of ability, though it is on the light side for intermediate skiers. Located at the foot of the Bear Mountain parking lot is Killington's most famous, some might say infamous, run: Outer Limits. This is a steep, heavily moguled run which can become icy due to the heavy skier traffic.

On cold, windy, or snowy days, relief from the elements can be found by skiing Bear Mountain. This is the most sheltered part of the Killington complex and also comprises some of its best expert terrain.

Average snowfall is 225 inches (602 cm).

Due to Killington's low elevation the weather sometimes does not cooperate, and snow can turn to rain or the accumulated snowfall can turn to slush or worse, to ice! Most western skiers condemn the East for its icy conditions. Though it is true that the East exhibits more icy conditions than does the West, its negative reputation is not deserved. Killington has a very sophisticated snowmaking program and, as long as the weather is below freezing, makes abundant quantities of snow. Seventy-five percent of the mountain can be fully serviced with snowmaking, and an early base is always applied to help conserve the natural snowfall.

According to John Okalovich, Director of Killington's Ski School, the conditions are not considered "icy" unless one cannot "set an edge." Skiers unaccustomed to eastern conditions should, therefore, make every effort to keep their edges razor sharp and have their skis tuned frequently since eastern conditions are "less forgiving" than typical western conditions.

The average daily temperatures during the season are

Nov.	28°	(-2° C)
Dec.	26°	(-3° C)
Jan.	17°	(-8° C)
Feb.	16°	(-9° C)
Mar.	26°	(-3° C)
Apr.	34°	(1° C)

Lift Ticket Prices 1993-94

$ 39 Daily(Last year's price, new prices not available at press time)
$ 77 2-Day Consecutive
$116 3-Day Consecutive
$155 4-Day Consecutive
$172 5-Day Consecutive
$206 6-Day Consecutive
$241 7-Day Consecutive

Rates for children 12 and under, and seniors 65 and over are half of the adult rate.

Killington has joined the trend other major ski resorts are pursuing in attempting to entice clients to extend their visits by offering discounts for longer stays. Lift ticket prices for Killington are only slightly less confusing to figure out than the IRS's 1040! Skiers planning a visit to Killington, or any other resort for that matter, should carefully review their options regarding available packages. Typically, lodging and lesson packages at Killington reduce lift ticket prices significantly.

Hours of Operation

9:00 A.M. to 4:00 P.M. weekdays
8:00 A.M. to 4:00 P.M. weekends

After Thanksgiving Killington offers the first half-hour of skiing FREE. This serves two purposes: first, it offers skiers the option of testing the mountain before investing in a lift ticket.

Second, the local managers and staff of lodging establishments are encouraged to take a run or two first thing each morning so they can be knowledgeable about the conditions on a day-to-day basis and be able to answer clients' questions with confidence.

How to Avoid Crowds

As previously mentioned, Killington can become crowded. This is natural because it is the largest and the most complete resort on the East Coast. Its close proximity to New York City and Boston make it natural for skiers to frequent the resort.

There is no substitute for local knowledge. The mountain must be skied frequently in order for skiers to learn how to minimize the effects of so many people on the slopes. Prudent skiers will do everything they can to avoid the Snowshed and Killington Peak base areas. These two areas are the most convenient to the lodging and, therefore, the most crowded.

Avoid eating lunch during the traditional period of 11:30 A.M. to 1:30 P.M. This may be the best time to ski those runs serviced by the Killington Peak Double Chair because most people eat at the base or at the restaurant at the top of this lift. After 2:30 the rush to the parking lots at the bottom of these two bases can resemble the Tokyo subway. On the other hand, if skiers have parked at one of the other bases, they will not be significantly inconvenienced by crowds.

Ski School

Adult classes begin at 9:30 A.M. and 1:00 P.M. daily and last for two hours. Class registration occurs at either the Snowshed base or the Killington Peak base. Individuals interested in lessons should make advance reservations by telephoning (802) 773-1330. The need for reservations is due, of course, to the large number of skiers who frequent Killington.

Killington has a terrific ski school that teaches what it refers to as the "Accelerated Ski Method." The ski school boasts it can teach most people enough technique in two hours for them to enjoy skiing most of the beginner runs. Indeed, Killington has made a major commitment to teaching new skiers. The ski school director has authority to demand service from the mountain maintenance crews as he feels it is needed. In addition, he controls two runs used solely for the ski school. One of these runs is a relatively long trail that runs from the Killington base to the Snowshed base. This extremely easy trail is designed to teach beginners very specific exercises. The slope is divided into twelve teaching stations. The beginner is instructed in balance and control, how to step from one ski to the other, and how to form a wedge into a turn. After completion of these exercises, students are ready to follow their instructor up the mountain and commence sharpening their newly acquired skills.

To simplify the ski lesson process, Killington also has divided its adult lessons into three classifications: Introduction, for beginners and novices; Mountain School, for novices to advanced skiers;and Master School, for advanced and expert skiers.

The Introduction classes cost $45 for a 2-hour lesson, which includes a lift pass at Rams Head and Snowshed, and even rentals. This is a good deal for beginning skiers!

Mountain School classes include 2 days of 2-1/2 hour lessons, including a lift ticket for all six mountains for $117, $59 for seniors 65 and older, and children, 6 to 12. A $15 rental option can be added.

The Master School for advanced skiers costs $140 for 2 days of 30-hour lessons, including a video review of your skiing, ski tuning, and a all-mountain lift ticket. The price for children and seniors is $70. A rental option can be had for $20.

For the 6- to 12-year-old set, Killington has the **Superstars Ski School,** in either full or half day sessions. Classes are grouped by age and ability. For a one day 2-1/2 hour lesson, the price is $46, $61 including equipment. Two days of half-day Superstars lessons include 2-1/2 hours of morning or afternoon lessons and lift tickets for $59, with rental equipment, $75. For two full day lessons, including 2-1/2 hours in the morning and the afternoon, lunch and lift tickets, the cost is $130 or $154 with rental equipment. Holiday rates increase slightly. If your child enrolls in this program and needs to rent equipment, please arrive one hour before class time so he or she can be fitted for skis and boots. These are 1993-94 rates.

Equipment Rental

Rental-equipment shops are conveniently located at Killington's five base areas: Snowshed base, the Gondola base, Bear Mountain and Killington bases, and the Sunrise base. Daily prices for 1993-94 were not available at press time, but a 2-day rate for lift tickets and equipment is priced at $125, and at $63 for seniors, 65 and older, and children 12 and under.

Last year rental skis were Elan. Bindings were either Look or Salomon, and boots were either Salomon or Nordica. High-performance skis also may be rented at any of these locations, if desired. The 1992-93 rates(new rates not available at press time) were $25 per day for adults and $17 per day for juniors. Special rates were available for those skiers who visit Killington on package plans. A $100 deposit was required, or a valid driver's license. In lieu of cash, a credit card may be used to post the deposit.

Numerous ski-rental shops are also located at the foot of Killington Mountain in the town of Sherburne.

Ski Tuning and Repair

Tuning and repair services are available at all five base areas from the same shops that provide rental skis. Tuning is critical to achieving satisfying skiing in the East. It is important to have ski edges sharp and the skis structured. Serious skiers are advised to seek out local shops that can not only flat file and sharpen their skis' edges, but which can also "structure" skis. Find a shop whose techniques utilize a man-made stone wheel to flatten and finish the ski bottom. In many cases, this is the identical equipment ski manufacturers used when they originally finished their skis.

The use of this type of equipment for tuning the skis eliminates the "whiskers" associated with sanding. It also applies a pattern or structure to the ski's bottom which is extremely important in reducing the friction on the bottom of the ski itself. Imagine trying to separate two sheets of wet glass. It is difficult to do because the water causes suction. The same thing occurs in varying degrees when skiing. The friction caused by the ski's gliding over the snow creates heat which causes the snow to melt and become water. When this happens, suction occurs and unless it is broken up by structuring the ski's bottom, it will slow the skis down and make turning more difficult. Individuals involved in ski racing will actually determine the skis' structure on the day of the race by evaluating snow conditions, temperature, and course conditions and then dictate the exact structure they want. Portable machines are available and tuning can take place just prior to the race.

Mountain Dining

Cafeterias can be found at six lodges: Rams Head Lodge, Killington Base Lodge, Snowshed Base Lodge, Gondola Base Lodge, Sunrise Mountain Lodge, and Peak Lodge. Don't expect to find any outdoor barbecues here. State law prohibits restaurants from cooking on open flames. Apparently this is due to a fear that an errant cinder could ignite a forest fire.

Lounges serving beer, wine, and spirits are located on the second floor of the **Snowshed** base facility, the first floor of the Killington Peak base, at the top of the **Killington Peak,** and at **Bear Mountain Lodge**.

Fine dining and individual seating is available at the Snowshed base. Just adjacent to the cafeteria is **Pogonips.** This is a bright, airy dining room with a nice view of the beginner runs going down Killington Peak. The restaurant specializes in pasta which is creatively served. Try its fresh pasta with dill.

Another charming restaurant located at the foot of Northeast Passage is the **"Back Behind Saloon Restaurant."** Featuring steaks and fresh seafood, the chef augments each day's selections with his unique specials. The restaurant is a great place to relax and enjoy a break from the day's skiing.

Child Care

Child care is available to Killington guests at the **Friendly Penguin Children's Center** located in the Snowshed base area and is licensed by the state of Vermont as a day-care center. It accepts children from six weeks to 6 years of age. The center has caretaker to child ratio of 1 to 4.

The Children Center's staff is trained to work with small children, and it has divided the center into specific areas of play such as the reading corner, the block-building area, a gross motor skills area, and a fine motor skills area. Indoor and outdoor activity is planned, and parents are advised to make certain they bring adequate clothing. Formula and diapers for infants six weeks to 24 months should also be provided by the parents.

Enrollment in the day-care program is by reservation only, and a fifty percent non-refundable deposit is required. You may cancel your reservation 14 days before your arrival. Any less time and you will forfeit your deposit. Also, for security purposes, parents will need two forms of identification to pick up their children.

During 1993-94, a full day of day care will cost $43, including a lunch provided for 2- to 6-year-olds. A half day, either morning or afternoon will be $29. Lunch is not included in half-days, but can be purchased for $5.

Children three to eight years old can enroll in the beginner ski program, **First Tracks**. To enroll, a child must be toilet trained, weigh at least 30 pounds, and wear a shoe at least size 8. For a half day lesson and day care (without lunch) the cost is $38, and for a full day with lunch, $57. Both prices include the price of equipment.

The Children's Center is open every day and operates from 8:00 A.M. to 4:30 P.M. Special rates are available for children visiting for more than one day.

For all information concerning the Killington children's center programs, call (802)422-6222.

Medical Facilities

Medical facilities at Killington are limited to five first-aid stations located at each base area. Injured skiers determined to need professional medical treatment are transferred to the Rutland Medical Center located only sixteen miles from the mountain. The Medical Center has a completely staffed emergency department manned 24 hours each day. This is a full-service hospital whose staff is able to perform identical services to those found in any large, metropolitan-area hospital.

Cross-Country Skiing

The Vermont countryside is among the most scenic in the United States. Unfortunately, there is no cross-country skiing available at Killington Mountain proper. However, numerous operations are adjacent to the resort. Two of the largest such facilities are Mountain Meadows and Mountain Top.

Accommodations

As a full-service resort, Killington offers its guests all the lodging amenities one would expect. Hotels and condominiums abound near the lifts and base lodges. However, there are no accommodations that can be considered ski-in/ski-out. It is necessary for lodging guests to drive to one of the base areas or to take one of the complimentary shuttles that run approximately every twenty minutes between the lodgings and the mountain. If a guest is not staying at Killington proper, some of the surrounding accommodations will provide transportation to the mountain's gateway points.

There are two hotels located at the bottom of Killington's slopes: the **Mountain Inn** and the **Cascades Lodge**.

The **Mountain Inn** is a contemporary building with comfortable rooms, not unlike rooms in any moderately priced hotel. Each room has cable TV, a telephone, radio and private bath. Guests will appreciate the hotel's whirlpool, sauna, game room, and pool table. The Mountain Inn's literature states that it is within walking distance to the lifts but with ski boots and carrying skis you might want to take the complementary shuttle.

The Mountain Inn rates $98 per night midweek, based on double occupancy and including breakfast. For the regular season, two weekend nights with breakfast cost $260. Children under 12 stay free in room with their parents.

The Mountain Inn has a small but very nice dining room, called the Aspens Restaurant. Its lounge is dark with a warm fireplace and the area becomes a nice evening gathering place crowded to hear the live entertainment.

Just across the street from the Mountain Inn is **Cascades Lodge**. Its hallways are decorated with charming antique ski memorabilia. The rooms are not unlike those found in the Mountain Inn, but the management and service personnel seem friendlier and more caring about their guests. Dining in the lodge's restaurant, "Dine with a View Restaurant," is warm and intimate; the food and service are pleasant.

The Cascades also has an indoor heated swimming pool, two whirlpools, a sauna, and a Universal Gym as well as an exercycle, stairmaster and rowing machine, just in case the skier did not get enough of a workout on the slopes! The Cascades during the 1993-94 ski season Dec. 20 to Mar.20 will charge $125 for a room with two double beds midweek and including breakfast.A 2-night weekend visit will cost $316. The lodge also provides changing rooms so that its guests can check out on time, ski, and then change clothes for the drive or flight home. This is a 3-diamond AAA rated lodge.

Killington Village has an abundance of available condominiums. The flagship of the condos at Killington is **High Ridge**. Constructed from New England clapboard on Killington's highest promontory and surrounded by woods, High Ridge's setting is spectacular. Many units have views of Killington Mountain. Some of the condos have saunas and whirlpools; the fireplaces are faced in Vermont marble or stone, and the living rooms feature cathedral ceilings. Amenities include icemakers, microwaves, self-cleaning ovens, and TV's equipped with VCR's and stereos. There is also a large, heated indoor swimming pool located in the center of the development. Shuttles are available for going to the mountain, and if the snow is good you can ski back to these condos.

A two-bedroom, two-bath deluxe High Ridge condo with indoor hot tub and sauna rents during the 1993-94 ski season for between $1,296 for a ski week, excluding weekends. Peak weekend rates and holiday rates are higher. A 2-bedroom, 2-bath condo without the hot tub and sauna will cost $1,096.

Those skiers who are vacationing with their families may want to avoid staying at the **Whiffletree** condominiums, as this is the only complex at Killington that rents to college groups such as fraternities.

Families might consider the **Trail Creek** condominiums, which are located close enough to the Snowshed Base Lodge, where the ski school is located, to ski in and ski out for the day. Ski week prices for a 2 bedroom will cost $1,149. These units have a master bedroom with a queen-size bed, a second bedroom with twin beds, and a sleeper sofa in the living room, bringing maximum occupancy to 6.

The Woodstock Inn is a 30 to 40 minute drive from Killington, but well worth the drive. Located at 14 The Green in Woodstock, the resort offers 146 luxurious rooms, suites and townhouses. The sports facilities include a large cross country ski center with 60 km. of trails, racquetball, squash and tennis facilities, and two heated pools.Relax in their steam room, sauna and whirlpool or have a massage. Prices are $145 to $270 per night depending on the season. (802)457-1100.

For a complete list of accommodations both at Killington and in nearby Rutland and its environs, telephone (800) 621-MTNS and request their free *Accommodation Guide* and/or *Your Guide to Lodging, Dining, Entertainment & Recreation in the Killington Area.*

Restaurants

No one should ever go hungry at Killington. There are marvelous restaurants throughout the area. Whether one's taste is for burgers or exotic seafood, there is a restaurant to satisfy the most demanding patron.

Hemingway's Restaurant is located not far from the base facilities on Highway 4. Established in an exceptionally well renovated old farmhouse complete with a stone-walled wine cellar, Hemingway's offers Continental cuisine, enhanced by its chef's special touch. Hemingway's is the recipient of numerous culinary awards including the Mobil Guide AAA rating and an award from *Travel-Holiday*. *It also has received a 4-diamond AAA rating. Call (802)422-3886 for reservations.*

Churchill's House of Beef and Seafood, across from the Cortina Inn on Route 4 West, won the Korbel Dine-Around award during 1989 and 1991. It offers delicious food and has a loyal valley following. (802)775-3219.

On the more rustic side and if you are looking for good nightlife, visitors should eat at **The Wobbly Barn Steakhouse** at least once during their vacation. Located just down the hill from the Snowshed base, Wobbly Barn is a Killington institution. Featuring mesquite-grilled steaks, chops, and seafood, this moderately priced restaurant is a local favorite. People are served on a first-come, first-served basis. The nightclub upstairs is well-known for its live entertainment.

Across the street from the Wobbly Barn is **Casey's Caboose** on Killington Road. Constructed from what appears to be an old railway caboose with a snowplow attached to it, the restaurant features steak, chicken, seafood, and fresh Maine lobster. The atmosphere is casual and the bar personnel are accommodating. This restaurant was rated the best family and casual dining restaurant in the Northeast by Parade Magazine. Call (802)422-3795 for reservations.

Back Behind Saloon and Restaurant, at the junction of Route 4 and 100 South, at the foot of Killington's Sunrise Mountain, offers a casual atmosphere and fresh seafood, steaks and chef's specials. (802)422-9907.

Cobble House Restaurant, is and 1864 Victorian Inn in nearby Gaysville. Enjoy French and Northern Italian cuisine in an intimate fireside atmosphere. Chef owned. (802)234-5458. Reservations are recommended.

The Grist Mill Restaurant is a popular happy hour spot, located on Killington Road by Summit Pond, an ice skating attraction. Live entertainment and a free hot or cold buffet is available daily, as well as a light bar menu. (802)422-3970.

During the holidays all of the restaurants in the area have long waiting lines. If the restaurant takes reservations, be sure to book them at least one day in advance. If reservations are not taken, expect to wait at least an hour before being seated.

All of the restaurants accept credit cards but not all take American Express. Prudence would dictate that visitors make certain to carry Master Card or Visa if planning to charge meals.

Two places that come highly recommended for night life, dinner and dancing are **The Pickle Barrel** and **The NightSpot**. The Night Spot is located at the top of the Killington Access Road, under the yellow awning. This great apres ski spot is know for its wood-fired pizza and caesar salad. Open from 3 p.m. to 2 a.m. during the ski season, the Night Spot has live acoustic music in the Outback and inside a DJ and dancing.

Activities

The Green Mountain Health Club is located in the Mountain Green Resort condominiums. This is an excellent facility for those who want a little more from their resort. Every exercise need and desire can be fulfilled at the Health Club with its lap pool, sauna, whirlpool, eucalyptus steam room, racquetball courts, and exercise room with Universal Gym and free weights. Aerobics classes are also held daily, and a telephone call will secure a reservation.(802)422-3113

Other activities include ice-skating, sledding, sleigh rides, movies, and winter camping. Additional health clubs and an assortment of bowling alleys are found in nearby Rutland.

Services

A full complement of sporting goods stores, apparel shops, pharmacies, grocery stores, liquor stores (state run), furniture, bath, florist, ice cream, and other specialty shops is within the immediate area.

MAMMOTH MOUNTAIN

Post Office Box 24
Mammoth Lakes, California 93546

(800) 367-6572 Reservations
(619) 934-2571 Information
(619) 934-6166 Snow Report

New For 1993-94

Mammoth Mountain celebrates its fortieth year in the ski resort business this year! Chair 18 has been remodeled, in an effort to improve traffic flow. In addition the resort has purchased six new snowcats to keep the trails in great condition. This year Snow Country readers voted its terrain as the best in the west, and its snow surface as one of the best.

The Mammoth Inn, owned by the McCoy family who founded this beautiful resort, is undergoing a renovation in honor of the 40 years of skiing on this mountain. The Inn is extensively remodeling its east-west building. Some of the standard rooms are being removed to make two bedroom condominiums. A general upgrading of decor and furnishings in the rooms also is underway.

How to Get There

It has been said that Mammoth Mountain is hard to reach: Whoever said that was right! Mammoth is hard to get to, but once there, it is a terrific town and a terrific mountain. The spirit of cooperation between Mammoth Lakes Resort Association and Mammoth Mountain's management is readily apparent. Mammoth Lakes is almost as large as Aspen and runs as well, too.

Currently the only way to get there by plane is to fly Alpha Air from one of the following gateway points: Burbank, CA., Orange County, CA., Los Angeles, CA.. Since certain restrictions apply and schedules change, persons contemplating flying to Mammoth should telephone (800) 421-9353 for information and reservations. To reserve a car at Mammoth/June Airport, call Eastern Sierra Rentals at (619)935-4471.

Skiers from outside California should consider flying to Reno Cannon International Airport, renting a car, and then driving to Mammoth. Reno is approximately 160 miles from Mammoth. The drive is primarily through high desert that rarely experiences any snow, so it is easy. From Reno take U.S. Highway 395 south to the Mammoth Lakes turnoff; turn right onto Highway 203 and follow it into town.

Those arriving from Los Angeles should plan on allowing at least six hours for the drive. Take CA. Highway 14 to U.S. Highway 395 north to Mammoth Lakes; turn left onto Highway 203 and take it into town.

From San Francisco and Sacramento, skiers should take Interstate 80 to U.S. Highway 395 south to Mammoth Lakes, turn off left onto Highway 203, and follow it straight into town. Greyhound also drives directly to Mammoth from the gateway points. For more information, telephone Greyhound at (800) 237-8211.

Mammoth Mountain receives bountiful snowfalls each year. All cars going into the high Sierras should be equipped with snow tires; chains are definitely recommended as well. Should the snow become too deep to drive on without snow tires, a few businesses along the approach routes will rent snow tires. However, they rent out quickly in winter situations, to say nothing about the prices charged!

Once in town, it is convenient to have an automobile because the distances between restaurants, shops, and the slopes are considerable. It is five miles from the town of Mammoth Lakes to the main mountain's base area. Local shuttle service is reliable, clean, and operates until 5:00 P.M. For specific information, telephone the Mammoth Area Shuttle (MAS) at (619) 934-0687. Shuttle service is free.

Mountain Information

It takes great people with vision to create great ski areas. Mammoth is the product of such vision. Since Dave and Roma McCoy installed a humble rope tow in the 1940's, Mammoth Mountain has been their brainchild and love. The first chairlift was erected and opened on Thanksgiving Day, 1955. Since then Mammoth has continued to grow and thrive under the guidance of Dave McCoy and his son Gary. Today Mammoth boasts thirty lifts consisting of

14   double chairlifts
1 high speed detachable quad
4   quad chairlifts
7   triple chairlifts
2   gondolas
2   surface lifts

These lifts crisscross the mountain forming various patterns that transport skiers over an incredibly large 3,500 acres (1,416 ha). The lift system is capable of moving 43,000 skiers per hour. Most of its business is conducted on weekends and holidays. Therefore, destination skiers from other parts of the country are advised to avoid as many weekends and holidays as possible when skiing Mammoth. Rather than scheduling a trip from Saturday to Saturday, plan on a Sunday-to-Sunday visit. That way there will only be one Saturday crowd to endure. Be sure to make lodging reservations far in advance, as it is virtually impossible to find last-minute accommodations over a weekend. As crowded as Mammoth becomes on weekends and holidays, it remains very underutilized during the week. Its lift capacity far exceeds the usual weekday crowds, assuring skiers there will probably be no lift lines Monday through Thursday.

Mammoth's base elevation is 7,953 feet (2,424 meters) with its summit at 11,053 feet (3,369 meters), providing a vertical drop of 3,100 feet (945 meters). Surprisingly, the timberline on Mammoth Mountain is relatively low considering the southern latitude of the mountain. This has blessed Mammoth with an exceptional mantle of snow-covered bowls, similar in topography to Whistler and Blackcomb in British Columbia. Mammoth Mountain's statistics show that fully 30% of the available skiable terrain is rated for skiers of advanced ability, 40% for intermediates, and 30% for beginners.

Beginning skiers are advised to ski Sleepy Hollow to Lupin, positioned right off Chairlift 15. At 2 miles

(3.2 km),this is the longest beginner run at Mammoth. The longest intermediate run is St. Anton, also 2 miles (3.2 km) long. Expert skiers should take Dragon's Back, a 2 mile (3.2 km) run from the top of Chairlift 9.

All beginner runs and most intermediate ones are on the lower part of the mountain. The higher elevations are almost exclusively advanced or expert. Whereas there is nothing on the mountain classified as double black diamond, there are areas which definitely qualify. Most expert skiers will want to ski the myriad runs among the bowls and couloirs that comprise the uppermost parts of the mountain and are reached by chairs 3, 5, 23, 25 and Gondola 2. Runs from the cornice area are assigned names and indicated on the trail map; however, expert skiers will quickly find out that the runs are not trails at all but huge expanses of skiable terrain. Experts will relish selecting different routes down the front face each time. This is not a mountain with which they will become quickly bored, as it will continue to challenge them as long as the conditions keep changing.

Intermediates will especially want to ski Roadrunner Ridge atop Mammoth mountain with its expert runs down the north face. From the top intermediates can follow the ridge and ski White Bark Bowl or take a quick left just opposite Cornice Bowl and ski wide-open meadows down Mammoth's backside with its panoramic view of the famous Minarets. Vistas from the top of Mammoth typically rival the views of the Maroon Bells from Aspen Highlands. Mammoth is really a great mountain for all skiers. Intermediates will enjoy all the runs off the number 9 and number 29 chairs. A taste of open bowl skiing can be found by skiing the number 3 or 5 Chairlift off Gondola 2.

Beginning skiers can hone their skills while traversing the broad, tree-lined runs near the Main Lodge and off the number 6 and number 11 chairlifts. Hut II base area offers substantial beginner terrain that frequently is less crowded than the more traditional Main Lodge area.

Mammoth Mountain has a long season, commencing in early November and running until June. Over the last twenty years Mammoth has averaged over 335 inches of snow annually. Its average snowfalls are

Nov.	34"	(86 cm)
Dec.	58"	(147 cm)
Jan.	64"	(163 cm)
Feb.	66"	(168 cm)
Mar.	61"	(155 cm)
Apr.	29"	(74 cm)

Because Mammoth is so far south its weather is more temperate than that typically found at ski resorts. The average base temperatures for Mammoth Mountain are

Nov.	45°	7° C
Dec.	45°	7° C
Jan.	40°	5° C
Feb.	40°	5° C
Mar.	45°	7° C
Apr.	50°	10° C

Mammoth's upper elevations are usually open and skiable until June or July.

Lift Ticket Prices (1993-94)

$ 40	Adult Daily
$ 20	Child Daily, ages 7-12 (6 and under ski free)

$ 30	Adult Half-Day
$ 15	Child Half-Day
$180	Adult, 5-Day, non-holiday
$ 90	Child or senior, 5-Day, non-holiday

Discount lift tickets are available by joining the **Mammoth Club**. If you ski Mammoth often, pay $60 for an adult, $30 for a child or seniors, to get lift tickets for $30 and $15, respectively. Also this will save you money on Alpha Air flights to Mammoth, and discounts on lodging, ski school and sport shop. If you ski only six days this will be worth the price!

Hours of Operation

8:30 A.M. to 4:00 P.M. Midweek
8:00 A.M. to 4:00 P.M. Weekends & Holidays

Lift Ticket Purchase Locations

Lift tickets may be purchased at the Main Lodge base, the Warming Hut II base, and at the base of chairlift 15. During weekends and holidays lift tickets may also be purchased at the bases of chairs 4, 10, and 2.

How to Avoid Crowds

At most major resorts people tend to ski certain chairlifts more than others, so avoiding crowds is only a matter of figuring out which chairs are used least. Unfortunately, this is not the case at Mammoth. Mammoth skiers tend to ski from east to west in the morning and then back again in the afternoon. The best way to avoid crowds, therefore, is to ski the lifts in the middle of the mountain early, the east end in midmorning, the west end in midafternoon, and the middle again during the waning hours of lift operation.

The Main Lodge and Warming Hut II areas get crowded at the end of the day. Ending the day at chairlift 15, 4, 20, 10, or 2 will greatly improve one's ability to hop a shuttle back into town or to get out of the parking lot without difficulty. Many people who drive from their accommodations to the mountain will back into the parking spaces when they arrive in the morning. They do this so they can leave in the evening without having to back up against traffic. Enlightened skiers will reduce their frustration levels and improve their digestion if they do as the locals do and back into the parking spaces, too.

Ski School

Mammoth Mountain's ski school specializes in teaching the American Teaching System (ATS). Its more than 300 certified instructors are pleased to work with both never-ever skiers and experts seeking specialty skills, such as mogul or deep-powder training. Ski-school classes meet every day at 10:00 A.M. immediately in front of the Main Lodge and Warming Hut II. Registration opens at 7:30 A.M. on weekends and 8:00 A.M. on weekdays. Registration closes at 4:00 P.M. Students should register at the ski school desk on the second floor of the Main Lodge or the third floor of Warming Hut II. All group lessons are from 10:00 A.M. to 12:00 P.M. and from 1:30 P.M. to 3:30 P.M. daily. Ski school rates during the 1991-92 season are

$ 38	Adult, all-day
$ 25	Adult, half-day
$175	Book of five all-day group lessons, transferable
$ 60	Private, one-hour
$180	Private, half-day
$360	Private, full-day

$ 54   Adult, First-time (beginners only) one-day "learn-to-ski" package, with rentals.

$210   Several special 5-day clinics are available throughout the year including the Advanced Ski Clinic; Senior Ski Camp and Women's Ski Seminar.

All of the above lessons are offered also to teens 13 to 17 years of age.

For children from 4 to 6 and 7 to 12, divided by age and ability, the   Woollywood Ski Academy is the place to be. Mammoth Explorers can take all day classes without lunch for $38, or an all day class with lunch and supervision for $58. A half day lesson is $25.

Private lessons must be reserved in advance. To make reservations or for information, telephone (619) 934-0685 or (619) 934-0787.

Equipment Rental

Numerous shops that rent ski equipment are located both at the mountain and in the town of Mammoth Lakes.

At the mountain for 1993-94, a standard package of skis, boots and poles will rent for $16, $12 for a half day. A performance package will cost $20 for a full day, $15 for a half. A snowboard package will cost $30, 22.50 for a half day.

The following prices for 1993-94 were not available at press time, but the managers said they would not change a great deal.

Sandy's Ski and Sport on Main Street offers a unique selection of brands for their ski packages. Rossignol Edge, Dynastar, Kastle or K2 skis, Dolomite, Nordica 500 or Tecnica T-3 boots, and Tyrolia binding rentals during the 1992-93 season were $16 per day or $11 per half-day. Rentals for five or more days include a free day—equivalent to a 20% discount!

Sandy's Sport Package includes Dynastar HPI skis, Rossignol STS, 750 LS (ladies only), or K2 TRC, LTP (ladies only), Nordica 500 or Tecnica T-3 boots and Tyrolia 490 RDR bindings. This package is estimated to be available for $22 per day or $15 per half-day, with five or more rental days receiving the fifth day free.

The High-Performance Package offered by Sandy's includes any of the skis for sale in the shop. In fact, any ski can be considered a high-performance rental with one day's rental fee applied to the price of the ski should the skier decide to purchase them. Among the top-of-the line products offered are the K2 TNC and 8.3, Rossignol 7S. Boots include the Nordica Grand Prix. The binding of choice is the Tyrolia 490 RDR. Any of this equipment is estimated to be available for $35 per day or $25 per half-day. Rent any of the above for five or more days and receive the fifth day free. Sandy's also has one of the largest selections of children's rental skis in the Mammoth area. Reservations for equipment are suggested and may be made by telephoning (619) 934-7518.

One of the largest ski shops in Mammoth Lakes is **Kittredge Sports** located on Main Street, next to the post office. Kittredge offers three packages for skiers to choose among. The recreation Package is $16 per day or $11 per half day and features Rossignol STS Carbon skis or the 65 LS ski and Salomon SX 71 or SX 81 boots. Their Performance Package features Rossignol 4M skis or any of the ski brands they retail and Salomon SX 82 boots. Performance Packages rent for $24 per day. Kittredge's Demo Package feature Rossignol STS Carbon skis or the 650 LS ski and Salomon SX 71 or SX 81 boots. The Demo Package rents for $33 per day or $25 per half-day. Other rental packages include the junior and children's which rent at a lesser rate. A damage waiver for $ .50 per day must accompany all rentals except Demo, which is $1. A toll-free reservation number for southern California residents is available at (800) 441-3331. Skiers from all other areas should make their reservations by telephoning (619) 934-7566.

Ski Tuning and Repair

Tuning and repair services are available at all ski rental shops, sporting goods stores, and at the mountain. Following is a short list of some shops and their estimated rates during the 1992-93 season:

Sandy's Ski & Sport

$ 5	Hot wax
$15	Flat file edges
$35	Full tune (minimum)

Kittredge Sports

$ 6	Hot wax
$30	Mount bindings
$15	Adjust bindings
$28	Full tune-up
$30	P-Tex, per hour

Mountain Dining

If there is any disappointing aspect to Mammoth Mountain, it could only be its mountain dining. The food service is all cafeteria-style and geared to moving huge quantities of skiers in and out of the food line. The cafeteria at **Warming Hut II** seats 900 skiers! The food is commendable and, considering the crowds served, the service is good, too. However, seating is at the typical long tables where food, clothing, and beverages are jumbled together in confusion.

In the back bowl near Chair 13, there is an outdoor-only restaurant. That is, it is only open on clear, warm days and offers no inside seating whatsoever. Like the Warming Hut, the cafeteria in the **Main Lodge** is large, evidencing the resort's name: Mammoth! **Mid-Chalet** located between Gondolas 1 and 2 is the third enormous cafeteria. It is also accessible from chairs 1,2,3,5,9,18, and 23. Food service here is probably the poorest of all the cafeterias. Skiers who prefer sit-down table service should try dining at **Mountain Inn**, directly across from the Main Lodge.

Child Care

Small World Day Care center is licensed by the state of California and specializes in the care of infants through preschool age children. Located in the Mammoth Mountain Inn across from the main lodge, it is only a few steps from the base of Chairlift 1. Parents may place their children in the school for full days (8:00 A.M. through 5:00 P.M.) or half-days. Newborn infants through two and a half-year-olds are cared for during the 1993-94 season for $45 per day or $30 per half-day. Preschoolers aged two and a half through twelve are $40 per day and $30 per half-day. When two or more children in the same family enroll, the second child receives a $5 discount.

A combined day care/ski school package is also available during the season. Preschool children who enroll enjoy day care from 8:00 A.M. through 10:00 A.M. and 12:00 P.M. through 5:00 P.M. A ski lesson is taught between 10:00 A.M. and 12:00 P.M. Total cost of this program including lunch is $60 per day. Small World Day Care recommends that parents be certain to provide their children with warm underclothing, snowsuits, hat and gloves, sunglasses or goggles, face scarves or ski masks, and a change of clothing. Newborns and infants must also have their own formula and diapers. The facility is open seven days per week during the entire season, and reservations are strongly suggested. For more information or to make reservations, telephone (619) 934-0646.

Medical Facilities

For ski injuries, the ski patrol will only render emergency aid. The patrol will administer trauma treatment, stabilize broken bones, and transport injured skiers downhill by sled either to the clinic located at the base of the mountain in Main Lodge or the one at Warming Hut II. Seriously injured skiers are transported to the full-service hospital located in Mammoth Lakes.

Cross-Country Skiing

Several cross-country touring centers are located within the Mammoth Lakes metropolitan area. The largest is situated six miles west of town at Twin Lakes. Tamarack/Rossignol Nordic Ski Center is located at Tamarack Lodge-Resort and offers 40 km of groomed tracks for all ability levels. Also available at the ski center are Rossignol rental skis, ski school, and food service. For more information, telephone (619) 934-2442.

Also close to town is Sierra Meadows Ski Touring Center with almost 45 km of groomed tracks. For more information, telephone (619) 934-6161. Other cross-country ski areas close by include June Lake and Rock Creek Canyon. The Forest Service Visitor Center also provides maps of the immediate area for back-country skiers.

Cross-country ski rentals are available from most ski rental shops in town.

Special Events

Mammoth has a reputation for being dedicated to developing ski racers. In pursuit of this goal, the race department has developed its Custom Coaching Concept which separates skiers according to ability levels, defined as Intro, Sport, and Expert. Each ability level has a specific racing and training objective. Rates vary from $28 per day to $12 per session. Telephone the racing department for more information at (619) 934-2571, ext. 3242.

NASTAR and Marlboro Ski Challenge courses are set each day on Bowling Alley, located at the top of the T-bar lift at the base of the Main Lodge. NASTAR race entry fee during the 1991-92 season is $5; second runs are $1. The Marlboro Ski Challenge is a coin-operated slalom race course and is open daily between 9:30 A.M. and 3:00 P.M. Cost is $.50 per run.

Accommodations

The only hotel accommodations actually on or adjacent to the ski mountain are found at **Mammoth Mountain Inn** which, like the resort itself, is owned by Dave McCoy and his family. Mammoth Mountain Inn is a well-maintained, full-service hotel. A large porte-cochère protects guests as they enter or exit the main lobby. Courteous bellmen greet arriving guests, help with luggage, and arrange for storing and tuning skis. The large lobby is dominated by a multi-story stone fireplace and gracious staircase leading to the mezzanine level.

Rooms at Mammoth Mountain Inn were redecorated not too long ago, and this year the hotel is again going through a renovation. Their decorating colors tend to follow the popular Southwest trend: mauves, teals, sea foam, etc. Hotel rooms and suites are available year-round, and while small, all have adequate closet and dresser space to store bulky ski clothes. TV with remote control is standard, and there are three hot tubs on the premises. During the 1993-93 ski season (November through April) single or double hotel rooms rent during the week (Sunday through Thursday) for $80 and $325 per night depending on the size of room, which range from single hotel type rooms, to deluxe rooms with a view of the slopes, two bedrooms and a loft, and suites.

Among the nicest condominium properties for rent at Mammoth Lakes are the **Snowcreek** condominiums a few miles southeast of town. Five phases of condos have been constructed, with many more planned for the future. The more recent the construction, the more updated and perhaps the better the accommodations. Snowcreek IV is available in five floor plans from two bedroom with two baths to three bedrooms with three baths. Exterior construction is of stucco and wood in a style reminiscent of Tudor.

The interior of a typical rental unit at Snowcreek follows the same stucco theme. Walls are dressed in barnboard; ceilings soar; and the wood-burning fireplaces are finished in impressive native-stone hearths. Typical units have all the living quarters on the entry level with bedrooms and laundry facilities on a lower level. Some units also have lofts above the main living quarters. These lofts are unusual because they are open on two sides, rather than the usual one side. This provides a view from the loft into the kitchen area as well as the living area.

Excellent storage abounds with large closets, cupboards, and dressers. The master bedroom is decorated in Southwest colors, has exposed rafters, and oak furniture. The master bath contains double sinks and an extra large bathtub and shower. The other bedrooms are decorated in a more traditional mountain style including brown carpet, stucco walls, barnboard, and Quaker-pattern patchwork quilts on the beds.

Guests will enjoy the convenience of a small powder room adjacent to the entry. The living area includes a separate dining area and a large kitchen with all the modern appliances one could need, including dishwasher, disposal, and microwave oven. Remote-control units and VCR's are available for guests who request them when making their reservations. A hot tub is found within walking distance of every condo, and the units are on the shuttle bus route. As with most condominiums, check-in is late (in this case 4:00 P.M.) and checkout early–10:00 A.M. Since there is never any shortage of renters on the weekends, Snowcreek, like all rental property in Mammoth, has one rate for weekdays and another for weekends. Weekday rates during the 1991-92 season are $105 per night for a standard one-bedroom unit, $180 per night for a two-bedroom with loft, and $225 per night for a three-bedroom with loft. Management requires a minimum two-night stay. Rates are substantially higher during weekends and holidays.

One of the best features of the Snowcreek condos, however, is not even in them; it is the exclusive **Snowcreek Athletic Club**. This is as fine a club as one could hope to find in a major metropolitan area, with its snack services, bar, and amenities all housed in a structure that blends in with the environment. The facility is available to guests renting Snowcreek condominiums. Among the facilities and services available are eight racquetball courts, an extensive free weight room, Nautilus equipment, Lifecycles, Tunturi bikes, treadmill, stretching bar, anti-gravity machine, and rowing machine. If this were not enough, there is an enclosed fifty-six foot lap pool, a full-sized gymnasium for volleyball, basketball, badminton and a full aerobic/exercise schedule. The tastefully finished locker rooms feature steam baths and hot spas. Snowcreek Athletic Club information is available by telephoning (619) 934-8511.

Close to the shuttle bus stop and within walking distance to most shops in Mammoth Village is **Snow Goose Inn**, a nineteen-room bed and breakfast establishment. Snow Goose is known among locals for its excellent breakfasts including freshly baked quiches, muffins, croissants, granola, and fresh fruits. Each afternoon around 4:00 P.M. wine and cheese are served in the breakfast room and common living area. The common area also features a large screen TV and comfortable seating. This is one of the few rental establishments anywhere that allows pets!

Each room in Snow Goose Inn has a telephone and TV, twin queen-size beds, paneled walls, and a very tiny dresser. The clothes storage situation is the only shortcoming of this otherwise excellent bed and breakfast hotel. All rooms have a bathtub and shower.

Mammoth's only ski-in/ski-out condominiums are also its newest and perhaps its most luxurious. **The Bridges**, just a half-mile above chairs 15 and 24, are truly lovely. They are available in a number of configurations from two-bedroom, two-bath to four-bedroom, loft, four-bath units. Views from the Bridges are exceptional; windows overlook the valley and mountains to the east of Mammoth. Each unit has been professionally decorated in warm, comfortable colors. Kitchens are immaculate and feature all the amenities one expects from a first-rate property. Wood-burning fireplaces, open, beamed ceilings, private decks, and wood paneling are only a few of the amenities offered at The Bridges.

Nestled among tall Ponderosa Pines back a few hundred yards from Minaret Rd. is the reasonable **Alpenhof Lodge**. A throwback to bygone days when tourist cabins were in vogue, the Alpenhof rooms and suites are well-maintained, if somewhat dated, accommodations. Hotel rooms feature color TV's with HBO and direct-dial telephones. The main lodge houses one of Mammoth's best restaurants, **The Matterhorn**, and also offers an indoor therapy pool, laundry room, recreation room, and sauna. Suites are larger than hotel rooms and have wood-burning fireplaces.

Restaurants

Ocean Harvest is an excellent seafood restaurant located at the corner of Old Mammoth and Sierra Nevada roads. A large restaurant, it features a decor that cannot seem to make up its mind if it wants to be "old mountain mining town" or nautical. Its ceiling and walls are rough-sawn cedar; the seating is comfortable captain's chairs. Old nautical photographs juxtaposed between contemporary photos decorate the walls.

Diners frequent the Ocean Harvest because of its quality seafood, all of which is broiled over mesquite wood. A sampling of its menu would include Pacific red snapper, Norwegian salmon, blackened mahi mahi, calamari steak, Australian lobster tail, Canadian scallops, and swordfish—all fresh. An extensive wine list is available to complement any dinner. Downstairs from the restaurant is a raw bar which features a DJ and dance floor for après-ski. Telephone (619) 934-8539 for reservations.

Those skiers who would like a taste of the Orient should sample the food at **Shogun**, located on the second floor of the Sierra Center at the southwest corner of Old Mammoth Rd. and Minaret Rd. Shogun is a family-oriented restaurant with authentic Japanese cuisine. Try the miso soup for starters; it's excellent with tiny bits of tofu floating in the broth. The tempura is lightly battered and the vegetables that traditionally accompany this dish are equally enjoyable. Sukiyaki is prepared in a piping hot cooking bowl and served steaming with onions, mushrooms, morels, and Japanese noodles. For reservations, telephone (619) 934-3970.

Reportedly one of the finest dining spots in Mammoth Lakes is **Whiskey Creek** at the corner of Main Street and Minaret Summit Rd. Housed in a modern structure complete with track lighting, a gas fireplace, and trendy photographs, Whiskey Creek is primarily noted for its beef items. In addition to a special daily menu, there is a regular menu that includes prime rib, top sirloin, roast rack of spring lamb, baby back ribs, and chicken sierra. A sampling of a daily menu would include items such as fresh Norwegian salmon, calamari, mesquite-grilled fresh yellowtail, roast duckling, and Greek prawns. An extensive wine list is offered. For reservations, telephone (619) 934-2555.

Skiers will confirm they are definitely in California when they take a look at **Nik-N-Willies Take-N-Bake pizza** carry-out menu. Nik-N-Willies only sells take-out pizza, so it will be of interest only to those skiers who are staying in condos or have access to an oven. Although the usual pizza toppings are offered, there are a few that are best described as "offbeat," such as salami, pineapple, mandarin oranges, anchovies, jalapenos. This menu is a riot—you gotta see it!! Find Nik-N-Willies in Ivey Square at the corner of Tavern and Old Mammoth roads or telephone (619) 934-2012. The restaurant also sells sandwiches and pizza to take home to bake or hot to go.

If one's palate is hungering for Italian dishes other than pizza, try **Slocum's Italian & American Grill** on Main Street in downtown Mammoth Lakes. Situated in a very identifiable green and white frame building, Slocums offers fine Italian cuisine and terrific après-ski. All the traditional favorites such as spaghetti marinara, tortellini primavera, and lasagna genovese are prepared daily from fresh ingredients. Seafood, chicken, and veal dishes are also available. Italian and Californian wines are always available. Telephone (619) 934-7647.

Activities

Dog sled rides are available from Dog Sled Adventures, featuring Sierra Meadows Loop Ride, Minaret Vista Lookout Ride, or individually planned wilderness adventures. Telephone (619) 934-6270 for information.

Champagne breakfast hot air balloon rides are staged by High Sierra Ballooning, who also specialize in aerial photography and "Nordic cross-country skier drop-offs"—what a fall! Telephone (619) 934-7188.

Mammoth Adventure Connection offers guests an unusual night out on the town called Wintermoon Dog Sled dinner rides. Wrapped in warm blankets and sipping champagne, guests depart on full-moon evenings from Mammoth Mountain Inn and enjoy the spectacular Minaret vistas, ending the evening with dinner at Mammoth Mountain Inn's Grill or Yodler Restaurant. For information, telephone (619) 934-0606.

Snowmobile rentals are available from either DJ's Snowmobile Adventures at (619) 934-4480, Mammoth Lakes Snowmobile Rentals at (619) 935-4263, or Center Street Rentals at (619) 934-4020.

Helicopter skiing is available from Mammoth Heli-Ski at (619) 934-4494.

Snow-cat skiing is offered by Cat-Ski at (619) 932-7598.

Services

A good selection of sporting goods stores, apparel stores, pharmacies, grocery stores, liquor stores, furniture, bath shops, and specialty stores are all within Mammoth Lakes proper. In addition, there are antique shops, massage services, bakeries, hair salons, bookstores, florists, banks, churches, dry cleaning, optical services, and baby-sitting.

PARK CITY SKI AREA

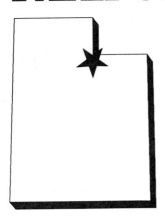

Park City Ski Corp.
P.O. Box 39
Park City, Utah 84060

(800) 222-PARK Reservations
(801) 649-8111 Information
(801) 649-9571 Snow Report

New For 1993-94

This year marks the debut of King Con at Park City -- a high speed detachable quad chairlift which will whisk 1,300 more people per hour up the former site of the King Consolidated triple chair. The lift serves a section of beautiful intermediate runs, including Courchevel, Chance , Climax and, of course, King Con. The lift ride has been shortened from 11 minutes to five minutes. The resort had the old triple chair rebuilt, renamed Eagle and moved to the front of Ski Team Ridge. Its base is near the 3 Kings lift. The Eagle lift has a mid-way unloading ramp which will access two new runs. This area will be set aside for race training at Park City. The top of the lift is near the top of Gotcha run.

How To Get There

One of Park City's outstanding features is its accessibility. Located thirty-two miles from Salt Lake City on I-80, an all-weather, six-lane highway, Park City is accessible from the Salt Lake Airport in under one hour.

Many Park City visitors who arrive by air arrange ground transportation with one of several companies. Lewis Brothers Stage has buses or vans which depart Salt Lake International Airport every 60 to 90 minutes from 9:30 A.M. to midnight. Return trips are made every 60 to 90 minutes between 6:30 A.M. and 9:00 P.M. Lewis Brothers Stage charges $14 each way, $26 round trip, and half-fare for children under twelve during the 1993-94 ski season. Share Ride Vans also are available from this company for $18 one way, $34 for round trip. The vans will load within 30 minutes of when the luggage is loaded to accommodate the different arrival times of flights.   Telephone (801) 649-2256 in Salt Lake City and Park City, or (800) 826-5844 to book reservations.

All Resort Express also provides private van service for $80, 1 to 4 passengers minimum and $20 for each additional passenger, up to $160. one way. The driver will stop at a liquor or grocery store for your convenience. Call (801)649-3999 or (800)457-9457 for reservations.

Once you are at Park City, if you would like to visit Snowbird or Alta, the **Canyon Jumper** shuttle provides service going to the other resorts every morning, and returning late afternoon for $18 round trip. Call All Resort Express for information.

Taxis, limousines, rental cars, and even helicopters are available from the airport to Park City.

Once you are in Park City the Park City Free Transit provides a free shuttle bus service on a regular daily schedule between lodges, shopping, Park City Ski Area and throughout the town. Hours are 7:45 A.M. and 12:30 A.M.

Car rental agencies located at the airport include

Agency	(801) 534-1622
Alamo	(801) 575-2211
Avis	(800) 221-1212
Budget	(801) 363-1500
Dollar	(801) 596-2580
Hertz	(800) 654-3131
National	(800) 328-4567

Mountain Information

Park City is a wonderful family mountain with a good mix of beginner, intermediate, and expert runs. This is the only resort reviewed that is not on National Forest property. The land is leased to Park City Ski Corp. by mining concerns. In fact, prior to lift installation, skiers were taken near the top of the mountain by means of underground mining carts. Once at the end of the tunnel, the carts were lifted up by an elevator. The remains of this transportation system still may be seen. Today the old mining shafts are filled with water which is used for Park City's artificial snowmaking equipment. During fall and early winter the water is pumped out of the shafts, and in the spring when the snow melts, it runs back into the shafts. This is a self-contained ecosystem.

Park City has 2,200 acres (890 ha) of skiable terrain. Of this, 375 acres (133.5 ha) can be covered with man-made snow. There are 82 trails varying in length from one-quarter mile (.4 km) to three and one-half miles (5.6 km). Fourteen of the trails are rated by the resort as easier (beginner), 40 as more difficult (intermediate), and 28 as most difficult (expert). The longest beginner run is "Easiest Way Down" at 3½ miles (5.6 km). The longest intermediate run is Payday at 4,890 feet (1,490 meters). The longest expert run is Shaft at 3,830 feet (1,167 meters).

The lift system at Park City consists of

3 Quad Chairs
5 Double Chairlifts
5 Triple Chairlifts
1 4-passenger Gondola

The gondola at Park City is very unusual. Not only is it the longest gondola in the western United States, but it also makes a turn halfway up the mountain. Actually, the gondola changes cables at a halfway house called "Angle Station."

Park City's base at 6,900 feet (2,103 meters) and summit at 10,000 feet (3,048 meters) yield a vertical drop of 3,100 feet (945 meters).

The lift system at Park City is capable of transporting 22,200 skiers per hour, and skiers can anticipate less crowding than one would likely find at Aspen or Vail. If crowds are relatively evenly spaced, the queuing for lifts should not be excessive.

The mountain will remind skiers of Aspen Mountain and Aspen Highlands. Like each of these, Park City is a mountain on which the lifts go up a ridge and where skiers ski down the sides of the ridge. However, the expert runs off the ridge at Park City are not nearly as steep as the ones on Aspen

Mountain. Mountains such as these possess a lot of character. Because the trails emanate from ridgetops, they expose several fall lines. Typically they also have long run-outs from the bottom of the runs back to the lift stations.

Park City's mountain does not require a great deal of snow to be skiable. It does not have the rocky conditions one would find at a resort such as Jackson Hole or Snowbird. Park City receives an annual average of 350 inches (889 cm) of snow, the majority of which is received late in the ski season. The late snowfall is typical of the Rocky Mountains' winter. Last year, like much of the West, Park City received a blizzard bonanza in the form of more than 600 inches of snow!

Average monthly snowfalls are

Oct.	19"	(48 cm)
Nov.	41"	(104 cm)
Dec.	43"	(109 cm)
Jan.	46"	(117 cm)
Feb.	52"	(132 cm)
Mar.	59"	(150 cm)
Apr.	26"	(66 cm)

The average daily temperatures at Park City are quite temperate for a ski resort:

November	26°	-3° C
December	31°	0° C
January	27°	-3° C
February	31°	0° C
March	37°	3° C

One of Park City's nicest features is that a beginning skier can ski from almost the top of the mountain all the way to the bottom by skiing along the Gondola to Angle Station, taking a left onto Sidewinder, and following it to the gondola base station. Another interesting thing to do at Park City is to take the Town Lift up from the town of Old Park City first thing in the morning. This is an unusual and beautiful ride among the historic old homes and lodging accommodations. In the evening skiers take an intermediate run down either Quit'n Time or Creole back to Old Park City. The intermediate runs along the King Consolidated lift are excellent. Some of the runs are always groomed for cruising while others have moderate bumps for those who want to work on technique.

None of Park City's expert runs are beyond the reach of most competent recreational skiers. That is to say, there are no double black diamonds. The best expert runs have to be the trails in the bowls, of which there are several. The ski are has 650 acres of bowl skiing. The largest is Jupiter Bowl. Most of the bowl trails begin on open snow fields and end on gladed runs. They are never groomed, so depending on conditions, they can have serious moguls. Another interesting expert run is Blueslip Bowl, a small but steep bowl. It derives its name from the staff members who were terminated for skiing it before the current owners decided to expand avalanche control and open it for recreational skiing. The "blueslip" was the equivalent of corporate America's "pinkslip."

Deer Valley

In addition to all the excellent skiing at Park City, Deer Valley is only one mile away. A great ski mountain in its own right, with the reputation for great quality of service nad the ultimate in skiing luxury, this area is growing and adding new services every year. The runs at Deer Valley are easy to intermediate and are meticulously groomed. The resort proper is among the most beautiful in America. However, it is a small mountain and would not normally retain one's interest for more than a few days.

Since last season, Deer Valley has added a new high speed quad, carved 8 to 10 new runs, and increased its snowmaking capability on Flagstaff Mountain. The area has added 6 new snowcats to its fleet and added a new double chair on Bald Eagle Mountain's Wide West run.

Deer Valley has 3 mountains, including Bald Mountain with a summit of 9,400 feet; Bald Eagle Mountain which reaches 8,400 feet; and Flagstaff Mountain, to 9,100 feet. Comprised of 1000 acres, with a vertical drop of 2,200 feet, Deer Valley has 66 runs serviced by

2 high speed quads
9 triple chairs
2 double chairs

In the other direction from Park City, only minutes away, is ParkWest. Primarily a day-ski area, it does not have a great many amenities associated with a destination resort. However, it is worth one's time to ski there. The mountain is about two-thirds the size of Park City. Taken together, the area forms one of the largest ski resorts in the country.

Guests staying in Park City can experience an European style of skiing found almost nowhere else in America. It is possible to ski from Park City to Snowbird via the **Interconnect**. The 1992-93 season price for the five- or four-area tour is $95 per person. The Interconnect takes eight hours to ski its twenty-two mile length and passes through five resorts. Strong intermediates to experts can qualify for this great experience. Only skiers in good physical condition should consider this trip, however. The trip is generally easy until one reaches the "Highway to Heaven" between Solitude and Alta. Highway to Heaven is located at about ten thousand feet and is approximately one-half mile long. This is a trek one never forgets. One misstep can create an avalanche or take the trekker into a remote valley whose only exit is via an uphill hike. After skiers arrive at the top of Alta, they are assured of powder skiing all the way to the base. Then expert skiing ability is required in order to ski to Snowbird. Upon their arrival in Snowbird, skiers are met by a van which returns them to Park City. Shorter variations of this trip are also possible. Telephone (801) 534-1907 for information and reservations. Trips only depart on days when there is no avalanche danger. Skiers are grouped according to ability and are well supervised.

Night skiing is available on Pay Day and First Time. Night-skiing lift tickets are good from 4:00 P.M. through 10:00 P.M. The 1993-94 fee for night skiing is $9 per adult and $5 for children twelve and under. Night skiing is free with the purchase of an afternoon half-day lift ticket or with multiple day passes.

Park City Lift Ticket Prices (1993-94)

Standard Daily Rates

$44	Adult, All-Day
$20	Child, All-Day
$30	Adult, Half-Day
$15	Child, Half-Day
$22	Ages 65-69
Free	Over 70
$8	Round trip gondola
$5	child, round trip gondola

Multi-Day Pass Packages

$120	3 of 4 Day Pass
$156	4 of 5 Day Pass
$190	5 of 6 Day Pass
$228	6 of 7 Day Pass

Child, 12 and Under

$ 54	3 of 4 Day Pass
$ 71	4 of 5 Day Pass
$ 88	5 of 6 Day Pass
$104	6 of 7 Day Pass

Multi-Area Books

$205	Adult, 5 of 6 Days
$ 90	Child, 5 of 6 Days
$246	Adult, 6 of 7 Days
$108	Child, 6 of 7 Days

Multi-area lift tickets are good at Park City, Deer Valley, Alta, Snowbird, Brighton, Solitude, and Sundance. However, because each area is owned by a different company and has different lift-ticket prices, it is necessary for skiers purchasing these tickets to go daily to the resort's ticket window and exchange their book's ticket for the specific area's lift ticket. At those resorts with higher fees than Park City, the purchaser must pay the difference at the time of exchange. If the area to be skied is less expensive, then the skier probably will have to accept the difference in coupons exchangeable at the resort for food or some other similar purchase.

Deer Valley Lift Tickets (1993-94)

$45	Full Day Adult
$33	Afternoon, 1 to 4 p.m.
$25	Child, 12 and under
$30	Senior, 65+
$18	Child, afternoon
$21	Senior, afternoon

Hours of Operation

9:00 A.M. to 4:00 P.M. daily
4:00 to 10:00 P.M. Night Skiing

Lift Ticket Purchase Locations

Lift tickets may be purchased at the ticket office located near the Gondola at the Resort Center. Alternatively, tickets may be purchased at the base of the Town Lift in Old Park City.

How to Avoid Crowds

Crowds are at their worst during the Christmas–New Year's holidays. They can also be bad during Spring Break and on the weekends. The population of Salt Lake City has the same effect on the ski resort on weekends that Denver has on Keystone, Breckenridge, and Copper Mountain. However, during congested times, delays can be avoided by taking the Town Lift to the Crescent lift and skiing down one of the intermediate runs on the north side of Lost Prospector lift. From the top of Lost Prospector, the entire resort opens up for skiers.

Skiers staying near the Resort Center should avoid taking the Gondola. Instead they should take the Ski Team lift and ski down to the Lost Prospector lift. From the top of Lost Prospector it is possible to ski the entire mountain.

However, on crowded days it is important to avoid the Lost Prospector and Prospector lifts just before and after lunch time as these two lifts then become the most popular on the mountain.

Ski School

Park City employs 250 certified ski instructors who teach the American Teaching System (ATS).

Beginning and low intermediate skiers meet at the Base Meeting Area at the base of the Pay Day chairlift. Intermediates and advanced skiers meet at the Summit Ski School Meeting Place located near the top of the Gondola. All-day classes meet at 9:45 A.M., break for lunch, and regroup at 2:00 P.M. Afternoon classes meet at 2:15 P.M. Prices do not include lift tickets.

$ 40	Adult
$ 33	Adult, Half-Day
$113	Adult, 3-Day
$178	Adult, 5-Day
$ 70	Adult, 1-Hour Private
$168	Adult, Half-Day Private

Park City offers an attractive Early Bird Private Lesson from 8:45 to 9:45 A.M. at the Base Ski School for only $45, and an additional $10 for each additional person.

For high intermediate to advanced skiers, the **Mountain Experience** is a wonderful way to ski less frequented areas of the mountain and possibly learn something as well. This 4-hour excursion with the company of an instructor/guide takes you into high bowls and glades and less traveled areas of the mountains. The prices is $40. These classes emphasize different ski techniques for skiing assorted snow conditions. Classes meet at the Summit Ski School Meeting Place at 10:00 A.M.

Children's Classes, Ages 7 to 13

$ 40	Full-Day
$ 33	Half-Day, 2-hour
$ 64	All day lesson with supervised lunch

These prices do not include the cost of a lift ticket.

The Deer Valley ski school is located next to the ticket office in the Snow Park Lodge. The 1993-94 adult group lessons are $55 for a 5-hour lesson. A beginner special from 9 a.m. to 10 a.m. is offered for

$60 for 1-2 people, $75 for 3-5 people. Children's group lessons for 6- to-12-year-olds last year were $60 for 5 hours, $78 with a lift ticket. For 4- to 5-year-olds, 5 hours of instruction cost $65,or $78 with a lift ticket. For 3- to 5-year-olds six hours of child care, a one hour private lesson and lunch cost $80.

Equipment Rental

There are numerous ski-rental companies in Park City. Most offer three types of rental equipment. The basic package offered is usually termed "Recreational." It is designed for novice or low intermediate skiers who will probably spend considerable time in lessons. The second package usually offered is called a "Sport" package. This is an upgrade of the recreational ski. The boots and the bindings are usually the same. However, the ski is always different and is typically a little stiffer. The third type of ski package is called "Performance" or "Demo." There is frequently a significant up-charge for this type of equipment. Many times the rental shop will offer more than one type of ski or boot. The equipment is almost always the manufacturer's top-of-the-line. Some examples of the rentals available in 1993-94 follow:

Breeze Ski Rentals

Skis, Boots, Poles, & Bindings for $14 Per Day
$60 Per 5-Day Package
Children's rate is $11 per day, $45 for 5 days.

Equipment offered includes Pre, Rossignol, K2, Olin skis, Nordica & Salomon boots, and Salomon bindings.

Cole Sport, Ltd.

Junior package	$10 for 1-3 days
Sport package	$13 for 1-3 days
Pro package	$13 for 1-3 days

Ski Tuning and Repair

There are substantial differences in the charges for tuning and repairing skis throughout the Park City area. Estimated costs for the coming year will be approximately

$ 7	Hot Wax
$10	Deburr
$20	Sharpen Edges
$35	Full Tune
$28+	P-tex

Mountain Dining

Park City has three mountain restaurants. The largest is **Summit House**, a cafeteria located at the Summit where the gondola terminates. This is a rustic restaurant whose shelter is typical of most ski resorts. It is open from 9:00 A.M. to 3:00 P.M.

The **Mid-Mountain Lodge** on Pioneer was built around the turn of the century for Silver King Mining Company. Originally the lodge was a boarding house for miners. Later for a short time, it was the U.S. Ski Team's training center. In what has to be one of the most difficult house-moving jobs ever performed, the two-story structure was relocated uphill intact with the aid of five bulldozers. After extensive renovation, the former boarding house was converted to a full-service cafeteria. A large outdoor deck was added to the structure and the upstairs was converted into several large rooms to accommodate groups. The restaurant is open from 10:30 A.M. to 3:30 P.M. No credit cards are accepted.

The **Snow Hut** is located at the base of Prospector Double Chair. Often crowded during peak periods, Snow Hut serves cafeteria-style meals and an assortment of beverages including wine and beer.

At the base of the ski area in the Gondola Building is another restaurant, **Steeps**, open from 8:00 A.M. to 1:00 A.M. A cafeteria on the first floor serves soups, stews, salads and a baked potato bar. The outside deck offers burgers and sandwiches. And upstairs is the Steeps Private Club which offers a full service lunch and live entertainment for apres-ski.

Child Care

Day care for newborn to age 3 is difficult to find in Park City. Once children begin to take skiing lessons the ski school has accommodations for them, but before that time, skiing parents must look elsewhere. The prices quoted are from 1992-93, updates were not available at press time.

In Park City, Miss Billie's Kids Campus,is located across from ParkWest Ski Resort on Highway 224. A licensed preschool and child care center, Miss Billy's will take care of children from newborns to age 12. The center has 40 year-round students and holds open less than a dozen spaces for "drop-in" visitors. Costs are $40 per day for children under 1, and $45 per day for those older than 1. A 1 percent discount is offered to those parents with more than one child enrolled. The center also offers transportation to and from the center for $10 a day. Call (801)649-9502 for a brochure and information.

Creative Beginnings, with a center for infants and toddlers at 180 Prospector Ave., and for 3- to 12-year-olds at 2180 Sidewinder Drive, also is a licensed pre-school and child care center. It usually has only 3 or 4 open spots for daily or weekly visitors. For infants and toddlers, the price is $50 per day, and for 3-year-olds and up, $40 per day. For five hours or less, the half-day cost is $30 and $25, respectively. Call (801)645-7315 for more information.

The Deer Valley Child Care Center is a state licensed facility which will care for children 6 to 24 months, and 2 to 12 years of age.

Medical Facilities

Several medical emergency services are available in Park City, as well as Holy Family Health and Emergency Center. Holy Family is affiliated with Holy Family Hospital in Salt Lake City.

Skiers injured on the slopes are cared for by the ski patrol. The patrol will treat trauma and stabilize injuries such as fractures. Further treatment is rendered at Holy Family Health and Emergency Center. Injured skiers are taken to one of the two emergency clinics on the mountain. Selection of clinics is determined by the location where the injury occurred and the severity of that injury. The ski patrol has complete treatment centers at the Summit House and at the Resort Base. If treatment is rendered at the Summit, the skier will be transported after stabilization to the base by gondola.

If an injury or illness is too extreme for the local hospital to treat, air ambulance service to Salt Lake is available.

Cross-Country Skiing

A great deal of cross-country skiing is available in the Park City area.

The Norwegian School of Nature Life can provide day or night tours into the back country. Call (801) 649-5322 for information about nordic/cross-country ski lessons or cabin/snow cave overnights.

Located five miles northeast of Park City is the **Jeremy Ranch Cross-Country Ski Area**, just off I-80. The Ranch has three tracks including a 3 km course for beginners, a 7 km course for intermediates, and an 11 km course for advanced and expert three-pin skiers. Its telephone number is (801) 649-2700.

Just twenty minutes south of Park City is the **Homestead Resort** with 10 km of track on the Wasatch Mountain State Park Golf Course. There is also a one-half kilometer training track.

All cross-country areas offer complete lessons, equipment rentals, and apparel. Prices are nominal.

Accommodations

Park City has accommodations for every budget. The best selection of upper-end properties is found at Deer Valley Resort one plus mile from Old Park City.

The **Yarrow Hotel** with its red brick tower is somewhat of a landmark in Park City. As visitors approach the resort, it is one of the first resort properties seen. There are 179 rooms in the Yarrow. The hotel, at 18 Park Avenue, serves breakfast, lunch and dinner. The Pub, a bar on the premises serves hors d'oeuvres and drinks.

The Yarrow is a full-service hotel whose large central lobby features a fireplace and nicely appointed furnishings. A ski-rental shop is on the premises, as well as a Delta Airlines reservation desk and an Alamo car-rental agency. Additional amenities include a swimming pool, sauna, hot tubs, concierge service, room service, daily maid service, valet service, and a complimentary shuttle to the mountain with hourly departures. Double occupancy hotel rooms during the 1993-94 season rent from a low of $85 to a high of $159 per night.(800)327-2332 or (801)649-7000

is a jewel of a hotel. With only twelve rooms, each furnished differently, it is difficult to secure reservations on short notice. Located at the corner of Main Street in historic Old Park City, the Silver Queen has one and two-bedroom condos. All have Jacuzzi baths, fireplaces, and washer and dryers. The kitchens are fully equipped so entertaining is easy. During the 1993-94 season the condos rent for between $75 and $295 per night for a one-bedroom unit. The two-bedroom unit is between $95 and $375 per night. Telephone (801) 649-5986 for reservations and information.

One of the nicest and most convenient hotels in Park City is the **Silver King Hotel**, only a few steps from the base of the gondola.

The Silver King is a condominium hotel which features numerous amenities. In other words, the units are privately owned, but the facility is operated like a hotel. There is a nicely appointed lobby with a large lacquered fireplace and big bright windows. The Silver King's underground parking is really appreciated on cold snowy days. The hotel also provides a heated indoor/outdoor swimming pool, therapy pool, sauna, valet service, laundry, daily maid service, cable tv, ski ticket sales, conference and meeting facilities and more.

Although the units are individually furnished, there is a commonality to them. Some units may have a blue color scheme while others have a white one. All are furnished in country French. Even the smallest studio units are unique. Dining room ceilings are constructed out of glass, providing enjoyable views of the falling snow. What a cozy setting for relaxing in front of the crackling hearth!

The largest units are two-bedroom penthouses which occupy two floors and have their own private spas. Large kitchens, living areas, entertainment areas, and spacious bedrooms complete these marvelous accommodations.

Silver King accommodations are priced during the 1993-94 regular season from a low of $120 per night for a studio to $520 per night for a DeLuxe penthouse. Telephone (800) 331-8652 for reservations and information.This is a AAA 4-diamond resort. As at almost all ski area facilities, prices will go up according to the season.

For truly unique accommodations, comfort-seeking skiers should consider the **Washington School Inn**, which is listed on the National Register of Historic Places. The building was originally constructed in 1889, and as its name implies, was "school" to hundreds of students until 1931. A major renovation costing in excess of $1 million was completed in 1985, when the current fifteen-room bed and breakfast hotel was opened. Furnished in early American tradition and boasting some authentic period antiques, the Washington School Inn is a treasure. Each of its rooms has been decorated individually, and returning guests will no doubt have a favorite. The rooms and suites are named after former school teachers. The Miss Urie suite, for example, is a lovely example of the hotel's finest accommodations. It features its own television, wet bar, and a decor of burgundy carpeting and yellow, rose-patterned wall and bedcoverings. With its large, four-poster bed campaign chest, desk, and full-length mirror, the suite represents the epitome of a late nineteenth century hostelry.

The hotel's lobby and public areas, graced with their potted palms and gas fixtures, are reminiscent of a long-past, more restful time. One of the nicest spas found anywhere is available in the basement. Sunlight streams through a small casement window and focuses its light on the steam emanating from the tub. Thriving poinsettias, palms, and ferns are everywhere. The floor is constructed from flagstones which have been sealed but look permanently wet. Adjacent to the spa is a ski locker area and a men's and women's bath and locker room - all immaculate!

Washington School Inn rental rates during the 1993-94 season range from a low of $75 per night, double occupancy, to a high of $225 for a single guest room. Deluxe suites range from $120 to $275. This hotel received the AAA 4-diamond rating in 1993. For reservations or information, telephone (800) 824-1672.

The Stein Eriksen Lodge is located at mid-mountain at the Deer Valley Ski Resort and is a luxurious hotel with an emphasis on service. The Mobil Travel Guide rates a 4-star inn, while AAA gives it its highest 4-diamond rating. The lodge has ski in\ski out access to the mountain, jacuzzi, sauna, heated outdoor pool, a weight room and a free shuttle around Park City. A ski rental and repair shop is on the premises as well as concierge service and an award winning restaurant, the **Glitretind**. Prices range from $89 per night during the low season to a high of $1750 during the holidays.

The Goldener Hirsch Inn, with only 20 rooms also is a beautiful place to stay at Deer Valley.

Restaurants

Amici Ristorante is located in the heart of Park City's "old town" on Main Street. Its welcoming ambiance promises delightful food and service. Amici's modern Italian architecture is intriguing because all the marble, granite, and antique finishes are faux. They were created for the restaurant's owner by a local artisan and are guaranteed to fool all but the most observant. Dinner at Amici is a thing to be savored; diners should be prepared to spend up to one and a half hours enjoying such delectable favorites as arrosta di maiale (roast pork loin crusted with mustard and peppercorns) or canestrelli di carciofi (sea scallops with artichoke hearts and herbed butter). Consistent with the European style, Amici serves its salad after the main course. Dinner is "il prezzo é fissato" and there are only two seatings per evening. Menus change from year to year, but it is always special. Prices are comparable to those of other good restaurants in Park City. For reservations telephone (801) 649-5883.

On the more plebeian side, try **Yen Jing** located in the Resort Center. The shredded pork and garlic is as excellent as the hot and sour soup is inferior. The service is attentive and the prices are moderate. A word of caution: do not accept a table near the entrance. The door's constant opening and closing makes diners at these tables uncomfortably cold.

Cisero's, a fine Italian restaurant, is located in delightful Old Park City. Patrons often must wait in its downstairs bar, as it is a popular place and no reservations are accepted. To compensate for the wait the restaurant will pay the club fee mandated by Utah liquor laws. However, one is expected to pay for the drinks consumed while waiting. The bar, located in a basement, is quite typical of others in mountain restaurants. The noise level is about twice what normal ears can stand, and the acoustics are non-existent. All these negatives somehow work well together, and the bar is a popular gathering spot for locals.

The upstairs restaurant is furnished in eclectic mountain style with both tables and banquettes. The menu features pasta dinners, veal dishes, and seafood. Specials include stuffed lumaconi, eggplant parmigiana, lasagna, Joe's vegetarian casserole, chicken cacciatore, and a daily beef special. The prices are low to moderate and the service attentive. Credit cards are accepted.

Situated one-half mile north of Park City is **Adolf's Restaurant**. This is frequently touted as one of the best restaurants in Park City. The interior is pseudo-Swiss featuring a large public dining area festooned with various colorful flags and posters. Menu items include a variety of beef, veal seafood and Swiss specialties.

If one's dining preferences lean toward the hard-to-locate, intimate restaurant, try **Alex's**. Located on Main Street in historic Old Park City, entrance to Alex's is almost hidden between two retail shops at street level. Once the entry has been located, follow the steep steps down into the dining area itself. A careful scrutiny of the walls confirms that the building housing the restaurant is very old. In the dimly lighted and softly decorated atmosphere, diners involuntarily hush conversation. Each table is graced with a delicate floral piece. Starched table linens are white and burgundy and set with French tableware.

Alex's food preparation is excellent! Consider trying the grilled half-chicken roasted with herbs or the three fish platter. The menu is either à la carte or fixed price, whichever the diner prefers. For reservations, telephone (801) 649-6644.

Sitting long-neglected at the foot of the historic district is the old **Union Pacific Depot**. It has finally been renovated by Frody Volgger into one of the city's better après-ski spots and dining rooms. The Depot faithfully maintains its heritage and culture. Its bar area still contains the original freight scale and the walls are graffiti-covered and decorated with slightly bawdy drawings. The Depot features fourteen different beers on tap. Après-ski appetizers include weinerschnitzel, bratwurst, hungarian goulash, and a marvelous bunderfleish.

The dining room is as contemporary as the bar is rustic. Oak flooring, plaid upholstered walls, and fine table settings complete the ambiance. Chef Volgger's talents are evident from the first serving of salad: a composée of red cabbage, carrots, potato salad, beets, and smokey white beans. Entrées include Austrian specialties such as schlachtplatter; smoked pork chops, sauerkraut, Tyrolian dumplings and potatoes or Jaeger schnitzed; sauteed veal cutlet, hunter style with wild mushrooms in a light cream sauce. Other, more traditional entrées include roast duckling, trout fillet des tages, and Depot chicken. The Depot should be on every skier's agenda. Telephone (801) 649-2102 for reservations.

For European style and luxury, try the **Glitretind Restaurant** at the Stein Ericksen Lodge. (801)649-3700, reservations are recommended.

Also recommended is the **Goldener Hirsch** restaurant at the inn of the same name, modeled after the Goldener Hirsch in Salzburg Austria. Reservations are required (801)649-0010.

Other fine dining in Park City includes **Ichiban Sushi** for ethnic Japanese, the **Barking Frog** for Southwest cuisine, **Pastabilities** for Italian, and **Imperial Café** for traditional French dining.

Activities

Non-skiing activities abound in Park City. To find out about hot-air balloons, sleigh rides, snow cat tours and much more, call A.B.C. Reservations Central at (801)649-ABCD. Among them:

Snow tours on snowmobiles or snow-cats. Telephone High Country Adventures at (801) 649-1217 for more information.

Guided snowmobile tours through the Wasatch high country. Telephone Snowmobile / High Country Tours at (801649-FUNN.

Helicopter skiing in some of the best country around Park City. Telephone Utah Powderbird Guides for more information at (801) 649-9739.

Facials, pedicures, massage, acupressure, manicure, and make-up applications at the Vie Retreats. Telephone (801) 649-6363.

Grocery shopping or gourmet basket delivery services from "At Your Service." Telephone them at (801) 649-6700 for more information.

Hot air balloon rides around Park City. Call Balloon Biz at (800)448-2138, or Balloon Affaire at (801) 649-1217 or Park City Balloon Adventures at (801) 645-8787.

Sleigh rides to a distant mountain cabin for dinner. Telephone Park City Sleigh Co. at (801) 649-3359 or Soup's On at ParkWest at (801) 649-1217 for information.

Other activities include legitimate stage performances in the Egyptian Theater in Old Park City or Gambling Tours to Nevada. Mrs. Field's Cookies is headquartered in Park City, and tours of the production facilities can be arranged.

The shopping here in one of America's finest restored mining towns is really excellent. Everything one could want is to be found on Main Street such as art galleries, tee shirt shops, restaurants, bars, hotels, and much more.

Services

Because Park City is a year-round, self-contained city, all the services one normally expects in a town can be had. There is a full complement of churches, sporting good stores, apparel shops, pharmacies, grocery stores, liquor stores, indoor tennis courts, ice-skating, athletic clubs, aerobics classes, movies, dentists, gas stations, and optometrists.

Town Map

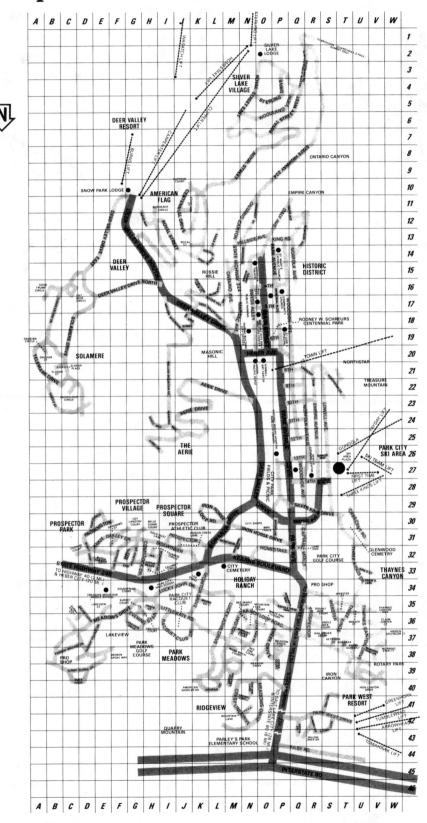

This spectacular tram carries up to 125 skiers to the summit of Hidden Peak at Snowbird resort, 3,100 vertical feet above the valley, offering a variety of intermediate and expert runs. Photo courtesy of Snowbird Resort.

SNOWBIRD/ALTA

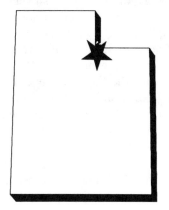

Snowbird, UT. 84092

(800) 453-3000 Reservations
(801) 742-2222 Information
(801) 742-2222 Snow Report

New For 1993-94

While Snowbird is best known for its vast steep terrain, this year the resort has decided to put the emphasis on some of its easier runs, by specifying two areas on its mountains as out of bounds for the "bombers" who speed down the runs as fast as they can at every ski hill. These "Family Ski Zones" will be prominently marked and easy to find so that those who choose to ski slowly can relax without fear that an uphill skier will zoom by.

The area's new trail map also will reflect where these designated zones will be. These are long runs! From the top of the tram, Chip's Run down through Peruvian Gulch to Whodunnit will lead all the way back to the bottom of the tram. The other run can be accessed from the top of the Gad II chairlift, and it follows the Election and Bassackwards runs to the bottom of the mountain.

How to Get There

Like Park City, one of Snowbird's best features is its accessibility. Located almost against the back wall of Little Cottonwood Canyon, Snowbird is only 29 miles from Salt Lake International Airport.

Taxis, limousines, rental cars, and even helicopters are available from the airport to Snowbird and Alta. Canyon Transportation works with Snowbird resort and will provide a van round trip to the resort for $30 during the 1993-94 ski season. Reservations are advised. Call (800)255-1841.

Car rental agencies located at the airport include

Agency	(801) 534-1622
Alamo	(801) 575-2211
Avis	(800) 221-1212
Budget	(801) 363-1500
Dollar	(801) 596-2580
Hertz	(800) 654-3131
National	(800) 328-4567

Driving to Snowbird for the first time is something of a challenge. The Mormon Temple is considered the center of the city. Actually, however, it is located on the north side of town and is considered as "zero" for Salt Lake's street-numbering system. Little Cottonwood Canyon is south of the city center. Take I-15 south from the airport or from the Temple about three miles. Watch the brown signs that indicate the Snowbird turnoff at 90th South. There are only a few of these signs, so keep a sharp eye out. Turn east onto Highway 209 and follow this road through commercial and residential properties until it ends at a 7-Eleven convenience store at the corner of 7th East. The streets are not marked, but it is necessary to make a right turn here. Proceed to the next traffic light and turn left. This road meanders through a residential area and is called Little Cottonwood Canyon Road. Drivers will know they are on the correct road when they see a large electronic sign indicating road conditions for the rest of the trip up the canyon. In periods of heavy snow, snow tires and/or chains will be required. Due to avalanche danger, there are times when the road is temporarily closed while road crews blast away the snow. Snowbird is located in the Wasatch Range which frequently receives snow in abundant quantities, so skiers should be prepared for delays.

On clear days, and when the air pollution in Salt Lake City is not too thick, the drive down the mountain back into the city is beautiful. Be sure to take a camera because there are ample opportunities to photograph Salt Lake from the roadside.

Mountain Information

Snowbird is a great ski mountain with character and variety. There are steep, wide open runs, gladed runs, bump runs, and super powder runs everywhere.

Snowbird boasts 2,000 acres of skiable terrain and has a total lift capacity of 8,810 skiers per hour. The base is located at 7,900 feet (2,007 meters) and the top of the tram is located at 11,000 feet (3,353 meters). This provides a vertical drop of 3,100 feet (787 meters).

The mountain is serviced by

1 Aerial Tram
7 Double Chairlifts

Crowding is usually not a problem at Snowbird even though it is close to a major city. This lack of crowding is primarily because there are a number of other day ski areas in the vicinity. It must also be noted that Snowbird is not an easy mountain. Its beginner and intermediate terrain is both more limited and more challenging than at most other resorts.

Twenty percent of the mountain's runs are classified as easiest; 30 percent as more difficult; and 50 percent as advanced\expert. The trail rating used at Snowbird can equate with those of Jackson Hole, Sun Valley, and Telluride, but not with those of areas such as Keystone, Aspen, and Snowmass.

All beginner runs are located along the lower portion of the mountain and typically are catwalks. The main beginner run and teaching hill is Big Emma, named after a famous Alta madam during the height of the mining era. Big Emma is a great beginner run. It is wide and long, with a pitch so gradual that instructors can control their students' speed by limiting how far up the hill they take them.

Most of the intermediate runs are steep. However, the resort closely monitors the development of moguls and does an excellent job of cutting them before they present problems. Any intermediate who skis Snowbird will leave a better skier. The top of Chip's Run is steep. Most intermediates will be able to ski down it if they stay in control. It is an excellent run, and intermediates might find that by skiing it several times they will build their confidence and gain the strength and courage to try other areas of the mountain for them.

By and large, Snowbird is for experts and aspiring experts. It is a mountain that requires a lot of snow. Fortunately, it receives over 550 inches (1,397 cm) annually. Its monthly snowfalls are

Nov.	65"	(165 cm)
Jan.	76"	(218 cm)
Feb.	84"	(213 cm)
Mar.	107"	(272 cm)
Apr.	75"	(191 cm)

Snowbird Mountain can be skied very differently depending upon snow conditions. During lean periods of snow, the runs are heavily moguled. They are best skied immediately after a heavy snowfall when the steepness is needed in order to maintain forward momentum.

The longest beginner run is Big Emma at 550 feet (168 meters). The longest intermediate run is Chip's Run at two miles (3.2 km), and the longest expert run is Silver Fox at 1.7 miles (2.7 km).

It should be pointed out that although Snowbird considers Big Emma to be its longest beginner run, some other resorts featured in this book have selected catwalks as their longest beginner runs. If Snowbird were to do the same, it would have several runs over one mile (1.06 km) in length. Likewise, it should be pointed out that Silver Fox is expert for the entire 1.7 miles!

Snowbird's terrain varies. The Cirque near the terminus of the tram is one of the world's greatest ski runs. It is a large bowl that catches abundant snowfall. The only problem is accessibility. The Cirque Traverse is a difficult run. It is narrow and steep: its sides drop off dangerously. First-time skiers on this run should use appropriate caution and remain in control. The back side of the Cirque is locally referred to as "Restaurant Row." Access to it is from Regulator Johnson. Ski about one-third of Regulator and begin traversing to the right. By doing this, skiers can ski under the Gad Chutes and can enjoy exceptional tree skiing.

As with most mountains that are steep, there are many possible runs and trails not indicated on the trail map. Virtually all the area within the resort's boundaries is skiable. Many of these unnamed runs require the services of a guide until one learns the ins and outs of the mountain. Any of Snowbird's snow hosts or hostesses will assist interested skiers in locating infrequently skied areas. After major storms it is easy to see where locals have skied, but it remains difficult to surmise how they got there.

Many first-time visitors to Snowbird spend so much time skiing the Aerial Tramway, Little Cloud, and Gad lifts that they completely ignore the runs near the bottom of the mountain. This is a mistake because many fine runs such as Blackjack, Adager, and Harper's Ferry East are well worth their time. This is especially true if the wind is blowing and the temperature is dropping. During inclement weather the only shelter may be on the Peruvian, Mid-Gad, and Gad-II lifts.

Snowbird's average temperatures during the winter are

Dec.	23°	-5° C
Jan.	21°	-6° C
Feb.	22°	-5° C
Mar.	25°	-4° C
Apr.	27°	-3° C

Alta Mountain - Information (801)742-3333

Snow Report (801)572-3739
Lodging and Reservations(801)942-0404

Alta is included with Snowbird because Snowbird lacks adequate intermediate terrain to completely satisfy destination skiers. Likewise, Alta cannot be considered a destination ski resort because it lacks so many amenities found in the other resorts featured in this book. However, Alta is a great ski resort in its own right and if the accommodations and amenities found at Snowbird are taken into account, the two resorts together definitely do qualify for inclusion in *The Greatest Ski Resorts in North America.* Alta is within a mile of Snowbird and transportation between the two mountains is provided by Utah Transit Authority.

At Alta last year the Sugarloaf lift was upgraded to a triple chair from a double. The lift was extended upwards 2-300 feet to give skiers more access to the ridge, and easier access to the top of Germania Pass. In addition the base area transfer tow also has been changed to extend from the bottom of Wildcat to the bottom of Albion, saving people a lot of leg work. The high-tech tow was especially designed for Alta by YAN.

Base elevation at Alta is 8,550 feet (2,172 meters) and top elevation is 10,550 feet (2,680 meters), providing a vertical drop of 2,000 feet (508 meters). This is almost a third less vertical feet than Snowbird and, no doubt, accounts for the exceptional beginner and intermediate terrain.

Best morning ski conditions are generally found off Sugarloaf chair. Most of the runs here are intermediate or expert. Yellow Trail and East Greeley are highly recommended expert runs. Deep powder can usually be found even a week after a big storm. In fact, there is almost always fresh powder to be found somewhere at Alta. Although Alta is crowded on weekends, during the week there is never crowding and there are more ways down the slopes than skiers to ski them. In the afternoon experts should ski West Rustler off the Germania lift. Intermediates will love the long runs off Supreme chairlift, particularly Rock 'n Roll and Big Dipper. Beginners enjoy getting a mile-long run down Crooked Mile which is serviced by Albion lift. The Albion and Sunnyside lifts serve primarily beginner terrain. These runs are almost never disrupted by fast skiers, except late in the afternoon when some of the more aggressive expert skiers head home after skiing the Supreme and Sugarloaf lifts.

During periods of flat light or heavy storms, expert skiers should consider confining their skiing to the runs off Germania lift, specifically West Rustler, Eagles Nest, and perhaps North Rustler. Intermediates should stick to the runs emanating from Collins lift, and beginners should be comfortable on any of the trails off the Albion or Sunnyside lifts.

To ski from the Albion side to the Germania side, skiers of intermediate ability or better should take Baldy Traverse located at the top of Sugarloaf lift. This traverse deposits skiers at the top of the Germania lift. There is also a lateral rope tow running from Albion Day Lodge to Alta Lodge.

Snowbird Lift Ticket Prices (1993-94)

Snowbird does not have a "high" or "low" season rate. There is only one rate.

$ 38   Adult All Area (Includes Tram)
$ 31   Adult, All Chairs
$ 23   Children, 12 & Under (Includes Tram)
$ 23   Seniors, 62 - 69 (Includes Tram)
Free   Seniors, 70+

Half-Day Prices

$31   Adult, All Area (Includes Tram)

$23   Adult, All Chairs
$18   Child, Senior, All Area (Includes Tram)
$14   Child, Seniors, All Chairs

Morning half-day lift tickets are valid from 9:30 A.M. to 1:30 P.M. Afternoon half-day lift tickets are sold from 12:30 P.M. until closing.

Alta Lift Ticket Prices (1992-93)

The 1993-94 prices were not available at press time.
$23   Area day pass (regardless of age)
$17   Area half-day pass, A.M. or P.M.
$21   Albion, Sunnyside, and Cecret ten-ride pass
$17   Albion Day pass
$11   Albion, half-day pass
Alta accepts only Mastercard, Visa or cash.

Hours of Operation

Snowbird-   9:30 A.M. to 3:45 P.M. (Tram)
9:30 A.M. to 4:30 P.M. (Lifts)

Alta's hours of operation are from 9:15 A.M. to 4:30 P.M.

Lift Ticket Purchase Locations

The main ticket office is located just outside the Aerial Tram station on Snowbird's Plaza Deck. There is also an auxiliary ticket office in The Cliff Lodge. You can also buy tickets at all front desks at lodges in Gad Valley.

There are two lift ticket sales locations at Alta. The main ticket window is located adjacent to the main parking lot near the base of the Collins and Wildcat lifts. Another ticket sales location is next to Albion Day Lodge near the Lower Albion parking lot.

How to Avoid Crowds

Crowds are not really a problem at Snowbird. The only area that is subject to occasional crowding is the Aerial Tram. It is possible, however, to ski virtually all the mountain without taking the tram. Adequate chairlifts service most of the area.

Most crowding at Alta occurs on weekends. The Germania lift seems to be the most plagued by crowds and should be avoided. The Collins lift is usually the least crowded, as is the Wildcat lift for experts. Experts will find the least crowds in the Westward Ho area.

Ski School (1993-94)

Snowbird employs more than 125 PSIA instructors certified in the American Teaching System (ATS). Classes are available seven days a week for every level of ability. The ski school has instituted a policy of "eight is enough," meaning that you never will have more than 8 people in an adult group lesson, Christmas and President's holidays excluded.

For the younger set, the Child/Super Teen's classes begin at 9 a.m. and end at 4 p.m., The cost is $65 and includes, lunch, group lessons and supervision.

Adult beginners and children meet at the Chickadee Ski School sign just west of the Cliff Lodge near the Chickadee Lift. Adult classes meet at 10:30 A.M. and 1:30 P.M., while children's classes usually meet at 10:00 A.M. and 1:30 P.M.

$ 50	Adult All-Day
$ 40	Adult, Half-Day
$125	Adult, 3-Day, Mon.-Wed., Consecutive days only
$225	Adult, 5-Day
$ 65	One-Hour Private
$165	Half-Day Private (3 hours)
$ 40	Early Bird (9 to 10 a.m. only)

$250	All-Day Private
$ 90	One hour for 2-5 people
$ 40	Early bird private specials

Snowbird offers its **Mountain Experience Program** to those skiers who are advanced or expert. These classes emphasize technique and handling assorted snow conditions. Mountain Experience guides are also available to competent expert skiers who would like to learn more about Snowbird's famous out-of-bounds skiing. Classes meet in front of the tram station on the Plaza at 10:00 A.M. These classes are five hours in duration.

$ 65	One-Day
$290	5-Day

Children's Classes[1]

$ 60	Full-Day
$ 40	Half-Day
$165	Three-Day
$250	Five-Day

For 3- to 4-year olds, Snowbird's Chickadee program pairs 2 children of similar ability alone in a class so that they get extra individual attention and learn more quickly. The cost is $40 per 1-1/2 hour session, and reservations are required.

Sign up for ski lessons at the ski school ticket offices located in the Cliff Lodge on level 1, the Snowbird Center on level 3 or call (801)742-2222, ext. 5170.

Equipment Rental

Three rental shops are located in Snowbird: **Breeze** and **Cliff Lodge Rental Shop** and **SportStalker**. Prices were unavailable at press time but Breeze estimated its costs would be $13 per day for skis, boots, poles and bindings. Cliff Lodge rentals start at $16 per day in 1993-94 for a basic rental package of skis, boots, and poles. For the sport package, the price is $21, and for high performance skis, boots and poles, it will be $28. Children's rental packages cost $16 per day. Rental rates are discounted at The Cliff Lodge if equipment is rented for longer than two days.

---

[1] Lunch and supervision are available at an additional cost.

Ski Tuning and Repair

The rates at the Cliff Lodge Rental Shop for 1993-94 are $35 for a complete tune up; $22 for sharpening and waxing of skis; and $6 for wax only; and $15 for binding testing and adjustment.

Mountain Dining

Mid Gad restaurant is located at the top of the Mid Gad lift. This structure is built of timber shipped to the mountain from the Pacific Northwest and is quite handsome. This is a cafeteria-style restaurant featuring short-order foods and hardy dishes such as beef stew, ribs, and so forth.

The best mountain restaurant is not on the mountain itself but rather is located next to the Aerial Tram base station. It is called **Forklift**. The Forklift has table service and an excellent menu. The restaurant's floor-to-ceiling windows overlook Hidden Peak. Diners can watch the Aerial Tram or perhaps the porcupine that sometimes lives in the trees outside the windows.

Try the stir-fried shrimp and oriental vegetables. It is a delicious entrée and not too filling, just right for the active skier's lunch.

There are three cafeteria restaurants and one sit-down restaurant on Alta's slopes. The newest cafeteria is located at Albion Basin and is appropriately called **Albion Grill**. Hot foods, deli sandwiches, and salad bar are available daily. All food is well prepared and attractively served. 3.2 beer and wine coolers are the only alcoholic beverages served. The Albion Grill is Alta's largest on-mountain restaurant.

The Alpenglow cafeteria is located at the base of Sugarloaf chairlift in Albion Basin. Its broad deck boasts beautiful panoramic views of the Greeley Area. It is best know for its "avalanche burger."

Located at the base of the Germania lift is **Watson Shelter**. This is the oldest and most picturesque restaurant in Alta. It features two levels, the first of which is a typical ski resort cafeteria, while the second features a delightful sit-down full-service restaurant called **Chic's Place**. Whether conditions are severe or mild, Chic's offers a comfortable place in which to dine. On cold, wintery days there is a warming fireplace by which to relax and enjoy a delicious meal. On warm, spring days skiers enjoy lunching on the outside deck with its gorgeous views and delightful service.

Typical meals at Chic's include a daily pasta special, reuben sandwiches, chili, or the catch of the day. A California-style entrée of seafood and sprouts is popular and well prepared. Prices are moderate and wines and beers are also available.

Child Care

Child care for children 3 years and older is available at **Snowbird Children's Center**, located on the first level of The Cliff Lodge on the ski services floor. This is a licensed day care facility with caretaker to child rations of 1 to 3 for infants, with a floater also in the room; 1 to 5 for 2- and 3-year-olds; and 1 to 10 for 3- to 12-year-olds. During the 1993-94 season child-care rates are $50 per day for 6-week-olds to 24-month-olds. For toddlers, 2- to 3-year-olds the price is $48. For toilet trained 3-year-olds and older children, the price is $36 per day. If there is space available, an hourly rate of $9 will be charged for shorter periods..

On Friday evenings, the Snowbird Children's Center offers **Kids Club**, an evening of child care featuring child-oriented entertainment, such as a magician, "pet lady", musician, or movies. This program is for children between three and eleven; its cost, including dinner, is a modest $23.

The Friday Kids Club activities begin with a party on New Years' Eve, whether it falls on a Friday or not. A special Holiday Bash will be planned for that evening. The party will last from 6:30 until 12:15 and the charge is $30 for the first child, and $26 for each additional child. Teens 11 to 15 will have a party in a separate room for the same price.

Enrollment in day care or any of the special programs may be made by telephoning (801) 742-2222, ext. 5026.

Medical Facilities

The medical emergency center is located in the Snowbird Center on level one. This facility, affiliated with Alta View Hospital of Salt Lake City, has a fully staffed emergency room that can handle acute emergencies and injuries and is equipped with X-ray equipment. Serious trauma cases are transported by ambulance or helicopter to Alta View Hospital. The emergency center's hours are from 9:30 A.M. to 6:00 P.M.

Cross-Country Skiing

Due to Snowbird and Alta's steep surrounding terrain (after all, it is a box canyon), there is no cross-country skiing at either resort.

Special Events

Every Tuesday, Wednesday, and Thursday at noon, National Standard Races (NASTAR) are held on Snowbird's Wilbere Race Course. This course, located between Big Emma and the Wilbere chairlift, also has a coin-operated self-timer course set up on the same hill. It is open the entire day. Each April the Rights of Spring are celebrated at the Snowbird Spring Wine Festival.

Accommodations

The Cliff Lodge and Spa is as impressive as the towering peaks which surround it. Constructed of raw, rough concrete and natural clear fir, The Cliff appears to have burst from solid rock to soar ten stories.

The winding Little Cottonwood Canyon Road leading to Entrance #4 twists down a small cliff and around The Cliff. Valet parking is available at The Cliff's lowest level.

A short escalator ride takes guests from the lower level up to a spellbinding main lobby. The massive lobby is ten stories high and furnished with quality contemporary furnishings. Oriental objets d'art complete the decor. The sheer size of the public rooms is overwhelming, and thus its decorations, such as plants, are extremely large. Floral baskets hanging in the **Golden Cliff Restaurant** are large enough to contain palm trees!

The size of everything in The Cliff dictates use of strong textures such as those found in the textiles displayed in its wall coverings, wall hangings, and furniture covers. As a counterpoint, the designer wisely selected warm pastel colors to complete the design. Sea foam, mauve, peach, and similar colors predominate.

The spacious rooms are well lighted and furnished with quality furniture. In fact, visitors could say the single most significant impression they receive from Snowbird is its dedication to quality. Whether it is in the furniture or the chairlifts, no corners have been cut nor expense spared in making Snowbird a truly world-class resort.

The Cliff Lodge has many amenities one normally would not expect to find at a ski lodge. There are coin-operated laundry facilities on each floor, and steam irons and ironing boards may be borrowed from the front desk. There is an art gallery on Level C. Cribs and roll-away beds are available from housekeeping and stamps may be purchased from the front desk. A gift shop and small variety store are located on Level C.

Skis are not permitted in the rooms, but a free ski check is provided on Level 1. Cable TV in each room receives all the networks plus ESPN and PBS. There are also Channels 11, 12 and 13 which broadcast current information regarding Snowbird. Items like road conditions, weather, places to visit, or restaurants in which to eat are frequently featured. Cliff Lodge rental rates during the 1993-94 season start at $103 for a canyon view bedroom, $400 for a 2-bedroom suite per night during low season, increasing to a high of $178 and $756, respectively, during Christmas week.

Condominium accommodations are available at **The Lodge at Snowbird**. Do not confuse The Lodge at Snowbird with The Cliff Lodge. On Little Cottonwood Canyon Road, The Lodge at Snowbird is located just west of The Cliff Lodge.

The Lodge at Snowbird is twelve to fifteen years old and is beginning to show its age. Its architecture is very striking and in keeping with other Snowbird properties: it seems to fit perfectly into the environment. The lobby with its large stone fireplace is very attractive.

Rooms in The Lodge are charming, however. Each has a granite fireplace and cable TV. The Danish modern furnishings need replacing, but the recently remodeled kitchens are well equipped with all the appliances one could need except for microwave ovens and ice makers.

Staircases to the upstairs bedrooms are exceptional and a testament to the original architect's concept of gracious mountain living. The master bedrooms are constructed as lofts; consequently, they are open to the living area. This can be a problem if more than one family or a family with children occupy the unit. For example, if the occupants of the master bedroom want to sleep and the other guests want to stay up and watch TV, the volume will be just as great in the bedroom as it is in the living room, presumably an undesirable situation.

The units' upstairs and downstairs baths are complete with tubs and showers. There are also dressing rooms attached to the bathrooms; closets are spacious.

Although The Lodge at Snowbird consists primarily of one-bedroom units, some may be converted to two-bedroom units by utilizing an adjoining room. 1993-94 rates for The Lodge at Snowbird start at a modest $83 per night and peak at $161 per night during Christmas week.

Other accommodations include **The Inn** with sixty-five DeLuxe rooms and the Iron Blosam Lodge. The Iron Blosam is an interval ownership condominium and, as such, rooms are rarely available.

When children twelve and under stay in the same accommodations as their parents, they can stay and ski free.

Nestled in an aspen grove between Snowbird and Alta are **The View** condominiums. These are privately owned and managed by Snowbird Realty. These condominiums probably have the best view in all of Snowbird and Alta. Their windows provide a panoramic view of Snowbird and Salt Lake City. On clear evenings the lights of the city sparkle, and traffic driving up the Little Cottonwood Canyon appears to be a continuous ribbon of color. Each condo in The View is individually decorated, but all tend to be contemporary. Available in one, two, and three bedrooms, each unit is constructed of first-class materials. Brass fixturing, marble tables, berber carpeting, Jacuzzi tubs, and lots of closets make living in The View easy and fun. Although it is possible to ski-in and ski-out to Snowbird, one must take the shuttle to ski Alta. It is possible for strong skiers to ski-in to The View from Alta by traversing Wildcat and Westward Ho. All units in The View include laundry rooms with washers and dryers, satellite T.V., V.C.R. with remote control, fireplaces, and on-site management. There is also an indoor hot tub and changing rooms for guests. For information and reservations at The View, telephone (800)274-7172.

In roughly the same area as The View are the more traditional **Village at Sugarplum** condominiums. These units are just far enough off the slopes that it is necessary for guests to use the shuttle service which runs directly in front of the units to get to either Snowbird or Alta. Landscaped units are arranged picturesquely in duplex groupings, each reached by a winding path. Built among aspen and birch trees, The Village at Sugarplum creates an ambience similar to that found at Sun Valley.

Condos are available in one or two-bedroom configurations or two and three bedrooms with loft. Each unit is furnished differently, but all contain Jenn-Air ranges, Magic Chef dishwashers and disposals. Typical interior finish-out is in natural oak. Although more units are being constructed each year, many of the units on the rental program are several years old and are beginning to look a little dated with furniture that may be more utilitarian than designer specified. Depending on one's taste and needs, it would be a good idea to telephone the management company and ascertain the description and age of any units being contemplated before actually renting. The toll-free number is (800) 562-2888. Village of Sugar Plum 1993-94 winter rates range from a low of $225 to a high of $525 per night, depending on the size of the units. (800)562-2888.

Powder Ridge is on the Alta side of the mountain. All condominiums at Powder Ridge are three bedroom, three and one-half baths. Constructed to fit in with the environment, all units have great views of Alta and are contemporary. Soaring ceilings and large windows dominate. There are fireplaces, spas, and fully equipped kitchens with plentiful storage and brand-name appliances. Even garages are provided so guests are assured their cars will start each morning, regardless of the temperature. Powder Ridge condominiums rent during the 1993-94 season for $325 per night during low season and $500 during high season. Telephone (800) 562-2888 for additional information or reservations.

Restaurants

Everything at Snowbird is first-class. This is particularly true of the restaurants. The finest dining is found at **The Aerie Restaurant** located on the top floor of The Cliff Lodge. This is a formal restaurant with soft lighting, unique ceilings, Oriental screens, and entertainment. Its tables are set with fine china on white linens. A display of antique Chinese kimonos frames the entrance. The views are spectacular!

Service is attentive and the food is excellent. Consider ordering lamb. It is raised locally in Utah and served with an excellent Dijon mustard sauce. Order salad dressings and other sauces on the side, as the chef seems to have a heavy hand when he applies them.

A hot breakfast buffet is offered in The Cliff Lodge's **Atrium Restaurant**, also located on Level B. While enjoying breakfast and gazing out the ten-story high windows, listen for the ski patrol setting its four-pound avalanche charges. As the charges detonate, the windows reverberate.

The eleven-story Atrium is obviously an extremely vertical room due to the soaring height of windows and open lobby adjacent to it. Large ficus trees dressed in Italian lights establish a pleasant mood. To further enhance the ambience, soft Strauss or Vivaldi music is piped in.

Another fine restaurant has just been renovated in The Lodge at Snowbird and is called, appropriately enough, **The Lodge Club.** During the day the restaurant is brightly lighted by the snow's reflections through the Club's greenhouse windows. One entire wall is a glass-fronted, climate-controlled wine cellar with several hundred bottles of very fine varietal wines.

Meals here are well prepared and presented by amiable waiters and waitresses. Appetizers include such selections as escargot, Manila clams, smoked salmon, duck paté, or baked brie. Salads feature fresh spinach and Belgian endive. Entrées include breast of chicken, Norwegian salmon, pork tenderloin, filet mignon, and rack of lamb. Wonderful desserts and after-dinner drinks are also available.

Visitors may have heard horror stories or exaggerated claims about Utah liquor laws. Most of these stories are mere fabrications. Liquor may be purchased in state-controlled liquor stores and taken into any restaurant. The restaurant may charge the diner for a setup such as cola or 7-Up. Restaurants may charge a "corkage" fee for wines that are brought in. A package store is conveniently located in the Snowbird Center.

Activities

Because Snowbird is located in Salt Lake City's watershed area, restrictions are imposed on the activities allowed. No dogs or other domestic animals are permitted in the watershed. Therefore, no sleigh rides or dog sled rides are permitted here. In fact, the laws governing activities at Snowbird are so strict that the resort is not even allowed to construct high tension lines in the valley to bring in electricity; it has had to create its own energy. Consequently, Snowbird has built one of the country's largest co-generation energy plants. Natural gas fires an electric generator to provide electricity. The excess heat produced by the gas fire is used to heat The Cliff Lodge.

Snowbird is well known for is its Spa, located in The Cliff Lodge. In very spacious quarters, one can exercise, enjoy a massage, or receive a beauty treatment. There is even a café which features low calorie and low cholesterol meals. Complete packages, such as those offered by the finest spas in the world, are available to skiing and non-skiing guests alike. Owner Dick Bass is committed to providing an environment where one can be physically, mentally, spiritually, and emotionally renewed.

Some of the deepest powder helicopter skiing in the country is offered by Wasatch Powderbird Guides. Reservations can be made in Snowbird Center or by telephoning (801) 742-2800. In the spring it is a unique experience to try their Cornball Special which consists of four runs in corn snow followed by 18 holes of golf at the Wasatch State Park Golf Course. Prices start at $350 per person. The season runs from Dec. 15 through May 15, and the helicopters make it possible for skiers to access 80,000 acres of powder glades and bowls.

Services

Within Snowbird guests will find churches, sporting good stores, apparel shops, a pharmacy, a grocery store, a bank, and a liquor store.

Ski Hosts and Hostesses provide free guided tours of the mountain. Meet at the "Free Guided Skiing Tour" sign on the Plaza deck. Tours leave at 9:00 A.M. and 1:00 P.M. every day.

Wildcat Base Area, Alta Ski Lifts

SQUAW VALLEY/Alpine Meadows

Squaw Valley Ski Corporation
Post Office Box 2007
Olympic Valley, Ca. 96146

(800) 545-4350 Reservations
(916) 583-6955 Information and Snow Report

New For 1993-94

Last year Squaw added one double and two new triple chairs to its vast area, and this year continues to realign lifts to facilitate the flow of traffic.

Both the Mainline and Headwall double chair lifts have been repositioned this year to alleviate crowding in the mid mountain areas. Add this to last year's new triple chair serving the High Camp Bath and Tennis Club and the Silverado Triple Chair bowl area opening up 800 acres of terrain, and one can see that Squaw's management is putting its efforts into moving skiers quickly all over its mountains.

This year a 12,000 square foot **Children's World** Facility will open at the base of the mountain. It is conveniently located near to the one-year-old "Papoose" lift.

As it started to do last year, Alpine Meadows Ski Area has teamed up with some Lake Tahoe lodges to offer ski packages which will assuredly entice eager skiers to visit. Especially attractive is the "Dawn of the Season" package available until Christmas Eve. For $49.50, visitors can find double occupancy lodging, breakfast and an all-day lift ticket at Alpine. Call 1-800-949-DAWN for information.

The Hyatt Regency Lake Tahoe in Incline Village and Alpine offer a season-long offer for $59.

How To Get There

A regional airport is located in South Lake Tahoe. American Eagle has flights from San Jose and San Francisco to S. Lake Tahoe, and Alpha Air flies from Los Angeles. If travelers from the East Coast want to fly directly into Tahoe rather than into Reno, it is necessary for them to overfly Squaw, land in San Francisco, and catch another flight to Tahoe. Hertz and Avis both have cars to rent at this airport, but please make reservations.

The nearest major airport to Squaw Valley is Reno Cannon International. Located 45 miles from the resort, it is served by twelve major carriers. The Reno Airport is very convenient, and because of its desert location, it is relatively immune to the variances of winter weather.

Numerous car rental agencies are located in the baggage claim area of the terminal as well as just outside airport property. Taxi and limousine services are also available. Car rental agencies represented in Reno include Alamo, Avis, Budget, Dollar, Hertz, National, and Thrifty.

If skiers intend to rent a car from one of the major companies at the airport, they should plan to pick up the car from the lot without their luggage. The rental lots are located about one-quarter mile from the baggage claim area, and there are no shuttle buses. Unless skiers can find one of the few porters at the airport, they will probably become exasperated trying to carry their luggage to the car. It is much easier to drive the car around to the baggage claim area and load the luggage there. Upon returning, it is likewise extremely important to unload the luggage **before** returning the car to the rental parking area.

It is usually less expensive to arrange for a rental car in the city where it is to be rented, rather than going through the toll-free 800 number. Rates established locally are typically lower than those established nationally. A way to secure a better rate without the risk of not getting a car is to telephone the local rental agency 24 hours in advance of need. By doing this, the consumer is assured of both a low rate and an available car.

Because the police in the Sierras may require that all vehicles have snow tires and chains, it is imperative that the car be so equipped. Check the equipment before accepting the rental car.

Although snowfall in the Sierras tends to be sporadic, it is prodigious whenever it occurs. Should the skier arrive in Reno during one of these major dumps, it may be necessary to drive to Squaw via Carson City, rather than taking the more direct route on I-80. Be certain to check road conditions with the rental agency before departing.

There is no regular shuttle between Reno Airport and Squaw Valley. To charter a bus will cost more than $100 per person, so really it is more cost efficient to rent a car at the airport.

Skiers who wish to combine skiing with a little gambling and stay in Reno can catch the airport shuttle bus. It leaves the baggage claim area each hour on the half hour for the major hotels and casinos. Prices were not available at press time, but judging from the previous years prices, it will be less than $10 round trip.

In the past daily shuttles departed Reno's hotels for Squaw Valley and Alpine Meadows between 7:00 A.M. and 8:00 A.M. At press time, no definite arrangements had been made for this service for the 1993-94 year, but there probably will still be a service. Please call Sierra Nevada Grey Line at (702) 329-1147 to check out when or where these buses will be leaving and returning, and to make reservations.

Accommodations are limited at Squaw Valley, as is true at all California ski resorts. Therefore, many skiers have to stay in lodging somewhat removed from the resort itself. To help accommodate these guests, Squaw runs free shuttle buses between the resort and hotels on the north shore of Lake Tahoe, the south shore, Tahoe City, and Truckee. Telephone Squaw Valley's toll-free number, (800) 545-4350, and request a bus schedule in advance because one may not be available at the airport or at the guest's hotel.

Mountain Information

Squaw Valley is the largest destination resort in California. It is also among the best ski mountains in the United States—possibly the world. Every conceivable type of terrain is located at Squaw. Rather than consisting solely of trails, the resort offers six peaks that are skiable. There is certainly adequate terrain for all ability levels.

Squaw Valley is BIG! Consisting of more than 4,000 acres, Squaw is only one-third smaller than Vail with its huge back bowls. The vertical drop is 2,850 feet (869 meters). Squaw's uppermost summit is 9,050 feet (2,758 meters), and its base is at 6,200 feet (1,890 meters).

Thirty-three lifts including one aerial tram and one gondola serve this extremely large area. Twenty-five percent of the lifts service beginner areas, forty-five percent intermediate, and thirty percent expert. The mountain naturally divides itself into areas of specific ability levels, thus making it possible to position lifts to exploit this natural phenomenon. The only other mountain that comes to mind with this natural division of ability levels is Copper Mountain in Colorado.

Like all great mountains, the names and numbers of trails are insignificant because the entire area is skiable. In fact, a review of Squaw's trail map will merely reveal names of the lifts. The only list of trail names, to this writer's knowledge, exists in the ski patrol's office to help patrolmen locate and evacuate injured skiers.

One of the most unique features of Squaw is that the beginner slopes are at the top of the mountain rather than at the base. Novice skiers can access the slopes by taking either the aerial tram or gondola and exit the same way after lessons or after free skiing. The longest beginner run is off the Riviera lift[1] at 387 feet (118 meters). The longest intermediate run is The Mountain Run which is three miles (4.8 km), and the longest expert trail is KT-22 at 1,753 feet (534 meters).

KT-22 is an interesting run. It is very steep and tends to become heavily moguled. Prior to the founding of Squaw Valley, the owner and his wife were dropped by helicopter on top of what was to become KT-22. The wife's name was "Katie," and she reportedly said it took her 22 kick turns to get down the hill. The name stuck! Not only is KT-22 one of the most difficult runs in America, but the chairlift may also qualify as one of the most frightening. The lift before its terminus is at least as high as the Loges Peak lift at Aspen Highlands. However, the view of Lake Tahoe is breathtakingly beautiful.

The unique and wonderful thing about Squaw is that many of its expert runs can be made relatively easy or extremely difficult depending on where one begins to ski them. For example, if one takes the Granite Chief lift and skis the runs underneath, the run is primarily easy expert. All that is required is the ability to ski bumps. A strong intermediate could competently handle this terrain. However, it takes a real expert to ride the Emigrant lift and go around Emigrant Peak to the top of Granite Chief. Once around the backside, skiers find themselves on a cornice looking at anywhere from a three or four-foot jump onto the slope to a ten-foot jump, depending on snow conditions.

Most of the intermediate runs are gathered around the area just above the gondola and tram. These are the Emigrant Peak and the Shirley Lake areas. The runs are almost always groomed, and it is possible to really cruise these trails. More adventurous intermediates will enjoy the thrills awaiting them under Siberia Express. This is a large bowl, quite steep with moderate moguls.

Squaw Valley averages over 450 inches (1,143 cm) of snow annually. Most of this snow comes infrequently, but in prodigious amounts. Its monthly snowfalls are

Nov.	52"	(134 cm)
Dec.	54"	(138 cm)
Jan.	71"	(181 cm)
Feb.	80"	(202 cm)
Mar.	77"	(194 cm)
Apr.	35"	(89 cm)

---

[1] The longest runs can only be identified by the lift serving an area because Squaw Valley only names lifts, not trails.

Because of the snowfall pattern, Squaw Valley experiences really excellent powder skiing during and immediately after a snowstorm. The remainder of the time, conditions are packed powder. The snow at Squaw tends to be more moist than that found in Colorado primarily due to Squaw's location relative to the Pacific Ocean. Spring snows can be very heavy; therefore, more physical conditioning is required to ski Squaw than the Rocky Mountain resorts.

Squaw Valley's average temperatures at the base are

Nov.	31°	0°	C
Dec.	31°	0°	C
Jan.	31°	0°	C
Feb.	33°	1°	C
Mar.	34°	1°	C
Apr.	41°	5°	C

If Squaw Valley's total acreage is divided by its uphill lift capacity a relatively high figure results substantiating the most frequently heard complaint about Squaw: it's crowded! In an effort to counter this negative image, the management has done something unique. It guarantees lift lines of no more than ten minutes in duration or the cost of the lift ticket is refunded, and skiers may ski the remainder of the day free. Beware, however, of seemingly ironclad offers. Actually, in order to participate, skiers must register and purchase what amounts to an insurance policy for $1. Further, they must state their ability level because the offer only applies to lifts of similar ability. All lifts are continually monitored and waiting times noted. In reality, what happens is that all the waiting times of all the lifts of a particular ability level are added together and divided by the total number of lifts to determine the wait. For example, there are ten intermediate lifts. The actual waiting times for each lift are added together and divided by ten for the average wait. If this figure exceeds ten minutes, a refund is granted. However, what often happens is that a skier may be skiing one intermediate lift and experience a fifteen-minute wait. When he goes to collect a refund, he is told that although a fifteen-minute wait existed at the lift he was skiing, there was only a five-minute lift line on another lift (even though it might be a great distance away from the area being skied). However, because there was an intermediate level lift with a wait of less than 10 minutes, the skier is not eligible for a refund.

Lift Ticket Prices (1993-94)

$ 41	Adult, All-Day
$ 28	Adult, Half-Day
$ 78	Adult, 2-Day
$114	Adult, 3-Day
$180	Adult, 5-Day
$ 5	Child, Under 13
$ 5	Adult, 65+

Interchangeable lift tickets are available at Squaw Valley and other ski areas around Lake Tahoe including Alpine Meadows, Northstar, Homewood, Sugar Bowl, Mt. Rose, Ski Incline, Heavenly Valley, and Kirkwood.

Hours of Operation

9:00 A.M. to 4:00 P.M. daily, except weekends and holidays when the lifts open at 8:00 A.M. The aerial tram and gondola cease up-loading operations at 3:45 P.M. daily. Night skiing on Fridays and Saturdays only from 4:00 P.M. to 9:00 P.M.

Lift Ticket Purchase Locations

Additional ticket portals have been added at Squaw Valley during the past two years, so some of the crowding during peak periods should have been alleviated. Tickets may be purchased at base area of the mountain and at The Resort at Squaw Creek.

How To Avoid Crowds

Crowd control at Squaw Valley is a serious matter. In spite of its tremendous size, there is only one way down the mountain at night, and that is via the three-mile long Mountain Run. The only other alternative is to ride down in either the gondola or the cable car.

This is a bad situation, but it is handled as well as possible by the ski patrol. Commencing as early as 2:00 P.M., ski patrolmen, some with bull horns, are positioned along the length of the mountain cautioning skiers to slow down and to ski in control. However, once skiers get down the mountain the confrontation with crowds is just beginning. During peak seasons it can take more than one hour just to get out of the parking lot. If the skier's accommodations are located anyplace other than at Squaw, he will have to fight traffic the length of Highway 89. If the ultimate destination is South Lake Tahoe and the weather is bad, this can turn into a Steven Spielberg nightmare.

Ski School

Squaw Valley Ski School employs over 150 trained professionals. These PSIA instructors teach the American Teaching System (ATS) which is almost universal in the United States. Students taking ATS lessons at any resort may confidently visit other areas where the same method is taught, thereby not becoming confused by a different approach.

This year the ski school offers something new. Beginner skiers to those learning parallel turns will follow a 4-station network, and can register anytime for an all-day lesson for $26. The ski school is located at the base of the Exhibition lift, next to the rank of lift ticket wickets. Private lessons this year will cost $50 for one hour, or $115 for a half day, and $225 for all day. The all-day rate is the same whether there is one person or a maximum of three persons.

Squaw offers first-time skiers the opportunity to ski for free. This is an attempt to encourage more people to take up skiing. The program is totally free: free lift ticket, free ski rental, and a free orientation lesson. The program is offered on weekdays only, and a $38 deposit is required. The deposit is refunded upon return of the rental equipment. This is an excellent program to help develop new skiers, and, hopefully, it will be initiated at other resorts in the future.

Squaw has a **Children's World at Papoose** for children under 12. All-day packages will cost $55, half-days will cost $35, and equipment rentals are $6. Packages include lunch, snacks, activities, instruction and lift pass. The area will be served by 3 surface lifts, a double chair and its own rental center, to simplify everything for parents and kids.

For younger children aged 6 months to two years, Squaw Valley also provides licensed day care for the same price.

Squaw also offers a variety of special clinics, including the **Just For Women Ski Clinic.** All the instructors are women. The classes are limited to 5 women of similar abilities and consist of daily ski instruction, classes about ski selection and equipment care and individual video feedback. The program strives to provide a positive learning environment with a supportive atmosphere. During 1992-93, a 3-day program will cost $395 and a 5-day, $600.

Call the ski school at (916)583-0119 for more information.

Equipment Rental

Despite of the size of the mountain, Squaw Valley Village at its base is quite small. There are not a great deal of duplicated services here. Rental equipment is available from the **Company Store** located on the Squaw Valley Mall, near the entrance to the Gondola. The Company Store rents recreational and high-performance skis. Most recent rates were not available at press time.

Ski Tuning and Repair

The **Granite Chief Service Center** is located on the access road into Squaw Valley. This is one of the best tune-up and repair shops to be found anywhere. Granite Chief's employees are all expert skiers who know Squaw Valley intimately. They have state-of-the-art Montana Crystal Glide tuning machines, and they can also expertly tune skis by hand. In 1993-94, their fees are expected to be approximately

$35......Tune
$ 5......Wax
$10......Hand Wax Du Jour
$15......Binding Adjustment

Mountain Dining

Two mountain restaurants are located on the mountain itself. The **Gold Coast** restaurant is situated at the top of the gondola. This restaurant closely resembles a stage setting for the Nutcracker Suite. One expects Prince Nutcracker to walk out at any moment. Gold Coast is an extremely large restaurant occupying three floors, and it also boasts a considerable amount of outdoor deck area.

The cafeteria-style meal service and food are excellent. Fresh salads and "make your own" sandwiches are featured. The bright colors and heraldic flags promise to lift the spirits of even the most blasé skier.

What was formerly **High Camp** restaurant is now dubbed **Bath and Tennis Club.** Located on the mountain top where the tram docks, it was completely rebuilt and enlarged during the summer of 1989. Included in its facilities are **The North Bar, Terrace Café,** and **Poolside Café.**

The newly created **Bath and Tennis Club** is the best dining spot on the mountain. In addition to an expansive salad bar, table-side service is offered, including daily specials as well as brochettes and burgers. The brochettes include beef sirloin, marinated chicken, jumbo shrimp, or vegetarian offerings. A children's menu is also available. Prices vary from $5 to $6 per item except for the swordfish which is market-priced daily.

Child Care

Child-care facilities are located in the brand new 12,000 square foot Children's World at Papoose. Day-care services are provided for infants from six months to three years of age. Diapers and special formulas should be provided by parents. Snacks and lunch are served, and the fee for all day in 1993-94 is $55. Half-day sessions are $35. Reservations are requested; telephone 1-800-545-4350 or (916)583-6985.

Medical Facilities

For ski injuries, the ski patrol will only render emergency aid. Patrolmen will administer trauma treatment, stabilize broken bones, and transport injured skiers downhill by sled to the clinic located at the base of the mountain, two doors down from the ski school. The clinic is managed by the

Tahoe/Truckee Medical Group. Competent physicians and nurses are always present throughout the day. Should an illness or an injury require more than emergency care, patients will be transported nine miles to the Truckee Hospital for further treatment.

Cross-Country Skiing

Squaw Valley Nordic Center is located near the base of the Papoose lift system. There are 25 kilometers of dual groomed trails for every ability level. Should the skier wish to cross-country ski off groomed tracks, several kilometers of wilderness trails are also available.

In addition to the usual cross-country lessons offered at most resorts, the Nordic Center offers instruction in telemark skiing. Lessons include all the turns such as wedge, skate, parallel, step, and telemark normally executed in cross-country skiing.

For unusual ski-touring experiences, consider a moonlight tour or a catered gourmet lunch tour. Contact the Nordic Center at 1-800-327-3353 for details and prices.

Alpine Meadows Mountain Information
1-800-441-4423

Alpine Meadows is a 2,000 acre (809 ha) day-ski area located adjacent to Squaw Valley, just one mile south on California Highway 89. Since the 1961-62 season, Alpine Meadows has been catering to Sierra skiers. It is a good day area and a complement to Squaw. Alpine Meadows has everything one has learned to expect from this rugged, snowy terrain. As at Squaw there are runs for every ability level and for every weather condition.

Alpine Meadows base is at 7,000 feet, and its summit is at 8,700 feet. It averages 400 inches of snow a year. More than 100 runs cover this beautiful mountain offering plentiful snow well into June many years. The mountain has

1 high speed express quad
2 triple chairs
8 double chairs
1 surface lift

During the warm spring days that bring corn conditions, skiers should flock to the bowls on the south-facing slopes. Lakeside and Sherwood are sunbathers' paradises. The runs in the Lakewood bowl area are almost exclusively intermediate, while Sherwood bowl's runs tend to be more expert. The definition of "expert" at Alpine Meadows is approximately the same as it is at Squaw. The runs thus designated tend to be steeper and/or more bumped than at most Colorado resorts. Visitors not familiar with trail nomenclature should pay attention and be careful until they have determined that they can, indeed, ski these runs with impunity.

The best snow at Alpine Meadows is found on the north-facing slopes. These runs are primarily served by the high-speed Summit quad and the slower Roundhouse Chair. On the typically crowded weekends, skiers are advised to avoid Summit Chair at all cost, as it is always the most crowded. Ski Lakewood Chair or Yellow Chair. Alpine Bowl Chair is also a good bet. Some of the northern Sierra's worst crowding occurs on Highway 89 just outside of the parking lot. The best way to reduce the tension created by the highway crowds is to park smart at Alpine Meadows. This means that when arriving in the morning, park close to the Subway Chair. If parking along the sides of the lot, back in, avoiding the necessity of backing out in the evening. Ride Subway Chair at no charge to the base area and purchase lift tickets there. Parking in this manner will at least give you a chance at surviving the weekend rush!

Expert skiers will want to consider skiing Wolverine Bowl and Beaver Bowl off Summit Chair. There is also an area locals refer to as "Idiot's Delight." Idiot's Delight is an extemely steep chute and should be avoided by all but the best and/or craziest skiers. All three of these areas are reached by climbing along the top of the Pacific Crest Trail which is located just above and to the skier's right as he exits Summit Chair. A fifteen-minute climb accesses acres and acres of incredible skiing. Like all runs at Alpine Meadows, though, the runs are short, almost never longer than 1,550 (472 meters) vertical feet. Super expert skiers will want to test their mettle on the Palisades and its surrounding terrain, including such runs as Our Father and Scott Chute. Also in the same area is Keyhole; ask a local where it is and take a look at it from the Roundhouse Chair before attempting to ski these most difficult runs. Keyhole is about 500 feet long and 18 to 20 feet wide at its narrowest point. The slope is a rakish 45°! Surprisingly, despite this recitation, the majority of Alpine Meadows runs are intermediate. Management does a terrific job of keeping most of the slopes groomed, and intermediates can get a real kick skiing Alpine Bowl from top to bottom numerous times each day. This is cruising ground!

Alpine Meadows does not allow snowboards, nor has it set up any Nastar or Marlboro self timers.

Lift Ticket Prices Alpine Meadows (1992-93)

$39	Adult, All-Day
$26	Adult, Half-Day
$13	Child, 7-12
$ 5	Child, 6 and under

Hours of Operation at Alpine Meadows

8:30 A.M. to 4:00 P.M.

Accommodations

Squaw Valley is one of only a handful of Sierra resorts offering on-site accommodations to its guests. The available accommodations are limited in relation to the size of the mountain being served, but the facilities Squaw has built are exceptionally nice.

The Resort at Squaw Creek is the last word in ski resort accommodations! The 1993 Mobil Travel Guide awards it 4 stars, and AAA awards it four diamonds. It offers without question the finest hotel accommodations available in a North American ski resort. Consisting of 405 rooms and built at a cost of over $125 million, it ranks as one of the country's most costly ski hotels. Its meticulously crafted exterior is reminiscent of Frank Lloyd Wright's style, yet remains contemporary with its towering six stories of black glass. The hotel lobby is dominated by a soaring tray ceiling and distinctive waterfall-inspired lighting fixtures. A large native Sierra granite fireplace has been placed at an acute angle to the floor-to-ceiling windows which overlook Squaw Valley's slopes. At night one can watch the gaily illuminated aerial tram ply its way between the base facility and High Camp, site of the Bath and Tennis Club. Granite columns skillfully inlaid with Italian indigo marble soften and lend tactile sense to the room. The lounging area of the lobby is delineated by the use of a beautiful Edward Field-crafted carpet woven from teal, blue, and fuscia yarn. All soft seating is custom built for the designer and represents an extension of the hotel's basic design which strives to combine city sophistication with mountain informality. The lobby's reception area is constructed from cherry with a contemporary natural finish. Brass, bronze, and glass act as transitional materials between the coarse granite and the inviting, warm cherry paneling.

The hotel has five different types of rooms: Deluxe Guest Rooms ranging from $250 to $275 per night; suites ranging in price from $350 to $375 per night. All rooms, suites, and penthouses feature many of the same amenities such as in-room ski and boot fittings, easy ski in/ski out access to the slopes, homemade cookies at check-out, limousine and airport transfers, video check-out, seven-day laundry and dry cleaning, 24-hour room service, ski concierge, on-site Hertz car rental service, video cassette players, service bars, and two plush bath robes per unit. The hotel also offers some package rates which include a full breakfast buffet, deluxe guest room, room tax, and daily lift tickets. To pay the package rate, a guest must stay at least two nights. Rates are higher during the holiday season. Call the hotel at (800)327-3353 for reservations or information.

Rooms are decorated with custom-designed cherry furniture continuing the Frank Lloyd Wright theme which dominates the lobby. All walls are fabric covered and the color palette tends to burnt mauve shades. Deep, large bathtubs and granite bathroom counters testify to the elegance of the resort's appointments. Every guest need has been anticipated. There is even a telephone in each room with a built-in modem port. The T.V. boasts 22 free channels, 8 pay-per-view movies; in addition rental VCR's and movies are available from the concierge.

The Resort at Squaw Creek is not just a hotel—it is truly a world-class resort. Connecting the lobby to the tower suite is an arcade of wonderful shops, a deli, and specialty stores.. **RSC Traders** is a whimsical variety store which has a little of just about everything including wines, spirits, books, mineral waters, toiletries, and cosmetics. **Sports Tahoe** is a quality apparel shop whose lines include Descente, Spyder, Killey, North Face, and Polo. **High Altitudes** is a quality haberdashery for men and women. Seasonal resortwear and designer brands such as Silverado, Berck and Randy Kenyon are complemented with a large assortment of fine leather goods, such as luggage. **Imports** carries a complete line of designer tee shirts, knits, caps, etc.—all the souvenirs a Squaw Valley skier could want. A cute toystore for tykes is affectionately called **Lilliput**. It specializes in hand-crafted wooden toys and children's books. Across the pedestrian way from Sports Tahoe is **Sweet Potato Deli**, a delightfully cheerful place to enjoy a leisurely breakfast or to just sit with a cup of coffee and read one of the many newspapers offered daily. In addition to homemade pastries, gourmet coffees, tasty soups and sandwiches, Sweet Potatoes has available for purchase an array of the resort's signature chutneys, relishes, jams, jellies, and sauces.

No resort would be complete without an art gallery and **The Gallery at Squaw Creek** easily meets this requirement. Oils, pastels, prints, serigraphs are plentiful; many well-known west-coast artists exhibit at the gallery.

Another of Squaw's premier properties is **Squaw Valley Lodge**, also awarded four diamonds by 1993 AAA Tour Books.It is located just under the aerial tram on Squaw Peak Road. The Lodge is within easy walking distance of all base lifts, the Olympic Village shops, and restaurants. This is a new facility, built as condominiums but run as a hotel.

Lodging consists of studios and studios with lofts. Guests may specify whether they want units with one or two baths. All units come with General Electric appliances including dishwashers, microwaves, refrigerators, and disposals. Fireplaces are not included in any housing units at Squaw because local ordinances prohibit them. The rooms are comfortably decorated in earth tones and fine oak. Upon entering any room at the Lodge, one is immediately impressed with the beautiful oak slab flooring in the foyer and kitchen. All cabinets in the kitchen and living area are constructed from riff-cut oak in a natural finish. Ski storage is in the foyer, and a large, well-lighted closet is also handy. Bright throw cushions and accessories invite guests to consider these accommodations home during their ski holiday. The beds are of European manufacture and consist of a thin mattress on a box spring. Thick but lightweight down comforters make sleeping very comfortable.

While staying at the Squaw Valley Lodge, guests should be certain to use their key to lock the door behind themselves when leaving. These doors do not lock automatically upon closing. Guests should also note that thermostats in the rooms are locked and cannot be adjusted without a special key. If room temperature is uncomfortable, visitors must telephone the front desk; the staff will send a technician to adjust the thermostat to a different comfort setting.

Staying in the Squaw Valley Lodge has advantages. There is a large, heated outdoor pool, a therapy pool, covered parking, an exercise facility including aerobic instruction, on-site ski and clothing rentals, and elevator service. The spacious lobby is a great place to meet with friends after a hard day of skiing. It is also comfortable to relax in front of the lobby's large fireplace while enjoying a cocktail or other beverage.

During the 1993-94 season, rates for staying at the Lodge range from a low of $150 to a high of $295. When booking reservations, please note that the reservation office does not open until 8:00 A.M. Pacific Time.

The **Olympic Village Inn**, referred to locally as the OVI, was originally built for the 1960 Olympics as housing for participating athletes. Now, twenty-eight years and some $40 million later, the OVI has been renovated and greatly expanded to provide luxury accommodations for Squaw Valley guests. The old dormitory rooms have been creatively converted into guest suites with private balconies and gourmet kitchens. Although the resulting layout of the suites is unusual, they do have a charm not easily duplicated. Entrance to each suite is through the bedroom. In order to go from the bedroom to the living/kitchenette area, it is necessary to go through a small hall, off which the bathroom is located. This configuration resulted from the original dormitory's layout of two rooms sharing one common bath. In the newly configured suites, one former dormitory room has become a bedroom while the other has become a living/kitchenette area.

Each suite has been decorated with Laura Ashley prints and fine country French furniture. Although the rooms are small, they are quaint and more comfortable than many larger rooms. There are two telephones per unit, and a stereo system is pre-wired throughout. The reception desk has a library of tapes available to guests.

The complex features a heated outdoor pool with a waterfall and five hot tubs. There are two on-site restaurants, and the lobby with its large stone fireplace and comfortable seating is massive. Floor-to-ceiling windows overlook the ski slopes and surrounding countryside. In the evenings, entertainment featuring comedians, country-western or contemporary musicians is provided in the lobby.

Although Olympic Village is within walking distance of the lifts, complimentary shuttle service is available every five or ten minutes. Rates for 1993-94 are $165 during the week for a one bedroom suite for four with a kitchen, $195 on the weekend. For a similar suite with a fireplace, $225 during the week, $250 during the weekend. (916)581-6000.

Situated at the other end of the lift complex at Papoose lift is **Squaw Tahoe Resort**. These are older, more traditional condominiums than either the Lodge or the OVI. Squaw Tahoe Resort has a total of thirty-two condominiums, but a third of them are time-share units not normally available for rental. Accommodations consist of studios, one, and two-bedroom units. All units have fully equipped kitchens with GE appliances. Some units have fireplaces. Those units with fireplaces burn chemical logs which burn cleaner than natural wood. This is necessary in order to comply with local fireplace codes. Should a room with a view of the slopes be desired, be certain to request an odd-numbered room. The even-numbered rooms all face the Olympic Village or the meadows. Studio units have queen-size Murphy beds, while the full-size units have regular queen-size beds. The Squaw Tahoe Resort has underground parking and a clubhouse with outdoor spas and an exercise room. The equipment in the exercise room consists of free weights and progressive resistance equipment.

Squaw Tahoe Resort is located adjacent to one of the mountain's equipment barns. Light sleepers may want to request accommodations on the other side of the complex.

The 1993-94 rates for Squaw Tahoe Resort are between $125 and $250 per night. For information call (916)583-7226.

For lower prices, try the **Best Western Wildwood Inn.** 619-934-6855, From November to April,, prices range from $59 to $84 for single occupance, and $64 to $94 double occupancy.

Restaurants

Although there is considerable night life in the Lake Tahoe region, there is almost none at any of the Sierra ski resorts. Fortunately there is activity at Squaw Valley, though somewhat limited when compared to destination resorts in the Rocky Mountains.

Dining activity at Squaw Valley revolves around the **Olympic House** situated at the gondola base. This building has two levels and contains many restaurants and bars as well as other services, such as clothing stores and specialty shops. In the afternoons, activity centers around **Bar One.** Located on the second floor of the Olympic House, Bar One features a large outdoor deck facing Squaw Peak. In the spring many patrons sit outside and enjoy the tanning power of the late afternoon sun. Another gathering spot for the après-ski crowd is found on the second floor of the Olympic Plaza building. This building abuts the Olympic House and appears to be a part of it. Here the **Olympic Plaza Bar** features continuous Warren Miller films or other ski-related movies on wide-screen TV. Its outdoor deck which faces KT-22 and Red Dog is sheltered from the wind; parts of it are in the shade of huge California redwoods.

The Olympic House and the Olympic Plaza have an arcade feel to them. Numerous fast-food restaurants feature various specialty foods such as oysters, tacos, ice cream, pizza, and deli-style sandwiches which may be enjoyed in any of the bars. Seating is also available next to the glass-enclosed gondola house.

Table-service dining is available at **Jimmy's,** located on the second floor of Olympic House next to Bar One. Open for breakfast and dinner, Jimmy's specializes in California-style fine dining. In addition to daily specials, it features freshly prepared appetizers and entrées such as calamari steak, oysters Rockefeller, artichokes, sashimi, tournedos of beef, teriyaki brochette of beef, prime rib, rack of lamb, roast chicken with lemon & fresh dill, fettucini with chicken, shrimp and sausage. The wine list includes many California varietals such as Cabernet Sauvigon, Zinfandel, and Chenin Blanc. Champagnes and dessert wines are also available.

Jimmy's is the only Plaza restaurant that accepts major credit cards. Squaw's fast-food establishments accept only cash.

Locals enjoy **Le Chamois Bar and Pizza Restaurant** located next to the aerial tram's base station. The food is good, and the service is congenial. Paul, who has tended bar there for several years, knows the local history as well as anyone. For a taste of a regional snack, ask Paul for a "Squeeler." This is a little hot sausage that comes with its own "kit." The kit consists of a napkin, hot cajun mustard, and a stick to spread the mustard on the squeeler.

Fine dining is the specialty of the **Creekside Restaurant** located in the Olympic Village Inn. Its ambience is soft and warm. Lighting is diffused through an intricate, redwood ceiling lattice. Tables overlook the swimming pool and waterfall which are both illuminated in the evening.

Entrées typically include farm-raised game such as venison and seafood. The three bean soup is spicy and the green beans are al dente. The venison is excellent, and because it is farm raised, it does not have the wild taste normally associated with game.

Squaw Valley Inn's new management has provided a unique hunt decor in **Benton's**. The central feature of the restaurant is a wall painting depicting foxes dressed as hunters, Garth Benton's whimsical parody on hunting. Although Benton's menu is rather ordinary, the food is prepared expertly and served with style. Entrées may include bleu cheese filet, cajun beef prime rib, roasted cornish game hen, or grilled swordfish. This à la carte restaurant is convenient and will not disappoint.

The Resort at Squaw Creek's restaurants are likely to become the mecca for fine dining throughout the entire North Lake Tahoe region. The resort's flagship restaurant, **Glissandi**, features neo-classical French selections served in an elegant ambience. According to Chef Jean-Pierre Doignon, "neo-classical food" might best be described as haute cuisine created by using only fresh ingredients to achieve a lighter, more contemporary style than that of traditional French fare. While similar to nouvelle cuisine in terms of colorful presentation, the neo-classical menu is heartier.

Although selections change daily, Doignon's menu always includes a five-course offering, as well as à la carte selections. Some examples of this creative chef's wizardy are terrine de foie d'oie au Sauterne et ses toasts briochés (a terrine of homemade fresh goose liver) or cassoulette de moules fraiches demi-poulette (fresh mussels with a cream sauce) as an appetizer. The house salad is typically asperges de saison et jeunes poireaux aux truffes fraîches (asparagus and baby leek with fresh truffles). Entrées may include pot au feu de pigeonneau aux morilles (squab with fresh vegetables and morel mushroom), homard du Maine et poisson frais a l'orange (live Maine lobster with orange butter), or filet de porc a l'anis etoilé à la mode Chinoise (pork tenderloin served Chinese style). Stylized desserts are a hallmark of the Resort at Squaw Creek and at Glissandi, they are not only delicious, but also a feast for the eyes. A sample offering might include l'assiette du chocolatier (a combination of three different chocolate desserts), a banane rôtie au café (baked banana with coffee), or galettes orientales (ginger and honey galette with raspberries).

Reservations are required at Glissandi, which received a 4-diamond rating from AAA. It is open from 6 to 10 p.m. and is closed on Sundays.

Cascades is a less formal dining room than Glissandi, but is nevertheless quite able to stand on its own reputation. Lovely cherry-paneled walls and huge windows provide diners with a constantly changing panorama of outdoor activities. From just relaxing and watching skiers complete their day of skiing to enjoying the splashing going on in any or all of the Resort at Squaw Creek's three pools and hot tubs, the Cascades is the place to be. A buffet and à la carte format includes grilled meats prepared on an open hearth, hearty soups, a salad bar, and a wonderful dessert kiosk. Open for breakfast, lunch and dinner, it is an ideal gathering place.

Wolfdale's at 640 North Lake Boulevard, Tahoe City is one of the most incredible restaurants to be found anywhere! Its American chef studied in Japan where he developed a love for Japanese cuisine and the finer cultural points of this ancient civilization. Chef Douglas Dale has brought to Wolfdale's an amalgamation of East and West. For example, appetizers may include such mouth-watering morsels as sashimi with ginger and wasabi wild mushrooms timbale with smoked trout and baby greens served spectacularly on glazed oriental pottery and decorated with a miniature tree trunk. Even the simple spinach-radicchio salad with smoked bacon is rendered terrific by the addition of Morbier croutons.

But the entrées are what set this eating establishment apart from all the rest. Imagine sautéed sturgeon with calico scallops, pancetta and red wine sauce or crusty quails stuffed with wild mushrooms, brioche, and herbs. If this is not enough, try grilled spicy salmon with crispy leeks and arame couscous.

All dishes have a distinctive Japanese flavor to them. Prices are moderate; however, the wine list is lacking. A special short menu is available for bar patrons. Reservations are imperative; telephone (916) 583-5700.

Only a few steps from Wolfdale's, near the landmark large tree which sits in the middle of the road, is an intimate, excellent bistro called **Christy Hill**. This restaurant defines its cuisine as "California nouvelle." It is indeed an apt description. The charming ambiance is enhanced by the warmth of a fireplace and the soft illumination emanating from decorative wall sconces. Knowledgeable waiters offer an excellent wine list which features six or more varietals (available by the glass) and extensive additional choices (by the bottle) that naturally lean heavily toward California vintners.

Christy Hill, though not specializing in seafood, does emphasize it. For appetizers, consider the fresh Hog Island and Olympia oyster combination, served raw on the half shell with salsa fresco, fresh Florida rock shrimp, P.I.E. mussels, or smoked salmon plus Maine lobster with fresh fettucini pasta and an olive oil sauce of braised fennel, garlic, roma tomatoes, fresh basil, and Parmesan cheese.

Dinner entrées at Christy Hill may include fresh Hawaiian mahi-mahi, lightly blackened with three peppers and served with a sauce of fresh tangerine juice, sun-dried tomatoes, jalapeno, and cilantro. Another delicious choice might be Australian lamb loin, broiled and finished with d'Anjou pears, ginger chutney with fresh tarragon, and wild rice. For reservations, telephone (916) 583-8551.

For inexpensive Mexican food which the Mobil guide calls a good value, visit **Gringo's**, on Main Street, 619-934-8595.

Activities

Activities at Squaw Valley have steadily increased over the last two or three years. A cinema located in the Opera House features full-length first-run movies. The Bath and Tennis Club, situated at High Camp atop the Cable Car terminus, contains the Olympic Ice Pavilion which is not only olympic size, but also the highest artificial ice-skating rink in the world. The Bath and Tennis Club also has two outdoor heated tennis courts available year-round. In an unusual twist, the plant that will create the ice for the ice rink will also be used to produce an artificial surface for summer skiing adjacent to Bailey's Beach lift! A Marlboro self-timer practice race course is positioned at the top of the Shirley Lake chairlift. Several snowmobiling companies work out of Tahoe City and offer daily tours, as well as hot air ballooning and mountain tours via snowcat.

Twice each day the Tahoe Queen plies the waters of Lake Tahoe between the casinos located at South Lake Tahoe and Squaw Valley. Guests staying in South Lake Tahoe may take the 8:00 A.M. shuttle and arrive around 10:00 AM in Squaw Valley for a full day of skiing. Departure in the evening for the return trip is at approximately 4:00 P.M. Full breakfast, dinner, and cocktails are available at extra charge. The Tahoe Queen is a large, paddle-wheel boat graciously furnished in Victorian style.

Services

A full complement of sporting goods stores, apparel shops, pharmacies, grocery stores, liquor stores, furniture, bath, and specialty shops is within the immediate North Lake Tahoe area. In addition, there are antique stores, massage services, art galleries, bakeries, beauty salons, book stores, florists, movies, theaters, banks, churches, alterations, dry cleaning, optical shops, and baby-sitting services.

The views of the immense valley below Steamboat's Mt. Werner are breathtaking. The mid mountain restaurant shown here is Rendezvous Saddle.
Photo by GuideBook Publishing

STEAMBOAT

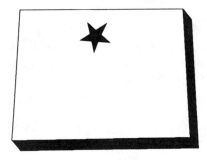

2305 Mt. Werner Circle
Steamboat Springs, CO. 80487

(800) 922-2722 Reservations
(303) 879-6111 Information
(303) 879-7300 Snow Report

New For 1993-94

This year, Steamboat Resort is adding a warming shelter and restaurant near the top of the Four Points lift on Storm Peak. For a quick bite and a rest, skiers will be able to stop at the new facility to use rest rooms, snack bars and telephones.

No other new facilities have been added this year, but last year two new high-speed detachable quad chairlifts with bubbles and foot rests were added. Storm Peak Express and Sundown Express have improved traffic flow in two heavily traveled areas.

How To Get There

The Yampa Valley Airport, 23 miles from Steamboat Springs, is served by Continental, American Airlines, Northwest Airlines, United, and Mesa\United Express Airlines. American flies daily non-stops from Chicago and Dallas/Ft. Worth and on Saturdays from Newark. Northwest serves Steamboat with daily flights from Minneapolis. Continental flies to the Yampa Valley on Saturdays from Houston and Cleveland. United provides two daily flights from Denver, and Saturday flights from Chicago, Los Angeles and San Francisco. Mesa\United Express has daily flights from Denver as well. Ground transfers during 1993-94 season are provided by both Alpine Taxi and Panorama Taxi. Both charge $34 round-trip with children twelve and under half price.

Air service is also available from Denver to the Steamboat Springs Stolport, 5 miles from town, via Continental Express on DeHavilland-7, 46-passenger aircraft. Continental flies 10 flights to the Stolport daily. The Stolport is opening a new terminal this year. Budget, Hertz, Avis and National all have desks available for car rentals.

The Sheraton Steamboat Resort & Conference Center offers complimentary pickup from the STOLport, as do several other lodging companies. When booking accommodations, verify pickup. Alpine Taxi also is available for $16 round trip, $8 one way, and $12 for same day service.

Alpine and Panorama also both provide service to and from the Denver airport to Steamboat Springs. To reserve a spot, call Alpine Taxi at 1-800-343-RIDE, 1-800-232-RIDE in Colorado, or 879-2800 in Steamboat. Call Panorama Steamboat Express at 1-800-545-6050 or, in Steamboat, (303)879-3400. Panorama provides two vans per day between Denver and Steamboat. The week day round trip price is $82 per person, and on weekends that rises to $98. Children ride for half price.

Alpine will also provide vans between Denver and Steamboat, on a chartered bases. The price is $275 per van, with the price dropping to $55 per person for six or more.

Traveling to Steamboat by car is easy and convenient. From Denver travel due west on I-70 through the Eisenhower Memorial Tunnel and take the Silverthorne exit at Colorado Highway 9 north. Follow Highway 9 along the Green River to Kremmling. In Kremmling turn west onto U.S. Route 40 and proceed directly into Steamboat.

A scenic drive of 157 miles under most conditions, the trip should not take longer than two and a half hours. However, during heavy snowstorms, the drive over Rabbit Ears Pass can be memorable. Should weather be a consideration on the day of travel, telephone (303) 639-1234 for road conditions. If the road should be closed overnight, ample hotel rooms are available in the town of Kremmling.

Approaching Steamboat from the west is as simple as taking I-70 east to Colorado Highway 131 at the Wolcott Interchange. Turn north and continue until the U.S. 40 Interchange, then follow the signs to Steamboat. This is a very picturesque drive through low mountains and open range --look out for deer on or near the road! Should heavy snow conditions prevail, you may want to consider an alternate route from the west. Instead of taking the Wolcott exit off I-70, take Colorado Highway 13 out of Rifle and go around the mountains. In the town of Craig, take U.S. 40 east to Steamboat. This alternative route is slightly longer, but in bad weather it will be much faster and safer.

Mountain Information

Situated in Routt National Forest, Steamboat has four mountain peaks available for recreational skiing: Thunderhead Peak, Storm Peak, Sunshine Peak, and South Peak. Taken together, these peaks offer 3,685 feet of vertical, the second highest vertical in Colorado. (The highest is Aspen Highlands). Base elevation is a moderate 6,900 feet (2,103 meters) and Steamboat's highest peak is 10,585 feet (3,200 meters). There are 2,500 skiable acres (1,012 ha) and over 50 miles (80 km) of trails. Of these, fully 1,551 acres (628 ha) are groomed. Snowmaking can reach 385 acres on 29 runs.

Steamboat is served by twenty lifts comprised of

1 8-Passenger Gondola
1 Quad Chairlift
2 Express Quad Chairlifts
6 Triple Chairlifts
7 Double Chairlifts
1 Ski School Lifts (1 Surface, 1 Double Chairlift)
2 Surface Lifts

The longest beginner run is Why Not at 3 miles (4.8 km). This trail begins at the top of the Silver Bullet Gondola and winds its way down to the base area. The longest intermediate run is High Noon at two and a half miles (4 km). High Noon begins at the top of Sunshine Peak, at the terminus of the Priest Creek and Sundown chairlifts. Skirting the Rendezvous Saddle restaurant, it continues down to the base of the Elkhead lift.

The longest expert run is Shadows, which runs parallel to the Sundown chairlift on Sunshine Peak. It is a gladed run, just under one mile (1.6 km) in length.

Steamboat skiers are able to get to the top of the mountain twice as quickly as they used to because of the installation of two high-speed, detachable quad chairlifts with bubbles and foot rests for protection and comfort. The new lifts replaced triple chairs, making the Storm Peak Express and Sundown Express. Other changes include removing the WJW chairlift and the Four Points Chair will become a triple lift using towers from the Old Storm Peak lift. The changes will give Steamboat an uphill capacity of 29,941 skiers per hour.

Each day at Steamboat a report on the snow conditions and a list of groomed runs are posted in the lift ticket sales windows. The information includes temperature, wind, snow depth, and recently groomed trails. Special events are also mentioned. Adjacent to the tram room at the base is a large trail map which is changed electronically to indicate the current status of all runs.

Steamboat is a diverse mountain where skiers of most ability levels can ski around the entire complex and enjoy the terrain's rich diversity. Its intermediate and expert runs are spread evenly among the four peaks. Most beginner runs, are located on Thunderhead with a few on Sunshine Bowl. The well thought-out lift locations make it easy and quick for skiers to find untracked powder or freshly groomed conditions. During periods of inclement weather, the mountain's even distribution of varied runs guarantees skiers good ski conditions. When the wind is blowing over Storm Peak and Sunshine Peak, it is best to ski the Four Points, Burgess Creek, Arrowhead, and Thunderhead lifts, or the Silver Bullet Gondola; all are protected from the wind.

Steamboat is as much a gentle mountain as Snowbird is a challenging mountain. In other words, Steamboat does not have many trails that are intimidating. In fact, no runs are designated double black diamonds. This is a great family mountain where the entire family can enjoy skiing together on numerous runs. However, the expert runs are not wimpy. They will challenge the expert, and in the right snow conditions (powder), they may be among the best in Colorado. Chute One and The Ridge can be very demanding!

Ski through the trees off Traverse, The Ridge, and Crowtrack or enjoy the frequent knee-deep "Champagne" powder that regularly graces this mountain. The term "Champagne" is reserved for the snow at Steamboat where the flakes are small and very light—just like bubbles in champagne. This kind of snow is effortless to ski. No doubt, the powder's lightness contributes to the ski school's active powder classes. There is probably not a better place to learn to ski deep powder than at Steamboat. Once powder skills are learned under these ideal conditions, they are easily transferred to other areas where the snow may be a bit heavier.

Steamboat's annual snowfall is 325 inches (825 cm). The monthly snowfall is

Nov.	27"	(69 cm)
Dec.	71"	(180 cm)
Jan.	63"	(160 cm)
Feb.	56"	(142 cm)
Mar.	57"	(145 cm)
Apl.	20"	(51 cm)

Average monthly temperatures during the season are

Nov.	28°	-2° C
Dec.	18°	-8° C
Jan.	15°	-9° C
Feb.	18°	-8° C
Mar.	26°	-3° C
Apl.	38°	4° C

Lift Ticket Prices (1993-94)

Like many other Colorado ski resorts, Steamboat has departed from a "high" season and a "low" season. Instead it has established a "regular" season and a "value" season. Value season rates are $5 less expensive than regular rates. The regular season commences on December 11 and runs until Apr.3.

Regular Season Lift Tickets:

$ 41	Daily Adult
$ 35	Half-Day Adult
$234	6 Days Out of 7
$200	5 Days Out of 6
$ 24	Daily (Age 65-69)
$Free	Daily (Age 70+)

All major credit cards are accepted. Value season rates are lower, with adult daily tickets costing $34 and youth, $24.

Hours of Operation

8:30 A.M. to 4:00 P.M.

Lift Ticket Purchase Locations

Lift tickets may be purchased at the Silver Bullet Gondola building located off the Plaza at the mountain's base.

Of particular interest to parents skiing with children 12 and under is the "Kids Ski Free™" program. In order to be eligible for this program, parents and their children must stay in lodging booked through the Steamboat Springs Chamber Resort Association for a minimum of five days and the parents must purchase a 5-or-more-day lift ticket. However, once this minimum criterion is met, children may stay free in their parents' room. Sorry, but if children require their own room, there will be a charge for the additional room. Also, this program is available one a one-to-one basis. One free ticket, for one paying ticket.

If parents also are renting skis for the same period of time, the children's ski rentals also will be free. This offer will not be valid between Dec. 19,1992 and Jan. 3, 1992.

How To Avoid Crowds

The principal areas of congestion at Steamboat occur at lower High Noon, at the base of the Elkhead lift, and in the evening along Heavenly Daze and Vagabond.

The ski patrol places gates constructed from fabric netting at trail junctions in order to slow down skiers coming off the trails. A frequent place for these precautions includes the Twister and Four Points junction where they exit onto Ego. The technique works and prevents really fast skiers from intimidating less aggressive intermediates on Ego.

Ski School

Steamboat's ski school employs 230 instructors trained in the American Teaching System. Most, if not all, credible resorts use this teaching method. It is important that a uniform teaching method be employed because skiers tend to move around and visit different resorts. For this reason, the ATS has become an American standard.

At Steamboat two basic group lessons are available to guests: two-hour lessons and all-day lessons. A two-hour lesson during the 1993-94 season is $32 while an all-day lesson is $48. Beginning skiers will be delighted to learn that lift tickets are not required while skiing with an instructor.

Classes meet in back of the Sheraton Village Hotel between the Preview and Headwall lifts. A 1-hour private lesson will cost $70.

For children, Steamboat offers the Kids' Vacation Center which has skiing and nonskiing programs. The Kiddie Corral will have child care for ages 6 months through kindergarten for $48 for a full day, $33 for a half day without lunch. A skiing program for ages three and a half through kindergarten will cost $50 for a full day lesson, and $35 for a half day.

The Buckaroos will include a full day of child care, including a one hour private lesson, lunch and indoor games for children two and a half to three and a half will cost $90.

Reservations are required; telephone (303) 879-6111, ext. 218 for more information.

Special ski classes available for those who have specific skills they want to hone include the Mt. Werner Challenge Series, an intensive one-day program for advanced and expert skiers. Class sizes are limited, and the 1991-92 fee is $42. Meet at the top of the gondola at 10:15 A.M. Classes are organized for adults.

A two-hour NASTAR race clinic is offered for adults and children. These classes meet daily except Sunday at 11:00 A.M. at the Bashor Race Area; cost is $36. Take the Christie III chairlift to get to the race area; exit the chair to your left.

Bump and powder clinics are also available at Steamboat. Powder clinics are held every morning when there is at least six inches of new snow. Personally, this author does not believe the lessons are worthwhile unless there are at least nine to twelve inches of new snow. The technique for skiing six inches of champagne powder is not significantly different from that of skiing packed powder. However, at nine inches or more, the technique is definitely different and lessons would be a good investment. Cost of the powder clinic is $37; the bump clinic is $40 for adults.

Equipment Rental

Steamboat Springs' average rental prices for this year will be $16 per day for skis, boots and poles. For a sport package, prices will range from $16 to $21, and for high performance, $23-27.

Prices at the two **Sport Stalkers**, one located on Ski Time Square and the other on Gondola Square were not available at press time, but call for new rates at Telephone (800) 525-5520 for reservations and information.

Other rental stores with competitive prices include **Ski Haus International, Steamboat Select Inc./Pro Select, Terry Sports, Village Center Ski Rentals,** and **Werner's Storm Hut.** All stores accept major credit cards. Either a cash deposit or credit card imprint is required.

Ski Tuning And Repair

Tuning and repair services are available at all ski rental shops and sporting goods stores. The Sport Stalker has stone-grinding equipment manufactured by Montana, called Crystal Glide. Skis must be warm before waxing. Therefore, it is a good idea to drop the skis off at the end of the day and pick them up the next morning.

Mountain Dining

A convincing argument could be made that America's very best mountain restaurants are at Steamboat. The resort's flagship has to be **Hazie's,** located in the gondola building at the top of Thunderhead Peak.

Hazie's broad expanse of two-story high windows gives its diners an uninterrupted panoramic view of the Yampa Valley. Diners look out across sprawling Old Steamboat Springs and see the distant mountain that locals refer to as "the Sleeping Giant." Look carefully at the mountain. Can you see his chin? His chest? His feet? The Giant is lying on his back with his head facing south and his feet pointing north.

Begin a leisurely lunch by having a cocktail in Hazie's attractive bar constructed from mahogany and accented by deep green carpeting. The walls are glass and the fixturing is brass. Sample the bar's exceptional hors d'oeuvres such as sashimi (fresh yellowfin tuna, sliced thin and served raw); gravad lax ("buried salmon," Norwegian salmon cured at Hazie's); tuna grille aux poivre (fresh yellowfin tuna, rubbed with cracked black pepper, seared and served cold with a Roma tomato sauce); crab back (a Caribbean specialty, blue crab mixture stuffed into the shell and baked with lime butter). Several kinds of oysters including blue point, oysters nouvelle, or Moscow are also served. Hazie's freshly made and unusual gourmet pizzas are also worth a try.

From the bar, move to the adjoining restaurant which occupies two floors. The view from Hazie's windows is uninterrupted because the second floor is cantilevered off the interior wall over the first-floor dining area. The result is spectacular. Try to get a second floor seat. Table settings and service are first-class. Each table is decorated daily with fresh flowers, adding to the ambience.

Hazie's is open for lunch and dinner. A perfect night in Steamboat calls for an early evening ride on the Silver Bullet to dinner in the restaurant. For appetizers consider one of the following: curried Cajun seafood salad, Mozzarella salad, or Callaloo—a coconut cream-based soup of the Isles, abundant with fresh spinach and crab.

The nouvelle American cuisine dishes include such items as scallop pie in bonnet or salmon mousse. Hazie's salads often add unusual items such as calamari. Typical entrées might be veal roulette with wild mushroom stuffing or orange spicy shrimp. The menu at Hazie's is never predictable because the chef prepares different dishes each evening; all of them are very interesting and always excellent.

The diner can watch the evening lights come on in Steamboat Springs as the snow begins to fall gently, preparing the mountain for yet another day of that special Steamboat champagne powder.

Steamboat's other mountain restaurants seem to pale in comparison to Hazie's. However, these restaurants are still superior to those at most other resorts.

Located in Rendezvous Saddle at the top of South Peak is **Ragnar's** restaurant. This is smaller than Hazie's, and the offerings are different. Ragnar's is decorated in a style reminiscent of Old Steamboat. Weathered barnboard walls are decorated with many old photographs of the late Buddy Werner and other legendary skiers.

The menu at Ragnar's leans toward Scandinavian dishes such as Dages Fiske Ret (seafood special of the day); Grilleret Laks Norheimsund (fresh Norwegian salmon, mesquite broiled and served with light mustard dill sauce.); Stekt Lammekolle (oven baked leg of lamb served with fresh garden vegetables and drippings from the roast); Stekt Rodspaette Trondheim (fresh sole sautéed with asparagus, shrimp, and leeks in a butter lemon wine sauce).

Rendezvous Saddle Restaurant is located in the same building as Ragnar's; this is an excellent cafeteria which has menu items such as fresh fruit, pastries, and quality hot food. There is also a terrific outdoor sun deck where freshly grilled foods including barbeque are offered. Staff members are among the friendliest in Colorado, and they will make sure your luncheon experience is memorable.

The cafeteria at Thunderhead is called **Cafe Thunderhead**. The food service here is comparable to that of Rendezvous Saddle. The café provides a warm shelter in an occasionally hostile climate.

The Stoker Bar, located one floor below Hazie's, offers table service and is quite charming. Though not as elegant as Hazie's nor Ragnar's, it is very comfortable and a great place to grab a sandwich on those days when one does not want a full meal. Its coffee drinks are also welcome on cold, snowy days.

The **B.K. Corral** is located on the third floor of the gondola building. This fast-service restaurant is a cafeteria and home of **Charlie's Breakfast Club**. The term "Club" is a misnomer because Charlie's serves a full breakfast and is frequented by those serious skiers who want to be among the first on the mountain at rope drop. At noon the offerings feature pizza, hamburgers, hot dogs, and other typical American lunch items.

In the evenings ride the Silver Bullet to the **Corral** restaurant and enjoy a family-style Western barbeque, live entertainment, and dancing. The Corral features such traditional Western fare as baron of beef, Danish pork ribs, barbecued chicken breasts, baked potatoes, salad bar, dinner rolls, and desserts. Reservations are suggested.

All of Steamboat's mountain restaurants are relatively new and are meticulously maintained. Other resorts would be well advised to visit Steamboat and emulate its excellent food service.

Child Care

The child-care nursery at Steamboat is part of the **Kids Vacation Center** located on the bottom floor of the Silver Bullet Gondola at the mountain's base. The Kiddie Corral Child Care Center accepts children from six months through six years. Meals for younger children must be provided by parents. Diapers and other special items should also be provided by parents. Cost for nursery service is $48. Half-day care is also available for $33. All prices are current for the 1993-94 ski season. Telephone (303) 879-6111, ext. 218 for reservations.

Medical Facilities

The ski patrol will only render emergency aid for ski injuries. The patrol will administer trauma treatment, stabilize broken bones, and transport injured skiers downhill. Actual treatment, however, will be administered at the Routt Memorial Hospital in Old Steamboat Springs. Injured skiers are transported to the hospital via ambulance. This is a full-service hospital with several practicing physicians on staff.

Chiropractors, dentists, orthodontists, optometrists, pharmacies, and physical therapists are available in Steamboat Springs as well.

Cross-Country Skiing

The Steamboat Ski Touring Center offers 30 kilometers of groomed trails on the grounds of the Sheraton Steamboat Golf Club and its Robert Trent Jones-designed course. The facility is open from 9 a.m. to 5 p.m. daily, from Thanksgiving through mid-April, with trails closing at 4 p.m. At press time 1993-94 prices were not yet available, but during the 1992-93 season, a daily trail ticket for adults cost $9, and for children, $5. Half-day tickets are sold at 1 p.m. and cost $7.50. Rentals cost $10 for a full day and $8.50 for a half day for skis, boots and poles.

One-hour group lessons cost $23.50 and one-hour private lessons can be arranged for $40 per hour. 2-hour instructional tours are available for $34.50 per person.

In addition the touring center offers half-day and all-day back-country tours on Rabbit Ears Pass, with reservations made a day before. Half day tours cost $28.50 per person, full day, $37.50. For more information about any of these program, call the Steamboat Ski Touring Center, 303-879-8180.

Accommodations

Steamboat has old and new lodging to fit all budgets. Physically, the lodging and most of the restaurants are situated around the base facility. Old Steamboat Springs is downhill about two or three miles. City bus service between the two entities runs on a half-hour schedule from early morning to late evening.

Most of the prices quoted here do not include lower prices which often are available between Thanksgiving and Christmas, and during the April end of the season weeks.

Hotels

The largest hotel in Steamboat is the **Sheraton Steamboat Resort** located across from Ski Time Square. The lift system is just off the Sheraton's lobby, and the gondola is an easy two-minute stroll. The Sheraton's lobby is typical of other Sheratons and is rather nondescript. The common amenities include a heated swimming pool, whirlpool, laundry facilities, restaurants, and an après-ski lounge on the premises. All rooms have cable TV and coffee makers. Underground parking is also available. During the regular 1993-94 season, rooms at the Sheraton rent for between $219 and $279 per night based on double occupancy.

Just across the hill from the Sheraton is the **Ptarmigan Inn**. Located practically under the gondola cables, the Ptarmigan is managed by Best Western and is a ski-in/ski-out facility. The rooms at the Ptarmigan are spartan but clean, and the staff is very friendly. All rooms have cable TV, views of the mountain or of the outdoor heated pool. There are also individual ski lockers, a sauna, and a restaurant. Rates during the regular 1993-94 season run from a low of $169 per night to a high of $229 per night, based on double occupancy.

Condominiums

Right at the base of the mountain are the **Torian Plum Condominiums**, a very convenient ski in\ski out address. The complex provides an on call private shuttle, and every unit has two color televisions with standard cable and HBO, a vcr, in room safes on request, gas fireplaces, and washers and dryers.Conference facilities are available, and residents also have the use of an outdoor heated pool, hot tub and sauna. Rates are $295 to $455 for a one bedroom; $395 to $625 for a two bedroom; and $525 to $795 for a three bedroom.

The **Norwegian Log Condominiums**, located up the ski hill about 125 yards, are ski-in/ski-out units. The view from one side of the condos is of the ski mountain and from the other side of the Flat Top mountains. There are a total of eleven condominiums consisting of two and three-bedroom units. The fully equipped kitchens' amenities include microwave ovens, convection ovens, complete sets of dishes, serving pieces, silverware, and glasses. All accommodations have fireplaces, color TVw/HBO, balconies, and Jacuzzi bathtubs. Daily maid service, garages, and an on-site concierge add to guests' comfort.

The Norwegian Log Condominiums are about twelve years old. Although all the units are decorated individually, the theme is consistent throughout. Typical of the time they were built, they are beginning to show their age. The walls are knotty pine, and the dominant color is brown. The rooms are large and nicely furnished. During the regular 1993-94 season they rent for between $425 and $500 for a two bedroom; and $395 and up for a four bedroom per night.

Among the nicest properties at Steamboat is **The Meadows at Eagleridge**. Situated in an open meadow about 500 yards from the lifts, The Meadows is among the newest offerings at Steamboat. The stucco exterior is complemented by an extensive copper-clad roof which is just beginning to take on the green patina of aging. Access to the individual units is through the underground garage. Upon checking in, all guests are given an electronic door opener not only for their convenience, but also as a security device.

Although the Meadows has only eighteen condominiums, a concierge and daily maid service are on the premises. The complex features a beautiful, heated outdoor swimming pool and spa. Its ample deck area is a great place to have a party or to gather and meet other guests.

The condominiums are elegantly furnished, and five of the penthouse units have private elevators. Each living room has a large brick fireplace and recessed ceilings. All lighting is on rheostats so one can adjust the room's lighting to his own preference. Each dining room has its own private wet bar and Scotsman ice maker. The kitchen has gray stone flooring and contains a microwave oven, a convection oven, a Thermador grill, and an instant hot water tap. The grill is set in an attractive brick-arched alcove. The view from some of the kitchen windows is of Mt. Werner. Other rooms look out on the Sleeping Giant.

The rich Zolatone colors selected for the walls are accented with quality mahogany trim. The baths include Jacuzzi tubs, double sinks, tile counters, medicine cabinets, and all are well lighted.

Each master bedroom features a wood-burning fireplace. The master's king-size bed has reading lights built into the headboard as well as a remote control unit for the TV. All condos have central humidity control, walk-in closets, and private balconies off each bedroom. The balcony floors are heated so it is not necessary to shovel snow off them. Thus, the balconies can be used all season.

The 1993-94 rates are between $425 and $475 per night for two bedrooms and two bathsFor 3 bedrooms the range is $550 and $635.

The **West Condominiums**, on the inside of Mt. Werner Circle, a 3 or 4 minute walk to the gondola offers less expensive rates, an out door heated pool, hot tubs, washers and dryers within the complex, and gas fire places. Many of the units recently have been renovated. Prices range from $140 to $245 for a one bedroom; $200 to $365 for a two bedroom; and $280 to $525 for a 4 bedroom.

Another good condominium complex, located near to the cross country ski center is the **Ranch at Steamboat**, which is about 1-1/2 miles from the gondola, and has a very good shuttle service. Prices there are $440 for a two bedroom; and $540 for a 3-bedroom, 3 bath condo.

Also recommended are the Inn at Steamboat Bed and Breakfast, which is 3 blocks from the gondola and charges $169 for a room with two twin beds, breakfast included.

Many other hotels and condominiums are available. Before booking reservations, ask for a copy of *Steamboat's Travel Planner*, a free brochure with photographs of the properties and descriptions of their amenities. A review of this brochure will insure that guests know in advance the quality and appearance of the accommodations.

Restaurants

All genres of restaurants are available in Steamboat, from the finest French restaurants to modest Mexican cafés.

The "in" place for après-ski is **The Inferno**, located downstairs at Gondola Square. This is a "down and dirty" old West bar and grill. The bar is dark, and when the music starts, it is the only thing anyone can hear. The central feature at The Inferno is its Wheel of Fortune. Occasionally, a bartender will spin the wheel and the number on which the arrow stops becomes the price for Corona beer! There is a small dance floor, and live entertainment is offered after 9:30 P.M.

La Montana Mexican\Southwestern Restaurant offers wonderful gourmet creations with a southwestern flare. Try the shrimp enchiladas, the red chili pasta, and other specialties. Busy, noisy and comfortable, this restaurant makes its own flour tortillas. The margaritas are very good. This is a very popular nightspot at Apres Ski Way and Village Drive. Reservations are recommended. 879-5800 ext. 1.

Andersons and Friends Good Earth Restaurant is moderately priced and known for it home made soups and fresh salads. It is big on sandwiches. Try the cashew and raisin sandwich! Downtown at 903 Lincoln. 879-0208. Kids eat free.

Another good restaurant for families is **Grubstake Restaurant and Bar.** Order you meal with a telephone.Specializes in steaks and chicken. It has great milk shakes. In Gondola Square. Open for breakfast lunch and dinner. 879-4448.

Cipriani's is a good small Continental restaurant. It is located in the Thunderhead Lodge and Condominiums across from Ski Time Square. Cipriani's is located in the basement of the lodge. With seating for only fifty-eight patrons within its setting of stuccoed walls and brass rails, Cipriani's has the flavor of an intimate left bank bistro.

The Italian menu features such delectables as Pesce Spada Graticola (freshly broiled swordfish topped with lemon butter, diced tomatoes, artichoke hearts, scallions, hearts of palm and shallots); Maré Alfredo (fettucini with clams, oysters, mussels, crab and Languestino topped with sauce Alfredo and bacon); Vitello con Funghi, Sugo di Galliano (veal scallopini, sauteed with leeks and wild mushrooms, topped with butter sauce and finished with butter).

Several other fine restaurants worthy of consideration are located in Old Steamboat Springs.

Two restaurants are located at 911 Lincoln (U.S. 40) and share the same ownership. The first, **L'apogee**, is Continental and pricey, while the other, **Harwigs Grill**, is less formal and features a more eclectic menu. Both restaurants feature one of the largest wine lists in Colorado with over 4,000 bottles cellared. At L'apogée appetizers may feature items such as saumon fumé or huîtres hercules. For entrées, select from a large choice of poultry, meat, fish, as well as daily specials. Typical entrées may include poulet aux artichout, medallions de veau aux morels, or melange a trois grillé. Prices are à la carte and relatively expensive.

Harwigs, on the other hand, features items such as Cornish game hens, Madras veggies, bouillabaisse, and jambalaya at prices well within most budgets. For reservations at either restaurant, telephone (303) 879-1919.

Activities

Steamboat offers an endless variety of activities:

NASTAR races are held daily (except Monday) on the Bashor race course area from 10:30 A.M. to 12:30 P.M. Adjacent to the NASTAR course is the Marlboro Ski Challenge, a coin-operated self-timer race course. Its hours are the same as NASTAR's.

Billy Kidd offers 2- and 3-day race camps throughout ski season. Open to all ages, a typical day includes two hours of free skiing with Billy or one of his specially trained coaches, five hours of race training, and one hour of video analysis.

The Norwest Bank Annual Cowboy Downhill is one of the largest media events in Colorado Ski Country. Originated by Billy Kidd and his buddy Larry Mahan, the six-time, All 'Round World Champion Cowboy, the Cowboy Downhill consists of over sixty events. One event not duplicated anyplace else includes running a slalom course, lassoing a ski hostess, saddling a horse, and crossing a finish line. This event always coincides with the National Western Stock Show held in Denver.

The Winter Carnival, another annual event, happens also to be the oldest winter carnival west of the Mississippi. For one week in February, the entire town of Steamboat participates in such events as racing, ski jumping, sled racing, a cross-country hot air balloon race, a parade, and many other events including a spectacular fireworks display.

Balloons Over Steamboat, hot air balloon rides. Telephone (303) 879-3298.

Over the Hill Gang. Skiers 45+ meet on Sundays and Mondays at their sign near the Sheraton. Participants should be intermediate skiers.

Jupiter Jones Powder Cats. Untracked powder skiing on Buffalo Pass in Routt National Forest. Intermediate through expert skills required. Free Coyote skis provided. Telephone (303) 879-5188 for reservations. (For more information on snowcat skiing and Steamboat Springs Powder Cats, see the special feature section of this book entitled *The Joys of Snowcat Skiing.*)

Dinner sleigh rides. Telephone (303) 879-0954 between 8:00 A.M. and 6:00 P.M. for reservations.

Snowmobile rentals. Telephone (303) 879-2062 or (303) 879-1551 for information and reservations.

Bowling, only two and a half miles from the slopes. Telephone (303) 879-9840 to reserve a lane.

Dogsledding. Telephone (303) 879-7199.

Ice-skating. Howelsen Hill Ice Rink. Telephone (303) 879-0341 for the operating schedule.

The Steamboat Health & Recreation Company. Thirty exercise classes each week consisting of acrobics, including low impact, stretching and toning, and yoga. There is also a weight room with free weights, Universal Gym, and stationary bicycles.

Services

A full complement of churches, sporting goods stores, apparel shops, pharmacies, grocery stores, liquor stores, furniture, bath, and specialty shops is within the immediate Steamboat area. Additionally, guests at any of the condominiums or homes may place orders for provisions directly with Nancy's Selective Shopping. Telephone (303) 879-5018 for food delivery prior to your arrival.

Village Map

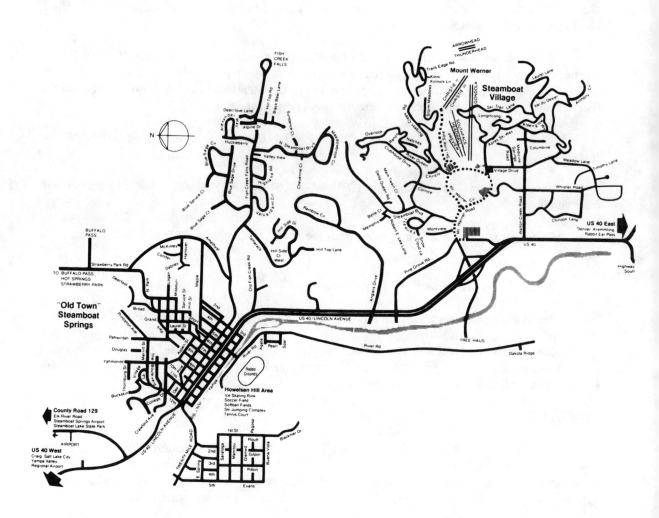

SUGARBUSH/Mad River Glen

Sugarbush Ski Resort
RR Box 350
Warren, Vt. 05674-9993

(800) 53SUGAR Reservations and Information
(802) 583-SNOW Snow Report

New for 1993-94

Sugarbush fans are looking forward to more certain skiing on the excellent runs at Sugarbush South this year, and even better next. In the past, during dry years it was difficult for certain areas of that mountain to have good snow coverage, and snowmaking had been thwarted by environmental concerns. This summer a compromise between the ski area and environmental groups means that around 40 percent of the mountain will be covered for this year, and for the 1994-95 season Sugarbush plans to install a $10 million snowmaking system that will cover up to 70 percent of Sugarbush South.

How To Get There

Sugarbush and the smaller Mad River Glen ski area are located almost next to one another, 45 miles south of Burlington International Airport in the town of Warren, Vermont. Burlington International Airport is served by Continental, Delta, United, U.S. Air, and TWA Express. Getting to Sugarbush or Mad River Glen is as easy as getting on Interstate Highway 89 shortly after exiting the airport, and following it to exit 10, Waterbury. After a delightful drive through the rolling Green Mountain National Forest, you will come to a fork in the road just after the town of Waitsfield; turn right onto highway 17. Stay on 17 until you reach German Flats Road which goes directly to the smaller of the two Sugarbush mountains—Sugarbush North, or continue to the main Sugarbush resort located on Sugarbush Access Road.

Travelers from the greater Boston area should take Interstate Highway 93 north to Interstate Highway 89 and exit at number 9, route 100B. Just south of Moretown, 100B joins Highway 100. Drivers should continue on this combined route number until just after Waitsfield where they will pick-up Highway 17, the direct route to both Sugarbush and Mad River Glen.

Skiers from the New York City area should take Interstate Highway 95 to Highway 91 (north). After Highway 91 ends at Interstate Highway 89, follow the instructions for travelers from Boston.

Guests driving to Sugarbush from the west can take any number of interstate highways to Interstate 87. Exit I-87 at exit 20 (route 149), and follow it to Route 4 (east), through Rutland, to Route 100. Continue on Highway 100 past Warren to Sugarbush Access Road.

Avis, Hertz, National, Budget car rental companies are all represented at the Burlington International Airport. Thrifty is located off site, as is Rent-a-Wreck, aka Rent-Rite. Ski racks are available and should be requested when booking. The ski racks provided are an inexpensive type that you must place on the car yourself. There is an up-charge for these racks, and you should be sure to park only in a secure places or remove your rack nightly, as you will be responsible if it is stolen.

It is recommended that all persons considering a multi-day stay in the Sugarbush/Mad River Glen area arrange for an automobile. Many of the better restaurants and accommodations are not located at the base of the resort, and unlike many western ski resorts, Vermont resorts do not have many (if any) hotel accommodations. They generally have some condominiums and several fine restaurants, but not enough to satisfy guests for more than a day or two. Many of the hotels, or more correctly "inns," offer shuttle service between their establishment and the resorts, but here one is subjected to operating on another's schedule, rather than his own.

Approximately 10 companies offer metered taxi services within a 100-mile radius from Burlington Airport, but prices are high. A one-way fare to Sugarbush will cost around $62.

For any ground travel questions, the Ground Transportation Information Center at the airport, which is open every day from 11 to 15 hours, will be happy to help you find an answer. The desk is located in the baggage claim area.

Mountain Information

Sugarbush is located in Green Mountain National Forest and consists of two mountains situated about five miles apart. The larger and main resort mountain is called Sugarbush South (formerly South Basin). It rises 3,975 feet (1,925 meters), providing a vertical drop of 2,400 feet (720 meters). The second mountain is called Sugarbush North (formerly known as Mt. Ellen). It is the highest mountain in Green Mountain National Forest at 4,135 feet (1,241 meters), with a vertical drop of 2,600 feet (780 meters).

The two mountains combined provide guests with 400 acres (160 ha) of skiing terrain. Of these 400 acres, 183 (91.5 ha) can be covered fully by snowmaking equipment. Snowmaking capabilities in the eastern U.S. are extremely important because eastern elevations are so low. One day's snow is frequently followed by the next day's rain. Conditions at eastern ski resorts are much more fickle than at western ones. While western resorts may experience "hardpack" because it has not snowed in a few days, it is not unusual for eastern resorts such as Sugarbush to have their hardpack converted to ice due to rain and/or melting and refreezing. Skiers unfamiliar with eastern skiing who contemplate a trip there should be certain to bring their heaviest and stiffest skis, ones that enable them to set an edge on the hard surface. Leave the Pres, Heli-dogs, and Quantums at home.

Sugarbush South

The best skiing for beginners is usually found off either the Village or GateHouse lifts. Sugarbush South has developed good skier separation, and few expert skiers are ever encountered racing down the Village and GateHouse-serviced slopes. This gentle terrain is excellent for beginners and less-experienced intermediates, allowing them to polish their form and "stand tall" in their boots.

The wide-open cruising runs so many skiers crave are found in abundance off the Spring Fling and Super Bravo lifts. From the Spring Fling lift, try Upper Snowball and Spring Fling; both are wide and groomed daily. This is a good place to work on form or just let the skis run. Sugarbush's longest intermediate run is Jester at 1,500 feet (457 meters). Jester runs from the top of the Super Bravo lift all the way to the base area. Its well-groomed and sheltered environment normally assures skiers of good snow conditions.

The best expert skiing at Sugarbush is found in the Castlerock area. Castlerock is served by the Castle Rock lift, and all the runs except for Troll Road are expert. Castlerock is closed frequently because it requires abundant snow coverage. Try Castlerock Run for the easiest expert runs; Rumble or Lift Line will provide more challenge. Regardless of snow conditions, there runs are tough. They generally are covered with skiers, and there are always many rocks and ice to avoid as well.

Eastern ski resorts generally cut narrower trails than do western ones. The principal reason for this policy is to allow the trees lining the runs to act as snow fences. These natural snow fences help the resort retain its snow. Snowstorms in the East are frequently accompanied by strong winds, and the trees help hold the snow while preventing it from blowing away. On the very worst weather days, avoid the top of Heaven's Gate lift. The wind and blowing snow can make this area extremely unpleasant. Wait until the storm passes, then enjoy the expert and intermediate runs emanating from it.

Although these resorts are typically busy, skiers can avoid crowds and enjoy the best skiing by avoiding the middle of the trails. Ski the sides where the trails will be the least crowded and the least icy. Avoid Gate House lift and Sugar Bravo, always the most crowded.

Sugarbush North

Sugarbush North is different from Sugarbush South in both appearance and "feel". The base area around Sugarbush South has been developed to include a sports complex, condominiums, restaurants, etc., but Sugarbush North has only a large parking lot at its base. Skiers who frequent Sugarbush North seem more laid back and typically ski more conservatively than those frequenting Sugarbush South. Sugarbush North is strictly a day ski area. It is half as large as South Basin but contains numerous runs that will challenge skiers of all ability levels. Upper F.I.S. is steep and usually heavily moguled. Between the moguls and on their backside, ice normally forms, tending to make skiers consider their turns cautiously. The total length of Upper and Lower F.I.S. is 2.5 miles (4 km), making it the longest expert run at Sugarbush. One of the most difficult runs on either mountain is Hammerhead—skirting along the west side of the Green Mountain Express, the world's fastest SuperQuad. This cantankerous run is narrow, icy, rocky, crowded, and just plain mean! Try it at your own risk.

Inverness is Sugarbush North's cruising run; ski straight down the fall line. It is always immaculately groomed, and is a great place to learn how to link your turns. Since no expert terrain is found off Inverness lift, Inverness also is the area favored by those who like to ski fast and (hopefully) in control.

Mad River Glen Mountain Information

Mad River Glen is a charming anachronism. Constructed in 1940, its trails have not since been modified, nor has much of the lift equipment been modernized. Chair A is still the same single-person chair that was originally installed and has been in continuous use since the 1940's. Mad River's narrow trails seem to amble, while other resorts' trails seem to "hurry". Mad River Glen is in harmony with the environment. Many trees have been left along the trails' length. It is as though the trails are foot-paths that weave among trees, rocks, and frozen waterfalls.

Mad River Glen is best known for its expert runs. As its bumper sticker flaunts, "Ski It If You Can!" Here there are no compromises—the skier must get down the mountain the best way he can.

Many knowledgeable skiers consider Paradise to be the most difficult run in the East, and with good reason! Paradise is not shown on the map, but it is located to the right of Fall Line and Creamer, looking uphill. To reach Paradise, ride Single Chair to the top and immediately upon exiting begin the short climb uphill (just behind the lift operator's shelter). Do not attempt this trek without a guide if no tracks are visible. However, if there are tracks, follow them. From here there are only two ways down: Paradise or Octopus Gardens. Most of the tracks probably will lead to Paradise. You will know you are on Paradise when, after your first few downhill turns, you ski over a frozen waterfall! There are still two more waterfalls to traverse before finishing what will definitely be memorable run. In addition to waterfalls there are large rocks, small rocks, trees, tree trunks, moguls, ice, and other skiers. Only the very skillful should attempt this run. No one will like it very much, but all will be proud they skied it.

Mad River Glen is owned and operated by Betsy Pratt, a delightful lady determined not to let modern technology interfere with the way she wants to run her resort. She contends that Mad River Glen is comprised of numerous small segments of what she terms "excellence." She believes that with all the various weather factors they have to contend with in Vermont, it is unrealistic to think that conditions in the entire resort on any given day will be perfect. However, she does believe there are always several areas of the resort which are exceptional. She believes that once a skier happens upon such an area, he should ski it over and over.

Antelope is one of the best intermediate runs in North America. It is a long run like those featured at many resorts, but what sets Antelope apart is its character. It is sinuous, slinking from a 3,637 foot peak (1,091 meters) to a 1,600 foot (480 meters) base; all the 2,037 foot (621 meters) vertical length is delightful. At the top of the run, it meanders through fir trees; further along its sometimes narrow and sometimes wide journey, the trees transition to maple. The trail twists and turns without another trail in sight until the very end. The lone skier should pause to listen to the wind as it blows through the tree branches and the melodious scrape, scrape of his skis' edges turning on the snow, savoring his solitude.

Although Mad River offers an abundance of expert terrain, it also has an equal number of beginner runs. Like all the other trails, beginner runs are skillfully woven into the fabric of the environment, primarily in an area know as Birdland. Here beginning skiers can learn the skills necessary to advance to intermediate level. Many ski resorts relegate their beginners to big, wide-open slopes. Here, however, the runs are narrow, gently in tune with nature. The same skills are taught by the ski school here as at other resorts. Somehow, however, the lessons seem gentler and promise to be more enduring because of the closeness to nature that one experiences in this environment. This resort is in distinct contrast to new resorts characterized by wide-open surfaces and surrounded by condominiums, restaurants, and ski shops.

Despite its day-skier status, Mad River Glen is necessary, convenient, and a wonderful enhancement to the Sugarbush experience. Each resort is counterbalanced by the other, because neither is strong enough to stand on its own as a destination resort.

Sugarbush Lift Ticket Prices (1992-93)

$ 35	Adult, All-Day (Weekdays)
$ 39	Adult, All-Day (Weekends)
$ 27	Adult, Half-Day (Weekdays)
$ 30	Adult, Half-Day (Weekends)
$ 66	Adult, 2-Day (Weekdays)
$ 70	Adult, 2-Day (Weekends)
$ 94	Adult, 3-Day (Weekdays)
$102	Adult, 3-Day (Weekends)
$145	Adult, 5-Day (Weekdays)
$174	Adult, 5-Day (Weekends)
$ 20	Junior, 7-12 Years Old & Senior 65 - 69

Free   Child, 6 & Under
Free   Senior, 70+

Multi-day tickets are non-refundable for any unused portion. Holiday rates are the same as the weekend rates. In addition, there is a Value Season commencing opening day through December 24 and from March 22 until closing day. During that period, midweek lift tickets will cost $15, and weekend tickets will cost $29.

Mad River Glen Lift Ticket Prices (1993-94)

$ 26   Adult, All-Day
$ 30   Adult, All-Day, Dec. 26 - Jan.2 & Feb 19 - Feb.21
$ 22   Adult, Half-Day, weekends and holidays
$ 16   Adult, Half-Day, weekends and holidays
$ 12   Adult, Half-Day, weekdays
$ 50   Adult, 2-Day
$ 74   Adult, 3-Day
$ 20   Junior, 6-16 Years Old & Senior 65-74
Free   Child, 5 & Under
Free   Senior, 75+

This year Mad River Glen is trying something new with its lift tickets. **If you purchase a 4-day ticket, you will be able to ski an additional 3 days for free!** The regular price for four days is $104, and during holiday periods it will be slightly higher.

Free skiing for everyone is offered daily during the first half-hour of operation. Pre and post-season rates are reduced.

Hours of Operation

8:30 A.M. to 4:00 P.M.
9:00 A.M. to 4:00 P.M. weekdays at Mad River Glen and at 11:30 A.M. on Christmas Day.

Lift Ticket Purchase Locations

Lift tickets may be purchased at the Gate House Base Lodge at South Basin or at the Mt. Ellen Base Lodge at Mt. Ellen. In addition, discount tickets are available from over 100 outlets including P&C grocery stores, Ski Markets, and numerous other independent ski rental shops throughout the Sugarbush area. Discounted tickets are usually priced $4 off the regular resort rate, except during the Christmas holidays.

How To Avoid Crowds

Crowd control at Sugarbush is a serious matter, as it has become everywhere. Skiers who are out-of-control or skiing too fast will lose their lift tickets. Generally speaking, however, there is not a serious problem with crowd control as there are numerous ways down the two Sugarbush mountains at the end of the ski day. Unlike many resorts that have only one or two downhill routes, Sugarbush has so many that there is no cross traffic and few areas where mixed levels of ability try to occupy the same space.

Mad River Glen does not have enough skiers for crowd control to be much of an issue.

Ski School

Sugarbush's ski school, under the direction of Peter Forsthuber, teaches the American Teaching System (ATS). All 110 instructors are members of the Professional Ski Instructors of America (PSIA), and, as such, are highly qualified to teach. The method used to teach skiing is the same method found in most major destination ski resorts throughout the United States. It differs only slightly from the technique taught in major Canadian resorts. Ski school classes meet in front of the Gatehouse at South Basin and behind the Base House at Sugarbush North. Classes are at 10 A.M. & 2 P.M.

Never-ever skiers or snowboarders can purchase the following special Guaranteed *Learn to Ski* packages. The purchasers of these packages are restricted to using the beginner lifts only. Most classes consist of six students. However, during peak periods some classes may consist of as many as eight students. In these classes, beginner skiers are guaranteed to learn how to ski under control on a designated novice trail by the end of the day, or the package is free until they do learn.

$39 Adult/Junior, Lift, Lesson, Rental Equipment

Other ski classes

$ 24 Class Lesson (2 Hours), All Abilities
$ 45 Private Lesson (1 Hour)
$225 All Day Private Lesson (9 A.M.–4 P.M.)
$310 All Day Semi Private Lesson (2–4 Persons)

Four through five-year-olds can be enrolled in the **Minibear Program**. This program organizes children by age and ability. Level-one skiers acquire basic skills on the Minibear ramp and then move on to level two which is an actual slope. By the time they are ready for level three, they will be on an actual beginner ski run. Depending on weather, Minibear children are outside for no more than two hours at a time, twice a day. The remainder of the time is spent in supervised day-care activities, such as rest or playtime.

Older children (ages 6– 10) may be enrolled in the **Sugarbear program**. Sugarbears learn valuable skills in the Land of the Mogul Mouse, a fantasy garden consisting of bumps, turns, tunnels, and cartoon characters designed to make children responsive to their lessons. Lessons consist of two 2-hour lessons each day, a two-hour supervised lunch, and a rest period.

$50 All-Day, Minibear Program (Day Care, Lunch, 2 Lessons, Equipment)
$32 Half-Day, Minibear Program (Day Care, 1 Lesson, Lunch, Equipment)
$40 All-Day Sugarbear Program, Lift & 2 Lessons, Child (6 years)
$60 All-Day Sugarbear Program, Lift & 2 Lessons, Junior (7– 10 years)

Add $6 per day if lunch is desired. Half-day sessions also are available.

Equipment Rental

Equipment rentals are available at both **Sugarbush South** and **Sugarbush North**. The equipment is identical at both rental locations. The 1993-94 rental price for recreational skis or snowboards is $22 per day, $16 for each additional day. A performance package will cost $30 per day.

Tuning and repair services are available from the rental shops at Sugarbush South and Sugarbush North. The most recent fee schedule was not available at press time, but expect it to be about

$35 Full Tune-up
$ 7 "Quick" Edge Sharpening

$ 4   Hot Wax
$ 7   Base Patch/Weld

Mountain Dining

Because Sugarbush's vertical is so limited, only Sugarbush North has an actual mid-mountain restaurant. All other eating facilities are located at the base of the mountain. Sugarbush South's regular cafeteria service is located in **Gate House Lodge**—a rather unremarkable facility, typical of 1,001 other day-area cafeterias with adequate food and reasonable prices. Except for its convenience, however, there is not a compelling reason to eat here.

Sugarbush South's best food service is found in **Valley Lodge House**, just a few steps east of Gate House Lodge and the main lifts. The **Mad Topper** (also know locally as "Mushroom" because of its shape) is a sit-down restaurant with table service. The menu features excellent pizza, grinders, calzones, and tossed salad. Service is prompt and courteous; prices are reasonable. Located just upstairs from Mad Topper in the same facility is **Castlerock Café**. This café features daily specials such as BBQ, wings, clam chowder, or chile. Meals are served buffet style; prime rib is caved to order daily.

The meal service at Sugarbush North is similar to that offered at Gate House. Mid-mountain Glen House is somewhat more limited in its selections.

Child Care

Licensed day-care is available for infants (from six weeks of age) and children up to ten years old. The facility is located in Sugarbush Village at Sugarbush South. This is the area's only day-care facility and it is adjacent, but not convenient, to the slopes. Parents are advised to drop their children off in the morning before entering the main parking lot at Sugarbush South or driving to Sugarbush North. The child-care center is open seven days a week, 8:00 A.M.—4:30 P.M.

Sugarbush Day School Nursery is completely equipped with climbing equipment, cribs, swings, and lots of toys. Lunch and snacks are included in the daily fee. Parents of non-toilet-trained children should provide at least six disposable diapers each day. Those whose children are on formula should likewise make certain to provide enough for the entire day. A change of clothes is also suggested. If your child has a special blanket or toy, by all means bring it. Children enjoy music, crafts, stories, arts, and outdoor activities. Telephone (802)583-2495 for reservations.

A parents' night-out is provided each Saturday evening from 7:00 P.M—midnight. Day-care rates are

$ 6   Hourly
$ 4   Lunch
$ 40   Full Day with Lunch
$175   Five Day Special

Medical Facilities

For ski injuries, the ski patrol will only render emergency aid. Patrolmen will administer trauma treatment, stabilize broken bones, and transport the injured skier downhill by sled to a clinic located at the base of the mountain. The clinic at South Basin is staffed by a University Orthopedic Clinic doctor and nurse. Should an illness or an injury require more than emergency care, patients will be transported by the fastest and most appropriate means to Montpelier, thirty miles southeast of Sugarbush.

Cross-Country Skiing

Perhaps it is due to the variances of New England weather, or perhaps due to the independence often associated with the frugal and soft-spoken Vermonters, but cross-country skiing is BIG back East! Although no cross-country skiing is available at either Sugarbush or Mad River Glen, the surrounding area is a cross-country mecca, particularly around Warren, Vermont.

A large track system in the area is **Blueberry Lake Cross-Country Center**, located on Plunkton Road in East Warren. It boasts over 29 km of trails and groomed track. The 1993-94 price were not available at press time. Rentals are available. For more information, telephone (802) 496-6687.

Still another cross-country ski area is located in Huntington, just north of Waitsville. Dave and Myra Brautigam own the **Camel's Hump Nordic Ski Center**. Camel's Hump has over 3000 acres (1,214 ha) of alpine terrain, 35 km of machine-groomed track, and 30 km of wilderness trails. A complete Nordic center, Camel's Hump offers lessons, rental equipment, and wilderness guide service. For additional information, telephone (802) 434-2704.

The **Sugarbush Cross-Country Ski Area** is located at the Pavilion (direct across the street from the Sugarbush Inn), one half mile south of the lifts. It is the closest cross-country area to Sugarbush South. Its 40 km. of trails are groomed; most of the terrain is rated beginner to intermediate. **Knickers**, a restaurant located adjacent to the trails, is open for the season to serve its Nordic skiers. For more information, telephone (802) 583-2301.

Accommodations

Unlike at most western resorts, no big-name hotels have been developed at any Vermont ski resorts. This no doubt due to the strong association of independent innkeepers whose members own most, if not all, the state's hotel accommodations. Ski resorts would experience the wrath of a very large segment of the local population if they were able to obtain zoning and building permits for large hotels. Thus hotel-type rooms are only available away from the resorts proper; condominium properties, however, have been allowed on ski resort land or adjacent to it.

Numerous inns are located within ten miles of both Sugarbush and Mad River Glen. Sugarbush publishes a list of many inns which have agreed to pay a fee to Sugarbush for bookings they receive. Most of these inns are small, and many include breakfast and dinner, usually served family style. This is a nice arrangement if you want to establish a close rapport with other guests. However, you will then, presumably, be giving up the opportunity to sample the many fine restaurants in the area.

The Sugarbush Inn is located on the Sugarbush Access Road and combines the decor and look of an established New England inn with all the amenities of a resort. The 46 2- and 3-bedroom units have cable television with HBO, private baths, bellman and concierge service. A guest shuttle will bring you to the slopes. The recreation facilities include two heated pools, saunas, whirLpool, and a health club. Rooms vary but range from $96 to $157 per night, depending on the size and season.

Weathertop Lodge is located on Highway 17 one mile south of German Flats Road, 2.5 miles from Sugarbush North, 4 miles from Mad River Glen and 5 miles from Sugarbush South. Its owners take great pride in the facility and the services they offer their guests. This is a small inn (only nine rooms) but unlike many inns, each room has its own bath, shower, and toilet. No TV's nor telephones are found in any of the rooms; courtesy phones have been installed on the first and third floors for guest use. A large common room with a blazing fireplace, TV, video games, books, and newspapers is the usual gathering place for après-ski.A hot tub where guests may soak their weary bones is located on the main floor. Of if hot tubbing sounds too "California" for you, a Finnish sauna is also available.

Those who feel they did not get enough exercise on the slopes can climb to the upstairs attic which has been converted to a small gym, complete with free weights, punching bag, ballet bar, and exercycle.

Each room is decorated with a quilt wallhanging that the owner's mother crafted especially for the Weathertop. Twin queen-size beds or double beds, adequate clothing storage, and hanging space complement each room, as does a small refrigerator for those who want to provide their own refreshments. All rooms recently have been redecorated. 1993-94 room rates for the Weathertop are $82 (plus tax)based on mid-week, double occupancy. At Christmas, the rate is $125 per night, midweek. Typically included in the room rate is a large country breakfast consisting of bacon, sausage, eggs, waffles, pancakes, and all the juice and coffee you can drink.

Mountainside Condominiums are located within walking distance of the Sugarbush South lifts in Sugarbush Village. These are somewhat dated units, furnished in natural oak, with tan or brown being the dominant colors. Mountainside units are available as one-bedroom plus loft or two-bedroom. The one-bedroom models are small and more typically fit the usual description of an "efficiency." The kitchens in all units feature Kenmore appliances and include a dishwasher and an electric range. There are no microwave ovens, electric can openers, or other amenities commonly found in better condominiums. Bedrooms contain a king-size bed and feature good storage space in the closets and dressers. The bathrooms are small (resembling the size one might find on a small yacht). No amenity packages containing soap, shampoo, or conditioner are provided. A wood-burning fireplace and a T.V. are the usual center of activity in these condominiums. During the 1993 season condo rates will vary between $130 and $300 depending on season and size.

Located a scant 1/3 mile from the slopes and offering guests reliable shuttle service, **The Bridges Resort and Racquet Club** is one of Sugarbush's most popular condominium complexes. The general facility features a private health club in which all guests receive courtesy membership. There are two indoor Har Tru tennis courts, an indoor lap pool, outdoor hot tub, and a full fitness center including exercise area for aerobics, Nautilus equipment, Stairmaster, a recreation room, locker rooms, and a poolside café featuring a fieldstone fireplace and windows overlooking the action at the pool. Each unit has a VCR and video tapes are available for rent at the front desk, providing young and old alike with the option of snuggling-up in front of a warm fire in the hearth and watching the likes of Batman defend Gotham against the tyranny of the Joker or Indiana Jones battle sinister characters in another desert adventure.

The largest units at The Bridges are three-bedroom condominiums. There living rooms are U-shaped with expansive windows overlooking the beautiful countryside or the slopes themselves. Kitchens are well equipped with Kenmore appliances; each includes a compactor, microwave, ice maker, lots of dishes, utensils, and electric range and oven. Washer and dryers are found in all units except one bedrooms.

Rental rates during the 1993-94 regular season range from $145 to $195 for a one bedroom; $190 to $340 for a 2-bedroom and $305 to $395 for a 3-bedroom. Prices are higher during the Christmas/New Year's period, and 30 per cent lower during the Value Season, November until December 18 and March 20 until the close of the ski slopes. 802-583-2922.

Southface represents some of the best accommodations available at Sugarbush South. These are actually duplexes with individual carports and hot tubs, although some units have saunas in lieu of hot tubs. Be sure to specify a preference when booking. A unique feature of these units is a miniature loft which accommodates a cable T.V., and two futons that can be folded to form seats. The loft is a great hide-away for children and is only accessible by a wall-mounted ladder. Each living room is large and flooded with natural light. All are complete with T.V.'s, stereos, lots of comfortable lounge seating, and dining bars which separate the kitchens and living areas. Fireplaces are more contemporary than are usually found in mountain condominiums; kitchens definitely provide what gourmet cooks demand.

Ranges and ovens are natural gas; microwaves, dishwashers, ice makers, and many, many utensils thoughtfully have been provided. Formal dining areas seat six comfortably and yield great views of the slopes. Southface units rent for $260 for a 2-bedroom and $336 for a 3-bedroom, mid-week during the 1993-94 regular season. Prices rise during holidays and on weekends.

Summit Condominiums are located at the very top of Sugarbush Village and doubtlessly derive their name from that fact. All units feature three bedrooms, two baths and have commanding views of Green Mountain National Forest. Their small, sunken living/dining areas with crate-like furniture are highlighted by wood-burning fireplaces. Harvest-gold kitchens with almond-colored appliances feature microwave ovens, compactors, dishwashers, and electric ranges. Some units also contain small washers and dryers. Summit Condominiums rent for $270 to $460 during the 1993-94 season.

Restaurants

At the new **Sugarbush Inn,** you can choose from two restaurants. **The Terrace Restaurant** provides a country inn setting for with a menu which changes its local and regionally-influenced dishes daily. Or try the **Grill Down Under** which offers a more casual atmosphere with freshly grilled dishes.

Sugarbush's best restaurant is **Chez Henri**. One of Vermont's oldest restaurants, Chez Henri has been in continuous operation since 1962. Located on the lower level of Sugarbush Village, it is an intimate bistro in the romantic style of Degas and Toulouse-Lautrec's Paris. On warm spring days, enjoy an appetizer with champagne in a creekside setting while working on your tan. What better way to spend the late afternoon than relaxing outside with moules marinière (mussels, white wine, shallots) or escargots en vol au vent (snails in puff pastry)!

If the weather is inclement, relax for après-ski in Chez Henri's famous marble bar. Soft candle-light, red and white checkered tablecloths, and black bentwood seating guarantee an intimate prelude to dinner. The extraordinary wine service and gastronomy is exemplified by les patés aux fruits de mer (seafood with linguini in herbed butter), les rognons de veau Robert (veal kidneys in Robert sauce), or l'espadon grillé (swordfish grilled with tomato coulis). All items are à la carte; all major credit cards are accepted. For reservations, telephone (802) 583-2600.

Nestled in a small valley on the east side of the access road to Sugarbush Village is **Sam Rupert's Restaurant.** A warm fire welcomes shivering skiers to a friendly milieu of musk-scented barnboard and burnt-umber clay masonry. Dine while watching gentle snowflakes fall on the verdant woods outside.

Sam Rupert's comprehensive menu and numerous daily specials offer great variety to even the most demanding guest. For example, one day last winter a few of the daily specials included five onion soup gratineé, Chinese chicken vegetable soup, fresh steamed mussels, herb and red pepper fetuccines with veal, beef and chicken, grilled swordfish with orange ginger butter, venison and Vermont quail with Chinese cabbage and red zinfandel sauce. Food like this is reason enough to visit Sam Rupert's, but it also periodically features a strolling magician who is terrific. He is guaranteed to make you marvel at his skill! For reservations, telephone (802) 583-2421.

A short distance from Sugarbush and only two or three miles from Mad River Glen is **Millbrook**, a small restaurant owned and operated by Joan and Thom Gorman. Millbrook is actually a country house with guest rooms. However, its restaurant is its best feature. Small, warm, and typical of Vermont's laid-back atmosphere, Millbrook provides dining individually prepared to guests' specific desires. Because Thom worked for some time in India, he has elected to feature several Indian dishes on his menu such as chicken brahmapuri (boneless breast of chicken cooked in a rich, spicy, village-style purée and served with rice and homemade tomato chutney) or badami rogan Josh (tender chunks of lamb, simmered in a rich curried sauce of cardamom, cumin, coriander, coconut, almonds, ginger, yoghurt, and tomatoes). Of course, if your palate tends to the more mundane, there are always the old stand-bys: shrimp scampi, garden lasagna, veal Roma, etc. For reservations, telephone (802) 496-2405.

Another local favorite is **The Common Man**, which is located in a beautiful old barn rebuilt and redecorated in a country European fantasy style. When the original barn burned down 7 years ago, proprietor Michael Ware moved this one board by board to the location and rebuilt. Try the fresh salomon, or cassoulet, or the Anatra in Agrodolce(roasted breast of duck, cut off the bone and dressed with a sauce of raspberry vinegar and Vermont honey). The menu is eclectic and creative. A wine list of 150 varieties and desserts baked on the premises complete the picture. Moderate prices. Children's menu available. Reservations are recommended(802)583-2800.

Activities

One of the best facilities for indoor sports in the East is Sugarbush Sports Complex, located at the entrance to Sugarbush Village. This large, modern facility features state-of-the-art exercise equipment such as Life Step, Stairmaster 4000PT, Life Row, and Concept II rowing machines. Free weights, aerobic classes, swimming, steam, sauna, massage, a hot tub, and tennis courts are only some of its numerous amenities. Lockers and a health bar complete the complex's facilities providing non-skiers with enough activity to while away the hours while their companions are on the slopes. Inquire about membership when booking lodging reservations; some units provide complimentary membership. Teenagers can use the Sports Complex each Saturday evening from 9 - 12 for only $5.

NASTAR and coin-operated slalom race courses are available at both Sugarbush mountains. The cost is $4 for the first run and $1 per each additional run.

Horseback riding and skijoring are available at Vermont Icelandic Horse Farm; telephone (802) 496-7141.

Ice skating and rental skates are available at the Sugarbush Inn; telephone (802) 583-2301.

Night club entertainment is featured at Blue Tooth, Chez Henri, Gallagher's, Mooselips Lounge, and Nipper's at Madbush.

Several companies offer sleigh rides. There are also snowmobile rentals, snowshoe rentals, and theater available. Check local literature upon arrival for telephone numbers.

Services

A full complement of sporting goods stores, apparel shops, pharmacies, grocery stores, liquor stores, furniture, bath, and specialty shops is within the immediate Sugarbush/Mad River Glen area. In addition, there are antique stores, massage service, art galleries, bakeries, beauty salons, bookstores, florists, movies, theaters, banks, churches, alterations, dry cleaning, optical shops, and baby-sitting services in the town of Waitsville.

A view of Sugarbush ski runs from the quaint town of Warren, Vermont belies all of the activity going on at the mountain. Photo courtesy of Sugarbush resort.

SUN VALLEY

Sun Valley Company,
Sun Valley, Idaho 83353

(800) 786-8259 Reservations
(208) 622-4111 Information
(800) 635-4150 Snow Report

New For 1993-94

During the past five years Sun Valley has undergone a total transformation, proving it will continue to be a model of good skiing and the good life. It has been two years since the resort installed what is touted as the world's largest automated snowmaking system at a cost of over $16 million. Last year Sun Valley installed a new high speed detachable quad on the River Run side of Bald Mountain, replacing a triple chair and speeding the trip up the mountain by one third.

For the 1993-94 season two new high-speed detachable quad chairlifts will be running, a new day lodge has been built on Seattle Ridge, and the River Run Plaza is beginning an expansion and renovation.

One of the new quads, the **Lookout Express**, leads from the top of the River Run Quad to an elevation of 9,036 feet, just 70 feet north of the Christmas Quad's terminus. From there skiers can ski down toward Warm Springs, ski in to Christmas or Little Easter Bowls, or hop on the Lookout lift for a ride to the middle of the Sun Valley Bowls.

Another new high-speed detachable quad chair will replace the triple chair leading up **Seattle Ridge**. At its summit skiers will find a new 17,000 square foot log and glass day lodge. It is scheduled to open December 1, 1993. Just last year, a new lodge was built on the other side of the mountain at Warm Springs to replace the old North Face Hut.

How to Get There

Compared to many American destination resorts, Sun Valley cannot be considered easy to reach. Its nearest commercial airport is in Boise, a distant 168 miles. Friedman Memorial Airport in Hailey, 12 miles south of Sun Valley, is served daily by Horizon Airlines with flights from Boise and Salt Lake City. Delta's connection SkyWest Airlines also offers daily flights from Salt Lake City. Avis, Hertz and National also provide rental cars at the airport. Private aircraft can be chartered at the Hailey Airport, if desired. Shuttles provided by the Sun Valley Bell Service will provide transportation to and from the airport for Sun Valley Company guests.

Horizon Air 1-800-546-9308
SkyWest Airlines 1-800-453-9417

Although somewhat inconvenient to reach, Sun Valley is well worth the inconvenience because once skiers reach the resort, its secluded location becomes an advantage. There are no weekend crowds, and the entire resort takes on a comfortable, family atmosphere.

The best way to reach Sun Valley by air is to fly into Salt Lake City Airport, a major airline hub. From Salt Lake it is a short flight to Boise on scheduled airlines, followed by a three-hour drive to Sun Valley. The drive is easy because the road follows mountain valleys and is virtually immune to inclement weather.

Take I-84 from either Boise or Salt Lake. This fine, all-weather divided highway bisects the Snake River Plain, and one is not even in the mountains until reaching the town of Bellevue about twenty miles from Sun Valley. In fact, the name "Sun Valley" is literal—it attests to the fact that the weather is usually sunny in the valley. Unlike many mountain resorts, Sun Valley experiences few long periods of gray sky and snowy days. Quite the contrary, it typically receives frequent, small snowstorms that assure boot-deep powder on a regular basis, and it usually enjoys clear, deep blue skies during daylight hours.

Charter bus services are available from Boise, Idaho Falls, Twin Falls, and Salt Lake City. Interested travelers should contact their travel agents for a list of services and times.

Car rentals are available at all the major and regional airports. Hertz and National will rent cars that can be dropped off at Sun Valley. All other rental agencies require drivers to return the cars to their original rental location.

Although a car is not a necessity at Sun Valley, it will certainly enhance one's visit. The resort itself is self-contained, but there are many other interesting places and towns to visit. The added flexibility and mobility that an automobile provides should justify the expense.

Mountain Information

Sun Valley like Aspen has two mountains: Bald and Dollar. Dollar Mountain is situated adjacent to the Sun Valley Resort, while "Baldy" is approximately two miles away. Shuttle buses run every fifteen minutes between both mountains. Shuttle service begins a half hour before the lifts open and runs until one-half hour after they close. In addition, the city of Ketchum provides shuttles which run continually between the mountains and the various hotels, condos, and retail establishments in town. For those wishing to drive between Sun Valley Resort and the mountains, ample parking is available at Dollar's base and at the River Run base of Baldy.

Dollar Mountain is primarily considered a teaching mountain. It is relatively small and very gentle. There is not a single tree on this hill, causing it to resemble Sestriere, the famous ski resort in northern Italy. Dollar's base is 6,010 feet (1,832 meters) and its summit is at 6,638 feet (2,023 meters), giving it a vertical drop of 628 feet (191 meters). The entire mountain consists of only 127 acres (51 ha) with uphill lift service for 4,800 skiers per hour.

Bald Mountain is a classic ski mountain, and it is the mountain for which Sun Valley is most famous. Baldy has all the elements intermediate and expert skiers look forward to in skiing! There are gentle rolling slopes, steep runs, moguled trails, and bowls filled with downy powder. At first glance, the trail map maligns the enormity and diversity of the terrain and considerably understates the quantity of runs. As at Jackson Hole, most of the terrain on the map is skiable, not just the illustrated runs. Also, the trails emanating from the upper ridge are large, completely open bowls.

Baldy's base is 5,750 feet (1,753 meters), the lowest of any resort located in the Rocky Mountains. Its summit is 9,150 feet (2,789 meters) giving it a vertical drop of 3,400 feet (1,036 meters).

During the past six years, Sun Valley has completely revamped its lift services on Bald Mountain by adding six high-speed, detachable quad lifts. One new lift, Look-Out Express, replaced the old Lower Warm Springs and Limelight lifts. The new Christmas lift replaces the former Christmas lift and the Ridge chairlift. The third new chairlift, Greyhawk, runs roughly parallel to the old Look-Out Express, except it terminates at the top of Upper Greyhawk trail. The addition of these new lifts greatly enhanced Sun Valley's uphill lift capacity by providing a total uphill lift capacity of 23,800 skiers per hour.

The total reported number of skiable acres is 1,275 (516 ha). However, Sun Valley significantly understates its skiable acreage by failing to take into consideration the entire terrain of its bowls. If Sun Valley were to include this immense bowl area in its figures, the total acreage would possibly double. Actually, Sun Valley is never crowded like Aspen or Vail. This is the reward one receives for skiing at a major resort away from any substantial urban area.

Sun Valley's trail map not only understates the available terrain for skiing, but it also creates the false impression that Baldy is an "easy" mountain. This impression is created by the use of the terms "easier," "more difficult," and "most difficult." Skiers familiar with other areas, particularly Colorado, are used to associating the color green with beginner, blue with intermediate, and black with expert. At Sun Valley, however, green is easier, but definitely not beginner. Beginning or low intermediate skiers are advised to confine their skiing to Dollar Mountain. Green runs such as Gretchen's Gold, Southern Comfort, Christin's Silver, and Siggi's Bowl, to name a few, are definitely intermediate and may be among the easiest runs on the mountain—relatively steep, but not moguled. In fact, that seems to be the major difference between the green "easier" runs and the "more difficult" blue runs. The "most difficult" black runs are upper intermediate and low expert. There are no truly "expert" runs here like the double black diamonds found at resorts such as Jackson Hole or Snowbird.

One of the greatest attractions to Bald Mountain is that it is a nearly perfectly formed mountain. There are almost no areas in or out-of-bounds that are avalanche prone. After a snowstorm many local skiers take off for out-of-bounds areas to ski untracked powder. Skiers interested in out-of-bounds skiing should always be accompanied by a knowledgeable guide.

Skiers who want to stay on the traditional runs after a major dump will find the best snow in Siggi's Bowl, Mayday Bowl, Lookout Bowl, Easter Bowl, Little Easter Bowl, and Christmas Ridge and Christmas Bowl. Because the wind normally blows from right to left (looking downhill), the best conditions are on the lee, or right-hand side of the bowls. During snowstorms or on rare days when Sun Valley gets flat light, stay out of the bowls and ski runs heavily lined with trees. The trees provide contrast and make it much easier for skiers to see moguls and other terrain features. Sun Valley's bowls are such broad expanses of white that contrast and definition are difficult to perceive.

Bald Mountain is located in such a way that one side is almost always in the sun. Most knowledgeable skiers will begin their day skiing the River Run side but after lunch will switch to the Warm Springs side.

Sun Valley's annual snowfall is 175 inches (445 cm)—small, but adequate by comparison with many other resorts. Neither Bald nor Dollar Mountain is excessively rocky, nor do they require extraordinary quantities of snow to cover their runs. Monthly snowfall figures are not maintained by Sun Valley.

Average monthly temperatures during the season are

Nov.	32°	0° C
Dec.	21°	-6° C
Jan.	19°	-7° C
Feb.	24°	-4° C

Mar.   31°   0° C

Lift Ticket Prices (1992-93)

Sun Valley has a two-tier lift ticket price structure. The cost of a daily lift ticket for Dollar Mountain is less than a Baldy ticket. However a Dollar skier can purchase a Baldy upgrade at anytime. The skier who purchases a lift ticket for Baldy may also ski at Dollar.

Baldy lift ticket prices during 1993-94 are

$TBA Adult, Daily
$129 Adult, 3-Day
$200 Adult, 5-Day
$225 Adult, 6-Day
$TBA Adult, Half-Day
$TBA Child, Daily
$TBA Child, Half-Day
$125 Child, 6-Day
$100 Child, 5-Day
$ 65 Child, 3-Day

Dollar Mountain lift ticket prices during 1992-93 were

$23   Adult, Daily
$16   Child, Daily
$16   Half-Day

Children's rates apply to children aged eleven and younger. Throughout the season Sun Valley stages seasonal promotions during which children 17 and under may ski free if their parents are staying at a participating Sun Valley area lodge, or the Ski Corporation offers various discounts for children. Interested skiers should check with the resort in advance to determine if there are any incentives or discounts to be offered during their planned ski holiday. Telephone (800) 786-8259.

Hours of Operation

9:00 A.M. to 4:00 P.M. daily

Lift Ticket Purchase Locations

Lift tickets may be purchased at either River Run Base or the Warm Springs base of Bald Mountain or the Sports Center in the village. Lift tickets for Dollar Mountain are available at Dollar's base. Additionally, tickets may be purchased at the Sports Desk located on the shuttle turnaround next to the Sun Valley Lodge. Tickets may be purchased anytime between 8:30 A.M. and 3:30 P.M.

How to Avoid Crowds

Because Sun Valley's uphill lift capacity greatly exceeds its average quantity of skiers, there are no crowds and, consequently, no need for crowd controls.

Ski School

Sun Valley's Ski School is more than fifty years old. Over the years the ski school has honed its teaching techniques to a fine edge and offers instruction for any ability level. It offers group lessons and private lessons; instructors will even customize a program to fit specific needs such as powder skiing, bump skiing, or racing.

Over 160 instructors are employed at Sun Valley. Sun Valley now has adopted the American Teaching System method for its instructors.

Novices and low intermediates are taught to ski on Dollar Mountain. Strong intermediate skiers are taught on Seattle Ridge or College, located on Bald Mountain. Advanced ski instruction is at the instructor's option and can take place on any of the runs on Bald Mountain.

Enrollment in ski school is easy. Its main office is located next to the Sports Center on the shuttle turnaround next to the Lodge. Skiers also can enroll at Dollar Cabin situated at the base of Dollar Mountain or at Warm Springs Lodge. Those skiers who decide on last-minute lessons can enroll at Lookout Restaurant atop the Challenger Quad.

The 1993-94 ski school rates are

$ 41	One-Day (3 Hours)
$109	Three-Days (12 Hours)
$ 55	Child's 4-hour lesson
$147	Child's 3 days of 4-hour lessons
$ 47	Race Clinics
$130	3-days of Race Clinics

The above prices do not include lift tickets. There are no class lessons available at Bald Mountain on Saturday or Sunday, except during the Christmas holidays.

Equipment Rental

There are 12 equipment rental shops in Sun Valley. One of the larger shops, **Sturetevants of Sun Valley**, has two locations: 314 N. Main Street in Ketchum and in the Greyhawk Alpine building located at the base of the Warm Springs lift. At press time, rates were not available, but expect them to be similarly priced when compared to other resorts. A standard package often goes for around $17 per day.

The High-Performance Package is primarily a demo rental program, considered a means for the store to generate equipment sales. Under this program, a skier can rent any brand or ski size in either shop for around $28 per day.

All packages must be accompanied by a damage waiver which is actually an insurance policy. Also, at the time of rental, the renter's credit card number is noted as is its expiration date. Neither an imprint nor a deposit is required.

Ski Tuning and Repair

Tuning and repair services are available at all ski rental shops and sporting goods stores. Sturetevants of Sun Valley has WinterSteiger stone-grinding equipment which provides a superior flat ski surface compared to other common methods of tuning.   Skis must be warm before waxing. Therefore, it is a good idea to drop the skis off at the end of the day and pick them up the next morning.

1993 Sturtevant tune-up rates were

$ 8   Hot Wax
$21   Edges Sharpened
$35   Complete Tune-up
$35+   P-tex

Sturetevants tries to be as cooperative as possible, and its staff will, therefore, be pleased to deliver customers' skis to either store for pickup.

Mountain Dining

There are three mountaintop restaurants on Bald Mountain. **Lookout Restaurant,** situated at the top of the Christmas and Limelight lifts, is a cafeteria. A large, clean, and nicely furnished restaurant, Lookout can be a refuge for skiers on cold, stormy days. On bright sunny days dining is available outside on a broad deck with a fantastic view of Sawtooth National Forest.

The other mountain restaurant is situated at the top of the Cold Springs lift and the base of the Christmas lift. This is a unique structure named after its shape: **"Roundhouse."** Cafeteria-style meals are available here, as is table service. The table-service part of the restaurant is by far the best of all the mountain restaurants reviewed. This part of the Roundhouse is named **"Averell's"** after Averell Harriman, former Chairman of the Board of Union Pacific Rail Road and ambassador to the Court of King James. Averell Harriman was responsible for both Sun Valley's development and the Roundhouse restaurant, which dates back to 1939.

The carte de vin at Averell's is peerless. Among the many varietals offered during the 1989-90 season were Grand Cru/Cabernet Sauvignon; Sterling/Cabernet Sauvignon; Rutherford Hill/Merlot; Glen Ellen/Proprietor's Reserve Chardonnay; Kendall Jackson, Chardonnay; Trefethen/ Chardonnay; Callaway/Fumé Blanc; and Pouilly Fuisse. Additional wine selections are also available by the bottle or by the glass. Domestic and specially selected foreign beers, coolers, and mineral waters can also be purchased. Dining at Averell's is definitely a treat not to be passed up!

This year a new restaurant will open at **Seattle Ridge.** A 17,000 square foot structure of glass and massive logs, every window offers panoramic views of the Sawtooth Mountains and the Big Wood River Valley. Some of the logs in the new restaurant are 30-inches in diameter. The wood was culled from massive dead timber that had burned in a forest fire or died of other natural causes and then stood in the weather for two to seven years before being purchased. Some of the logs came from the famous Yellowstone fire in the late 1980s. Outside, a 5,000 square foot terrace on the south and east will be a beautiful place to sit when the weather cooperates. Infrared heaters and windscreens will help to keep it warm. Inside, a wood burning oven for freshly made pizzas to order, an Idaho Potato Baker Bar, salads, and fresh pasta dishes and grilled meats will be available for hungry visitors.

Other restaurants are located at the base of Dollar Mountain and at the base of the Warm Springs lift on Baldy.

Child Care

Child care in Sun Valley is available from **The Sun Valley Co. Playschool** just north of the Sun Valley Mall behind the gift shop. Reservations are necessary, and to use the service you must be a guest of the Sun Valley Resort. During the 1993-94 season, the center will charge $27 for 3 hours of infant care, or $58 for all day care. For toddler, $21 will be charged for 3 hours, and $48 for all day. And for potty trained children and older the charge will be $18 for 3 hours and $39 for all day. All day includes meals. Otherwise, there will be a charge for meals and extra activities, such as skiing. The center will care for children six months to six years of age. Call 208-622-2288 for information.

Medical Facilities

Sun Valley's ski patrol will only render emergency service to injured skiers. The patrol will administer trauma treatment, stabilize broken bones, and transport injured skiers downhill by sled or helicopter.

After evacuation, skiers are transported to Moritz Community Hospital for actual treatment. The hospital is full service and has a 24-hour emergency room.

Cross-Country Skiing

Some of the greatest cross-country skiing in the country is available at Sun Valley. Principally, there are four companies that offer cross-country experiences.

Sun Valley Resort's Nordic Center is located just behind the indoor ice rink at the Lodge. Nordic skiers have complete use of the resort's two heated swimming pools, indoor and outdoor ice skating rinks, as well as all the amenities offered by the Lodge.

The terrain at the Center's trailhead is quite gentle, but as it continues on its 40-kilometer trek, it increases in difficulty. Three-pin skiers usually are not subject to high altitude sickness, the fatigue, or other ailments normally associated with Rocky Mountain Nordic skiing because of the area's relatively low elevation. Groomed tracks direct skiers through snow-covered meadows where they can either ski tour or experiment with the diagonal skating so in vogue today.

It is possible to rent or purchase all the equipment necessary for cross-country skiing at the Nordic Center. The Center also has a wax room and shop with all the accessories necessary for waxing and tuning. In addition, those alpine skiers who have purchased a multi-day ticket may exchange one day for a cross-country ticket. This is a good program for skiers who have never tried cross-country but who think they might like it. Pick a clear day and try skiing the green beginner course or better yet, take a lesson from one of Hans Muehlegger's certified staff; a one-hour group lesson was only $14 during the 1990-91 season.

The daily trail fee during 1990-91 was a modest $10 and only $5 for children six to twelve. Senior citizens were able to ski for only $6.50.

The **Nordic Center at Warm Springs Ranch** has 12 kilometers of groomed creekside tracks. One kilometer of track is even lighted for night skiing! A complete pro shop, day lodge, lessons, rentals, and off-track tours are available at Warm Springs Ranch. There is even a doggie track for those skiers who cannot bear to leave Fido at home. A word of caution, though: most resorts and condos will not allow dogs in their units.

Located only twenty-two miles from Sun Valley and situated in Sawtooth National Forest is **Galena Lodge**. A chef in the recently remodeled kitchen turns out freshly baked biscuits daily and offers complete breakfast and luncheon menus. The 40 kilometers of tracks are groomed daily by a newly acquired Piston Bully 170, assuring skiers of a smooth, firm surface regardless of weather conditions.

Galena Lodge charges $11 for adults using its tracks. Children under six ski free; ages six through seventeen are charged $7. The Lodge has an excellent ski school and a complete rental shop stocked with accessories. Transportation to Galena is provided Tuesday through Friday for a nominal charge. Telephone (208) 726-4010 for additional information.

For the cross-country skier who is really into experiencing the mountain environment, there is not a better way to do it than to arrange a tour to a Mongolian Yurt. **Sun Valley Trecking Company** offers a four to six-hour tour over easy trails to its Fishhook Yurt. Once at the Yurt, skiers will be treated to a lunch of culinary delights. This trip is especially memorable on New Year's Eve. New Year's Eve 1989 was celebrated by an evening tour to the Yurt where the host served a hot and spicy golden punch, homemade cream of chestnut soup, crème fraîche, and boned shoulder of lamb. A Bûche de Noël—a yard-long chocolate roll—was served for dessert.

Accommodations

There are inadequate adjectives in the English language to describe the graciousness and ambience that surround **Sun Valley Resort**'s guests.

If they arrive in the evening, guests entering the town of Sun Valley are greeted by a large lighted wreath on the side of a barn. The road leading to the resort itself is lined with split-rail fencing; its lighting creates a fairyland atmosphere. Upon entering the grounds of the resort, one is immediately awestruck by towering pines that frame the entrance. The main building of Sun Valley Resort and the guest's first stop is the **Sun Valley Lodge**. Under an immense porte-cochère, a valet will help unload the car and park it. One then enters the reception area and lobby through large double doors. Each afternoon high tea is served in the lobby while guests sit in front of the fireplace and watch skaters on the outdoor ice skating rink. The room is large and elegantly decorated from its hardwood floors with sculptured carpet in rose, flaxen, and silver to the rich, wood picture-frame paneling and gold-tone chandeliers. In a far corner of the room, a tuxedoed pianist plays show tunes and traditional favorites.

Adjacent to the lobby is the **Peter Duchin Room**. Its natural oak paneling and plush seating is reminiscent of a fine bar in New York City, rather than a mountain lodge. The bar is constructed of fine inlaid gray/brown marble and the service here is excellent. The spirits and wines offered are exceptional. However, the guest is cautioned to ask for the price before ordering the better varietals. It is not uncommon to order a glass of wine only to find out that it has cost as much as $9 a drink for a bottle that sells for $12 in a liquor store.

The Peter Duchin Room features piano jazz after 4:00 P.M. Later in the evening a band plays dance music. On occasion, a big name entertainer is presented and there is never a cover or surcharge.

The corridors leading to the rooms resemble a well-kept museum. Photographs of Hollywood notables and Washington politicians abound, as do full cases of trophies won by many of Sun Valley's residents and visitors.

Rooms in the Lodge are tastefully decorated with traditional flair. Not large by most standards, they nonetheless include amenities such as towel warmers and closets whose lights go on when their doors are opened. All the services of any world-class hotel are as near as the telephone: room service, massage, valet, and so forth.

The grounds of Sun Valley are meticulously maintained. Many of the evergreens are lighted, and walkways are always cleared of snow. A stroll through the picturesque village is delightful as one passes by the Opera House and the Mall with its tony shops. Sun Valley is probably the only resort where a skier can purchase a custom-made ski parka or ski pants. Staying at Sun Valley Resort is so pleasant one does not even have to put ski to slope to know this is as good as it gets!

Although Sun Valley Resort is the premier place to stay while skiing at Sun Valley, there are several other accommodations. Very nice accommodations at that! Not far from Sun Valley Resort is the **Radisson Elkhorn Resort**. Elkhorn is comprised of over 200 hotel rooms and condominiums. The style is Tyrolean modern and appears very comfortable with its surroundings. A small village is located in a semi-circle emanating from the lodge. Restaurants, shops, and galleries are all within walking distance of the accommodations.

A deluxe bedroom at Elkhorn Lodge during the 1993-94 season rents from a low of $88 during the Value Season (Oct. 1 - Dec. 20) to a high of $378, depending on the season. Less expensive rooms are available and two-bedroom condos run from $138 to $378 per night. Telephone (208) 622-4511 for reservations.

If staying at the base of the lifts is a consideration, pickings are limited at the River Run base. This may change with the renovations planned there during the coming year or two. Within walking distance is the **Tyrolean Lodge**, managed by Best Western. This is a medium-priced hotel, and its location is somewhat removed from town and other resorts in the area. During 1993-94, rooms rent for between a low of $65 and a high of $110 per night.

Numerous condominiums are available at the base of the Warm Springs lift area. Directly across the street from the Greyhawk and Challanger lifts are the **Edelweiss Condominiums**. As one might expect, Edelweiss has an Austrian motif; its exterior stucco walls are decorated with paintings of the Austrian countryside. Inside, the rooms are clean and well maintained. Guests will appreciate the new furniture and tan carpeting. Cooking in these units is limited, since the range is small and there are no microwaves nor dishwashers. Available as studio lofts, these condos accommodate up to four persons at $150 per night. The upstairs lofts normally contain twin beds, but management will convert these to one queen-size bed upon request. Edelweiss Condominiums have underground parking, a sauna, an outdoor heated swimming pool, hot tub, ski-waxing room, and laundry room. Rental can be arranged by telephoning Warm Springs Resort at (800) 635-4404 or the central reservation number listed on page 195.

Greyhawk Condominiums, only a few steps west of the Edelweiss Condos, are among the newest units in Warm Springs. Unfortunately, their entrance is very dark and foreboding, a pity because the individual units are quite nice. Interiors are decorated with kelly green carpeting, oak furniture, green marble fireplaces, and entertainment centers. Some units even display mounted elk heads over their fireplaces. Soft, supple leather couches and scottish plaid seating complete the units, giving them the warm, secure feeling of a British gentlemen's club. Two-bedroom units with two full baths and kitchens fully equipped with G.E. appliances (including washers and dryers) guarantee guests pleasant stays here at the foot of Baldy. Skiers will appreciate the fenced-in, heated outdoor pool and hot tub in which to soothe away minor aches and pains. A two-bedroom Greyhawk condo will cost $295 per night during the Regular Season. Reservations may be made by telephoning Warm Springs Resort at (800) 635-4404.

The base area around Warm Springs is very congested. Parking is extremely limited; therefore, guests staying in this area should make certain when booking their reservations that parking is included in the rental cost. Skiers staying in areas other than Warm Springs should not drive to the area but should take one of the shuttles provided by Sun Valley Resort or by the city of Ketchum. Should parking privileges be necessary, expect to pay as much as $15/day at Warm Springs.

Restaurants

If the skiing on Baldy and the beauty of Sun Valley Resort are not enough to entice skiers to Idaho, then the restaurants will. Although restaurants are plentiful around Ketchum, none is finer than the **Lodge Dining Room** found on the second floor of Sun Valley Lodge. Those skiers who have been fortunate enough to enjoy the cuisine at The Ranch in Keystone will be delighted to discover another restaurant equally worthy of their praise. Evening dress and a coat and a tie are **strongly** suggested for dining in the Lodge Dining Room. Beautiful table settings, attentive service, and outstanding food make an evening at the Lodge a treat. Diners should sample the trout meunière and some of the sinfully sweet confections. On Sunday, rest and attend the Lodge's buffet presented among beautiful ice sculptures. Enjoy a leisurely meal accompanied by harp music and more delectable dishes than one could possibly eat.

For less formal occasions, numerous restaurants are located around the resort, principally on the Mall.

The **Christiania Restaurant** was established in 1959, and continues to serve innovative continental cuisine. Located on Sun Valley Road, Christiania across the board is an excellent restaurant. The chef prepares excellent local lamb and fresh fish. Call 726-3388 for reservations.

One such restaurant, **The Ram**, is decorated in Swiss/Austrian decor with scythes, ox yokes, and cowbells on the walls. Chandeliers constructed from antlers complete the image. The chef labors over guests' orders on an open brazier. Waitresses are costumed in Bavarian attire, and the menu offers a complete list of meat and fish dishes. Naturally, a restaurant of this type offers several game dishes on its menu, including elk with lingonberries. The native trout with pea pods, cauliflower, cherry tomatoes, baby carrots, and wild rice is excellently prepared. The vegetables are always al dente, and the rolls are served hot with honey butter.

An even less formal restaurant is the **Konditorei**. Featuring its own takeout bakery, the Konditorei is a comfortable establishment. While waiting to be served, one can read a complimentary newspaper and catch up on the world's events. Order one of the ice cream specialties or just enjoy a hot cup of coffee. The Konditorei is the equivalent of a New York City hotel's snack bar or short-order grill.

The **Evergreen** restaurant in Ketchum gets rave reviews from its excellent wine list to its modern French cuisine. Reservations are recommended (208)726-3888.

Located on a side street in downtown Ketchum is **Peter's Restaurant**. Peter's is a modern Tyrolean restaurant. Its white stucco interior is subtly lit with track lighting, making it warm and inviting. The walls are sparsely decorated with local artists' water colors, which are for sale. Many veal dishes featured here are typical of the fare served in eastern Europe's montainous regions. The Gulyas soup is a Hungarian dish prepared with tomatoes, beef strips, and paprika. Try the excellent watercress salad with orange tarragon dressing. For an entrée, taste the veal with paprika complemented with spaetzle, red cabbage, and fresh green beans with almonds. Meal service is well paced, and some of the waitresses have a theatrical air which is very pleasant. Although the acoustics could stand some improvement, Peter's rates an "A" for food and service.

On the north side of the street, in a second-floor location just across from the Warm Springs lifts is **Barsotti's Mountain Cafe**. This is a charming restaurant with lots of open spaces, high ceilings, and contemporary oak furnishings. Its California-influenced menu is broad and complemented daily with specials from the chef. The extensive wine cellar features over forty wines. For appetizers enjoy the roasted garlic and crostini or the polenta sticks with gorgonzola sauce; for entrées try the linguine with pesto, carbonara, or capellini. Barsotti's is good food, good value, and good atmosphere. Try it! Telephone (208) 726-3838 for reservations.

An inexpensive fun place to try is **Grumpy's Beef and Burger** in burger. This casual restaurant serves 32-ounce schooners of beer and big burgers. Please remember, no dogs inside!

Those who have had enough haute cuisine should try **Louies Pizza & Italian Restaurant**, located in the old church on Leadville. The only resemblance this restaurant has to its original architecture is its facade and gothic arches. The banquet seating resembles pews but is infinitely more comfortable. Louie's is always crowded; expect to wait up to one-half hour for a table. The wait is worth it, however, as the food is excellent and the service good. In addition to pizza, Louie will make spaghetti, lasagne, fettuccine, or manicotti for his guests. Reservations are not accepted.

All told, twelve quality restaurants are located on Sun Valley Resort property and over fifty other restaurants are found throughout Ketchum. Meals of every type and description from hot dogs to fine Continental dining are available. Try any of the restaurants; very few will be disappointing.

Activities

For skiers who would like to find out just how good they really are, National Standard Races (NASTAR) are held on Baldy every Tuesday through Friday on the face of Warm Springs. A coin-operated Marlboro self-timer practice race course is also located on Warm Springs Face.

Sun Valley Helicopter Ski Guides will fly powder hounds to back-country skiing. Five full runs per day totaling 15,000 vertical feet are achievable. Too much? Try three runs and 9,000 vertical feet. For more information, telephone (208) 622-3108 or 788-4884.

Mulligan Snowmobile Tours offers tours with catered lunches every day of the week. Telephone Mike Mulligan for more information at (208) 726-9137.

Ice-skate to the sonorous strains of Bolero on either of Sun Valley's two ice skating rinks. Admission during the 1990-91 season is only $4.95, and skates can be rented for $1.25.

Take a dinner sleigh ride in the Sawtooth Mountains. Telephone R. J. or Glenda Lewy for reservations at (208) 622-5019.

Beautiful, clear, sunny days in Sun Valley were made for soaring! Scenic soaring tours in a glider are available from Soar Sun Valley. Telephone (208) 788-3054 for information and costs.

The Comedy Club at the Ram Bar in Sun Valley Resort is a fun place to check out in the evenings.

The Sun Valley Health Club on First Avenue in Ketchum is the place to "flex the plex." This is a new, modern facility featuring all the amenities one expects from a first-class health club. Nautilus, free weights, aerobics classes, karate, ballet, Stairmaster, stationary bicycles, treadmills, and rowing machines are all there. A complete pro shop can provide any items needed but forgotten at home. There is even a twenty-yard, four-lap indoor pool close to a sauna and steam room.

No need to let small children interfere with an exercise schedule; the Athletic Club will entertain them right on the premises with toys and trained supervisors. Telephone (208) 726-3664 for more information.

Finally, enjoy fabulous shopping in the Sun Valley Mall. Among the many fashionable shops you will find are The Kitzbühel Collection and Panache, specializing in ladies' clothing and furs.

Services

A full complement of sporting goods stores, apparel shops, pharmacies, grocery stores, liquor stores, furniture, bath, and specialty shops is within the immediate area. In addition, there are antique shops, massage services, art galleries, bakeries, beauty salons, bookstores, florists, movies, theater, banks, churches, alterations, dry cleaning, optical shops, and baby-sitting services.

At Taos, visitors get a good look at the challenging terrain on Al's Run from the Taos Ski Valley Resort Center.
Photo by Robert Reck/Courtesy Taos Ski Valley

TAOS

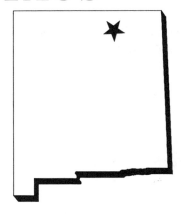

Taos Ski Valley, Inc.
Taos Ski Valley, NM 87525

(800) 776-1111 Reservations
(505) 776-2291 Information
(505) 776-2916 Snow Report

New For 1993-94

The new owners of the Hondo Lodge at the bottom of Taos Ski Valley have transformed the 50-year-old local institution into a modern, enlarged hotel. Renamed **The Inn at Snakedance** for the run which it faces at the bottom of the slope, the new facility has 60 new rooms all equipped telephones, televisions, and small refrigerators,and many with wood-burning stone fireplaces. The decor, of course reflects the New Mexican surroundings and much of the furniture was made locally.

This is the first new building in Taos since 1966. It also offers guests a spa with a large hot tub, exercise equipment and sauna, ski storage and built-in boot dryers. The owners have tried to retain the hunting lodge flavor of the original building, and of course it still is located with ski in\ski out convenience at the bottom of the #1 quad chair lift. A bar and restaurant also will be on the premises. One interesting note -- the new hotel will not accept children under the age of 6 because of plumbing problems they experienced in the past with flushed diapers. Hotel rooms will range in price from $90 per night to $395, depending on size and season. Call 800-322-9815 for details.

On the mountain, Taos Ski Valley has widened some runs this season. The base of Willy Tell has been enlarged at the bottom of chair 8. The area had been a bit of a bottleneck in the past. A run named Baby Bear also has been widened.

How To Get There

Taos Ski Valley is located in the southern Rocky Mountains' Sangre de Cristo Range. It is 147 miles north of Albuquerque and approximately 20 miles from the picturesque town of Taos. Because most of the area around Taos is high desert, the roads are usually clear. On occasion, however, wind-driven storms can cause hazardous driving conditions. If driving and weather conditions are suspect, it is always a good idea to check road conditions before setting out.

With today's interstate highway systems, it is easy to reach even a secluded area like Taos. Traveling from Texas, use I-40 out from Amarillo to Albuquerque and take I-25 north to Santa Fe. From Santa Fe take Highway 84/285 to Taos. Go through town to Highway 150 and turn right. The road ends at the ski valley.

From farther North and East, take the interstate system to Denver and then follow I-25 south to exit 18 (the second Walsenburg exit). Continue west on Colorado Highway 160 over La Veta Pass, a well-maintained, all-weather highway to Fort Garland. At Fort Garland turn left onto Colorado Highway 159, which becomes NM Highway 522 as the New Mexico stateline is crossed. Continue on

NM 522 through Questa until you see a blinking yellow light, then turn left onto NM Highway 150. Highway 150 will end at Taos Ski Valley fifteen miles later.

From the West take I-40 east to Albuquerque and then I-25 north to Santa Fe. From Santa Fe, take Highway 84/285 to Taos. Go through town to Highway 150; turn right and you will arrive at Taos Ski Valley in about twenty minutes.

Reaching Taos by air is as easy as booking a ticket on any of the major airlines to Albuquerque's International Airport. A car can be rented at the airport, or Mesa Airlines offers commuter service to the Taos Municipal Airport. Cars may also be rented at Taos Municipal Airport.

All the major car rental agencies at the Albuquerque Airport are located near the baggage claim area on the terminal's lower level. It is a good idea to have a car in Taos. Without one it is difficult to enjoy the town of Taos, due to its distance from the ski valley. And, because Taos is the oldest continuously occupied city in the United States, it has a great many features which visitors to the area will surely want to enjoy. Car rental selections in Taos are more limited than they are in Albuquerque.

When renting a car, be sure to insist that it has been *skierized*, i.e. equipped with snow tires and ski racks. Vans and four-wheel drive vehicles are also available. Due to the latter's popularity, however, it is prudent to reserve one far in advance. Most rental agencies, and resorts for that matter, begin accepting reservations in August. For peak holiday seasons, the availability of cars and accommodations can become limited by September.

Shuttle service to Taos Ski Valley from either Taos Airport or Albuquerque Airport is provided by Faust's Transportation, Pride of Taos, and Greyhound. For current rates and information, telephone (800) 345-3738 in New Mexico and (505) 758-3410 from outside the state for Faust's Transportation. Call Pride of Taos at (800) 821-2437 or Greyhound at (800) 992-7669. Reservations are required and will be canceled if not confirmed at least 30 minutes prior to departure. When departing Taos, plan on arriving at check-in at least 30 minutes prior to departure. The check-in at Albuquerque Airport is across from baggage claim areas A and B.

Skiers staying in the town of Taos will find that buses to the ski valley run daily on a timely schedule. Transportation is provided by Pride of Taos. For reservation or information, telephone (505) 758-8340.

Mountain Information

Taos enjoys a justly deserved reputation as an expert's mountain. However, it is so much more! Taos is an experience not to be found at any other American ski resort. This resort was built from the dreams of one man, Ernie Blake. Taos was founded just after World War II when Ernie and his family single-handedly developed the mountain and its village. The resort has maintained its quaint and unique style right into the 1990's.

Taos's guests are strongly encouraged to enroll in a week-long ski program consisting of instruction in the morning and free skiing in the afternoon. Taos's ski instructors teach skiers of all ability levels. Unless guests are staying in a condominium, all the accommodations are American plan. This means that guests take all meals in their lodge. A camaraderie is quickly developed among skiers, many of whom return year after year for the same weeks. The same camaraderie is fostered during lessons. Instructors encourage people to learn together and to develop friendships that will last throughout the week. Refusal or non-participation in this program will make guests feel like "odd man out." Everyone else at the resort will be making friends and enjoying their holiday, while non-participants will still be trying to understand the trail map.

Taos is unlike those mountain resorts that illustrate all available runs on a trail map. Many of Taos's runs are not illustrated at all! Just like at Snowbird and Jackson Hole, there is an entire group of runs not shown on the map. It is much better to ski them for the first time with instructors who will make certain skiers do not find themselves on slopes beyond their ability level. Instructors will also help skiers improve their technique. By the end of one week, skiers will inevitably be better than they were prior to enjoying the Taos experience.

However, Taos is not only for expert skiers. Absolute novices who have never skied before are taught to turn very early because this is the best method to slow down. Taos's beginner hill is similar to Big Emma at Snowbird and is one of the steepest beginner hills of any resort. Nonetheless, Taos is an excellent resort at which beginners can learn to ski. Not only is ski instruction among the best available anywhere, but the natural steepness of the terrain forces people to become competent skiers sooner than would be possible at a resort with more gentle topography.

Taos also boasts a good deal about its intermediate terrain. The designation "intermediate" equates with intermediate elsewhere. So one need not fear that all Taos's skiing will be tough. Some of the best intermediate cruising grounds are found off Kachina Peak. Runs like Shalako, Hunziker Bowl, and Honeysuckle are terrific! Powderhorn which runs the entire length of the mountain is a long, dream run. All intermediate runs are continually groomed, and errant bumps are scrupulously removed.

The elevation of Taos at its summit is 11,819 feet (3,602 meters). With its base at 9,207 feet (2,806 meters), the vertical drop is 2,612 feet (796 meters). Of the seventy-one runs illustrated on the trail map, thirty-six (51%) are classified as expert, eighteen (25%) as intermediate, and seventeen as (24%) beginner.

The longest beginner run, Whitefeather, is 3.1 miles (5 km); the longest intermediate run is Honeysuckle/Rubezahl at 5.25 miles (8.4 km). Honeysuckle/Rubezahl is actually one run but was given two names to facilitate the ski patrol's need to quickly identify injured skiers' locations. The longest expert run is Longhorn, at 2.05 miles (3.3 km).

Taos is a mountain of extremes; when it snows, it usually snows prodigious amounts, and when it is not snowing, the weather is usually clear with bright, warm sunshine. Receiving over 323 inches (820 cm) of snow annually, its monthly average totals are

Nov.	40"	(102 cm)
Dec.	36"	(91 cm)
Jan.	58"	(147 cm)
Feb.	37"	(94 cm)
Mar.	63"	(160 cm)
Apr.	39"	(99 cm)

Taos's southern location gives it a rather temperate climate. The average monthly temperatures at the base are

Nov.	27°	-3° C
Dec.	21°	-6° C
Jan.	22°	-5° C
Feb.	28°	-2° C

| Mar. | 32° | 0°C |
| Apr. | 39° | 4°C |

The United States Forest Service will not allow Taos to sell more than 4,800 lift tickets per day. With an uphill lift capacity of 12,400, the slopes are never very crowded. Because there are only 900 beds at Taos Ski Valley, it is essential that most guests stay in the town of Taos and drive to the resort. Once there, however, adequate facilities accommodate the skiers. In fact, it is interesting to note that the uphill lift capacity is almost twice the number of skiers the Forest Service permits to ski each day. It should also be noted that the actual number of skiable acres open, which is not necessarily represented by the official trail map, is 1,100.

Lastly, it should be pointed out that Al's Run is indeed as formidable as previously reported by others. First, it is steep; second, it has some of the largest moguls that skiers will ever see. The mogul field is most formidable at the top. As skiers work (and it is work) their way down Al's run, the severity of the bumps diminishes. Near the top, however, the bumps are frequently waist-high with their backs chopped off.

Lift Ticket Prices (1993-94)

The lift ticket prices reported at Taos are day ski rates. Actual rates for guests staying in one of the lodges will be lower because multi-day lift ticket discounts are included in the lodging and lesson packages.

$35	Adult, All-Day
$32	Adult, Multi-Day
$20	Child, 12 or younger, All-Day
$18	Child, Multi-Day
$12	Seniors, Ages 65-69
Free	Seniors, 70 and over
$29	January adult price, except Jan. 1-2. 14-16
$22	End of season, adult price, Mar. 28 to Apr. 10

Multi-Day tickets are for a minimum of three consecutive days. A child is anyone 12 or younger.

Hours of Operation

9:00 A.M. to 4:00 P.M.

Lift Ticket Purchase Locations

Lift tickets may be purchased in the Ski Valley near the parking lot's shuttle bus stop in the center of the village, just below the #1 Lift, and in the town of Taos at the downtown ticket office next to Michael's Kitchen.

How to Avoid Crowds

Most crowds at Taos will be encountered in the day skiers' parking lot as visitors leave after a day of skiing. This is not as bad as at Squaw Valley, but during holiday periods, it can be annoying.

Crowding on the mountain is rare; however, the potential for crowding exists on lower

Whitefeather and Rubezahl. Both of these runs are low on the mountain and form the most convenient routes down the mountain at the end of the day. The only way to avoid crowding on these runs, should it occur, is to take Al's Run down in the evening.

Ski School

The Ernie Blake Ski School, now managed by Max Killinger, is justifiably acknowledged as one of the best, if not the best, ski school in the country. No doubt, this reputation is due to the large numbers of expert skiers it trains daily. Under the direction of Ernie Blake until his death in January 1989, the ski school remains a family affair. Family members share teaching responsibilities with the hired staff. Ernie believed it to be imperative for Taos's owners to stay constantly in touch with their clientele. His family feels that one of the best ways to achieve this goal is through their active participation in the daily teaching and area operations.

The more than 100 PSIA-certified instructors teach their own technique which is similar to the American Teaching System (ATS). The Taos system differs only in small details. Because so many Taos students are advanced, many of the lessons are actually refinements of techniques for learning how to ski specific conditions or situations. For example, a class may work on moguls, powder, chutes, or whatever the instructor and class agree is needed on a particular day.

Because most of the guests staying at Taos are participants in the "Learn to Ski Better Week" program, six days of intensive instruction are included in their lodging package, which also includes three meals per day and seven nights' accommodations. For those not participating in this program, group or private lessons are available.

Group lesson participants meet daily at 9:45 A.M. and at 1:45 P.M. Lessons are two hours, and during the 1993-94 season cost is $26 or $22 for 3 or more consecutive days.
Private lessons are $60 per person per hour. All-day is $350 or $200 for one half-day private lesson. For each additional hour in a private class, the cost is $40. For each additional person, $20.

For the *never-ever-before* skier, Taos offers its "Yellow Bird Program." Under this program, beginners receive four hours of daily instruction, use of the Poma, and rental equipment for $47 per day. Cost of the program without rental equipment is $42 during the 1993-94 season.

While some areas still do not cater to parents with very young children, Taos offers "Bebekare" a full day program for $45 for infants 6 weeks to 1-year-old. a half day is $30, or $9 per hour.
For the 1- and 2-year-olds, for the same price, Taos offers Kinderkare, a full day program with play programs and meals.

Taos's children's ski school is divided into two groups. Both Junior Elite groups meet at the beginners slope at Strawberry Hill in the A Frame. The younger group is open to children aged three through kindergarten. A very well-conceived program, it typifies the individual attention skiers of all ages receive from Taos's instructors. It is important for parents to register their children in advance, particularly during the holiday seasons.
Children enrolled in this program should arrive at the indoor facility at 8:30 each morning. A 1-hour less will be held in the morning, lunch will be provided, and children can play indoors and outdoors in the morning and afternoon. The program closes at 4 p.m. 1993-94 price is $50.
For children aged six through twelve there is a parallel program from 9:30 a.m. to 2:45 p.m. Check in is from 9 to 9:30 a.m. Meet on Strawberry Hill where the adult lessons meet.

This year the Taos Ski Valley will start offering a Masters Ski Week for people 50 years and older. Two hours of lessons every morning will be included, as well as evening seminars focusing on health and fitness and financial planning.

Equipment Rental

Four rental shops are located at Taos Ski Valley, and numerous others are found in the town of Taos.

At the resort proper, **Taos Ski Valley Rental** is located at the base area just below the #1 Lift. During the 1993-94 season, three rental packages are offered. The first is the Recreation Package designed for beginning and intermediate skiers. The fee for this equipment is $8 for the first day.

A port package is offered for $12 a day, $10 for multi-day.

The other package offered is called the Demo Package. The skis are the same kind as those in the Recreational Package, but the models are designed for more accomplished skiers. These rented for $20 the first day and $18 for three or more days.

Children's rentals were $7 the first day and $6 for three or more days.
Call (505)776-2291 for reservations or more information.

Cottam's, located near the covered bridge on the path to the parking lot, has a full line of recreational, sport, and high-performance ski packages. The 1992-93 prices are listed. Sports packages include Atomic, K2, and Dynastar skis, Salomon SX 41 or Nordica 500 boots, Salomon 337 or 447 bindings, and poles for $15 per day or $13 for three or more days. The high-performance package consists of almost any brand ski imaginable. Some of the more often requested include Dynastar, Atomic, Blizzard, K2, Pre, Volkl and Salomon. Boots are either Salomon SX 71 or Nordica 482 and bindings are Salomon 977. High-performance packages rent from $25 per day or $18 per half-day. To reserve skis in advance, telephone (800) 322-8267 or in-state (505) 776-8540.

Ski Tuning and Repair

Fine tuning is available at Taos Ski Valley Rental, which has Montana Crystal Glide ski structuring equipment.

New rates were not available at press time, but during the 1993-94 season, tune-up rates were expected to

$ 5	Hot Wax
$20	Flat File
$35	Complete Tune-up
$25	Crystal Glide stone grind Tune-up

Hand tune-ups are available at **Looney Tunes**, located along the path to the parking lot. Tune-up rates vary from around $25 to $35.

Mountain Dining

Taos has one and "one-half" mountain restaurants. The full restaurant, located at the base of the Kachina Lift, is a relatively new facility designed to blend in with the towering pines of the Carson National Forest. Constructed of rough-hewn timbers and enhanced by numerous windows, the **Phoenix Restaurant** is always bright and pleasant. The cafeteria-style food service is presented well, and there is ample variety. The lack of a sit-down dining area is regrettable, particularly because so many skiers at Taos do not stay in Ski Valley lodges. The Phoenix is really the only place on the mountain where skiers can go for a full meal.

The other restaurant, mentioned with tongue-in-cheek, is **Whitefeather Whistlestop**, located at the base of the #6 Lift. This small facility offers pizza, sandwiches, hot and cold drinks, and snacks. It also has the only sanitary facility on the upper front side of the mountain.

The **St. Bernard Hotel**, located directly to the right of the #1 Lift looking uphill, is primarily for lodging guests, but it also has a small, excellent food service adjacent to the dining room. If someone should suggest lunch at "the Dog," the St. Bernard Hotel is what is being referred to.

A brand new 35 thousand square foot resort center which houses **Rhoda's**, was opened for the 1989-90 season. It is located at the base of the new quad lift and contains a 300-seat cafeteria, Tenderfoot Katies and a 75-seat table-service restaurant and lounge.

Child Care

Taos's management is concerned that all its guests enjoy themselves. This concern is readily apparent in the lengths to which the owners have gone to provide excellent child care.
See the ski school section of this chapter for information about Bebekare and Kinderkare.

Medical Facilities

The ski patrol at Taos Ski Valley renders emergency service to injured skiers. The patrol will administer trauma treatment, stabilize broken bones, and transport injured skiers downhill by sled to the new Mogul Medical Center located at the base of the #1 Lift. It is a full service medical clinic. From the clinic injured skiers will be taken by ambulance to Holy Cross Hospital in the town of Taos.

For illnesses other than ski injuries, there are numerous doctors and clinics in the town of Taos. Consult the local Yellow Pages for listings.

Cross-Country Skiing

There are no cross-country skiing tracks nor lessons available at the Taos Ski Valley. Telemark skiers are welcome to ski on the mountain, however. Cross-country skiing is available throughout the greater Taos area, particularly in Carson National Forest. Groomed tracks as well as back-country skiing are abundant. All ski rental shops in Taos provide cross-country skis and can advise intermediate skiers as to suitable locations.

Special Events

Taos is a small resort compared to mega resorts like Vail and Aspen. Professionally staged races can cost as much as $100 thousand to sponsor. It is therefore unrealistic to think that a small, privately held company such as Taos Ski Valley with its restrictive capacity could compete for major events. Not that the mountain would not lend itself to such competition! If the moguls were cut on Al's Run, it would become an awesome downhill course, and several areas could accommodate slalom races, such as Powderhorn or Maxie's in the Kachina Basin.

In spite of not hosting World Cup nor professional race events, Taos has managed to create its own brand of events, including the Plymouth All-American Ski Races, Taos Pueblo Deer/Buffalo Dance, Taos Pueblo Turtle Dance, and Christmas Eve Torchlight Parade. At the end of the season, Bump/Bolt/Bike Races are staged.

NASTAR races (National Standard Races) are held almost daily under the #7 Lift, also the site of the coin-operated Ski Challenge self-timed practice race course. Visitors should check with Guest Services for the daily hours of operation.

Accommodations

Hotels

At press time , 1993-94 rates were not available. For updated rates and other information, call Taos Ski Valley call 1-800-776-1111.

Throughout this review, the reader has been told that Taos is different from other ski resorts. Its four main lodges are the primary reason for this difference. Their emphasis on guests' forming a close-knit group is unique in America.

The **St. Bernard** situated at the foot of the #1 lift is owned and managed by Jean Mayer, one of Ernie Blake's oldest acquaintances. The exterior of these accommodations resembles any of the numerous cow barns found on the slopes of Ernie's native Switzerland. The interior, however, is warm and inviting. Walking into the Dog's bar or dining room is like stepping back into a less complicated time when skis were made of hickory and ski clothing was baggy. Testimony to the St. Bernard's popularity is that it is usually fully booked by August for the ski season. Only a last-minute cancellation will yield a room for the first-time guest. Management offers returning guests the chance to re-book their rooms during the month of June, and many of them do. In July the remaining rooms are open for reservations. Call (505)776-2251 for information and reservations.

All rooms at the St. Bernard rent for the same amount: $1,300 double occupancy for a six-day ski week, including the prices of lift tickets, lessons and 3 meals. There is also a $70 charge per adult, and $40 per child, for all tips at the end of each guest's stay. Although all rooms are well maintained, it must be noted that they are small and their furnishings are dated. There is limited storage space for all the parkas, sweaters, etc. skiers take with them on trips. It is not the accommodations that make the St. Bernard famous: it is host Jean Mayer and his dining room. Meals are exquisitely prepared and served family-style.

The **Hondo Lodge**, now rebuilt and expanded and opening in November 1993 as **The Inn At Snakedance**, was the first accommodation facility built at Taos Ski Valley. Located only a few steps from the St. Bernard and built in 1955, the Hondo had a grotto-like quality about it. It is a very comfortable establishment where the warm, yellow glow of candles and soft, diffused light emanating from stained glass windows soften the Swiss decor and immediately set skiers at ease.

See page one of this chapter for a more detailed description of this new hotel.

The largest lodge, the **Thunderbird**, is situated on the banks of the Rio Hondo and is only a short walk from the lifts. This modern, well-maintained hotel is owned and operated by Tom and Elisabeth Brownell, who take a personal pride in knowing their guests and responding to their needs. The Thunderbird consists of three separate chalets constructed in the Swiss style typical of the entire valley. The main lodge building consists of twenty-four rooms, a dining hall, a recreation room, ski-tuning room, sauna, hot tub, and the **Twining Tavern**. The two other chalets, which have larger rooms than the Thunderbird, are within steps of the main complex.

The rooms in the Lodge are small and somewhat utilitarian when compared to accommodations at other major resorts such as the Lodge in Sun Valley or the Sonnenalp in Vail. However, all lodging accommodations at Taos are relatively small. What sets the Thunderbird apart is its cleanliness and adherence to the original design concept. All rooms have humidifiers and are well insulated against outside noise. Their decor is developed through the use of knotty pine, stucco, and Laura Ashley prints. Each room is different but always complementary to the whole. The bathrooms are misnamed since they do not contain bath tubs; instead, they have showers with copious quantities of hot water.

There are neither televisions nor telephones in the rooms. Children are served in the dining room before adults, and after dinner many of the guests' children head for the recreation room which contains a large-screen TV, VCR, games, and books. Should guests' skis need attention, there is a well-stocked ski tune-up room with a bench and vise. Unlike many tune-up rooms, this one is spotlessly maintained, with only a hint of hot wax in the air.

Whereas most resorts have a hot tub and perhaps a sauna, the Thunderbird has a "bath department." The department consists of separate men's and women's locker rooms. The indoor hot tub room is abundantly decorated with ferns and other tropical plants. Adjacent to the tub is the massage room where a resident masseuse is on call to administer to guests' assorted aches and pains. Each locker room has its own sauna and attendant. During après-ski, cocktail service is available.

The large Twining Tavern features a dance floor. Each year the Thunderbird hosts its famous Jazz Festival, which is described in the *Activities* section of this review. The dining room and tavern are gathering spots for guests who engage in congenial conversation, usually centering around the day's ski activities. Meals are served family-style, and the tables accommodate six to eight persons. The tables' large size promotes guests' interaction. Many visitors will share ski classes and quickly become acquainted with one another. The gathering of guests during and after dinner is common to all the lodges. Many of the lodges also host mountainside picnics during the ski season, weather permitting. The picnic luncheon served by the Thunderbird could grace the pages of *Gourmet*. Its picnics typically include fresh flowers, table cloths, and silver service. Wine, beer, soft drinks, and freshly baked goods accompany the kitchen's creations, which are always excellent.

Seven-day Ski Week Packages at the Thunderbird during the 1993-94 season are $1,170 per person based on double occupancy. Chalet rates are $1,268 per person per week. These prices stipulate check-in at 3:00 P.M. Saturday and check-out at noon the following Saturday. Included in the rates are seven nights' accommodations, twenty-one full meals, six days use of all lifts, a free NASTAR race as well as all the amenities of the Lodge. Guests are advised to leave $80 per person upon check-out, rather than tipping individually. Tips are evenly divided among staff members. The Thunderbird is the best place to stay in Taos Ski Valley. For reservations telephone (505)776-2280.

Located next to the beginner's hill, the **Edelweiss Lodge** is another Swiss/Austrian establishment whose watchword may well be attention to every guest's needs. Its small, intimate lobby is accented by a large rock fireplace. The faint scent of burning wood is inviting to guests who choose to sit in one of the comfortable chairs, enjoy a libation, and relax before contemplating the evening's activities.

Rooms in the Edelweiss are small but well appointed. Most rooms have views of the mountain, and there are neither televisions nor telephones in them.

The hot tub area, located indoors on the second floor, has a balcony where guests frequently romp in the snow while alternately enjoying the tub's steaming water. This is a very unusual hot tub room. Decorated with ferns and tropical shrubs, it has a very large tree growing through the floor and out the ceiling. A sauna is also available.

Edelweiss's **La Croissanterie** is a fine restaurant specializing in French and Austrian pastries. Situated directly on the slopes and decorated with antique skis and ski memorabilia, La Croissanterie offers a perfect setting for the mid-day meal.

Hotel Edelweiss rates during the 1992-93 season for a hotel room on the Ski Week Package for two adults are $1,200 per person. These rates include breakfast at the La Croissanterie and dinner at the St. Bernard as well as all lift tickets, a free NASTAR clinic, and race.

One of the newest additions to the quality hotel scene at Taos is **Salsa del Salto**, operated by Mary

Hockett and Dadou Mayer. This bed and breakfast, formerly a private home, features breathtaking sunset views of the surrounding mountains and high plateaus. During the past year the Mayers added two rooms to the hotel, increasing their capacity to 8 rooms. Amenities include a central living area with television, large fireplace, and an outdoor hot tub. Après-ski features complimentary snacks and salsa from which the lodging's name is derived.

Each morning Dadou prepares breakfast which can only be described as a gourmet event, ranging from simple granola to elegant eggs benedict with perfect hollandaise sauce. The rooms at Salsa del Salto are furnished in the Southwest colors and designs for which Taos is famous. Handmade furniture from Old Santa Fe Furniture Company is accompanied by Stevens & Co. Zuni pattern linens and duvets. The master suite is finely appointed and large enough to include a private balcony, fireplace trimmed in brass, exposed-beam cathedral ceiling, and a separate seating area. The master suite's bath is exceptionally large with two sinks, Jacuzzi tub, large shower, ample vanity, and bidet.

Although located on New Mexico Highway 150 fifteen minutes from the ski valley, Salsa del Salto participates in the various winter packages. New rates were not available, but in 1992-93 the Learn to Ski Better Week package during high season was $855 per adult, $478 for junior elite, $408 for kinderkafig. The master suite rented for $160. In addition, three and five-day packages are also available. Dinner is no longer included in this price. For reservations telephone (505)776-2422.

Condominiums

For those guests who do not want to stay in one of the lodges or for those who want to ski Taos but cannot book accommodations in a lodge, there are several condominiums to choose from. The **Kändähar Condominiums** are situated high on a hill overlooking the Strawberry Hill beginner ski slope and base facility. Climbing to the uppermost units from the base parking lot requires energy and determination as there are no fewer than 122 steps. Most guests only make this trek once! The easy way to arrive at the Kändähar is to ski down Raspberry Hill or across Strawberry Hill. If walking to the base area or other accommodations, it is easier to walk diagonally across the lower portion of Strawberry Hill than to walk all the way down the steps and then across the bottom of Strawberry Hill.

The Kändähar is built so beautifully into its environment that its buildings appear to be cantilevered out over the Ski Valley. All units have balconies off their main living areas, as well as rear balconies accessible through the kitchen's Dutch door. The rear balcony is used for convenient firewood storage, which also helps keep the units clean. Walking along the rear balconies is similar to walking in an ice cave. Due to the steepness of the hill on which the buildings are located, tarpaulins have been strung from the roof's eves to the floor of the balconies. These tarps prevent snow from filling up the balconies and also help keep the firewood dry. After enough snow has accumulated, the tarpaulins are removed, thereby creating the ice tunnels.

The Kändähar two-bedroom models have bedrooms along with a full bath on the lower floor. The kitchen, dining, living areas, and another bath are found upstairs. The kitchens are fully equipped and appliances include Jenn-Air ranges, microwaves, disposals, and dishwashers. A counter which serves as an extra dining area separates the living area from the kitchen. All units have color cable TV and, unlike the lodges, have telephones. Decor is typical of the Southwest with emphasis on Indian art and culture. The fireplaces are stucco with an arched opening, a style also common to the area.

During the 1992-93 season rentals were available as either hotel rooms, studios, one-bedroom or two-bedroom condos. The nightly rate for a one-bedroom unit was $250 double occupancy. Call (505)776-2422 for information or reservations.

Guests staying in Taos's condominiums are encouraged to enroll in the Ski Week Program in order to improve their skills and to meet other guests.

Across the slopes from the Kändähar near the Thunderbird Lodge are the **Sierra del Sol Condominiums**. Situated on the banks of Lake Fork Creek and overlooking the Carson National Forest, these 18-year-old condos are about 80% refurbished. When guests are booking into the Sierra del Sol, they are advised to only book the refurbished units. Fireplaces are made of free-standing metal on a brick pad. The kitchens are fully equipped with dishwashers, disposals, and all the amenities necessary to prepare daily meals during a guest's stay. Because not all units contain microwave ovens or stereos, if such items are important, guests should specifically request them at the time of booking. None of the units have telephones.

Sierra del Sol condominiums are available as studios, one-bedroom, or two-bedroom units. The refurbished units are decorated in warm hues including mauve, sea foam, and teal. New rates were not available at press time but, 1992-93 rates varied each month. Prices range from $65 to $115 per night.

A new group of condominiums have been added to the base of Taos. **Alpine Village** condominiums are located conveniently and offer mountain views, kitchenettes, tv and phones. Rates range from $78 to $260 nightly.

Other accommodations available at the Taos Ski Valley are the **Innsbruck Condos**, **Hide & Seek Apartments**, **Twining Condominiums**, the **St. Bernard** condos, and the new **Holiday Inn Don Fernando De Taos**, Ramada Inn, Best Western and Park Inn.

Restaurants

There are no restaurants available for evening dining at Taos Ski Valley other than those serving guests staying in the lodges. Condominium guests are expected to prepare their own meals or to go into the town of Taos for meals. Occasionally the lodges will have dining space available for a few people. If dining in the various lodges is desired, condominium guests will need to telephone them in advance.

Take-out pizza is available from **Dolomite Pizza** until 9:00 P.M. every evening.

Casa Cordova, located in Arroyo Seco, between Taos Ski Village and the town of Taos, is known for its fine food and wine list. This family owned restaurant is decorated with paintings by well-known Taos artists. (505)776-2500.

Called a great value by the Mobil Travel Guide, **The Chile Connection**, is an inexpensive place for dinner. It offers children's meals, has a brewery on the premises and specializes in Chicken chimichangas, chile rellenos, buffalo fajitas. 505-776-8787.

Brett House, located at the junction of NM 522 and 150, Southwestern style menu, with beer and wine. This restaurant is known for its fresh fish, lamb and veal dishes. It is found inside an interesting adobe house built in 1946 by artist Dorothy Brett. It has a beautiful mountain view. 505-776-8545

Also well thought of are **Doc Martin's** at the Taos Inn and **Villa Fontana**.

Activities

The town of Taos is a Southwest cultural center. As such, many cultural and artistic events are staged there monthly. Among them are native Indian dances such as the Deer or Buffalo dance and the Turtle dance. A lecture series offers subjects like "Healing with Crystals," "Hinduism and the Hanuman Temple," "Floral Arrangement," and "Stoneware." There are demonstrations such as papermaking, the lost wax process for bronze, weaving, Old Master painting technique, Navajo saddle blankets, watercolor techniques, sculpting in alabaster, masterworks of Colonial silver, and gold and silver jewelry making.

Theatrical musical entertainment is also available and has featured artists such as Michael Martin Murphey, John McEuen, Josh White, and Tom Chapin.

Visitors will enjoy Taos's shops and art galleries, some of the Southwest's finest. Movies are shown at Taos Plaza Theatre. Other activities include hot mineral baths at Ojo Caliente Mineral Springs and sleigh rides at the Taos Indian Horse Ranch. Lastly, fine museums such as the Kit Carson Home and Museum, Martinez Hacienda, Blumenscheim Home, and Millicent Rogers Museum can be found at Taos.

Services

A full complement of sporting goods stores, apparel shops, pharmacies, grocery stores, liquor stores, furniture, bath, and specialty shops is within the immediate Taos area. In addition, there are antique shops, massage services, art galleries, bakeries, beauty salons, bookstores, florists, movies, theatre, banks, churches, dry cleaning, optical clinics, and baby-sitting services.

TELLURIDE SKI RESORT, INC.

P.O. Box 11155
Telluride, Colorado 81435

(800) 525-3455 Central Reservations
(303) 728-3856 Information
(303) 728-3614 Snow Report

New for 1993-94

Telluride continues to experience growth in its mountain village and many people who love it express the hope that it can retain its quiet, remote character and still prosper. This year the readers of Ski and Snow Country magazines have rated its scenery the highest of any other ski resort in the U.S. or Canada! That speaks volumes for this area's picturesque surroundings. Ski readers also voted Telluride's Sunshine Peak as the best place or beginner skiers to learn how to ski in North America.

For skiers looking for a bargain the good news is that Telluride is joining another Colorado resort, Crested Butte, in promoting an early and late season **Ski Free Program**. Between Nov. 24 and Dec. 18 or Apr. 2 and 10,during this normally quiet time the resort will try to lure skiers to the slopes with free lift tickets if they are staying at participating area lodges. Most Telluride lodges are participating in the promotion. This could be a good way to try this area out if you've never been there.

In conjunction with this promotion, Telluride also is sponsoring a **Winter Festival Series** of bluegrass and country music at bars and night spots throughout the mountain village and town. Visitors and residents alike have enjoyed this series during other years.

The $9 million gondola which will deliver people from the town of Telluride to the ski lifts will most likely open a little later than originally planned, sometime during the summer of 1994. When it is completed, skiers no longer will have to drive the 7 miles from the Town of Telluride to Telluride Mountain Village, but can access the resort via the gondola. The 8-passenger eggs will climb to 10,450 feet on top of Coonskin Ridge, traveling two miles in 12 minutes. It will be a free mass transit system for the town.

How To Get There

Telluride may be reached on clear days by flying directly into the Telluride Regional Airport, located five miles from the slopes. This is the highest airport in the United States served by regularly scheduled airlines. Skiers visiting Telluride should book tickets directly to the Telluride Airport but should understand that they might land in Montrose, 64 miles from Telluride. Until 1989 Telluride Airport was strictly limited to operating in totally clear weather. However, since then the airport authority has spent in excess of $1.2 million in navigational instruments and built an FAA tower. These improvements have enabled the airport to service over 90% of its flights. Should deviation be necessary to Montrose, complimentary bus service to Telluride is provided by the airlines on which passage is booked.

During the ski season, daily service to Telluride or alternatively to Montrose is provided from Denver via Continental Express and United Express. Continental uses planes especially designed for short runways and high altitudes. America West Airlines provides service from Phoenix nd other southwest cities to Durango, 120 miles from Telluride.

Daily shuttle service to and from the Montrose Airport is available, but reservations should be booked at least 24 hours in advance. A one-way fare of $20 during the 1993-94 season is charged by both of the regular services, **Telluride Transit**, 1-800-800-6228, charges that fare if at least 4 people ride the van. For fewer than that number, $80 is charged for use of the 13- or 14- person van. **Skip's Taxi**, 1-303-728-6667, provides service in suburbans and other 4-wheel drive vehicles from 8 a.m. to 5 p.m. Transportation information from other locales is available from Telluride Central Reservations or Telluride Transit. Both companies charge $5 per person to the town of Telluride from Telluride, and at least $5 more a trip to the mountain village. **Mountain Limo** also provides a local airport service for $5. Call 303-728-9606.

All major car rental agencies are available at Telluride's regional airports including Avis, Budget, Hertz, National, and Thrifty. Once in Telluride, a car is more of a hindrance than a convenience. Transportation within the town of Telluride is amply provided by Telluride Transit which runs every twelve minutes throughout the town and every fifty minutes to the Meadows Day Lodge.

Mountain Information

By anyone's definition, Telluride Mountain is awesome! Located in the Uncompahgre National Forest deep in the San Juan Mountains, its ski trails offer terrain for skiers of every skill level. The view from the top is unequalled anywhere in the United States. The charming old mining town of Telluride, a National Historic District, lies with its back against the most breathtaking box canyon imaginable, nestled at the base of Ajax Peak. The majority of the trees surrounding the town and lining its trails are lodgepole, but unlike those at resorts closer to Denver, these trees are towering. Perhaps the size of the trees is due to the heavy annual precipitation received in this region.

Telluride Mountain has 3,165 vertical feet. Its base is located at 8,725 feet and its summit is at 11,890 feet. The skiable terrain comprises 1,050 acres (297 ha) and is serviced by

    1 Detachable Quad Chairlift
    6 Double Chairlifts
    2 Triple Chairlifts
    1 Poma Lift

The longest beginner run is Telluride Trail, situated on Telluride Face traversing from the top of the Coonskin lift to its base. The longest intermediate run is See Forever, and the longest expert run is the Plunge.

Telluride has installed the longest detachable quad in the world. Its 2.85 mile (4.58 km) length serves what many feel is the best beginner terrain in North America. Double Cabin and Galloping Goose are gentle, gladed trails located on Sunshine Peak and served by this long quad. They are situated away from the hustle and bustle of the rest of the ski resort. Here beginners are almost never intimidated by fast skiers. In these ideal conditions, beginners can work on establishing the rhythm necessary in order for them to advance to intermediate level.

Due to the diversity of terrain at Telluride, its mountain management has decided to deviate from the usual method of identifying trails by using circles, squares, and diamonds to denote a slope's difficulty. Telluride has expanded upon these graphics and has added double circles, double squares, and double diamonds in order to assist skiers in carefully choosing trails suited to their ability.

In total, there are 45 trails of which 21% are considered beginner, 47% are intermediate, and 32% are expert. These figures do not tell all, however. Of the 32% comprising the terrain defined as expert, a healthy percentage is beyond the typical 40-year-old expert's ability. Several runs are nothing more than avalanche chutes (such as Electra), and skiing them not only requires skill, but also stamina and endurance. Even some of the intermediate trails can be considered only marginally intermediate. What is expert at Vail, Copper, and Aspen is frequently considered intermediate at Telluride. For example, one of the few intermediate runs down the face of Telluride Mountain is Coonskin. This is a double blue square which, under all but the best conditions, skis like an expert trail. It has large bumps and is relatively steep.

A great deal has been written and said about the difficulty of Telluride's expert runs. They do deserve their reputation for making Telluride a tough mountain. What sets it apart from other areas' expert terrain is the unforgiving nature of its runs. Whereas most expert runs at other resorts contain areas within the trails that are intermediate, none exist on the front face of Telluride. Once a skier starts down, the trail is expert from top to bottom. Skiing the front face demands strong conditioning. If skiers are in shape though, they are rewarded with some of the best skiing available anywhere in the world.

Telluride's annual snowfall is 300 inches (762 cm). Its monthly average snowfall is

Nov.	20"	(51 cm)
Dec.	53"	(135 cm)
Jan.	50"	(127 cm)
Feb.	37"	(94 cm)
Mar.	66"	(168 cm)

The town of Telluride is totally dominated by its mountains. First-time visitors to Telluride may well suck in their breath and ask themselves, "What have I gotten myself into?" The view of the skiable terrain from town can only be compared to the view of terrain at Taos, New Mexico. One's field of vision is totally filled with the highly vertical and legendary front face. Beginners and intermediates should take comfort in the knowledge that somewhere up there is easier skiing. Access to the gentler slopes can best be reached by taking one of the two chairlifts bordering on downtown. These chairs are high and provide spectacular views for photography or gripping the chair, depending upon how well one handles heights. On a typical day the snow under the lifts may be pock-marked with the charcoal gray stain of an exploded mortar from the previous evening. Due to the steepness of the front face, constant attention is paid to the snowpack by the highly qualified ski patrol.

The ride up the mountain ends at See Forever, where the backside is exposed and a vast network of intermediate and beginner slopes opens up. The abundant snowfall, complemented by snowmaking as needed, assures quality conditions every day. Ice is something that never seems to be a problem in Telluride due to its exceptionally consistent natural snowfall and the meticulous grooming performed each day and night. For those who do not like moguls, long runs such as See Forever, Sundance, and Cabin Trail are over two miles each and are as smooth as silk. For the typical expert there are challenging trails such as the Plunge, the Spiral Stairs, Zulu Queen, Kant Mak-M, Dynamo, and Apex Glades. As the saying goes, there is something for everyone at Telluride.

Helicopter Skiing

Helicopter skiing at Telluride should be on many skiers' agendas. Offered through **Helitrax** whose office is located in the lobby of the New Sheridan Hotel, day trips of 10,000 (3,048 meters) vertical feet are completed in four runs. Helitrax has been operating under a U.S. Forest Service permit for nine years, and it has an unblemished safety record. Prior to departure, every client is instructed in helicopter safety, avalanche hazards, back-country travel, and the correct way to use a safety beacon.

Lest readers think they may not possess the ability to helicopter ski, Helitrax's records of previous clients indicate that 70% of the helicopter skiers have skied for 10 years and that 50% are between 30 and 40 years old, with a full 20% over 40!

Skiers generally make 5 runs in a full day of heli-skiing. Seventy percent of the terrain skied with Helitrax is in bowls above the tree line. The remaining runs are through the trees. Skiing commences atop towering 13,000 (3,962 meters) peaks, where the majestic peaks of Colorado, New Mexico, and faraway Utah are spread out in front of the skier! The price is $425 per person. Telephone (303) 728-4904 for reservations and information. Scenic flights also are available.

Lift Ticket Prices (1993-94)

$ 41	Adult Daily
$ 32	Adult Half Day
$210	6 Days Out of 7($35 daily rate)
$180	5 Days Out of 6($36 daily rate)
$152	4 Days Out of 5($38 daily rate)
$117	3 Days Out of 4($39 daily rate)
$ 23	Child (6 Through 12)
$ 23	Senior, 65 to 69
Free	Senior Citizen (70 and up)
Free	Toddlers (Through 4)

Lower lift rates come with certain packages and are available by booking lodging through Central Reservations.

Hours of Operation

9:00 A.M. to 4:00 P.M. daily
Mid-November through Mid-April

Lift Ticket Purchase Locations

Lift ticket purchase locations are conveniently located at the Oak Street and the Coonskin base lifts. There is also a purchase location at the base of Telluride Mountain Village, known as the Meadows Base Facility.

There is virtually never any waiting for ticket purchases. On those rare occasions when a line does exist such as the period between Christmas and New Year's, it is minimal.

How To Avoid Crowds

There are no crowds at Telluride.

Ski School

Whether skiers are just learning to ski or sharpening skills, they will find that Telluride's ski school is unique. It is directed by Annie Vareille-Savath who believes that skiers should not only be grouped by their specific levels of ability, but also by their learning styles. Therefore, Ms. Vareille-Savath divides her classes first by skill level and then further by learning style. The learning styles identified include those skiers who are intimidated by speed, those who "want to look good," and those who want to go fast. Each group thus identified is taught the proper techniques on slopes that will challenge their ability while developing their style. By bracketing classes in this manner, the ski school believes it can improve the learning curve of its students and increase their skill levels more quickly than with traditional methods.

The ski school meets in various locations depending on the classes selected. All five to twelve-year-old children's classes meet at the Meadows Base Facility, unless the children already know how to parallel ski. In the latter case, they should meet at the base of the Coonskin Lift. Access to the Meadows is via either the Oak Street or Coonskin Lift to the top of the front face and then by skiing down to the Meadows via See Forever, which is rated easy intermediate. In addition, a shuttle bus that circulates throughout the entire town every twelve minutes transports skiers to the Meadows Base Facility. For information and reservations, call (303)728-4424.

Ski school instructors add some local color to the children's ski classes by including stories about the Telluride's mining and skiing history and facts about the Ute Indians, and the area's geography and wildlife. The classes for 3- to 5-year-olds are part of the **Snowstar** program, and 6- to 12-year-olds enroll in the **Telstar** classes.

Adult classes usually meet at the Coonskin Base Facility in town. 1993-94 rates:

$ 35   Morning lesson with optional afternoon lesson add $15
$ 45   First-Time Skier or Telemarker (includes lift ticket and rental equipment)
$ 50   First-Time Snowboarder (includes lift ticket and rental equipment)
$ 35   2 1/2-Hour Clinic
$ 70   3 2 1/2-Hour Clinics

Telluride offers a wide variety of special classes for all levels of ability, as well as private lessons by the hour, half-day, or full-day. Among the special classes offered are snowboarding, NASTAR Clinic, Skill Building Workshops, Steep and Deep, and Bumps, Bumps, Bumps.

Equipment Rental

Olympic Sports shops are conveniently located at the base of all mountain lifts and downtown. Its 1993-94 rates for a complete rental (skis, poles, boots, bindings) vary from $15 per day to $30 per day for a high-performance package. "Ultimate Demos" which are all new '93-'94 skis and boots, can be had for $44 for a package, or $27 for skis only. Ultrawide powder skis by Evolution, Rossignol or Lacroix can be rented for $32 per day. Try these on a new powder day and you won't regret it!

Olympic Sports downtown shop boasts the largest selection of rental skis. Located in the heart of downtown Telluride on Colorado Ave. Telephone (800) 828-SKIS to reserve rental equipment.

Paragon Ski and Sport has four locations, including at the Oak Street Lift and the Coonskin lift, and at the Peaks of Telluride and on Main Street downtown. It has packages ranging from $13 to $19 per day. Additionally, it will allow skiers to demo top-of-the-line Elan, Völkl,Salomon, Kastle, Olin and Aughier skis for $26 per day. Telephone (303) 728-4525 to reserve rental equipment.

In addition to the above shops, two other sporting good stores are located in Telluride. These are **Summit Sports** on Oak Street and **Telluride Sports** on Colorado Avenue.

Breakage insurance or damage waivers are required at most ski rental establishments. Olympic also rents ski clothing, should the non-skier decide to give it a try.

Ski Tuning and Repair

All the ski rental establishments mentioned above will provide tuning and repairs. The rates for these services during the 1993-94 season were not available at press time.

Mountain Dining

As with most of the resorts featured, the food service and quality of the restaurants at Telluride is excellent. The crown jewel of the mountain restaurants is **Cactus Cafe**. Located in the La Chamonix condominiums at the base of the #3 and #4 lifts, the Cactus Cafe features dishes from the Southwest. The restaurant is tastefully decorated using bright colors such as dark green Mexican tiles and furnished with whitewashed pine tables and chairs. Terra-cotta accessories and plants add ambience to this well-lighted and comfortable restaurant. Full bar service is available during lunch, dinner, and après-ski. Try the veggie chili for a different warm-up during cold weather.

Situated one lift ride uphill from the Cactus is the **Gorrono Restaurant**. This is a collection of old weather-beaten buildings that provides the setting for one of the country's best mountain restaurants. Although the meals are served cafeteria-style, the quality of the food and the selection of items offered are equal to those of any sit-down restaurant. Full bar service is available. On fair weather days, the large deck is converted into several mini-food emporiums. One corner will have a service of hot, spicy shrimp and shish kebabs; in the other a full Bar-B-Que featuring hot dogs, hamburgers, spare ribs, coleslaw, beer and wine will be found. Sitting on the deck soaking up the sun's rays, watching others ski while enjoying the taped sounds of Paul Simon can soothe the soul and prepare one for an afternoon of mogul bashing!

Because it is difficult to ski from the Gorrono Basin area of the mountain to the front face, Telluride has located a small beer and pizza restaurant at the top of the #9 Lift. Although a minimal selection is available, the quality of the pizza is very good.

One other minimal mountain restaurant is located at the Meadows Base. The Meadows Base, where beginning skiers congregate, has basic amenities. The **Prospector Restaurant** has limited selections, and many of its offerings are pre-packaged fare. For those skiers who want their lunch to form a part of the total ski experience, this restaurant is not recommended.

Child Care

Telluride has located its child-care center on the first floor of La Chamonix in Columbia Place at the Mountain Village. This facility is clean and well maintained. Staff members are conscientious and appear to truly love children. The Mountain Village facility can accommodate a maximum of fifteen children up to and including three-year-olds. Parents are advised to provide diapers and the child's meals. Snacks such as crackers are provided by the nursery. The operating hours are from 8:30 A.M. until 4:30 P.M., and reservations are suggested. Telephone (303) 728-6727 or (800)544-0507. The rate for infants two months through one year during the 1992-93 season were $40 per day or $7 per hour. Rates for toddlers aged one year through three years were $35 per day or $25 per half-day. Toddlers' lunches are included. New rates were not available at press time.

Medical Facilities

Medical facilities at Telluride are of an emergency nature only. Should hospitalization be necessary, the seriously ill or injured skiers are transported to Montrose's hospital. Transport can be via either ambulance or helicopter, depending on the severity of the problem and weather conditions.

Cross-Country Skiing

Telluride has a network of 50 kilometers of tracks for cross country, much of it on high mesa ground with beautiful alpine views, and through the Telluride Town Park, along the San Miguel River Trail and

Valley Floor, on the Mountain Village Golf Course and on top of the Sunshine Express and its surrounding area.

The Nordic Center is located at The Peaks at Telluride. Telluride will exchange a downhill lift ticket for a Nordic ticket, and rental of suitable equipment is available for a modest fee. The 1993-94 rates for equipment are $14 per day for adults. On mountain access in 1993 will cost $12.

Various instructional packages are available starting at $25 for a beginner's group clinic, $35 for a private lesson for one. A gourmet lunch tour costs $45 and an overnight tour, $95. Call (303)728-5989 for information.

Accommodations

Last year the Doral Telluride Resort and Spa opened with much fanfare, and a reported building cost of $80 million. Many people have criticized the exterior of this hotel, but few would argue with the superior spa and good service it provided. However, the extravagant facilities did not arouse the interest expected during its first year, and so the company sold the hotel for a modest $27 million to the Westcorp development company from Phoenix. Reopened under a new name, **Peaks at Telluride**, its new management has increased the number of staff to serve its guests, and scaled down on restaurants. Still open will be Sundance, a southwestern style restaurant with beautiful views of the mountains. The Plunge restaurant will remain, but will operate as a bar and lounge.

The hotel promises the same or better level of service in its rooms and in the marvelous spa which includes 44 treatment rooms ready to provide massages, body treatments, facials and exercise programs including aerobics, racquetball, squash and weight training. This ski-in\ski-out convenience also includes and indoor\outdoor swimming pool, water slide, children's pool, 3 jacuzzis, saunas and steam rooms.

During the 1993-94 season, a deluxe room at the Peaks will go for between $345 and $395, except during the New Year's week when it will rise to a $235 per person rate, based on double occupancy for a 7-day package. **All guest room charges at the Peaks include the price of lift tickets and access to the spa.** A luxury suite, one bedroom and a living room with a pull out sofa and 2 full baths, will range from $725 to $925 per night.

Another beautiful small inn with a comfortable, homey atmosphere and spectacular views is **Pennington's Mountain Village Inn**, located on the 12th fairway of the Mountain Village Golf Course. Ski in and Ski out for 15 kilometers of cross country skiing, or use the free shuttle to drive 2 miles to the downhill slopes. This luxurious 12 room inn offers a gourmet breakfast every morning, and a hearthside happy hour every evening from 5 p.m. to 6:30. The European decorated rooms with have king or queen-sized beds, private baths, decks, and private guest lockers. Relax in a large hot tub or steam room after skiing. This is a particularly popular spot for weddings, and two of the rooms are large honeymoon suites. During the ski season, prices range from $150 to $250 per night. For information or reservations call (800)543-1437 or (303) 728-5337.

The **Telemark Condominiums** located in the Mountain Village are among the most opulent in Telluride. Here again, the Southwest influence dominates. Bleached oak cabinets, sea green carpets, mauve, and other complementary colors are exquisitely used. The Telemark overlooks Gorrono Basin, and visitors can relax in their condos while watching skiers return home in the afternoon, or they can soak in the hot tub while enjoying their favorite libations. Cathedral ceilings are accented by large, bleached beams that support the roof over the living and dining areas. The dining table comfortably seats six and should enjoy great use, because the kitchen is a gourmet cook's delight.

Appliances include Jenn-Air ranges, convection and radiant ovens, microwaves, garbage disposals and much, much more. All fixtures in these units are of the finest quality brass, kept at its shiniest by a conscientious maintenance crew.

Entry to the bedrooms is by a spiral staircase located adjacent to the tile and stucco fireplaces. There are double sinks in all the bedrooms. Custom-laminated cabinets in the baths attest to the developer's attention to detail.

The Telemark Condominiums are not located in the town of Telluride, and the prospective guest should be aware that there is little night life in the Mountain Village after the lifts close. The only restaurant within walking distance is the Cactus Cafe.

All Mountain Village properties share a common Southwestern influence in their furnishing selections and are relatively new, having been built only in the last two or three years. One of the newest condo developments is **Village Creek**, located across the parking lot from the Cactus Cafe. These well-constructed units have a breathtaking view of the canyon approach to Telluride and the towering peaks of the Uncompahgre National Forest.

White-washed oak flooring and Berber carpeting complements each units stylized individuality with a high level of good taste. All condos have wood-burning fireplaces, Kitchenaid dishwashers and disposals; other appliances are General Electric. Master suites contain a Jacuzzi tub, separate his and her sinks, and a queen size bed; all are beautifully appointed and appear spacious because of their soaring cathedral ceilings. Village Creek only consists of six condos, so reservations should be made well in advance.

True ski-in, ski-out convenience can be achieved by renting a condo in **Kayenta**. Constructed from millsap stone and stucco, these two and three-bedroom units are an architectural example of excellent Nordic mountain design. Located at the base of chair number 4 in Gorrono Basin, Kayenta offers all the conveniences of home away from home. Upon arrival, guests are treated to a survival amenities package typically containing such goodies as sausage, cheese, coffee, and fruit juices. Each bathroom features a separate amenities package containing shampoo and conditioner. Additionally, if guests should need the use of a blow dryer, toothbrush, knife sharpener, humidifier, or other incidental, the management company will be pleased to provide one promptly and at no additional cost.

Kayenta units are furnished with tea and oatmeal tone carpeting throughout. Wood-burning fireplaces in the living areas warm the soul, and appetites can be assuaged at the splendid dining tables which comfortably seat six. Conveniently located off the master bedrooms and adjacent to the kitchens are hot tubs and exterior decks. As expected, each unit has complete appliances and a luxurious master bath with a Jacuzzi tub, two sinks and a shower stall.

Aspen Ridge condos' striking exterior has been enhanced with extensive use of beautiful brass fixturing, stone, and bleached gray cedar siding. Guests will also be impressed with these units' interior finish, featuring clear maple tones, soaring cathedral ceilings, spacious living areas, and easy-to-use gas fireplaces. The upholstered furniture is reminiscent of Ralph Lauren's masculine style. Complete appliances and even a built-in T.V. assure guests of a pleasant vacation home. Skiers will certainly enjoy relaxing in the hot tub, sipping their favorite beverage while watching the wind tease the snow on the San Sofia range. These well-conceived units even provide garages with electric door openers.

Etta Place II condominiums are conveniently located near the base of the Coonskin Lift. Named after Butch Cassidy's girlfriend, Etta, these condos are within walking distance of all the town's restaurants, shops, and entertainment spots. Each unit in Etta Place contains its own private hot tub situated in the master bathroom; access to the tub is either from the bedroom or from the living room. Guests staying here will want to be certain to turn the tub off at night because its operation is quite noisy. These condominiums are very nice and are well maintained. From the moment guests enter the gray and white tile entry, they are aware of being in exceptional accommodations. Etta Place's kitchens contain all the essentials necessary to prepare family meals during a vacation. In addition to all the expected appliances, there are washer and dryers in each unit.

The dominant colors used in Etta Place are mauve, gray, and white. There is an outdoor heated swimming pool for guest use between the two buildings that comprise the complex. Sitting in the pool or in the hot tub and watching the snow fall on Woozley's Way is a great way to relax after a hard day of skiing and a wonderful prelude to an evening on the town.

Close to the Oak Street Lift and only two blocks from downtown Telluride are the **Manitou River Houses**. This project is available either as bed and breakfast or as two-bedroom condominiums. The project is eight years old and is nicely maintained. One of its central features has to be a handcrafted outdoor hot tub, situated in a wooden shelter with a lattice roof. The shadows in this area created by the full moon and reflections from the snow-laden slopes can create quite a romantic moment. This is a small condominium project with only ten condos. Priced well within the means of most people, the Manitou River Houses might well be one of the better housing bargains in Telluride.

The **Riverside Condominiums** are, as one would expect, along the San Miguel River. Medium priced and well maintained, these units include gas fireplaces, complete kitchens with Jenn-Air ranges and ice makers, steam showers, and a dining area that seats six comfortably.

The town of Telluride's best bed and breakfast is **The San Sophia** at 330 W. Pacific Ave., only steps from the Oak St. lift. Newly constructed to 1890's standards, it is a marvel to creative architecture. So many different angles have been used in construction, one knows it must have driven many carpenters to drink! The result of all the angles, however, is a very creative and interesting bed and breakfast. The rooms are quite small and the storage space limited. In spite of these shortcomings, though, The San Sophia is still highly recommended, because its management takes such care in assuring guests a first-class experience. The communal sitting room is complete with a well-stocked library of books, videos, and magazines. The breakfast provided as part of the tariff is best described as gourmet, and the après-ski of cheese, bread, and wine is always delightful. Rooms are furnished with antique phones, cable television, brass beds, and hand-made quilts. Outside a sunken Jacuzzi is housed in a gazebo. An intimate observatory, complete with maps and telescopes, is located on the top floor.

First-time visitors to Telluride should use caution in selecting their hotel or condominium. Many of the older condos have very poor acoustics, are poorly lighted and not well maintained. Some accommodations do not even have private baths or toilets.

For information and current prices for Telluride properties, call central reservations at 1-800-525-3455.

Restaurants

While all the resorts reviewed have great restaurants, Telluride seems to have more than its fair share. Of the outstanding eateries, **Silverglade** is the absolute best. Located in a basement on Colorado Ave., the Silverglade is furnished in a chrome and neon decor best described as California-style. Its menu is also California-inspired and changes year to year. Try their fresh fish entrees, the New York steak or the scallops sauted with soy, ginger, mushrooms and leeks. The vegetables are firm and fresh and the salads deliciously crisp. If you are adventurous, try the roast garlic, a la carte. An excellent wine cellar with an exceptionally large selection of California varietals will impress even the most jaded guest. The desserts fashioned by the pastry chef include such items as fresh raspberry white chocolate cheesecake or black bottom banana coconut cream pie.

The Continental Room in the **New Sheridan Hotel** is almost equal to The Silverglade. Those readers who have visited Aspen's Hotel Jerome will find The Continental Room comparable. The Victorian ambience of The Continental Room befits the period in which the hotel was built. The murals and statuary remind guests that they are in an Italian restaurant. The aroma of garlic wafts across the room as diners await the opportunity to order dinner. Service is friendly, and the choice of entrées is abundant. Fresh seafood is a daily menu item as are the lamb chops in Marsala sauce; the delicious chicken breast on spinach is laden with spicy Italian sausage. Prices here are moderate to high.

For some reason that escapes this author, breakfast is a major event at Telluride. For those readers who are big breakfast aficionados, there is no better place than **Leimgrubers von Telluride** on Pacific Ave. This restaurant is as German as the name suggests. It is one of the few places on or off the slopes where one will find a waiting line. The line begins to form about half an hour before Leimgrubers opens in the morning. This is due to the limited seating, also largely responsible for the ambience of the restaurant. The waitresses are large, amply endowed ladies who have a great sense of humor. The menu matches their exuberance. One should try the Belgian waffles with fresh strawberries or the freshly brewed coffee and omelet. One last word about Leimgrubers; if it snowed the evening before, arrive early and watch the waitresses shovel snow from the roof before opening the restaurant for breakfast. Leimgrubers is also *the place* for après-ski!

Located in an old ice house, **La Marmotte Restaurant Francais** deserves skiers' attention. Its old brick walls have been scrubbed clean, and its ceiling has been painted dark blue. A single wood-burning stove occupies a central location in the restaurant and offers a warm glow to chilly evenings. Each table at La Marmotte is graced with a single rose, and the walls and various shelves are decorated with strings of garlic cloves and wicker baskets bursting with mountain greenery.

As outstanding as La Marmotte's physical facility is, it is secondary to the food prepared there. Attention to detail is immediately apparent when the bread and butter arrive at the table: a solitary rose petal adds color to the butter service. The escargot, overflowing with delicious garlic, is served hot in its own indented pottery dish. The chunky tomato and mushroom soup is tasty and unusual because it is not a purée. Each evening the owners, Bertrand and Noelle Lepel-Cointet, offer special soups, appetizers, and entrées such as homemade pasta with smoked salmon, capers, shallots and cream sauce, chunky fish soup, duck confit and grilled breast, and braised leg of lamb with apple curry sauce.

La Marmotte is a small restaurant, accommodating only about fifty diners at the authentically French table setting. The views alone from La Marmotte are worthy of a visit—imagine the early evening sun setting on Ajax Peak. Unfortunately the bar is small and not convenient for casual cocktails. Reservations are a must because tables tend to fill up early. Dining is expensive.

Other fine eateries abound in Telluride, and there is not enough space in this chapter to list them all. However, a few worth mentioning include the **Floradora Saloon** (ask about the time someone tried to rob the bank next door by tunneling to it from the Floradora), and **Sofios** (the margaritas will provide stamina to ski the Plunge).

Activities

In addition to unparalleled skiing, Telluride offers its visitors sleigh rides along the San Miguel River.

Nightly movies are featured at the Nugget Theatre, as well as occasional concerts and live shows. At the Masonic Hall, a multi-image slide presentation of local flora and fauna is featured daily during the season.

Snowmobiling and sightseeing trips by Jeep or by air are also available.

The Telluride Athletic Club, located just outside of town on the road to Telluride's airport, offers visitors aerobics classes, handball/racquetball courts, gymnasium, free weights, and Biocycles. Complete locker room facilities are available.

Ice-skating at the town rink is open to the public on a scheduled basis. The rink also offers skating and hockey lessons. Skate rentals are available at Olympic Sports at 101 W. Colorado.

San Juan Balloon Adventures offer daybreak hot air balloon trips of one-hour duration and a champagne toast with the crew. Telephone (303) 728-4904 for information and reservations.

Services

A full complement of sporting goods stores, apparel shops, pharmacies, grocery stores, liquor stores, furniture, bath, and specialty shops is within the immediate town. In addition there are antique shops, acupressure services, art galleries, bakeries, beauty salons, bookstores, florists, flotation tanks, massage, and tanning studios.

Village Map

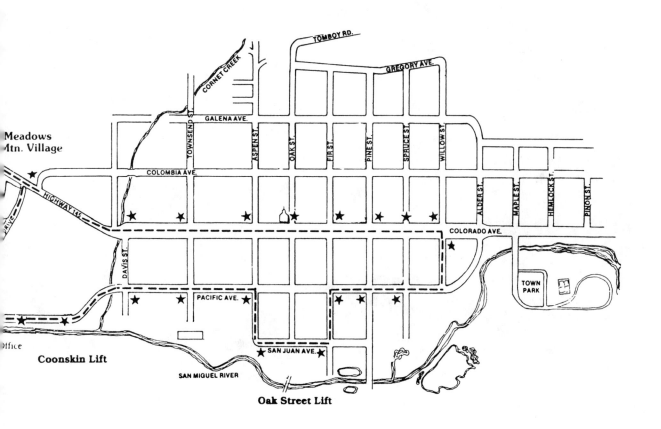

Two years ago Beaver Creek added Grouse Mountain to its area, increasing its stock of expert trails. This year the Spruce Saddle restaurant mid mountain is being renovated and expanded.

VAIL/Beaver Creek

P.O. Box 7
Vail, CO. 81658

(800) 525-3875 Reservations
(303) 476-5601 Information
(303) 476-4888 Snow Report

New for 1993-94

Vail Associates is adding a new high speed quad lift, **Pride Express**, on the Lionshead side of the resort. The bottom of the lift is about one quarter of the way up the mountain and leads all the way to the top at Eagle's Nest, where the gondola also ends. This may lead to more use on the Cheetah, Simba and Safari runs, some nice cruisers on the far west side of the mountain that often are neglected.

Vail, like other resorts, this year also is designating an area as a teaching area -- a place where skiers should recognize that slow skiing is de rigueur. This area will include the chair slow, teaching lift #15, which has been used for teaching for years, and the poma lift at GitcheeGoomee Gulch, but it will extend the protected area two runs to the east, including Ledges and Lodgepole runs. The area will be roped off, and anyone may ski there, but it will be identified for slow and learning skiers.

In addition, the old double chair # 9 at Lionshead will be shortened this year. The bottom of the chair will be moved up mountain to the junction of Minnie's Mile and Cub's Way.

Over at Beaver Creek a complete renovation of the Spruce Saddle Lodge at midmountain has been completed. An addition 290 seats are available, and a separate children's lunch room has been added. The restaurant now can seat 1,100 people. The decor has been renovated, on a western theme similar to Two Elk Restaurant at Vail.

Two new runs have been cut Beaver Creek. Between the Red Tail run and the Centennial Lift, a new run of 35 acres has been added, called Harrier. And farther up at Grouse mountain, Royal Elk Glades have been added to the legal terrain. This area was out of bounds last year, but so many people had been skiing it safely that its 45 acres was added to Beaver Creeks boundaries. Beaver Creek now has 1,125 acres of skiing.

And finally, Vail Associates this fall purchased the Arrowhead Ski Area in Edwards. Eventually, it is hoped that a new lift or two can be added to connect the area to the Beaver Creek runs, opening continuous skiing acreage to visitors at both mountains. Bachelor Gulch, an area between the two already has a run cut into its trees, but it has not been used. This could happen as early as the summer of 1994 and would 450 acres to the Beaver Creek total. Arrowhead is located at the Edwards exit, just one exit west of the I-70 exit, where Beaver Creek is located. It already is the site of a beautiful golf course, and an expensive housing development.

How To Get There

Vail and Beaver Creek are easy destination points to reach. Whereas so many major ski resorts test skiers' ability to endure fickle weather and unreliable air service, Vail is only a short 100 miles west of Denver. The resort is reached via I-70, a four-lane road scrupulously maintained by the Department of Highways. Crossing the Continental Divide is usually easy regardless of weather conditions because the Eisenhower Memorial Tunnel eliminates driving through the worst high altitude weather. The only potentially difficult portion of the drive is over Vail Pass, but it is also well-maintained and rarely impassable.

Traffic to Vail/Eagle County Airport continues to increase, making it easier to fly to within 35 miles of Vail, and 25 miles of Beaver Creek. American Airlines will fly non-stop to Eagle from Chicago, Dallas, Miami, Chicago and New York in 1993-94. Return flights to New York and Miami will stop in Denver. Delta will offer daily non-stop service from Salt Lake City. Located in a broad valley, Eagle County Airport actually is also very convenient to Aspen and rarely subject to the weather delays typical at Aspen's Sardy Field.

The airport also provides international flights from Taesa, a Mexican airline. The flights lead from Mexico City to Eagle County airport. All the flights stop in Laredo, Texas.

Once in Vail, it is not necessary to have an automobile because everything is convenient; in addition, shuttle service is provided. Guests at Beaver Creek, however, may want to consider car rental if they intend to frequent Vail proper during their stay.

If skiers neither want to rent a car in Denver or fly into the mountains, they can reserve space on any of several shuttle services. **Colorado Mountain Express** makes runs to the Vail area from the Denver airport every 30 to 45 minutes between 8:15 A.M. and 9:30 P.M. This service during the 1993-94 season costs $39.50 per person, Sunday through Friday. each way. On Saturdays, the trip will cost $42. CME also offers service to and from Eagle airport for $24 one way, $26 on Saturdays. To book reservations for this door-to-door service, telephone (800) 525-6363. Major credit cards are accepted. If you buy your airline tickets through CME, you may be able to get substantial discounts because the companies buy tickets in bulk.

Vans to Vail also provides a door-to-door service leaving Denver International or Stapleton beginning Nov. 24 at 6:00 A.M each morning and depart hourly until 7:00 P.M. Departures from Vail also begin at 6:00 A.M. and run through 6:00 P.M. An extra shuttle is added on Saturdays. The 1993-94 ski season shuttle rate is $39 to Vail or Beaver Creek until Dec. 18, 1993. After that date, prices rise to $44 one way Sundays through Fridays; $47 Saturdays and holidays. This is a per person rate, one way. Telephone (800) 222-2112 for reservations. All shuttle services require guests departing Vail to be ready for pickup 45 minutes before published departure time. This is necessary because there is only one published departure time, but individuals must be picked up from several locations within Vail. It is important to note that return reservations must be confirmed at least 48 hours prior to departure. This is especially important during peak periods such as Christmas and Spring Break.

Skiers who wish to drive from Denver will find the following major car rental agencies represented at Denver's International Airport:

Avis	(800)221-1212
Budget	(800)527-0700
Dollar	(800)421-6868
Hertz	(800)654-3131
National	(800)328-4567

Other car rental agencies are located outside of the airport property and offer free airport pickup and drop-off, among them:

Alamo	(800)327-9633
Enterprise	(800)325-8007
Thrifty	(800)367-2277

All rental agencies provide their clients with free maps. Due to possible road restrictions which may require chains or snow tires, travelers to Vail or Beaver Creek are advised to always rent a car that is *skierized*, i.e. equipped with snow tires and ski racks. For a slightly higher price, many rental agencies can also provide four-wheel drive vehicles. Travelers wishing to reserve these vehicles are advised to do so far in advance because the demand for them is great.

Although there is more than enough skiable terrain and activities to keep anyone busy in Vail, the added mobility of an automobile makes it easy to take a one-day side trip to either Copper Mountain, Breckenridge, or Keystone, all located approximately 30 to 40 minutes east of Vail.

Vail Mountain Information

Vail Mountain is unequivocally one of the greatest ski mountains in North America, so it is fitting that one of America's finest resorts has been established at its base. By anyone's definition, Vail Mountain is BIG, consisting of 12,500 acres (5,058 ha) of which 3,817 acres (1,533 ha) are developed trails. Vail is the largest single ski mountain in America. Unlike most resorts, Vail distinguishes between total number of skiable acres and developed trails, because its famous back bowls are so vast and totally skiable. The developed trails total 121 runs, the longest being Riva Ridge at three miles (4.82 km).

Located in the White River National Forest, Vail has a base elevation of 8,200 feet (2,500 meters) and rises to 11,250 feet (3,491 meters) at its summit. This equates to a 3,259 foot (991 meters) vertical drop.

This abundant terrain is serviced by the following lift equipment:

1 Gondola
1 High-Speed Enclosed Quadruple Chairlift, the Vista Bahn
7 High-Speed Quadruple Chairlifts
2 Quadruple Chairlifts
3 Triple Chairlifts
6 Double Chairlifts
5 Surface Lifts

Vail has more high speed detachable quad chairlifts than any other ski area in the world -- 8.

Vail's uphill lift capacity is 41,855 skiers per hour.

Vail's excellent mix of terrain offers challenge and excitement to skiers of all ability levels. The front face of the mountain, on which all of Vail centers, consists of 32% beginner trails, 36% intermediate trails, and 32% expert trails. The backside of the mountain presently consists of six bowls (Sun Down, Sun Up, Tea Cup, China, Siberia, and Mongolia), all of which are classified from advanced intermediate to expert depending on snow conditions. The mountain's back bowls are rated 36 percent intermediate and 64 percent advanced.

A seventh bowl, Game Creek, is undeniably intermediate and definitely not intimidating. It is reached by skiing down a catwalk from the top of the LionsHead Gondola or from the top of the Hunky Dory Lift.

Expert skiers enjoy skiing to the Game Creek Express Lift at the bottom of Game Creek Bowl by going off the side of the catwalk on runs such as Ouzo, Faro, and Deuces Wild. However, by following the catwalk to its terminus, easy, open skiing is available for intermediate skiers. Showboat has a double fall line, meaning it not only goes down but also (in this case) goes down right to left. This is a good area to ski when weather is cold and windy because the bowl protects skiers from the worst elements. The trails are short, though, and most people become bored with them after a few hours.

The six back bowls are much larger than Game Creek Bowl. Their runs are classified as expert, but in truth, a strong intermediate skier can handle them if conditions are ideal. These trails are long and bumpy and have double and triple fall lines. When it is snowing hard or if the light is flat, skiing can be difficult in the bowls even for experts. The good news, however, is that Vail enjoys sunshine a high percentage of the time during ski season. Due to the size of the mountain's bowls, powder can almost always be found somewhere, but the frequently skied tracks become packed shortly after a snowfall. The addition of China, Siberia, and Mongolia bowl during the 1988-89 season made Vail the largest single-mountain resort in North America. Shangri-la and Poppy Fields in China Bowl are continually groomed for intermediate skiers' enjoyment.

The front face of Vail Mountain may be roughly divided into three sections:

Golden Peak
Mid-Mountain
LionsHead

Golden Peak is the eastern-most area of Vail, and it is entirely beginner to intermediate terrain. Of all the areas at Vail, this is the least impressive. It is gentle and virtually treeless. Some have been known to call it dull. Many of Vail's beginner ski classes are held in this area.

The center of the mountain is unusual in that most of the beginner to intermediate skiing is on the upper portion, while the lower portion is expert. Returning in the evening, beginning skiers should stick to Gitalong Road, easy but safe. Intermediates will enjoy making Berries their final run of the day. More accomplished skiers should reserve enough strength to handle the very demanding Giant Steps, International, and Adios. These runs are so steep that until recently they were frequently closed. However, the recent acquisition of a winch cat has enabled Vail Associates to maintain these runs and keep them open most of the ski season.

The LionsHead area primarily consists of intermediate terrain. Many skiers who enjoy the upper portion of Mid-Vail take Eagle's Nest Ridge to return home in the evening. This is a run that begins at the top of Vail's #3 and #7 lifts. By taking Eagle's Nest Ridge, one can easily trek to the top of the LionsHead Gondola and take any number of intermediate trails to the LionsHead base. If it is cold or windy, Eagle's Nest Ridge can be very uncomfortable because it is totally open to the elements. However, once off the ridge, the skier is sheltered.

Vail, recognizing it had to do something about the habitual crowding of the LionsHead gondola, installed a high-speed quad in 1988-89 called Born Free Express. This chairlift runs parallel to the gondola and has taken a tremendous strain off it. However, in very cold weather or on extremely snowy days, skiers still prefer the comfort of the gondola. Further recognizing the need to transport skiers to the top of the mountain quickly and in comfort, Vail Associates next installed a seventh high-speed quad from mid-mountain to the summit of Eagle's Nest Ridge. It replaces chairs 2 and 17 and is called Avanti Express.

Some of the finest skiing at Vail is located in Northeast Bowl. Although actually a bowl, it is so broad that one's perception is that it is a face; skiers are not necessarily aware of skiing in a bowl as they are when they ski Sun Down or Sun Up bowls. Its runs are primarily intermediate with some expert trails arranged along the ridges that form the bowl. Extremely difficult double black diamond runs are found directly under the top of the # 11 Lift (Northwoods Express) and off the east side of

Prima. Unless skiers are very accomplished and fit, these runs should not be attempted. Unless you are an expert skier, avoid South Rim, North Rim, Prima Cornice, and Pronto.

The other double black diamond runs (Blue Ox, Roger's Run, Highline, and Prima), though difficult, are not dangerous. These runs are distinguished by their unending mogul fields. Bump skiers love them.

In order to leave Northeast Bowl in the evening, take chairlift #6 located at the base of Northeast Bowl up the backside of Golden Peak and ski into Vail Village via Follow Me. During the summer of 1988, Vail developed South Six Escape from the base of #6 which allows skiers to ski directly to Golden Peak Village, eliminating the necessity to ride up chairlift #6.

Due to the mountain's size and its natural terrain, Vail does not experience a great deal of congestion on many runs at the end of the day. No matter where skiers exit from the mountain, free shuttle service is available to transport them to other points in the village.

Vail Mountain receives an annual snowfall of about 300-350 inches (762 cm-889 cm). Its average monthly snowfalls are

Nov.	60"	(153 cm)
Dec.	62"	(157 cm)
Jan.	62"	(157 cm)
Feb.	54"	(136 cm)
Mar.	65"	(166 cm)
Apr.	34"	(86 cm)

Vail's snowmaking capabilities are substantial, though small in relation to the vastness of the mountain itself. Vail can cover 320 acres (130 ha) of trails with man-made snow.

The average daily temperatures at the summit during ski season are

	High	Low	High	Low
Nov.	28°	9°	-2°C	-12°C
Dec.	21°	5°	-6°C	-15°C
Jan.	20°	4°	-6°C	-16°C
Feb.	23°	5°	-5°C	-15°C
Mar.	28°	9°	-2°C	-12°C
Apr.	35°	13°	2°C	-10°C

Beaver Creek Mountain Information

Beaver Creek Mountain at 1,125 acres much smaller than Vail, but is growing. With the connection to Arrowhead pending it will grow by .... and it has a permit that covers 5,600 acres. Its trails are wide, impeccably groomed, and picturesquely cut into glades, glens, and gentle bowls. Beaver creek originally was designed with the intermediate skier in mind, but the addition of Grouse Mountain runs have added significant challenging terrain to its storehouse.

Beaver Creek does not enjoy the luxury of high-speed quad lifts, except for Centennial lift just off the main village plaza and the number 10 lift, the Grouse Mountain Express. It is amazing how quickly skiers have become accustomed to high-speed lifts, making every other lift seem tedious and boring by comparison.

Beginner trails are found both at the base of the mountain and at its summit. This is a relatively unusual arrangement but one that works very well, as it encourages beginning skiers by transporting them via chair lift over a large portion of intermediate terrain. When Vail Associates and the National Forest Service first collaborated and began laying out the mountain trails, they agreed not to build any trails wider than 100 yards, in recognition of the fact that deer and elk will not cross an open area greater than 100 yards. Today's trails thus take advantage of the diverse natural terrain without impacting wildlife's well-being. Beaver Creek's trails are a credit to those who designed them, as well to all those who cut them. Many trails take advantage of the natural glens found within aspen groves, particularly the northeast-facing slopes around Latigo. Open-bowl skiing on warm spring days is at its best in Larkspur Bowl. Here numerous intermediate runs are rimmed with a sprinkling of expert bump runs such as Loco and Lupine. Another smaller bowl is located east of Spruce Saddle, running to the base of the number 4 lift. This is Rose Bowl, and by any name, it is sweet! Rose Bowl is gentle and almost always freshly groomed, encouraging novices to work on style while allowing more accomplished skiers to cruise effortlessly.

Beaver Creek's trails are classified as 18 percent beginner, 39 percent intermediate and 43 percent advanced. The expert runs here are equivalent to Vail's black diamond trails, though not to those at Jackson Hole, Snowbird, Squaw Valley, Sun Valley, or Taos. Experts will enjoy Spider, Web, and Cataract off the number 4 chair, however. The junction of Web and Spider is interesting because it is a gully with a triple fall line—short and reasonably steep. Beaver Creek's most famous black diamond runs are the Birds of Prey—Peregrine, Goshawk, and Golden Eagle. The three runs are parallel to one another, and one seems pretty much like the other. All are long, similar to the Spiral Stairs or Plunge at Telluride and just as knee-crunching. They are difficult because they are so unrelenting; bump skiers will love them while "steep" lovers will not be impressed.

Lift Ticket Prices (1993-94)

These prices are the same at both areas.

$ 45	Adult Full-Day
$ 39	Half Day
Free	70+
$ 32	Child Full-Day (12 & Under)
$ 26	Child, Half Day

Multi-day lift tickets are discounted.

Hours of Operation

8:30 A.M. to 3:30 P.M. daily

Lifts 5, 21, 22 and the new Sun Up Triple Chair in Vail's back bowls close at 3:00 P.M.

Vail and Beaver Creek have posted lift status boards at the top of every lift, indicating how crowded each lift is currently. When the light on the board is green, the maze is not full. If the light is yellow, the lift line is approximately 20 minutes or longer. If the indicator light is red, the lift is closed.

Lift Ticket Purchase Locations

Purchasing lift tickets is simple at Vail. Ticket counters are conveniently located near all four uphill lift systems. Counters are also at the bases of Golden Peak, LionsHead, the Vista Bahn Express located in Vail Village, and at Cascade Village, a new location west of LionsHead.

Lift tickets may be purchased at the base of chair 12, just a few steps uphill from the Village Hall, home of McCoy's Bar and Restaurant. All Vail/Beaver Creek lift tickets are interchangeable. Next day tickets may be purchased between 3:00 P.M. and 5:00 P.M.

How To Avoid Crowds

A mega resort, Vail is the largest single ski mountain in the United States so there are bound to be crowds most of the time. However, Vail's new high-speed quad lifts transport skiers uphill faster than those at any other ski area in North America. Vail's terrain is vast enough to accommodate the additional skiers this system unloads. Excessive lift lines are, therefore, limited to the base areas from approximately 9:00 A.M. to 10:30 A.M. and from noon until around 1:30 P.M. The lifts from the Mid-Vail restaurants are also generally very crowded immediately after lunch. The crowds that previously formed at the LionsHead Gondola have been eliminated or greatly reduced with the addition of the new Born Free Express detachable quad and the Avanti Express to the top.

Skiers can avoid delays in the morning by skipping the Vista Bahn and the LionsHead Gondola and instead taking Giant Steps Chairlift to the Avanti Express or nearby Born Free Express.

The only way to avoid the ever-present lines at Mid-Vail is not to stop and eat there during the traditional lunch period. Eat earlier or later to avoid the crowds. An alternative to eating at Mid-Vail is to eat at one of the many restaurants at the base or at LionsHead. Except during weekends and holiday periods, Eagle's Nest cafeteria at the top of the LionsHead Gondola is generally uncrowded. The Wildwood Shelter at the top of Hunky Dory offers Italian food inside, and barbecues are set up outside on warm, clear days.

Generally speaking, Beaver Creek is not as subject to crowding as Vail. However, if there is crowding, it will occur at the Centennial lift generally around 10:00 A.M. when ski classes are making their way up the mountain. To avoid this line, consider using chair 12 and skiing Stacker or Larkspur Bowl until the crowds die down in the village. In the afternoon between 3:00 P.M. and 4:00 P.M. Centennial, Bear Tree Race, and Buckboard experience crowding. Be sure to exercise caution when skiing these runs late in the afternoon.

Ski School

Vail's ski school is among the best in the country. It is also the largest in the world with over 650 instructors, who have been credited with assisting in the creation and development of teaching methods employed by the Professional Ski Instructors of America. Ski schools are located conveniently at the base of Golden Peak, the Vail Village area (private lessons only), LionsHead, Eagles Nest (at the top of the LionsHead Gondola), Mid-Vail, and at the Two Elk Lodge in the Northeast Bowl. Beaver Creek's ski school is located in the Village Hall, just a few steps down from the Centennial Express lift or on mountain in Spruce Saddle.

Ski classes are divided into nine separate groups according to ability, from beginner through advanced. In addition, specialty classes are offered for style, racing, bumps, and powder. Vail also has developed its Mountain Guide and Super Mountain Guide programs for skiers of most ability levels. These guides take seasoned skiers to places known only to the locals and carefully match terrain with ability and interest. This is a great way to learn the mountain.

Ski programs may also be custom designed to meet specific needs. These can be on an individual or small, private group basis. 1993-94 prices start at $90 for one hour for 1 to 5 people and go to $370 for an all-day lesson for 1 to 5 people. Bookings for special classes or private lessons must still be made 24 hours in advance.

The 1993-94 ski season prices for lessons were as follows:

Adult

$ 75	One-Day, "Discover Skiing," lift and lesson
$210	Three-Day Intro, lift and lesson
$100	Adult, Intermediate to expert, lift and lesson, full-day
$ 90	One-Hour Private, 1-5 Persons
$255	Half-Day Private, 1-5 Persons
$370	All-Day Private, 1-5 Persons
$ 75	All Day, "Discover Boarding," lift and lesson
$ 60	Half-Day "Discover Boarding," lift and lesson

Children

At the Children's Skiing Center 3- to 6-year-olds meet from 10 a.m. to 3 p.m. for

$70	Mini Mice, "willing" potty trained 3-year olds lesson and lunch
$70	Mogul Mice, ages 4 to 6, can't stop on their own, lunch, lesson and lift.
$70	All-Day lesson and lunch for 6 to 12 year olds
$55	2-18 months infant care, or preschoolers 2-1/2 to 6 years, snow play and lunch.

Vail Associates has made every effort imaginable to ensure that young children have a good time while learning to ski at the resort. The mountain has been honeycombed with small theme parks which children can visit throughout the day. These include a "lost" silver mine, Devil's Fork Mine, Monstrous Mounds, and many other play areas designated for children only. The youngsters are even provided with their own trail map detailing the locations of the parks. Each week Disney's Sport Goofy visits the ski schools. There is even a weekly schedule of special Sport Goofy events, including Breakfast with Sport Goofy, Sport Goofy Challenge, and Kids' Night Out. Each week one of two programs scripted with the advice of Walt Disney Associates is presented by the ski school. These programs utilize costumed actors and actresses located in strategic areas of the children's parks. One script is entitled *The Ballad of Buckaroo Bob* and takes the children through a week-long odyssey that entertains them, teaches them history, and instructs them how to ski. It is a wonderfully crafted program which is bound to be imitated by other ski resorts in the near future.

For children too young to ski, Vail has the Children's Center at the base of Golden Peak. This facility accommodates children from two months through six years. The cost for the program varies from $55 per day. Diapers and special food should be provided by parents, and reservations are strongly advised. Prepayment of one day's fee is required to reserve a place.

Beaver Creek's Children's Adventure Center ski school is in the Village Hall. It offers the same programs as Vail. For infant care, the Small World Play School Nursery is creekside below the Activities Desk.

Equipment Rental

There are a great variety of rental shops in separate locations throughout Vail. During 1992-93, Vail Associates rentals for a regular package of skis, boots and poles generally will run about $14 per day. The following is a representative accounting of charges and equipment selections:

Vail's premier rental (and tuning) shop is located immediately in front of the Vista Bahn lift in the center of Vail Village. Joel Gros' **Colorado Ski Service** is located in the Golden Peak House and connected via underground tunnel with **Vista Bahn Ski Rentals**. Joel, the former chief tune-up technician for the U.S. Ski Team, operates both shops. Joel's Standard package offers Rossignol Edge Skis, Salomon bindings and boots for $15 per day, $12 per day for a 5-day package; The sport package consists of Rossignol QM and 3HP skis,reflex poles, Salomon bindings, Salomon, Nordica and Rossignol boots for $22 per day or $18 per day for five or more days. The High Performance/Demo package can include Rossignol 7SK, &XK, RSV, Volkl P.10SLC and Salomon 9000EXP Force 9 skis, or Axiom or LaCroix fat skis; Salomon 977 driver, or Marker SC1 bindings; and Rossignol, Nordica and Salomon boots for $32 daily or $28 per day for a 5- day package.

For information or to reserve rental equipment, telephone (303) 476-2566.

Another convenient shop in Vail is **Christy Sports,** the door of which is perhaps 50 feet from the Vista Bahn ticket window. They also offer three types of rental packages. The regular package will consist Rossignol 3XP skis, Salomon SX 61 boots, and Scott poles for $16 per day. The sport package will include Pre CS skis, Salomon SX 61 boots and Scott poles for $27 per day. And the premium package will cost $33 per day for any of about 20 different types of ski and several types of boots. Discounts are available for multi-day rentals. Christy's also has a store in Avon, near the entrance to the Beaver Creek resort.

Sports Stalker, Colorado Insight, Pepi Sports, Gorsuch, Breeze Ski Rentals and many other stores, including Vail Associates Rentals all offer rentals in Vail.Ski rental shops abound in Vail and area too numerous to list.

Ski Tuning and Repair

Vail boasts an enormous selection of companies and locations for ski repair. All rental establishments also repair skis but in addition, stores exist which only sell new skis and repair older ones. Almost without exception, all of their shops do a competent job of repairing or waxing skis. However, a few shops have state-of-the-art ski-tuning equipment and extraordinary technicians. All things being equal, skiers should consider having their equipment tuned or repaired where this up-to-date equipment and skill is available.

Colorado Ski Service (AKA Joel's Colorado Ski Service or Vista Bahn Ski Rental) is located at the head of Bridge St. in Golden Peak House. The combination of Tezzari stone-grinding equipment and Joel's extensive knowledge of ski tuning assures skiers of the very best tuning available in Vail. The 1993-94 cost of tuning is

- $ 8   Hot Wax
- $20   Edges Deburred and Waxed
- $25   Regular Tune
- $35   Tune with Stone Grind
- $ 8   Bindings Adjusted
- $ 5+   P-tex

Pepi Sports on Bridge St. in the center of Vail also uses Tezzari stone-grinding equipment. During the 1993-94 season their rates for tune-ups were

- $ 7   Hot Wax
- $25   Basic Tune
- $35   Full Tune
- $15   Bindings Adjusted with Torque Test

Vail Mountain Dining

Eleven mountain restaurants or pit stops have been conveniently located on Vail's slopes. In addition, over 100 restaurants are located within Vail Village. Most of these restaurants are accessible from the base of the mountain and should not be overlooked when it is time to stop for lunch.

Of the actual mountain restaurants, one of the best is located above the cafeteria at the terminus of the LionsHead Gondola at Eagle's Nest. **The Wine Stube** restaurant specializes in German cuisine but offers a savory selection of American dishes as well. Dining at The Stube is an elegant experience, complete with white table linens and silver service. The views from its windows can be breathtaking on clear days when one can see almost the entire New York Range. Reservations are recommended (303)479-2034.

The new **Two Elk** cafeteria on the east side of the mountain overlooking the bowls provides a large space for hungry skiers in a beautiful massive wood building with beautiful views and western mountain decor. It specializes in southwest, oriental and american cuisine. A full salad bar, baked potato bar and pasta bar also are available.

Located on the first level of Eagle's Nest is the **Eagle's Nest cafeteria**. The food served here is typical mountain fare, unremarkable but filling. During good weather the staff will arrange an outdoor Bar-B-Que featuring hamburgers, hot dogs, and ribs.

The **Mid-Vail** offers two levels (**Look Ma** on the upper-most level and **The Terrace** on the lower, or mid-level) of cafeteria-style dining. This mountain restaurant is the most crowded because it is at the top of the Vista Bahn lift and at the base of the Hunky Dory and Mountain Top Express lifts. Views from this restaurant are exceptional. On warm, clear days the staff will prepare an outdoor Bar-B-Que similar to the one at LionsHead. The outside service usually opens by the end of January, and it is very pleasant to linger outside a few moments, enjoying the sun's warming rays, while quenching your thirst with a hot or cold beverage.

Located below the Mid-Vail cafeterias is The **Cookshack**. It features a Southwest menu, informal ambiance, and attentive service. Reservations arc always suggested and become an absolute must during peak vacation periods. Telephone 479-2030.

The **Wildwood Shelter** is situated at the top of the Hunky Dory and Game Creek Express lifts. This restaurant is usually less crowded than either Eagle's Nest at LionsHead or Mid-Vail. However, its selection of menu items is also more limited. The vegetarian lasagna is good, and it also offers health food specials.

Trail's End offers daily specials and standard American fare of sandwiches and soups in the Lionshead Gondola building. Live entertainment daily is offered for apres-ski.

Golden Peak offers breakfast and lunch cafeteria style.

Three quick places to grab a bite are: **The Wok'n'Roll Express** at the base of the Orient Express Lift in China Bowl, a "ski-by pagoda" offering fried rice and "Yakitori," Chinese chicken, and other eastern specials; and **Dog Haus Express,** at the base of the Avanti Express, gourmet hot dogs,beer, wine and soft drinks; and **Pronto's Porch**, at the base of Northwoods Express, a vending-machine center.

If truly high-quality luncheons are desired, you should consider one of the restaurants in town. The trip back up the mountain after lunch is quite easy, thanks to the Vista Bahn lift or the LionsHead Gondola.

Beaver Creek Mountain Dining

The largest on-mountain restaurant is actually located at the base of the mountain: **McCoy's Bar and Restaurant**. This enormous self-serve restaurant, managed by the Hyatt Regency Beaver

Creek, is filled with numerous large tables covered with imitation leather oilcloth. Food served here is good, although a bit pricey. McCoy's menu is typical ski resort fare and does not reflect the imagination and creativity found at some of the other dining spots just a few doors away. However, the cavernous McCoy's remains a gathering spot for most skiers. It is open for breakfast, lunch, dinner, and après-ski, featuring live entertainment. Patio dining during lunch is available during warm weather in the spring. McCoy's is similar to—but cleaner than—The Village Cafeteria in Breckenridge.

Spruce Saddle Restaurant is fittingly located atop Spruce Saddle. This year it has been expanded and renovated, see the first page of this chapter. It seats 800 and offers a similar menu to the Village Hall's McCoy's. Also offers an outdoor barbecue in the spring. Located on the second floor above Spruce Saddle Restaurant is Rafters, a rustic sit-down, table-service restaurant. Like the Cook Shack at Vail, it is always crowded so be sure to book reservations at least a day in advance if you want to dine here. The menu may be defined loosely as "California chic" with a dash of the unexpected—sort of common but prepared unusually. Many skiers eat here just to enjoy the views, which are spectacular and definitely better than can be seen from anywhere in Vail. The best vista is to the northeast, with the Gore Range's soaring, majestic peaks touching the clouds. (303)949-6050.

Red Tail Camp is located at the base of chairs 9 and 11 and serves primarily as a warming hut. However, it is converted into an outdoor barbecue in the spring, enabling lucky diners to go home with a fantastic Vail tan.

Child Care

Child-care facilities are located at the base of Golden Peak (Vail's eastern-most mountain and the site of most beginner lessons) and also in the Village Hall at the base of the Centennial Express lift in Beaver Creek. Free transportation to Golden Peak is available via Vail's bus system, which makes convenient stops throughout the village. The **Children's Center At Vail** accepts children from two months to six years of age. Parents are advised to make children's reservations at the same time they book their accommodations because space is limited.

See the ski school section for more information.

Medical Facilities

Medical facilities at Vail are without peer when compared to other ski resorts throughout the United States. Vail has a complete hospital, fully staffed 24 hours a day. Conveniently located on Meadow Drive midway between LionsHead and downtown Vail, the clinic has the capability to care for critically ill patients and to perform surgery, should it be necessary. In addition, numerous specialists are in residence.

Skiers who are injured at Beaver Creek receive emergency service only. The ski patrol will administer trauma treatment, stabilize broken bones, and transport injured skiers downhill by sled for transport by ambulance to Vail Hospital.

Cross-Country Skiing

Three types of cross-country skiing are available at Vail: track, back-country, and telemark.

Track skiing is available on prepared trails over Vail Golf Course. The golf course's 10K dual track with skating lane meanders throughout Vail valley, just east of Golden Peak. While negotiating small hills and admiring the expensive homes lining the track's path, it is interesting to observe ice climbers who frequent the frozen cataracts just above the trail.

Back-country skiing is demanding because the skier traverses mostly flat terrain in specially selected areas of Vail. Guides and instruction for this demanding sport are available at the Vail Golf Course's cross-country headquarters. Call 303-845-5313 for information.

Telemark skiing combines skills necessary to ski downhill with equipment that is similar to that used in skiing the flat track of the golf course.

Cross-country instruction is available through the Vail/Beaver Creek Ski School. Classes meet at the base of Golden Peak. During the 1993-94 season all-day lessons cost $51.

The McCoy Park Track System is located atop the #12 Lift at Beaver Creek. McCoy Park consists of 32 km. of machine-groomed tracks of which 20% is advanced beginner, 60% is intermediate, and 20% is advanced. Cost for use of the tracks during the 1993-94 season is $15 for adults and $7 children. Half-day rates are $12 for adults and $5 for children.

At Beaver Creek rentals and instruction are available at the Cross Country Ski Center in Strawberry Park, next to the Strawberry Park lift, #12.

Vail Accommodations

With the exception of Aspen, there is no other American ski resort with a greater preponderance of quality accommodations. It is impossible to say which accommodations are best, but the list will definitely include the Lodge at Vail, Sonnenalp, Christiania, Doubletree Hotel Vail, Radisson Resort Vail, and the Westin Hotel, to say nothing of numerous luxury condominiums.

The original hotel in Vail, **The Lodge at Vail**, is on the slopes and in the middle of village activity. The Lodge is run as a condominium hotel with 60 guest rooms, and 40 suites. From its impressive porte-cochère to its large moss rock fireplace, the lodge ranks among the top resort hotels in the world. All units are decorated with mahogany and teak paneling or trim and feature marble baths. The view from the rooms is either of the mountain itself or of picturesque Vail Village. A few accommodations contain fireplaces, balconies, and fully equipped kitchens. The decor is Swiss/Austrian-style with warm, fabric prints and brass fixtures.Just this past summer, the Lodge has finished redecoration of its guest rooms, including reupholstering the furniture and adding new floral bedspreads.

By far, the most impressive feature of The Lodge is the number of amenities it offers guests. Not only is there concierge service, but a valet greets all returning skiers and takes their skis to night storage. The valet also arranges for ski waxing or tuning and is responsive to any other guest needs. The Lodge has a swimming pool and Jacuzzi on the premises.

After skiing, go to The Lodge and relax in **Mickey's Bar**. While enjoying a favorite beverage, be entertained by Mickey who plays the piano each evening. Later enjoy dinner in the Lodge's informal **Cucina Rustica** or splurge on a fine meal at the **Wildflower Inn** restaurant, one of Vail's finest eating establishments. Rates during the 1993-94 season range from $290 per night for a hotel room during the Value Season to $655 per night for a one-bedroom condominium during Christmas week. (303)476-5011.

The Radisson Resort Vail is considerably less formal than The Lodge. It has 350 rooms and frequently caters to the convention trade. Located near the Gondola at LionsHead, the Radisson offers both hotel rooms and suites. Its motel-style rooms are furnished with queen-size beds and traditional furniture upholstered in southwestern mauves and blues. Guests who want to upgrade their lodging can request a suite, many of which have balconies, fireplaces, and fully equipped kitchens. There are 3 restaurants on site: Luigi's, Windows and Gallery. Prices during the 1993-94 season range from a low of $125 per night for a valley view room to a high of $290. Prices for suites begin at $90 to $285, depending on size, and peak at between $350 and $930 during the Christmas\New Year's holidays.(303)476-4444 or (800)333-3333.

The Sitzmark Lodge with its fine location exemplifies lodging which encourages people to return to Vail year after year.   Located on Gore Creek only a few steps from Vail's finest retail shops, the Sitzmark has only 35 rooms, each complete with color TV, HBO, and refrigerator. All rooms have views either of the mountain or of the creek. They are accented in dark shades of brown and tan and are traditionally furnished with commercial hotel furniture. Daily maid service is provided, as is guest laundry service and underground parking. Complimentary breakfast is served daily in the lobby, and guests are advised to take full advantage of the resort's sauna, steam room, and outdoor swimming pool.

1993-94 rates range from a low of $105 per night to a high of $210 per night for a DeLuxe room with fireplace.(303)476-5001

Europeans and Latin Americans tend to favor the **Sonnenalp**, a truly world-class hotel with all the expected amenities. Recently renovated and expanded, its hotel rooms remind one of a Bavarian lodge high in the German Alps. They have been tastefully furnished with Bavarian furniture that to the untrained eye looks like country French. Gray wool upholstery with orange piping complements the wood's natural patina.

The Sonnenalp consists of three buildings with heated outdoor pools, a health spa complete with tanning beds, exercise machines, Jacuzzi, and a beauty salon for the guests' exclusive use. There are two excellent restaurants and the **Bully III Pub**. Try to finish a Spaten Beer while visiting the pub; it's a full pint and is imported from Munich. Add a slice of lime for additional flavor.

A hotel room in the Sonnenalp, based on the European plan, ranged from $175 to $265 per night during the 1993-94 ski season. DeLuxe rooms and suites are priced considerably higher.(303)476-5656.

One of Vail's finest hotels is the **Westin**, located at 1300 Westhaven Drive in Cascade Village, in West Vail. Those familiar with Westin hotels in the country's major cities will not be disappointed with Vail's Westin. It is impeccably appointed in a mock Empire style. The central lobby features a see-through glass fireplace which is always blazing. Charlie Brown marble flooring with brass reveal sets off mahogany walls and furniture. The repetitive use of unusual building materials is pleasing to the eye and the juxtaposition of rough and smooth textures adds depth to the image, creating a comfortable ambiance. This is a large hotel with 290 rooms. Alcoves arranged along long hallways are decoratively furnished with comfortable chairs and armoires, inviting guests to linger a moment and write postcards or read the newspaper.

The **Lobby Bar** is across the foyer and features live entertainment beginning at 3:00 P.M. each day. Adjacent to the Lobby Bar is **Alfredo's Restaurant**. The mahogany and marble motif flows from the lobby into the restaurant. Primary seating is in large winged chairs or on comfortable banquettes. One wall constructed completely of etched glass depicts the Colorado mountain columbine; this same pattern of flowers is woven into the burnt red carpet.

Rooms at the Westin are comfortably large with views of either Vail Mountain or Vail Valley. Decorated in teals, mauves, and sea foam colors, all rooms feature amenities one is accustomed to expect from better hotels such as a private, stocked refrigerator and service bar, terry bathrobes, complimentary shampoo, conditioner, tooth paste, etc.

Right next to the hotel is the Cascade chairlift which whisks guests to the new Pride Express Chairlift on the LionsHead side of Vail Mountain in under eight minutes. From there it is seven miles to the Mongolian surface lift, a traverse which can be skied in under one half-hour and indicates just how large and well configured Vail really is.

Not only does the Westin have its own ski lift, it also has seven-thousand square feet of retail shops, two outdoor thermal spas and swimming pool, an on-site movie theater, health club (Cascade Club), 24-hour room service, concierge, valet parking, in-room movies, and complimentary shuttle service to Lionshead and Vail Village. Hotel rooms in The Westin rent for between $250 and $400 per night depending upon the time of year.(303)476-7111

Situated along the banks of fashionable Gore Creek in West Vail is the **Black Bear Inn of Vail**. A beautiful handcrafted log inn, it is conveniently located on the town bus route. Its seclusion is a welcome respite for tired skiers and non-skiers alike. This small, quaint inn has only twelve rooms, each tastefully decorated. There are ten rooms with queen-sized beds and two with twin beds. Adjacent rooms can sometimes be rented, offering guests the opportunity to make up mini-suites.

All the rooms are large, comfortable, and immaculate. There are no televisions, VCR's nor other twentieth century intrusions in the individual rooms. Each room does have a telephone. However, guests can enjoy a variety of activities in the great room—reading, relaxing with their favorite beverage in front of the glowing antique stove, or watching T.V. Although guests are welcome to bring young children with them, they should take into consideration that no activities have been planned for youngsters and they may become bored with the adult ambience.

The Black Bear's fare is typical of most bed and breakfast establishments. Both hot and cold breakfasts are offered along with a daily chef's special. In the evening beer, wine, snacks and appetizers are served in the great room. Room rates vary according to season. Early ski season is the best bargain with rooms renting for $80 per night, based on double occupancy. Rooms rented between the end of November and mid-April closing rent for between $105 and $185 per night.(303)476-1304.

Vail offers a multitude of condominium accommodations for virtually ever taste and budget. Some of the most convenient and best quality are **Northwoods**, just to the east of Gold Peak; **Westwind**, **Landmark**, **Vail 21**, **Enzian**, and **Vantage Point**, all in Lionshead. Contact Central Reservations for information and reservations.

Beaver Creek Accommodations

Beaver Creek represents the embodiment of a well-designed and planned resort. It did not just spring up like Aspen, Crested Butte, or even Vail. As such all of its architecture has been individually designed to complement the whole. There are no oddities, shanties, nor budget lodging. Staying in one hotel in Beaver Creek is almost like staying at any other. All are furnished impeccably and in good taste—if not somewhat alike. To book reservations at Beaver Creek, telephone (800) 525-2257.

The hub of Beaver Creek's lodging facilities is the **Hyatt Regency Hotel** located directly at the foot of the mountain, close to Centennial Express lift, Village Hall, and the ski school. This hotel could be located anywhere; its style is similar to that of countless Hyatts spread throughout America. Its grand central lobby is large and impressive with fine wood paneling, high ceilings, and views of the slopes. The hotel has a comfortable European feel to it—as does the entire resort. Tapestries, hunt paintings, antler chandeliers, and ornamental ironwork complete the cozy ambience.This hotel epitomizes luxury and service, down to the young men who rush to help you get your skis off as you glide to a stop after an exhausting day on Grouse Mountain and a cruise down Centennial.

The hotel has a small, well-decorated and equipped spa for non-skiers or skiers who want to relax and treat their tired muscles to some soothing therapy. The heated outdoor swimming pool is accessed from inside the spa. Guests need only walk down a few steps and duck under the glass windows to luxuriate in the warm waters. There is also a co-ed hot tub for lazy après-ski soaking. For the more energetic, the spa features Keiser Cam II pneumatic resistance equipment, Stairmaster 4000 PT, Precor treadmills, Lifecycles, etc. Numerous body treatments are available in the Total Beauty Centre's alcove such as sports massage, deep tissue massage, Shiatsu, reflexology, stress-release back treatment, and numerous skin treatments.

Hyatt Regency's largest and most formal restaurant is the **Patina Grill**, located just off the lobby. Open for breakfast (buffet), lunch, and dinner, it features a traditional menu including New York sirloin, grilled veal chop, trout Meunière. A reasonable wine selection is available, as are daily special entrées.

Situated at the end of a long corridor on the west side of the building is **The Crooked Hearth**. This casual, family-oriented restaurant features fondues cooked at your table, pizza from wood-burning oven, soups, salads, and sandwiches.

The Hyatt's guest rooms are typical of Hyatt rooms everywhere. Their nicely decorated interiors include warm down comforters, marble baths, and spectacular views of Beaver Creek Mountain or the Gore Range. Rooms are priced from $385 to $475 during the 1993-94 season. During early April's Value Season, prices drop to $170 to $220.

Similar to the Hyatt, although not as plush, the finely appointed **Charter at Beaver Creek** offers 246 hotel rooms, one-bedroom and two-bedroom condos. From its massive entrance to its well-furnished rooms, The Charter is an excellent choice for Beaver Creek guests. Rooms and condos have all the benefits found in the best world-class hotels, such as concierge, valet, laundry, and retail services. Whether a room or condo is selected, the accommodations will include a fireplace, balcony, and living area. Oak woodwork, leaded glass balcony doors, and ceramic tiling create a very comfortable ambiance——all convenient to the slopes!

Condos have the best appliances available and include Sub-Zero refrigerators, self-cleaning ovens, electric ranges, microwave ovens, dishwashers, washing machines and dryers. All guests are welcome to use the Charter's spa and health club facilities as well as the heated outdoor swimming pool and **Forum** lounge.

Trappers Cabin, perched on top of Beaver Creek mountain, has spectacular views. For a fantastic treat, which will cost $2,200 per person daily, spend a week secluded on the mountain in this luxurious 4-bedroom, 4-bath cabin. All meals are prepared for you.(303)949-2308.

For something different, also consider the **Wildridge Inn Bed and Breakfast**, a Santa Fe style home located 3 miles from Beaver Creek's base. This is advertised as a special place to have a wedding. The home was designed by local architect Eric Vogelmann, with many special custom features such as beamed ceilings, kiva fireplaces, quarry tile or wide pine floors. The interior is special, but the exterior western look and its surroundings also are beautiful. Enjoy sitting on the 900 square foot flagstone patio which faces breathtaking views of Beaver Creek and the back bowls of Vail. Only 3 rooms are available, including the honeymoon suite with its own fireplace, step-up oval tub with view of mountains and another fireplace, beam ceiling, wide pine floors with oriental rugs, double walk-in shower, decorated with lace, tapestry and tiffany lamps. A full hot breakfast is served in the winter. Feel truly at home in the mountains on this one acre of sage and wildflowers which the deer sometimes sample. Winter rates range from $139 to $185, with a 6-night minimum.(303)949-6064.

Other fine accommodations at Beaver Creek include the **Post Montane**, the **Inn at Beaver Creek**, and the **Centennial**.

Restaurants

With well over 100 restaurants in Vail, it is impossible to do all of them justice. However, a few stand out and should be reviewed since they are of such high quality.

The best restaurant in Vail right now is **Terra Bistro**, located near the east end of the parking structure in the Vail Athletic Club. Serving an eclectic menu of creative American cuisine, this restaurant has something to appeal to every taste. It uses all organic and chemical free foods, including their range fed meats. Some vegetarian dishes also are offered. Try the vegetable spring room, the oven roasted trout with ginger and leeks, grilled, marinated pork chops with pineapple salsa and sweet potato samosas, or the sweet dumpling squash with herbed lentils and kale. The vegetables are cooked to crisp perfection and the spices are perfect. Reservations are recommended.(303)476-6836.

Located high on a mountaintop just west of Vail/Beaver Creek, the **Cordillera resort** presents **Restaurant Picasso**. Under executive chef Jacques Deluc's direction, Picasso has been awarded both Guide Michelin's coveted four stars and Mobile's five stars. *Esquire* magazine listed it as one of the best new restaurants in their November 1989 issue. Picasso is situated in a corner of the Lodge at Cordillera, a charming 28-room hotel designed by Leon Lamotte in the style of an European aubèrge. The restaurant has been designed with its namesake's Catalan heritage in mind. Bargello fabrics and several Picasso prints and etchings enhance the decor. Deluc's kitchen is managed by a young Belgian chef, Philippe Van Cappellen, whose work history includes stints in many fine Continental restaurants. Picasso's menu may include such mouth-watering entrées as red snapper with rouille or noisettes of lamb with fava beans. For reservations telephone (303) 926-2200 or (800) 548-2721. This is a very expensive restaurant!

Another new and delicious restaurant is **Chill's**, located at the East Vail Racquet Club. Opened by the owners of the renowned Chillingsworth's restaurant in Brewster, Cape Cod, Massachusetts, some of the east coast staff has moved west for the winter season. The original menu includes an extensive wine list. Try the fantastic wild mushroom soup. The preparations of the meat dishes and fresh fish are uniformly delicious.

The Wildflower Inn located in the Lodge at Vail is an Old-World style restaurant. It is circular in design and overlooks Vail Mountain and village shops. The walls of its tiled entry are lined with custom-built cherry wine storage cabinets. Tables in the light and airy dining room are set with fine linens and beautiful china. Large clusters of fresh-cut and silk flowers provide spectacular displays on tables, cabinet shelves, and even hang from baskets suspended from the ceiling. The expert architectural use of low steps creates a terraced effect, lending character to the room. The dominant color is white, and the contrast of the floral arrangements is stunning.

The Continental menu is equal to the ambience of the room; a variety of creative items is presented along with daily specials. Service is excellent. Due to the Wildflower's popularity, guests are advised to book dinner reservations during peak seasons two to four months in advance. For reservations telephone (303) 476-5011.

Another excellent dining choice has to be **La Tour**. Owned by Marie-Claire and Walter Moritz, La Tour is truly a family affair; Walter is the chef and Marie-Claire is the hostess. Because this restaurant is so popular, it is advisable to book reservations several days in advance (or longer) during peak holiday periods such as Christmas.

La Tour has a French menu and features several selections of veal, poultry, game, beef, lamb, and seafood in addition to daily specials. Walter's creations are served in an intimate dining room furnished in the Swiss/Austrian style so prevalent in Vail. Located at 121 East Meadow Dr., La Tour is in the center of Vail's activity. For reservations telephone (303) 476-4403.

In addition, gourmets should plan to visit **The Left Bank,** which serves excellent Continental and nouvelle cuisine. The Left Bank is located on Gore Creek Dr., Vail's Rodeo Drive. The Left Bank has been a traditional favorite of locals and tourists alike. Indeed, it has maintained its status as Vail's premier restaurant for over 25 years. The restaurant is owned and operated by Luc Meyer and his wife who assure diners prompt, courteous service. The Left Bank's extensive menu is dwarfed by the four-page wine list which would rival any restaurant's cellars. A broad offering of California and French wine dominates, but there are also representations from Italy and Australia. Reservations are obligatory; this restaurant is always crowded during the season. No smoking is allowed in the dining room; credit cards are not accepted but cash is perfectly acceptable! Before or after dinner it is always fun to take a short walk and look in the shops along this very exclusive street. For reservations telephone (303) 476-3696.

Sweet Basil, located at 193 E. Gore Creek Drive, is one of Vail's most popular dining spots. Featuring exquisite American cuisine, Sweet Basil is a must for the visiting skier. Typical entrées may include North Atlantic king salmon with a potato crust, grilled red onions, spinach, and cabernet butter sauce; grilled range chicken with roast garlic, peppers and eggplant, mustard vinaigrette, and parsley linguine; or striped bass sautéed with red and yellow tomato fennel relish, matchstick potatoes. For reservations telephone (303) 476-0125.

Only a few blocks from Sweet Basil on East Meadow Drive is **Alpenrose Tea Room & Restaurant**. This charming German/Austrian style establishment features many items from chef Claus's homeland, as well as traditional Continental items. Open for breakfast, lunch, and dinner, a visit to the Alpenrose should be on all skiers' agendas. On warm days, sit outside under one of the restaurant's colorful umbrellas and watch skiers from all over the world trek by. Make a dessert selection from the bountiful Confiserie-Patisserie display or select some fresh-baked goods to take back to the condo for later enjoyment. For reservations telephone (303) 476-3194.

Situated in a garret high above the Alpenrose Tea Room is **Ambrosia**, another of Vail's finest restaurants. Its medieval-inspired decor of dark paneling and tapestries provides the perfect setting for a fabulous meal. Typical offerings may include salmon béarnaise, côtes de veau aux champignons, elk steak "Diana", chateaubriand "Jardiniere", or noisettes d'agneau "Windsor". Telephone (303) 476-1964 for reservations.

Blu's at 193 Gore Creek Dr. is similar in ambience to Sweet Basil. It is, however, slightly more informal. There is a pleasant bustle about Blu's that is absent at Sweet Basil. Blu's menu can only be described as creative American. It features dishes such as sautéed sea scallops, veal forrestier, fresh fish in papillotte, "kick ass" California chicken relleno, two grilled fish with sauces, gypsy schnitzel, and scampi penne carbonara. Reservations are not accepted; it is not unusual at lunch and dinner to wait 15 to 45 minutes for a table. The waiting area and bar is limited, forcing diners to queue-up outside.

The Tyrolean Inn, located in the unusual looking building you pass on the way to Gold Peak on the east side of the parking structure, specializes in wild game. In fact the owner of the restaurant raises much of it on his ranch near Glenwood Springs. Their game and beef, lamb, pasta are all delicious, and the vegetables also are cooked crisp and presented beautifully. (303)476-2204.

Montauk, situated near the Lionshead gondola station, is the best seafood restaurant in Vail. A renovation has replaced its former nautical ambiance with a more contemporary design. Its open kitchen and airy interior are both casual and comfortable. Each day's fresh fish selections are listed on numerous chalk boards mounted throughout the restaurant and as might be expected, Montauk's menu changes daily. Although beef, poultry, and pasta are offered on the menu, most diners opt for seafood. Prices are based on market but are generally competitive with what anyone would expect to pay in Chicago, Dallas, or Los Angeles. For après-ski Montauk features a raw bar; in spring the restaurant's large outdoor patio is a frequent meeting spot for young adults. Telephone (303) 476-2601 for reservations. Only Mastercard and Visa are accepted.

Those diners adventurous enough to stray from beautiful Vail Valley will find several interesting "locals" restaurants within a ten to fifteen-minute drive. **The Gas House** is found just west of Beaver Creek in the small town of Edwards. This former U.S. Highway 6 Conoco station is one of the area's liveliest night spots. Around 9 P.M. each weekend evening, entertainment is provided to a packed house. The drink of choice here is beer; firehouse chile is a favorite menu selection.

The town of Minturn lies just west of Vail, two miles south of the U.S. 6 and I-70 intersection. Until recently it functioned primarily as a source of inexpensive housing for Vail employees. Today, however, the town has grown (only slightly) to incorporate a fine Tex-Mex restaurant, **Chilly Willy's**, a very popular and credible Mexican restaurant know only as the **Saloon**, an assortment of art galleries, espresso houses, and a charming bed and breakfast hotel called Eagle River Inn.

        Mirabelle at Beaver Creek Restaurant is a favorite of most Vail Valley visitors. Located at the entrance to Beaver Creek, this award-winning restaurant is owned and operated by the same people who own and operate Vail's Left Bank restaurant. Mirabelle's is believed to be situated on the site of Vail Valley's first home. The building was constructed in 1881-82; however, the actual restaurant part of the building was built in 1981, its style faithfully duplicating that of the original structure. The casual glance cannot discern where old and new meet. However, it is the food at Mirabelle's that is most memorable. The menu is decidedly French. Appetizers include such delectables as le fromage de chèvre (goat cheese en croute with red onions and a creamy goat cheese sauce), and les pâtés fraîches aux escargots (capellini past served with escargots, fresh herbs, tomatoes, and olive oil). Hot appetizers are just as creative—gravlax de saumon à la crème de moutarde et champignons (salmon cured with dill and cracked pepper, thinly sliced and served with a light dijon mustard cream and mushrooms) or la salade frisée de canard aux framboises (warm duck salad with raspberry and walnut dressing). Entrées may include feuilletés aux poissons et aux moules (assorted fish and mussels in puff pastry with a creamy herb sauce or carré d'agneau "provençale" (roasted rack of lamb with whole grain mustard, garlic, tomatoes, herbs and a light lamb sauce).

        Mirabelle's wine list is one of the valley's best, although all the selections are French. No credit cards are accepted; cash or approved checks are the only method of payment permitted. For reservations, telephone (303) 949-7728 after 1 P.M.

        For an adventure as well as a delightful evening, treat yourself to an evening at **Beano's Cabin**. This rustic, but elegant log cabin is tucked into Larkspur Bowl on Beaver Creek mountain. For lunch it is open to club members only, but in the evening, wrap up in warm clothes, have a schnapps before departure, and sit back on a sleigh ride drawn by a snowcat for a ride up the mountain. The sparkling interior lights invite you in as you arrive at the cabin. Check your coat and enjoy a six course meal and live music. Prices are $69 per person, $46 for children under 12. Alcohol and tip are not included.

        Laid back, comfortable service is the watchword at **The Bristol at Arrowhead**, a country club located only a few miles west of Beaver Creek. While the club itself is private, the Bristol dining room is open to the public. Guests will enjoy watching magnificent sunsets over the western high desert, as they peruse the excellent menu from their comfortable chairs. Featured appetizers may include baked oysters, angel hair pasta, steamed New Zealand green lip mussels, or the traditional favorite of escargot and artichoke hearts. Typical entrées may include blackened salmon, yellow-pepper linguini, grilled chicken breast, roast veal loin, or roast rack of lamb, priced competitively at $12 to $18 per entrée. Telephone (303) 476-0200 for reservations.

        The Gateway Center, located at Vail's main entrance, is home to three impressive restaurants: **The Siamese Orchid, Michael's,** and **Pizza and Páne**. These three restaurants offer foods as diverse as their names would suggest.

        Michael's is found on the third floor of Gateway Center; its tables overlook an atrium decorated with the creative woodcarvings of Dieter Menzel. An American version of the French bistro, Michael's decor is sophisticated and understated. Its inviting lounge is furnished with green marble tables and colorful pull-up chairs. Private wine lockers line its walls and provide amused diners with a subject of conversation.

        The restaurant's focal point is its open kitchen where skilled chefs hurry back and forth. Typical entrées may include delicious grilled breast of duck, tuna pepper steak with ginger, sea scallops with pistachio nut crust, grilled veal loin, or a perennial favorite - elk tenderloin! Additionally, several gourmet pizzas are prepared daily, as are numerous other specials. Michael's should be a "must" on everyone's list of places to eat. Prices are moderate to high; telephone (303) 476-5353 for reservations.

Gourmands and locals in-the-know head for Pizza and Páne, on the second floor of Gateway Center, to enjoy world-class pizza and pasta. Traditional Italian favorites, as well as creative, lighter entrées, are this restaurant's forte. Reservations are not accepted here; prices are moderate.

An inexpensive place in Vail for a quick lunch, dinner, drink or late night appetizer is the **Hubcap Brewery and Kitchen**, located in the Crossroad Shopping Center. They have some delicious varieties of original beers to sample and sandwiches and salads to eat.

The Fulton Ironworks is a moderately prices restaurant which offers steak, seafood, pastas, chicken and some vegetarian dishes. Unlimited house wine is offered for $3 per person, and guests may have unlimited fresh salad and homemade soup. Reservations are recommended, so call (303)476-4501 to reserve a spot and to ask how to find this restaurant, which advertises itself as "Vail's Hardest to find Restaurant!"

Other moderately priced casual dining establishments include the **Uptown Grill**, (best wine list in Vail), **Gasthof Gramshammer**, **Bart & Yeti's**, **The Chart House**, **Lionshead Bar & Grill**, **D.J. McCadam's**, **Cyrano's**, and **Ledges**.

Visitors should be aware that many Vail restaurants are closed on Monday and that (as previously noted) several do not accept American Express credit cards.

Activities

One of Vail's most popular activities is shopping. Other than Aspen, no other U.S. resort offers such extensive shopping selections. Most of the fine shops are situated along Gore Creek Dr. and include The Golden Bear, Fila, Ralph Lauren, Helga of Vail, Cartier, Benetton, and Crabtree & Evelyn. Numerous art galleries are also found throughout Vail, and visitors are always impressed by the many sculptures situated among the malls and walkways.

For the non-skier or for the person who just wants to take a day off from the slopes, numerous activities run the gamut from active to passive. Ice-skating is available daily at the indoor John A. Dobson Arena. Snowmobile tours are conducted through the White River National Forest. The staff will also provide a guide, if one is desired, as well as a warm suit and boots. Because weather conditions change rapidly in the mountains, be sure to take along warm mittens, goggles, and sunglasses. If you have never driven a snowmobile, it can be an exhilarating experience. Snowmobiles are as easy to operate as a lawnmower, so do not hesitate to try them on the basis of a misguided idea that they are difficult to operate.

Bobsledding is offered daily for $12 per person. The bobsled track is conveniently located adjacent to the number 2, (or Avanti) lift.

Unique activities include snowcat-drawn sleigh rides to Beano's Cabin in Beaver Creek, located 10 miles west of Vail. This is not only an enjoyable ride, but Beano's meals and service are peerless. What a truly great way to spend the evening!

Briefly, other available activities include

Heli-Skiing
Sleigh Rides

Snowcat Tours
Wildlife Tours
Hot Air Ballooning
Racquetball/Squash
Indoor Tennis
Swimming
Snowshoeing
Vail Library
Ski Museum

The most expansive health facilities are located across the street from the Westin Hotel at the **Cascade Club**. Comprising over 70,000 square feet, the Cascade Club is available to all Vail visitors for a $25 daily fee. If you stay at the Westin that price is $7.50 per day, and at certain other lodges, $15 per day. This club features four indoor tennis courts, four squash courts, two racquetball courts, a half-court, full Nautilus and free weight training center, indoor running track, aerobics studios and classes, gymnasium, year-round outdoor swimming pool and thermal spa, men's and women's steam rooms, individual massage rooms and suntanning studios, and a sports medicine center. The Cascade Club also has a very nice bar and short-order grill called Achilles Restaurant. The premises are kept clean and the equipment is well maintained. This club is truly as fine a health facility as can be found in any major American city.For more information call (303)476-7400.

Somewhat smaller, some would say more intimate, the **Vail Athletic Club** has recently been renovated, and its up-dated decor is quite fetching. The facility is located at 352 East Meadow Drive, convenient to Bridge Street and the Vista Bahn lift. Hoggan Camstar physical fitness equipment, a full range of free-weights, and numerous cardiovascular equipment is available to members and guests. In addition, personalized fitness consultations and instruction are available. A twenty-meter indoor lap pool, mens' and ladies' locker facilities, snack bar, aerobic and daily fitness classes complete the amenities. Unique to the Athletic Club is an indoor rock-climbing wall. Basketball, racquetball, squash and ping pong is available, as well as a full-service pro shop and retail center. Jacuzzi's and sundecks are just outside. As with any good club, child care is available, as are tanning beds, and various types of massage. 1993-94 fees for the daily guest are $25. For additional information telephone (303) 476-0700.

The magnificent **Spa at Cordillera** is one of those wonderful anomalies one can only find in the mountains. Situated high atop a mountain overlooking the New York Range's mighty peaks, this spa is peerless. In addition to a 2,000 acre "outdoor aerobics room" for cross-country skiing, hiking, and mountain biking, the following services are offered: an indoor lap pool, heated outdoor pool, Kaiser weight and aerobics room, exercise classes including aquatic aerobics, hydrobaths, massage, aromatheraphy, physical therapy, body and skin treatment. Personalized spa treatments are also available upon request. The spa offers "A Day Away" which consists of total use of the spa and fitness facilities, a nutritiously balanced lunch, massage, choice of a hydrotub or a facial, and a beauty salon choice of wash and blow-dry, manicure, or pedicure.

Located under the parking garage at LionsHead is the **Vail Teen Center**. The Teen Center is a two-story building with ping pong and pool tables on the second floor, while its main floor is divided into several unique restaurants. There is a snack shop with video games and an ice cream parlor with fousball. The music is loud, as befits such a facility. The Center is open for children and young adults aged six to nineteen.

Movies are shown daily at both the Crossroads Cinema and at the Cascade Theater. Ski movies such as those by Warren Miller are also featured at special times.

Services

A full complement of sporting goods stores, apparel stores, pharmacies, grocery stores, liquor stores, furniture, bath, and specialty stores is within the immediate town. In addition tourists can enjoy antique stores, acupressure services, art galleries, bakeries, beauty salons, bookstores, florists, flotations tanks, massage, and tanning studios.

Vail Village Map

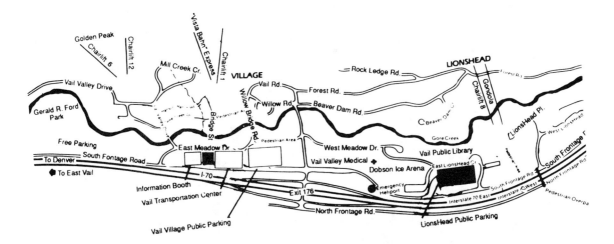

Beaver Creek Village Map_g

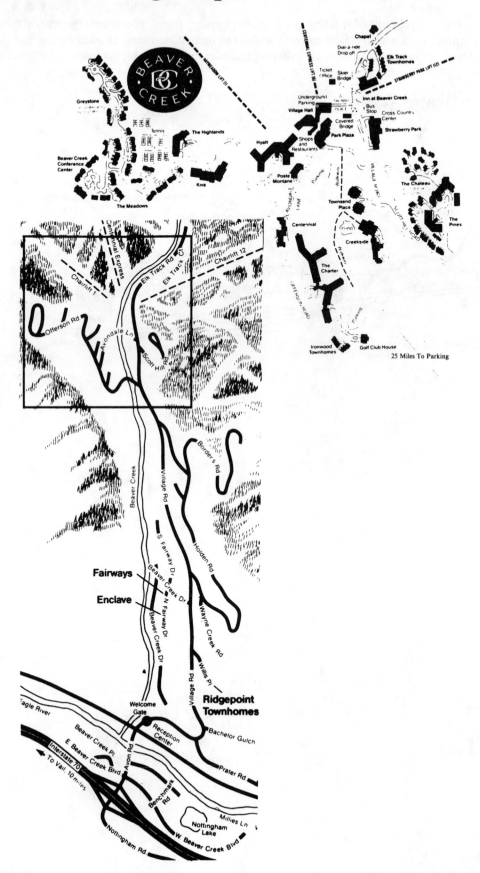

WHISTLER/BLACKCOMB

P.O. Box 1400
Whistler, B.C.
Canada V0N 1B0

(800) 944-7853 Reservations
(604) 932-2394 Information
Snow Reports
(604) 932-4211 Blackcomb
(604) 932-4191 Whistler

New For 1993-94

During the past two years, Whistler and Blackcomb have concentrated on improving lifts on their mountain, this year both have renovated restaurants on their mountains. At Blackcomb the resort has renovated Glacier Bite lodge, renaming it **Glacier Creek**. The restaurant and bistro combined now will seat 1,000, and a ski school desk and ski shop have been added to the structure. It is located at the bottom of the Glacier Express high speed detachable quad chair which was added to the mountain last year.

At Whistler, **Pika's** Restaurant has been doubled in size, adding 500 more seats. Massive new windows also have been added to enhance visitors views of their beautiful surroundings.

The World Cup Freestyle Championships will take place on Blackcomb Mountain Jan. 7 to 9, 1994. And Whistler Mountain will host the World Cup Down hill and Super G races March 5 to 6 and 12 to 13. Both men and women racers will be racing.

This year Whistler/Blackcomb resorts again were honored by the readers of Snow Country magazine, who voted the Dual Mountain area the number one ski resort in North America.

How To Get There

The gateway to Whistler and Blackcomb mountains is Vancouver, B.C., Canada. It is served by all major U.S. and Canadian air carriers. Vancouver International Airport is a modern facility situated on the south side of the city. Although located at the extreme edge of the North American Continent, Whistler/Blackcomb is relatively easy to reach. Vancouver proper is almost never shut down due to inclement weather. Protected as it is from extreme temperatures and snow by the Japanese current, its vegetation is similar to that found in traditionally more temperate areas such as Dallas, Texas.

From Vancouver, there are several ways to get to Whistler Village, the base facility strategically located at the foot of both Whistler and Blackcomb Mountains. Hertz, Avis, and Tilden car rentals are available at Vancouver International Airport. Individuals interested in renting automobiles should make certain their rental cars come equipped with snow tires and ski racks. The roads leading to the resort can be snow packed or even closed in sections. In order to experience minimum delays during periods of heavy snow, travelers are advised to carry tire chains.

Perimeter Transportation operates Whistler Express several times daily between the airport and Whistler Village. Telephone (604)266-5386 or 261-2299 for information and current schedules; reservations are required. During the 1992-93 ski season one-way fare between Vancouver International Airport and Whistler Village is $26.75 per adult and $14 per child[1]. Children under 5 are free. On request, Perimeter will stop at major Vancouver hotels. Passengers are urged to allow up to four hours for transport to the resort. However, when weather conditions are favorable, the trip generally only requires two and one-half hours.

Daily bus departures from downtown Vancouver can be arranged with **Maverick Coach Lines**. During the 1991-92 ski season Maverick has scheduled six departures beginning at 6:30 A.M and continuing through 7:00 P.M. for Whistler Village. The fare is only $13 one-way per person. For schedule information and exact pick-up locations, telephone (604) 932-5031.

Groups can charter buses through **Glacier Coach Lines**. Call (604)932-2705.

For a chance to do something a little unusual, Whistler/Blackcomb visitors should consider taking the ski train from the North Vancouver station. Tickets during the 1993-94 season are only $24.00 one-way for adults; $21 for seniors and youths 12 to 18; and $12 for chidren 2 to 11. For tickets leaving and returning to Vancouver on the same day, the fare will be $18 for adults; $15.75 for seniors and youths and $9 for children. Please call BC Rail at (604)984-5246 for information.

Even the most jaded traveler cannot fail to be impressed by the scenery in British Columbia. This is truly one of the world's most beautiful landscapes—jagged, snow-capped mountains, lush vegetation, rushing waterfalls, and the nearby straits all compete for the viewer's attention along the Sea to Sky Highway between Vancouver and Whistler/Blackcomb.

Regular shuttle bus service is available throughout Whistler Village, as well as other areas within the valley including Whistler Creek (the original base village at Whistler Mountain). Fare during the 1992-93 season is expected to remain at $1.50.

Mountain Information

Whistler/Blackcomb are two separate mountains each with different owners and individual operations. Nationally throughout Canada and the United States, however, the two mountains are marketed together in what is called the "Dual Mountain Programs." Both mountains are accessible from Whistler Village, and skiers may purchase dual-mountain ski passes or individual passes for each mountain. Although the mountains are adjacent to one another, they each enjoy their own character, and first-time visitors will undoubtedly select one or the other mountain as their personal favorite.

Whistler Mountain

---

[1] All prices quoted in this chapter are in Canadian funds. Visiting Americans and other foreign nationals will find U.S. currency readily accepted in all hotels, restaurants, etc. Exchange may also be purchased at Vancouver International Airport. At the time of this writing, the U.S. dollar was worth between $1.15 & $1.17 Canadian dollars.

Southern Californians will be struck by the physical similarities between Whistler Mountain and Mammoth Mountain. Both mountains are gladed on the lower slopes, and their tops are barren, snow-covered bowls.

Located in Garibaldi Provincial Park, Whistler has a total of 3,657 skiable acres (1,480 ha)and more than 100 marked trails, as well as a glacier and 5 alpine bowls where you make your own trails. The base elevation of Whistler Mountain is 2,140 feet (652 m.) and its summit is at 7,160 feet (2,176 m.). This provides skiers with 5,020 vertical feet (1,526 m.) of skiing. This mountain and Blackcomb both provide the two longest vertical drops in North American ski resorts. This terrain is serviced by

1 10-person high speed gondola
3 High-speed quad chairlifts
2 Double chairlifts
3 Triple chairlifts
2 T-Bars
2 Handle Tows

Whistler Mountain's trails are composed of 20% of its trails are expert, 55% intermediate, and 25% novice terrain, with its longest run of 5.8 miles leading from the Peak of Whistler through Symphony Bowl, Sidewinder and the Olympic Run to Whistler Village.

Whistler's uphill lift capacity has grown to 22,295, there are few lift lines.

Being the older of the two ski mountains, Whistler tends to have more double and triple fall lines than Blackcomb, and the trails through the trees are slightly narrower. Skiing at Whistler is exciting because the runs are so long. In fact, many of the runs are among the longest in North America.

Whistler boasts high-speed access to the high alpine skiing with its gondola and 2 new high-speed quad chairs. Service from the base at Whistler Village to the Mountain House Station three-quarters of the way up the mountain is by an unusual 10-passenger gondola called Whistler Express. What makes it so unusual is that passengers take their skis in the gondola with them. Around the interior perimeter is a narrow bench that passengers can lean against or "sort of" sit on. It takes eighteen minutes to travel 16,444 feet (5,012 m). Typical skiing on Whistler usually occurs off the various chairs serving the immediate terrain around Round House Station. Most skiers only ski the entire length of the mountain at the end of the day.

Two years ago at Whistler Mountain two new high-speed quad chairlifts, Redline and Quicksilver were installed. These two lifts are arranged one after the other; Quicksilver replaced the old gondola and Olive Chair and is fitted with a Porsche-designed plexiglass enclosure. The Redline replaced the old Big Red and Little Red chairs. Other changes at Whistler included a new $30 million day lodge, a 170-room hotel, and over 300 new condominium or townhouse units. Last year Whistler opened 5 kilometers of new trails on 25.5 new acres which increase access to the Whistler Creek side terrain.

Most of the chairlifts accessible from Round House Station are identified by color. Notable exceptions are Peak Chair and the Alpine T-bars, all situated on the uppermost part of the mountain. Experts will particularly love to ski Peak Chair. It serves Whistler Bowl and West Bowl. Both bowls are excellent examples of what single black diamond skiing should be like. The runs are steep but not too moguled, and there is lots of area in which to select a run. All the runs on the upper part of the mountain are in snowfields and so are totally skiable. During the week when the resort has fewer skiers, fresh powder can last for days because the area is so vast. West Bowl is reached by traversing across the midsection of Whistler Bowl. Upon arriving at the top of West Bowl, skiers may select the particular type of terrain they feel like skiing. To the left, a long traverse will center them in a large, snow-filled bowl. To the right, they can ski perfect gladed runs. The steepness and the extent of glades vary along the top ridge, so experience and conditions offer the experts unlimited tests of their skill.

Intermediates will find there is a tremendous amount of terrain to explore on Whistler. A good way to start to learn the ways of the mountain is to begin with a run down Whistler Glacier, which is accessible via either of the two Alpine T-bars. Smooth as silk and always groomed, the glacier is a great introduction to the wily charms of Whistler.

Intermediates will next want to examine Harmony Bowl, also at the top of the T-bars. This is similar to the expert terrain and provides excellent training for the intermediate who aspires to become an expert.

After skiing Harmony a few times, consider traversing along the upper portion of Harmony Bowl and ski into the remote and beautiful Burnt Stew Bowl. Although much of the 1,532 acres of high alpine bowls at Whistler present the skier with steep challenges, two beginner routes are maintained:the magnificent Burntstew Trail through Symphony Bowl and Highway 86 below West Bowl give skiers of all levels the chance to rest their legs and take in the stunning views. Burnt Stew Bowl provides intermediate skiers with a total feeling of back-country skiing. It is not skied as much as the rest of Whistler and is removed from the rest of the resort by the high calderas of Harmony Bowl. It is a place to be at one with nature and on a clear day, to marvel at the beauty of the numerous surrounding peaks and glaciers.

One of the best things about Whistler Mountain is that beginning skiers have the opportunity to ski all over the mountain's midsection. Beginner trails (not just catwalks) are woven into the pattern of the expert and intermediate runs emanating from the chairlifts around Round House Station. Also, beginners can develop a feel for skiing because the runs are long enough for them to begin to appreciate the natural rhythm developed by skiing uninterruptedly for lengthy periods of time.

Whistler receives an annual snowfall of about 360 inches (1,143 cm) per year.

Although Whistler Mountain has one of the longest vertical drops of any ski resort in North America, its base elevation is quite low. Because of this low elevation and the warm Japanese current just a few miles off the coast of British Columbia, Whistler occasionally gets rain instead of snow during its ski season. It can happen at any time, although most locals agree that the best snow conditions year after year occur during February or early March. However, should it rain during a visit, be of strong heart. Rain hardly ever occurs on the upper two-thirds of the mountain during the season and even on those rare occasions when it does, the rain is usually of short duration and followed by snow within a day or two.

Whistler has an extensive snowmaking capability from the bottom of the Red Chair to the base of Whistler Village and Whistler Creek. Snowmaking augments natural conditions during the early days of the season and extends the ability to ski to the base village at the season's end.

Blackcomb Mountain

Blackcomb Mountain is a much younger ski mountain than Whistler, having opened its gates in 1980. Whistler opened in 1965. This becomes readily apparent to most skiers when they take the time to ski both mountains. Blackcomb's runs are broader and straighter than are Whistler's. Some locals say Blackcomb is a more intermediate mountain than Whistler. Each skier should be his own judge on this matter, however.

The longest beginner run on Blackcomb is Mainline at 4.5 miles (8 km); the longest intermediate run is Cruiser at 3 miles (5 km), and the longest expert run is Gear Jammer at 1.25 miles (2 km). For a really long ride, try the longest run on the mountain: from the top of 7th Heaven to the bottom Cruiser is 7 miles (11 km.).

Like Whistler, Blackcomb is heavily gladed on its lower two-thirds. The upper one-third is primarily expert. Skiers can get to the upper third of the mountain by taking take the 7th Heaven

Express located on the west side of the mountain. From the midstation and Rendezvous Restaurant, interested skiers should take Expressway to the base of the high-speed quad. Most of the runs down the face of 7th Heaven Express are intermediate and begin in large, open snowfields and meander down to trails cut through the moss-laden Scotch pines. However, lying in a southwesterly direction is Xhiggy's Meadow which contains some expert runs. On fair weather days, experts sometimes hike to the cornice just above the meadow and enjoy untracked powder there when it is not otherwise available.

From the top of 7th Heaven Express, it is also possible to ski down onto the Horstman Glacier and enjoy its primarily intermediate skiing. Those who traverse across the top of Horstman Glacier or ski down the ridge from the snack bar situated at the terminus of the lift will find Saudan Couloir. Saudan Couloir is wide as far as couloirs go but extremely steep, with conditions that can change hourly depending on how frequently it is skied. This is one of several runs in the same area that rate double black diamonds to indicate that they are indeed more difficult than single black diamonds. From the top of the couloir and extending northwest towards Rendezvous Restaurant, a ridge called Blackcomb Ridge is both skiable and worthy of a double black diamond rating. Care must be taken to ski any of these runs only after the ski patrol has inspected them and deemed them safe. They are very avalanche prone and particularly in the spring must be watched on a daily basis. Other expert runs emanate off Secret Bowl and down into Jersey Cream Chair.

Last year's opening of the Glacier Express, a high speed detachable quad chairlift, has improved skier access to both the Horstman and Blackcomb Glaciers. Traveling 1,952 (595 m.) in just 6.5 minutes, the Glacier Express has the capacity to carry 7,700 skiers per hour in above tree line terrain. Blackcomb's total lift capacity is 26,400 skiers per hour. The resort's management says the new lift has eased lift lines on the 7th Heaven express and reduced turnaround time to the glacier and other high alpine areas.

Intermediate skiing at Blackcomb is terrific! Not only is there acre after acre of groomed runs, there is also the flexibility of being able to confidently ski the mountain top to bottom and see all types of terrain. From the top of Solar Coaster Express to the top of Wizard Express are some of the finest, wide-cut runs in North America. The fall lines are generally straight down the face of the mountain, and the moguls are kept to a respectable minimum by trail-grooming crews. In the spring intermediates are treated to a real learning experience as the conditions change every few thousand vertical feet. There may be soft, fluffy powder on the top of the mountain, soft pack one-third of the way down, hard pack halfway down, silky snow with a consistency of cornstarch two-thirds of the way down, and on the last third, heavy, wet snow.

On Blackcomb even beginning skiers can ski from top to bottom. From the Horstman Hut atop the 7th Heaven Express to the base at Whistler Village is the longest vertical drop in North America, and it can all be skied by beginners!

Blackcomb Mountain has grown to include 3,340 (1,352 ha) of skiable terrain.

Blackcomb's base elevation is 2,214 feet (675 m) and its summit is at 7,494 feet (2,284 m) giving it a total of 5,280 vertical feet (1,609 m) of skiing.

This terrain is serviced by

1   Covered quad chairlift (Wizard Express)
4   High-speed quad chairlifts
5   Triple chairlifts
1   Double chairlift
2   T-bars
1 Handle tow

Blackcomb's uphill lift capacity is 26,350 skiers per hour. The number of skiable acres divided by the maximum number of skiers transported per hour is .127. Crowding on the slopes should not be a problem.

The average monthly temperatures during the ski season at the summit restaurant elevation are

Nov.	25°	-4° C
Dec.	15°	-9° C
Jan.	16°	-8° C
Feb.	20°	-6° C
Mar.	20°	-6° C
Apr.	26°	-3° C

Of the over 200 trails on both mountains, 25% are expert, 55% intermediate, and 20% beginner.

Dual Mountain Lift Ticket Prices (1993-94)

Adult
(19 - 64)

3 days	$132
4 days	$172
5 of 6 days	$205
6 of 7 days	$234
7 of 8 days	$273
Blackcomb, Full Day	$44
Youth, 13 to 18, Blackcomb	$36
Daily Children, 7 to 12, Blackcomb	$19
Children under 6 ski free	

Hours of Operation

9:00 A.M. to 3:00 P.M. weekdays prior to February 1, 1993
9:00 A.M. to 3:30 P. M. weekdays after February 1, 1992

Lift Ticket Purchase Locations

Lift tickets may be purchased at the base of the gondola in Whistler Creek, the base of Whistler Express in Whistler Village, at Carlton Lodge across from the Fitzsimmons Chair, and at the base of Wizard Express covered quad.

How To Avoid Crowds

Because Whistler/Blackcomb are situated within a one and a half hour drive from a major city, it should surprise no one that these two mountains can become crowded during weekends. The best way to avoid weekend crowds is to plan a ski week beginning on Sunday and ending on Saturday. This way, there will only be one day of crowding to contend with, rather than two if the traditional Saturday to Saturday were selected.

When crowded conditions cannot be avoided, skiers are advised to concentrate on skiing the lower half of the mountains where runs are hardly ever crowded, except after 3:00 P.M. when most skiers begin the return to their accommodations. Also, on Blackcomb, ski the Stoker or Catskinner chairs. On Whistler, ski Redline, Orange or the Green chair. Black Chair can be a good choice for experts

choice for experts when Peak Chair becomes crowded. Although congestion exists along all lower runs late
in the afternoon, it is not nearly as bad as in many resorts because there are so many choices of ways down. All in all, both mountains are exceptional ski resorts.

Ski School

The combined ski schools of Whistler and Blackcomb employ up to 270 ski instructors. Recognized as two of the best ski schools in Canada, they offer numerous choices of instructional programs. Never-ever and novice skiers can enroll in either school's beginner programs. Blackcomb's beginner program is called **First Timers** and includes a two-hour lesson, all-day equipment rental, and an appropriate lift ticket. The cost for this program in 1991-92 was $39. Classes begin daily at 10:00 A.M. and 12:30 P.M. All beginner classes meet at Whistler Express or at the ski school located in Whistler Creek.

Skiers with little previous experience may enroll in Blackcomb's novice/intermediate program. Each lesson is for two and a half-hours and cost $31 in 1991-92. Classes meet daily on Rendezvous Ridge at 10:00 A.M. Blackcomb's private lesson during the same period was priced at $60 per hour or $290 for a full day.

In 1993-94, Whistler's ski school again offers beginners its **Learn To Ski** program which includes a two and one half-hour lesson, all-day equipment rental, and an appropriate lift ticket. Last year its price was $40. At press time, the new price was not available. Novice and intermediate lessons on Whistler Mountain were $32 for a two and one-half hour session. Lessons meet daily at 9:15 A.M.and 12:15 P.M. Students should meet their instructors in front of the alpine status board located next to the Whistler Express base station in Whistler Village. Private lesson fees at Whistler are the same as at Blackcomb. All ski school rates are subject to a 7 percent gst.

Both mountains offer a variety of specialty ski instruction programs which include the popular selections of bumps only, parallel perfection, powder clinics, and racing clinics. Interested prospective students should contact either ski school for additional information. Telephone Blackcomb at (604) 932-3141 or Whistler at (604) 932-3434.

Several years ago both Whistler and Blackcomb recognized that destination skiers would not choose between the two mountains, and that they should cooperate and promote a program in which skiers could utilize the assets of both mountain complexes. Out of this idea grew **Ski Esprit**. Ski Esprit is a dual-mountain program designed especially for destination skiers. Reminiscent of the "Ski Week" programs offered by Taos Ski Valley, Ski Esprit is a weekly ski program that utilizes both mountains and their respective ski school instructors. Group sizes are limited to no more than eight skiers. Skiers are first grouped with other skiers of similar ability. Through consensus the group tells its instructor each day what particular skills they want to work on. The day is then spent working on technique while skiing both mountains and learning about each area's terrain. People who have participated in this program give it high marks because they have left the program better skiers and made friendships they would not likely have made, left to their own devices. During 1992-93 the 3-day Ski Esprit program will cost $155, and the 4-day, $190. For more information on the Ski Esprit program, telephone (604) 932-3400.

For children at Blackcomb, three programs are offered. Register at the Kids Kamp at the base of the Wizard lift.

For children 2 to 3 years, **Wee Wizards,** is a program including one hour of skiing in the morning and one in the afternoon, playtime, lunch and snack and playtime, with occasion excursions to the fire hall or the chocolate factory. The price is $45 including boots, skis, lunch, lessons.

For children from 4 to 12 years of age, Blackcomb Kids Kamp offers a full day of ski lessons with lunch and lift ticket for $36.50

For the older set, 12 to 16 years, **Devo**, short for development, is designed to be attractive to teenagers. It can include any type of ski lessons desired, including powder, bumps, intermediate, or snowboarding. Rentals and lift tickets are separate, although kids will get a discounted ticket of $9.50 when they participate in this program. The daily price is $36.50.

At Whistler, A full day of ski lessons for children will cost $38. Lift tickets and rentals are additional. Call the ski school for more information at (604)932-3434.

Equipment Rental

Numerous rental shops are found throughout Whistler Village. Skiers planning trips during peak seasons such as Christmas, New Year's, and Easter are strongly advised to reserve their equipment in advance. Unlike U.S. resorts, Canadian rental shops do not use the terms recreational, sport, and high performance. Rather, they use only two designations: adult and high performance.

Blackcomb's adult package, priced at $24 per day during the 1992-93 season, consists of Kastle skis, Salomon boots, Salomon bindings and   poles.

Blackcomb's high-performance package, priced at $41 per day during the 1992-93 season, consists of various upper-end skis whose specific designations were subject to change. However, the general brand names were Fisher, Elan, Dynastar, Salomon, K2, Rossignol and Kastle skis; Salomon, Integra 1, Force 9 and Rossignol 800 and 900 boots, state-of-the-art high-performance Salomon bindings and poles.

Snowboards this year will rent for $24 per day. Call (604)932-3141 for more information.

Other rental shops in Whistler Village include **Whistler Mountain Gondola Rentals**, very conveniently located in the Gondola building. They have a completely new fleet of regular and high-performance equipment from Atomic and Salomon, children's equipment and accessories. Call (604)932-2311 for more information and prices.

Other stores which will carry downhill and cross-country ski equipment and children's equipment include **Village Ski Services** at (604)932-3659, and **Village Sportstop** at (604)932-5495. **Whistler Mountain Carleton Rentals** also will rent ski clothes. Call (604)932-6712.

Ski Tuning and Repair

Blackcomb Ski Shop offers Crystal Glide Finish by Montana. Montana manufactures ski-structuring and tuning equipment used by most ski manufacturers to finish their skis before shipping them to the ski shops. This year the shop has acquired a new robotic Montana tuning machine, probably the only one in North America. We'll fill you in next year on how it has worked. **Blackcomb's** estimated 1992-93 rates are

$ 9   Quick wax
$12   Hot wax
$39.95 Tune-up without repairs
$49.95 Major tune-up

Mountain Dining

Whistler Mountain has six on-mountain restaurants. Two are located at the top of Whistler Express. The original restaurant is called the **Roundhouse** because of its shape. Its food is served cafeteria-style and is quite good. In addition to the usual selections, it also offers a unique salad bar—unique because of the types of salads offered. For example, it is possible to have a delicious Caesar salad, Greek salad, or hot spinach salad. Daily specials are featured, as are a fine selection of homemade soups. Because

Whistler is located on the shores of the Pacific Ocean, indigenous varieties of salmon are frequently on the menu. Typically, one can order salmon grilled, poached, or sliced thin and served cold.

Just below the Roundhouse is another restaurant named **Pika's** which this year was expanded and renovated. The new huge windows will offer magnificent views of the valley below.

The Raven's Nest, at the base of the Redline Chair, is another restaurant with fabulous views. It serves pasta specialties, with a variety of sauce choices.

At the Whistler Creek base are the **Quicksilver Cafe** for breakfast and lunch buffets; Dusty's for lunch and apres-ski, inside and on a patio; and **Dusty's Den**, casual family dining in the evening.

At Blackcomb, six more eateries are available on the mountain or at its base.

The Horstman Hut, Crystal Ridge Hut and Glacier Bite each offer fast foods.
Merlins, a pub with sandwiches and other normal pub foods, is open from 11 a.m. to 8 p.m.

An elegant lunch inside or outside can be found at the Rendezvous Lodge on Blackcomb Mountain.

The Rendezvous Bistro offers a more casual choice for a quick meal during your ski day. A cappuccino bar also is available.

Child Care

Day care for infants and children under the age of two is extremely limited. *Whistler This Week* publishes a weekly list of persons available for baby-sitting in the various hotels and lodges. This book makes no representation as to the quality or reliability of any sitters selected.

Both Whistler and Blackcomb have implemented programs for children aged two through twelve. Whistler calls its program the **Ski Scamps**, and Blackcomb calls its program the **Kids Kamp**. Both mountains offer a variety of programs, and interested parents should telephone for specific information in order to determine which program is best suited for their children. Classes begin daily at 8:30 A.M. and last until 3:30 P.M. Whistler's location at the base of Whistler Express is very convenient, as is Blackcomb's at the base of Wizard Express. Reservations are necessary during peak periods and recommended all the time.

For children 18 months to 2 years, a non-skiing program is available for $50. It includes a snack, hot lunch and the ratio of caretakers to children is approximately 1:3.

Blackcomb Ski School Kids Kamp, telephone (604) 932-3141.

2 - 3 years of age	N/A half-day	$44 full-day
4 - 12 years of age	$27 half-day	$37 full-day

Whistler Ski School, Ski Scamps, telephone (604) 932-3434.

2 - 4 years of age	$48 full-day	
5 - 12 years of age	$28 half-day	$35 full-day

Medical Facilities

For injured skiers, the ski patrol only renders emergency service. The patrol will administer trauma treatment, stabilize broken bones, and transport the injured downhill by sled to a clinic located at the corner of Village Gate Blvd. and Blackcomb Way. Should additional medical treatment be necessary, patients are transported by ambulance or helicopter to hospitals in either Squamish or Vancouver.

Cross-Country Skiing

Whistler/Blackcomb have more than 15 km of trails in Lost Lake Park. This trail system meanders through varied terrain and accommodates all levels of ability. All trails have tracks set regularly as conditions require. The trailhead is located in the natural area between Blackcomb's and Whistler's bases, adjacent to the day-skiers parking lot. Trails also go through the golf course.

1993-94 rates were not available at press time, but were expected to be around $6.50 for adults. All ski rental shops in Whistler Village rent cross-country skis. For information about ski lessons, telephone (604) 932-6436.

Accommodations

Hotels

One of the premier hotels at Whistler/Blackcomb is **The Canadian Pacific Chateau Whistler Resort**, which is a ski-in\ski-out 343-room castle at the bottom of Blackcomb Mountain. Its complex not only includes an indoor\outdoor swimming pool, wading pool; saunas, whirlpools, and health club, but also two restaurants and a terrace barbecue, a Robert Trent Jones 18-hole Golf Course and conference facilities for up to 550 people. Prices this winter range from a low of $150 per night for two adults before Christmas, to a Christmas high of $250. All rooms have mountain views. AAA awarded this facility its four-diamond award for quality and service.

Whistler Timberline Lodge is located at the center of après-ski activity right at the bottom of the slopes. Located along the main pedestrian mall in Whistler Village, the Timberline is one of the resort's smaller hotels, with only forty-two rooms. One's first impression of this fine hotel is drawn from the intimate reception area finished in natural oak and accented by a two-story, natural-stone fireplace. Its Oriental carpet and camelback seating invite weary skiers to sit and relax a moment before trying the heated swimming pool or hot tub.

Despite Timberline's relatively small size, it offers eight different room configurations. Each room is tastefully decorated with berber carpeting, Navajo Indian design fabrics, and Southwestern-style furniture. All rooms are provided with fully stocked mini-bars, queen-size four-poster beds, jet bathtubs, built-in hair dryers (great for drying gloves and warming boots!), and complimentary personal amenities. Timberline's loft units feature fireplaces or terraces and pull out, queen-size sleeping sofas. Maximum occupancy of these units is four persons, and during the 1993-94 regular season they range in price from $55 per night during the value season in April to $300 per night during Christmas.

Other rooms include queen, double, bedsit-queen, bedsit-double, one bedroom, bedroom loft, and bedsit loft. Rental rates for these rooms vary with the season, and rates should be confirmed by telephoning the central reservations' number listed at the beginning of the Whistler/Blackcomb chapter.

One of Canada's most famous skiers, Nancy Greene, operates an exceptionally fine, full-service hotel. Located in the heart of the pedestrian mall only steps from Whistler Express and Blackcomb's Fitzsimmons Chairlift, the **Nancy Greene Lodge** doubled its size several years ago. Formerly the Nancy Greene Olympic Hotel, it became the Nancy Greene Lodge when its management acquired neighboring Crystal Lodge. The rooms currently are quite different from one hotel to the other—both nice, but different. It will probably be some time before this situation can be addressed and uniformity established. Meanwhile, prospective guests may want to specify which section of the combined hotel they want to stay in.

The original Nancy Greene Hotel has a warm, comfortable feel to it; the designer's liberal use of blues, tans, and burgundy is pleasing against the natural soft tones of rattan furniture. This subdued atmosphere provides a wonderful background for displays of Nancy's Olympic trophies—some of which are etched with the delicate patina of time. Adjacent to the lobby is **Nancy's Piano Bar**. Featuring live après-ski entertainment nightly and further enlivened by continuous large-screen TV skiing films, Nancy's Piano Bar is among the "in" places to be. The rooms in the original Nancy Green Olympic Hotel feature European-style extra-long beds, which can be placed together to form one large king-size bed. Be sure to ask for a king-size bed when booking reservations, if desired. Each room features a small sitting area, fully stocked mini-bar, wood-burning fireplace, and personal amenity package.

The new combined hotel has a total of ninety-seven hotel rooms and forty suites. Its amenities include a heated outdoor swimming pool, hot tub, and underground parking (actually, underground parking is available at all lodges and hotels, usually for a small fee added to the price of the room).

In the former Crystal Lodge area of the hotel, the rooms are all decorated differently; however most rooms have balconies, wood-burning fireplaces, small kitchenettes fully equipped with utensils, and a Murphy bed if additional sleeping accommodations are necessary. Interestingly, the rooms in this section of the hotel also contain safes. Each guest can program the safe with his/her personal code. The bathrooms are somewhat spartan, containing factory pre-built fiberglass enclosed tubs and showers. Most rooms have balconies and contain one and a half baths.

1993-94 prime season rental rates range from a low of $79 early and late seasons to a high of $170 during the holidays.Prices are $169 to $225 for a studio loft or single bedroom. Interested prospective guests should telephone Central Reservations for an exact quote for the time they are contemplating visiting Whistler/Blackcomb.

The Delta Mountain Inn is a large full service hotel in Whistler Village. The Delta Mountain Inn has 290 rooms, many of them one and two-bedroom executive suites. Balconies, fireplaces, refrigerators, safes, saunas, Jacuzzis, kitchens, and mini-bars are found in many rooms. Guest services include a concierge desk, room service, valet, laundry, and indoor tennis courts. Small pets are also welcome. Common facility amenities include a steam room, clothes washers and dryers, a heated outdoor pool, two whirlpools, exercise room, and non-smoking rooms. With all these features, it is no wonder British Columbia's Automobile Association awarded the Delta Mountain Inn its four-diamond award for excellence.

Eleven different room configurations are available at the Delta. The most modest is the regular double room which features a king-size bed, two lounge chairs, a small table, built-in desk, color TV, and a full bathroom. The most expansive of the configurations are executive suites which consist of a living area with queen-size sofa bed, TV, full kitchen and dining area, complete appliances, bathroom, dry sauna, clothes washer and dryer, balcony and fireplace; a separate bedroom boasts a king-size or two three-quarter size beds, bathroom, TV, desk, and lounge chairs. This year prices for a hotel room range from a low of $149 to a high of $235.

Condominiums

Situated in the middle of activity near the town's grocery store and liquor store is the **Hearthstone Lodge**. This is one of the older properties at Whistler Village, which is not to say it is very old at all. Although its lobby is small and nondescript, the rooms are among the most architecturally interesting in town. Roofs of the two-bedroom and loft units are partially glazed, providing abundant natural daylight and opening up these relatively small spaces. All two-bedroom and loft units have private balconies, fireplaces, bunk beds in the loft, and built-in banquette seating. Their master bedrooms contain a queen-size bed, dressing area, full bath and a sauna. In addition, there is a half bath off the entry. However, neither a swimming pool nor hot tub is available at Hearthstone. Telephones are available upon request.

One-bedroom units' decor varies according to the individual owners' tastes. All units, though, contain queen-size beds, one and a half baths, dishwashers, disposals, electric ranges, and most units have recently been renovated. Renovated condos typically include microwave ovens, too. Most of the guests at Hearthstone are families. Studios in 1993-94 range in price from $95 to $235; one bedrooms are $115 to $255; one bedroom with lofts are $135 to $285; and two bedrooms with lofts range from $189 to $475, all depending on the season and individual differences in units.

Glacier Lodge at the foot of Wizard Express on Blackcomb mountain is just a few minutes walk from the pedestrian mall of Whistler Village. Glacier Lodge was brand new in December 1988, and already discussions are underway for selected expansion. The central reservation area is decorated with mauve carpet; an elegant two-story, hammered-brass fireplace is its central feature. The walls are finished with natural-oak wainscotting and gray, bleached, rough-sawn cedar mullions.

Totaling 127 condominiums consisting of studios, one-bedroom, two-bedroom, and two-bedroom with loft units, all its rental units contain standard furniture packages consisting of the same mauve carpet found in the lobby, contemporary oak furniture, and complementary drapes. All units have a gas fireplace, cable TV, and a dining room table for four. It is surprising, however, that such new units would not also contain ice makers, microwave ovens, disposals, and compactors. An electric range and dishwasher are the only appliances included. All beds are queen size, and in the loft room, the space is quite cramped. Guests should be cautioned that the doors do not automatically lock behind them and should remember to use their key on leaving the room each time.

1993-94 winter rates for the Glacier Lodge during the regular season are $95 to $155 for lodge rooms, $105 to $175 for the studios, $145 to $245 for studio lofts, $255 to $410 for their largest accommodations 2 bedrooms with lofts. Glacier Lodge is managed by Blackcomb Hotels and Resorts who also manage numerous free-standing homes and condominiums in the area. There is good deal of ongoing construction at Whistler/Blackcomb, and persons wishing to rent condominiums or homes that are not being run as hotels should contact Whistler Chalets at (604)932-8700.

One of the more established condo hotels in Whistler Village is the **Blackcomb**. It is also the home of the **Savage Beagle Club** and **Araxi's** restaurant. Constructed in a more Alpine motif than most of the other accommodations, it has a unique ambience not found elsewhere in the Village. The Blackcomb has three types of rooms: lodge room with queen-size bed and satellite TV; studio with kitchen including all the features of the lodge room plus an additional single bed, fully equipped kitchen with dishwasher, and dining area; studio loft with kitchen and fireplace incorporating all the features of the studio plus a fireplace and an upstairs loft with twin beds. Color schemes for the units are basically blue and coral. Most rooms are beginning to appear dated, and it is anticipated that in the near future a renovation program will be undertaken to update the appliances, furniture, and upholstery.

Regular 1993-94 rates for lodge rooms are $75 to $125 double occupancy, $85 to $180 for studios with kitchens based on double occupancy, and $135 to $230 for the studio lofts based on quad occupancy.

Restaurants

One restaurant that is a must for everyone visiting Whistler/Blackcomb is **Rim Rock & Oyster Bar**. Located at **Highland Lodge** in Whistler Creek (also known as Whistler South or Old Whistler), it is a throwback to the old mining-era restaurants found throughout the U.S. Rocky Mountains. Rim Rock is decorated with assorted tables and chairs that defy period dating. Suspended high above the entry to the dining room is a very large marlin—no doubt caught by one of the owners. Hosts Bob Dawson and Rolf Gunther personally guarantee quality food and service.

At the time this was written, Rim Rock had two menus: a daily menu of specials and another menu which features standard items. The daily special menu contains items such as spring salmon, swordfish, baby coho, red snapper, Boston bluefish, mahi mahi, orange roughy, ahi tuna, dungeness crab, and lobster. All items are accompanied by the house salad, which is among the continent's best. Although a little heavy on the anchovies, three types of lettuce are accompanied by large, fresh strawberries, orange and grapefruit slices, Greek olives, sliced cucumbers, and a garnish of red and yellow pepper slivers.

An extensive wine list complements all entreés, and even the most demanding connoisseur will find a varietal to please his palate. It will be interesting for those skiers who are familiar with Canada's other major ski resort, Lake Louise/Banff, to contrast the quality of Whistler/Blackcomb's food service and wine selections with the dearth of them there. American skiers should be prepared for the seemingly high prices of wines and spirits in Canada.

Guests who do not enjoy fresh fish should try the rack of lamb off the regular menu. It is exquisite and includes seven full ribs with fresh Oriental snow peas, asparagus al dente, carrots, squash, etc--all dressed in a light sauce with just a hint of spiciness. The cajun prawn étoufée served on linguine with green peppers, snow peas, and acorn squash is also highly recommended. Telephone (604) 932-5565 for reservations.

Araxi's Antipasto Bar restaurant is situated on the ground floor of Blackcomb Lodge. It features international cuisine and is open for lunch as well as dinner. Its contemporary interior is paneled in natural oak, and the tables are covered with white linens. Each table is situated in such a manner that there are no bad tables. For dinner try the roasted sea bass with its herbal crust. Wonderful! A unique feature of the menu is that each entrée features a recommended wine to enjoy with the meal. For example, with the sea bass the chef recommends a California chardonnay or a French white bordeaux. Telephone (604) 932-4540.

Teppan Village, located on the mall level of Delta Mountain Inn, is an excellent choice for those diners who have tired of the ordinary and want a special night out. Although Teppan Village serves typical teppanyaki cooking, its decor is unique with a contemporary Oriental motif. Entrance to the restaurant is on one level while the actual restaurant is on another. The decor is all black and white with twentieth century interpretations of classical medieval Japanese themes such as samurai. Most people, hopefully, will find the environment fun and interesting. As with many restaurants of this type, the prices seem to be slightly higher than at other restaurants of similar quality. Telephone (604) 932-2223 for reservations.

There are two **Umberto** restaurants in Whistler Village. The original restaurant is Il Caminetto di Umberto Restaurant. When the owner was faced with consistently more demand for his food than he could supply, he decided to open a second restaurant—**Trattoria di Umberto**. Both restaurants are exceptional and both feature the same menu. Prices are moderate and the Italian food is excellent. Try the pasta and bean soup, pasta & fagiol, for starters and the salsicce contadine (Italian sausage with tomato sauce and mustard) for an entrée. All dishes are recommended. The wine list is adequate for most diners. For reservations at Umberto's, telephone (604) 932-4442 for Il Caminetto and (604)932-5858 for Trattoria.

Other family-style restaurants to visit include the **Cork & Cheddar Co.**, **Merlin's Restaurant**, **Nasty Jacks**, and the **Cactus Grill**.

Activities

Whistler/Blackcomb activities include

Tyax Heli-skiing Whistler; telephone (604) 932-7007
Whistler Heli-skiing; telephone (604) 932-4105
Helicopter tours; telephone Corporate Helicopters, Ltd. (604) 932-3512
Whistler Snowmobiling Tours; telephone (604) 932-4086
Dog sled rides; telephone (604) 932-5732
Scenic mountain flights; telephone Whistler Air (604) 932-6615
Aerobics workouts; telephone The Whistler Workout Co. (904) 932-4726

Services

Whistler Village is a complete resort with sporting good stores, apparel stores, pharmacies, grocery stores, liquor stores, and specialty stores. The village is convenient to most lodging, and window-shopping is a favorite visitor pastime.

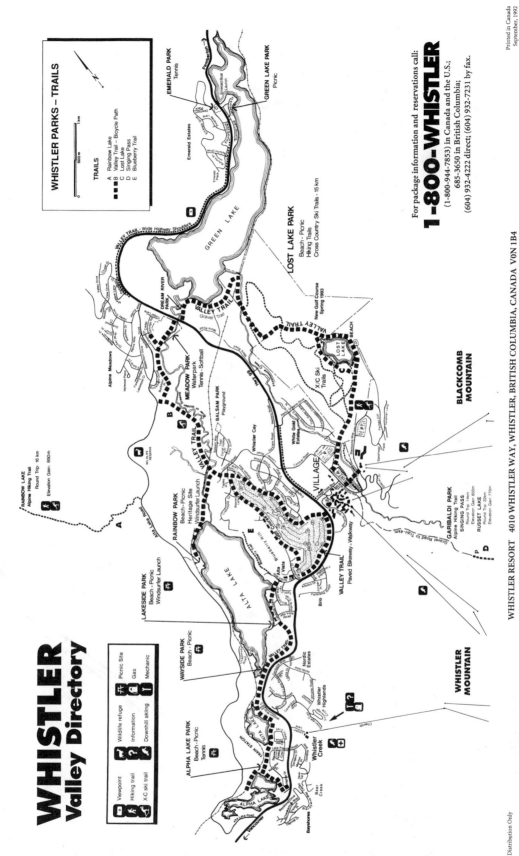

WHISTLER RESORT

WHISTLER
Valley Directory

Viewpoint	Wildlife refuge	Picnic Site
Hiking trail	Information	Gas
X-C ski trail	Downhill skiing	Mechanic

WHISTLER PARKS – TRAILS

TRAILS

A Rainbow Lake
B Valley Trail – Bicycle Path
C Lost Lake
D Singing Pass
E Blueberry Trail

0   500 m   1 km

Printed in Canada
September, 1992

For package information and reservations call:

1-800-WHISTLER

(1-800-944-7853) in Canada and the U.S.;
685-3650 in British Columbia;
(604) 932-4222 direct (604) 932-7231 by fax.

WHISTLER RESORT 4010 WHISTLER WAY, WHISTLER, BRITISH COLUMBIA, CANADA V0N 1B4

For Free Distribution Only

ORDER FORM

Order now your 1993-94 copy of *The Greatest Ski Resorts in North America* at the pre-publication price of only $14.95 plus $4.00 postage and handling. Virginia residents please add 4.5% sales tax.

        YES. Please send me _____copy(ies). Enclosed find my check or money order in the amount of $_____.

Ship Book(s) to:

Name_____

Address_____

City_____State_____Zip_____

Order by Phone: 703/476-5519

MAKE CHECKS PAYABLE TO: GUIDEBOOK PUBLISHING CO.

Mail to: GuideBook Publishing Co., 2465 Freetown Dr., Reston, VA 22091

ORDER FORM

Order now your 1993-94 copy of *The Greatest Ski Resorts in North America* at the pre-publication price of only $14.95 plus $4.00 postage and handling. Virginia residents please add 4.5% sales tax.

        YES. Please send me _____copy(ies). Enclosed find my check or money order in the amount of $_____.

Ship Book(s) to:

Name_____

Address_____

City_____State_____Zip_____

Order by Phone: 703/476-5519

MAKE CHECKS PAYABLE TO: GUIDEBOOK PUBLISHING CO.

Mail to: GuideBook Publishing Co., 2465 Freetown Dr. , Reston, VA 22091